Advances in African Economic, Social and Political Development

For further volumes:
http://www.springer.com/series/11885

Diery Seck
Editor

Regional Economic Integration in West Africa

Springer

Editor
Diery Seck
CREPOL - Center for Research on Political Economy
Dakar, Senegal

ISBN 978-3-319-37770-4 ISBN 978-3-319-01282-7 (eBook)
DOI 10.1007/978-3-319-01282-7
Springer Cham Heidelberg New York Dordrecht London

Printed on acid-free paper

Springer is part of Springer Science+Business Media (www.springer.com)

Introduction

In the wake of the recent global financial crisis, two favorable developments marked the African economies. On the one hand, African countries were deemed to have weathered the crisis better and emerged from it faster, than industrialized countries, and, on the other hand, they were credited with unusually high rates of economic growth over the last decade. As a result, there are signs that the continent is the next destination for foreign direct investment and future champion of economic vitality. West Africa has a sizable share of this seemingly new bonanza with a growth rate of nearly 7 % in 2012, and faces two issues of paramount importance. How to ensure that this high growth episode will not be short-lived? How to achieve a higher redistributive impact of the newly found greater economic prosperity? Considering that countries in the subregion of the Economic Community of West African States (ECOWAS) have endured decades of low economic performance and growth-impairing civil unrest if not civil war, it is natural to wonder what has recently changed for the better and what needs to be done to amplify this positive trend.

In many ways, West Africa is a land of contrasts. For instance it is commonly accepted that its private sector has played a key role in the ongoing economic boom and stands ready to continue its effort. Yet, it has not been successful at increasing incoming foreign direct investment or securing significantly higher levels of domestic bank credit which, in both cases, may hinder future growth prospects. A second notable contrast can be found in the subregion's inability to foster higher employment, especially for the youth, in the context of more vigorous economic activity. Consequently, it is not surprising that much of the civil unrest that plagues some West African countries is attributed by observers to the social exclusion that affects large fragments of their population. Policymakers have clearly identified this challenge as one of the most pressing policy goals to be pursued and are actively seeking remedial solutions. Finally, ECOWAS is arguably the African Regional Economic Community (REC) with the most ambitious agenda for regional integration and the loftiest stated policy goals backed up by the consensual support of its population and private sector. Yet, its cross-border transportation system is inadequate and the project of creation of the ECOWAS common currency union is at all but a standstill.

The underlying policy line is that, in order to maintain its current favorable development path, West Africa needs to satisfy three key arguments of its implicit growth function, namely private sector development, sound macroeconomic policy and effective regional integration. In July 2012, African scholars based on the continent and abroad met in Dakar to present and discuss research output that focused on these three key topics. These topics feature prominently among the priorities identified by the Summit of ECOWAS Heads of State in its recent meetings. All the manuscripts analyzed policies through the lens of regional integration or regional coordination, which constitutes a sizable contribution to the policy debate given the role assigned to ECOWAS's subregional institutions and their ambitious development agenda. While the process of restructuring of these institutions that will enable them to better tackle their new challenges is ongoing, the research output contained in this book will provide an opportunity for research to assist regional policy formulation.

The topic of the private sector is examined in two studies. Seck and Gaye (Chap. 1) conduct a continent-wide analysis of the impact of the recent global financial crisis on African countries in comparison with Arab countries. They report that African economies were mainly affected through their exports and real sectors with little effect on their financial and monetary indicators while Arab countries were hit faster and more widely with respect to all aspects of their economies. Arab states' high degree of openness and absence of anti-cyclical and cross-insurance policies made them acutely vulnerable to external shocks. However, they could lessen their exposure to shocks by investing more in African countries because their average correlation of export growth with African countries is lower than with other Arab countries. Deen-Swarray, Adekunle, and Odularu (Chap. 2) examine the state of transport infrastructure in West Africa focusing on ports, roads, airports, and railways with special emphasis on roads, and note the poor linkages among transport modes. They argue that this situation causes long delays and raises the cost of doing business. Furthermore, landlocked countries are not well connected to the regional transportation networks and there are inefficiencies in transport services caused by the strong level of protection of national transportation markets. This partly explains why intra-West African trade stands at less than 10 % of its regional GDP.

Regional macroeconomic policy is examined in five separate studies. In anticipation of the proposed monetary union of ECOWAS, Akpan and Udoh (Chap. 3) report attempts in recent years by some countries to design policies aimed at meeting primary and secondary criteria of nominal convergence set by ECOWAS. However, these policies are not properly coordinated and remain country specific and focused, thus defeating the essence of moving toward a monetary union. Their study shows that stability can be achieved through monetary union but at the cost of loss of ability to exploit monetary policy to boost output. Conversely, effective risk-sharing mechanisms and economic policy coordination within a holistic framework would smooth the process toward a successful monetary union. A number of preliminary structural reforms would provide the infrastructure for a more fruitful unification and would chiefly include regional fiscal policy coordination. Seck, Kemegue, and Kanda (Chap. 4) analyze the co-movement of African economies to assess the justification of monetary arrangements, mainly through the means of a common currency, during various business cycles. They find that the hypothesis of endogenous benefits of membership in monetary zones is not supported because developing countries' macroeconomic fluctuations have a weaker bond with those of other members of the currency union than with their respective main trading partners.

Tarawalie, Ahortor, and Umo (Chap. 5) conduct a number of econometric estimations to investigate the impact of real exchange rate volatility on export performance in the West African Monetary Zone (WAMZ) countries (The Gambia, Ghana, Guinea, Liberia, Nigeria, and Sierra Leone) using quarterly data for the period 1990–2010. Their empirical findings indicate that real effective exchange rate volatility has a significant negative impact on export performance in Liberia, Nigeria, and Sierra Leone, and a significant positive long- and short-run impact in the case of The Gambia. However, its impacts in Ghana and Guinea are found to be insignificant. It is also found that real effective exchange rate has a negative impact on export performance in the case of The Gambia, Ghana, and Nigeria, whereas a positive relationship is established in the case of Guinea and Liberia. While a positive relationship is revealed in the long run in the case of Sierra Leone, its impact is negative in the short run. They conclude that to improve export performance in the WAMZ, policies that will ensure stability of the real exchange rate should be pursued.

Ndiaye and Korsu (Chap. 6) seek to address the difficulty faced by many ECOWAS countries to satisfy the criteria of nominal convergence related to fiscal performance and, indirectly, the level of inflation. They investigate the determinants of tax revenue and construct an index of tax effort in ECOWAS countries based on stochastic frontier tax functions using annual data from 2000 to 2010. The results show that literacy rate has a positive effect on direct, indirect, and trade taxes; financial depth has a positive effect on indirect and trade taxes; agricultural share of GDP has a negative effect on direct and indirect taxes; and openness of the economies to import and GDP per capita have positive effects on trade tax. All the ECOWAS countries are found to be below tax capacity. Moreover, unlike other countries, Guinea Bissau and Nigeria have high tax efforts – more than 75 % – when natural resource related taxes are included in their respective total tax revenue, but with their exclusion the tax efforts of Nigeria and Guinea Bissau are as low as 25 and 7 %, respectively. Being below their tax efforts, ECOWAS countries could raise tax revenue with more effort. The potential of raising indirect and trade tax revenue is higher than for direct tax.

Nguena (Chap. 7) studies the domestic savings-investment causality in the WAEMU zone. It has been investigated in each country from a methodology based on co-integration. The existence of causality heterogeneity between savings and investment in the WAEMU zone suggests that one should consider a new model of fiscal coordination incorporating this heterogeneity, including adoption of a new budget rule that is more flexible and based on a structural fiscal balance without public investment.

Olofin et al. (Chap. 8) evaluate the determinants of effectiveness of ECOWAS at promoting regional trade in West Africa between 1995 and 2010. By estimating a modified gravity model (GM) that allows for the inclusion of country-specific and country-pair characteristics in addition to the traditional GM variables (income and distance). They find that economic size; distance; geographical factors such as common border, landmass, land-lockedness of countries; and socioeconomic variables like common language, political stability and availability of infrastructure significantly influence intra-regional trade within the ECOWAS region. They also find that the Francophone-dominated region (WAEMU) is exports trade creating while the Anglophone-dominated region (WAMZ) is trade diverting. Therefore, they argue that for ECOWAS to successfully facilitate intra-regional trade, current efforts at forming a synergy between WAEMU and ECOWAS should seek to promote trade between members, irrespective of colonial origin.

Fall, Vachon, and Winkler (Chap. 9) review the record of commercial regional integration over the period 1995–2010 in two Regional Economic Communities (REC), ECOWAS and SADC. Evolution of intraregional trade, measured by the ratio of intraregional exports over total national exports, as widely recognized, has remained low since 1995. Based on gravity equations and national data, their study disaggregates some determinants of intraregional trade. As expected, bad national infrastructures affect intraregional trade, as well as sectoral economic trends such as industrial and manufacturing growth. The study also examines the influence of regional leaders on intraregional trade and finds that adverse effects seem not to exist as the leading economies' performance appears to be positively correlated with intraregional trade. Conversely, overall economic performance of RECs' does not systematically translate into increased intraregional trade. Decomposition of exports by types of goods reveals more striking differences between levels of industrialization and development of RECs. SADC appears to be less regionally integrated and more open to global trade while ECOWAS and WAEMU are more integrated regionally but less integrated into global trade.

Elu and Price (Chap. 10) use a theory of rational terrorism, where a country's membership in a regional currency union conditions the cost of inputs that produce terror, and estimate the parameters of static and dynamic terrorism supply functions with Generalized Estimating Equation count data estimators for sub-Saharan Africa between 1974 and 2006. Their parameter estimates reveal that regional currency integration has counter-terrorism benefits as countries with membership in the CFA Franc Zone had fewer terrorism incidents than other sub-Saharan African countries. Their estimates also suggest that the CFA Franc Zone caused a decrease in terrorism. Considering that terrorism constrains important drivers of economic growth, these results suggest that another potential channel by which regional currency integration improves living standards in sub-Saharan Africa is through reduction of terrorism.

One may wonder why, given the abundant literature on Africa's economic situation, this book is necessary and, more importantly, adds something new. There are at least three main reasons. First, since the Oil Crisis that followed the Yom Kippur War in October 1973, between Israel and several Arab states, West Africa has seen the derailment of its growth path that arose from its initial years of independence. Thereafter, it started a downward economic spiral that several remedial donor-supported damage-mitigating programs sought to address. These programs spanned a period of nearly 40 years and included Structural Adjustment Programs (SAPs), the Highly Indebted Poor Countries (HIPC) external debt reduction Initiative, and poverty alleviation measures organized in national Documents for the Strategy of Reduction of Poverty (DSRP). After all these years of foreign-inspired programs, one can only note that West Africa faces a diverse set of country circumstances with several cases of economic stagnation, and the evidence shows that, as a whole, West African economies are not converging toward their industrialized or emerging counterparts, but rather diverging. This time it is about giving scientific contribution to economic growth in West Africa and not weathering the hardships of underdevelopment.

The second reason lies in West Africa's record as one of the most underprivileged areas in the world as reported by UNDP's Human Development Index – in 2010, five of the countries ranked among the last ten in the world are located in West Africa. Therefore, economic and social development, in any measure, is needed in this subregion more than anywhere else in the world. It is commonly agreed that most of its countries will fail to reach the Millennium Development Goals (MDGs) by the set date of 2015. But in a longer perspective, economic growth would create the added wealth that could help fund social programs in health and education as well as lay the groundwork for better economic and political governance. It would also make countries better prepared to tackle the challenges of climate change, social inclusiveness and gender equity, not to mention political stability and social cohesiveness. This book aims to participate in that quest for region-wide growth through regional integration, the collectively chosen strategy of West Africa's key players.

The third reason draws on the history of economic thought. Arguably, in order to be successful and enduring, thinking on development needs to be endogenous thus capturing all aspects of a society's evolution. This consideration is echoed by the recent increasing demand by West African policymakers for more research-based, homegrown policy recommendations, especially at the subregional level. Indeed, over the last few decades, policy has been almost exclusively focused on national challenges with regional initiatives taking the back seat and being mostly ramifications of the national priorities. This may partly explain the lack of balance of policy-oriented research between the two and the strong need for books like this one. One of the intended consequences would be the formulation and application of new theoretical models of growth and development that will inform policy and arouse consensual support of various categories of development stakeholders.

It is hoped that the body of evidence presented in this book and the new insight proposed on various issues related to the challenge of economic growth through regional integration will prove to be useful for scholars, policymakers, and institutions whose main mission is to promote economic and social development. It is also expected that the interconnection of policy analytics on West Africa's development agenda that emerges from this book will promote emergence of a new development paradigm or, at least, help deepen the existing ones.

May 2013 Diery Seck

Contents

Part III Regional Trade

Part I
Private Sector

The Impact of the Global Financial Crisis on Arab States and Sub-Saharan Africa: An Agenda for Growth-Inducing Collaboration

Diery Seck and Amie Gaye

Abstract The recent global financial crisis has generated considerable adverse economic repercussions around the world. It has also resulted in acute awareness of the variability of key economic indicators whose correlation with economic growth and population welfare underscores the need to manage risk nationally and internationally. Developing and small economies have proven to be highly vulnerable to economic adversities of a global nature in the absence of coping mechanisms that could take the form of compensation or aid. Arab countries and Sub-Saharan Africa (SSA) share this vulnerability to varying degrees and can be expected to suffer from it in the future but could, it is argued, reduce their respective levels of exposure through enhanced economic collaboration in trade and investment. The episode of the crisis has revealed that for governments and households the variability of income is as important a concern as its level. Therefore, it is expected that future economic policy will pay more attention to reducing economic risk than was the case in the past.

The purpose of the present study is to assess the impact of the recent global financial crisis on Arab and SSA countries respectively and to examine the scope for mutually beneficial trade and investment between the two regions. To this end, the investigation will focus on whether the same economic variables were affected and the extent of that impact. The link between exposure to the global economy and performance of the domestic economy will also be studied. Finally, sectors that could be targets for enhanced economic partnership will be discussed.

The underlying motivation of the study is multi-faceted. For Arab economies that typically are not members of any regional economic community or risk-mitigating alliance, the medium to long term strategic benefits of reinforced trade with, and investment in, SSA, are substantial. First, they give durable access to Africa-based non-oil natural resources that may serve as input in various industries. Even non-oil producing Arab countries' partnership with SSA provides diversification from traditional highly context-sensitive sources of revenues such as tourism

D. Seck (✉) • A. Gaye
Center for Research on Political Economy (CREPOL), Dakar, Senegal
e-mail: d.seck@crepol.org

D. Seck (ed.), *Regional Economic Integration in West Africa*, Advances in African Economic, Social and Political Development, DOI 10.1007/978-3-319-01282-7_1,

and worker remittances. The young and growing domestic markets of SSA can constitute opportunities for Arab industries.

For SSA countries, expansion of economic partners from new geographical regions in addition to Western Europe and North America, opens new prospects of growth and integration into the world economy. This could result in more market access in new higher income countries and opportunities for technological transfer. Furthermore, access to readily available capital from oil-exporting countries seeking to diversify away from oil, coupled with SSA's vast amounts of resources, could spur growth in Africa to considerably higher levels. The study gives insights into the external dimensions of regional integration in Sub-Saharan Africa, a key priority in the region, because it points to the gains from concerted management of external shocks on the one hand (IMF 2011) and collective attraction of foreign direct investment through collective provision of the benefits of geographical diversification on the other hand.

The study is organized as follows. The impact of the global financial crisis on Arab countries is examined in the first section. The same exercise is conducted for SSA countries in the second section. In section three, a historical overview of Arab investments in SSA is presented with respect to magnitudes, sectoral distribution and geographical areas of destination. In the same section a mathematical model of optimization of export-based investment is proposed and its implications drawn. The empirical evidence in support of the model is also presented in the same section. A brief conclusion ends the study.

Keywords Financial crisis • Arab economies • Sub-Saharan African economies • African economic development • African Arab trade • African Arab investment

1 Impact of Crisis on Arab Countries

1.1 Finance

Arab countries have been considerably affected by the global financial crisis.[1] During the 4 years 2007–2010, they suffered strong declines in their respective stock market indices, a process that took several years to complete. Indeed, of the 11 national indices, with the exception of Tunisia, all countries for which data are available experienced major declines in 2008. The worst affected ones were Egypt, Morocco and Lebanon. This adverse stock market evolution is also captured in Table 1. In spite of tangible recovery led by Egypt, Lebanon and Tunisia, some

[1] The empirical analysis has made use of considerable economic data and covered countries at the individual level. See the Appendix for the list of countries included in the study. However, the detailed results cannot be reported in this manuscript because of space limitation. Therefore, summary tables that display averages of countries are reported and comments made on individual countries whose data are used for the averages that are displayed.

Table 1 Selected average financial and economic indicators of Arab countries

Sectors	Variables	2006	2007	2008	2009	2010	Period average 2008–2010	Number of countries
Finance	Annual change in S&P global stock indices for selected Arab countries (%)	−3.7	41.0	−25.3	14.0	9.1	9.1	11
	Percentage change in stocks traded turnover ratio for selected Arab countries	6.2	3.2	27.9	−17.0	−33.2	−7.5	11
Money supply	Rate of change in money and quasi-money (% of GDP) in selected oil-exporting Arab countries	−1.7	10.7	−1.3	44.2	−3.7	13.1	8
	Rate of change in money and quasi-money (% of GDP) in selected non-oil-exporting Arab countries	0.9	3.0	−2.0	11.7	1.9	3.9	9
Credit	Growth of domestic credit provided by the banking system (excluding government claims)	0.1	0.1	0.1	0.1	−0.2	0.0	17
	Growth of domestic credit provided by the banking system to the public sector (% of GDP)	0.2	0.0	0.5	−1.2	0.1	−0.4	17
Trade and reserves	Current account balance as % of GDP of selected Arab countries	9.4	5.7	5.5	−1.1	−3.6	−2.3	15
	Growth in exports of goods and services (%) of selected Arab countries	9.6	8.2	5.7	−8.6	5.3	−1.6	7
	Growth of tourist arrivals in selected Arab countries in (%)	19.7	8.9	9.6	3.5	12.9	8.2	12
	Rate of annual change in reserves minus gold of selected Arab countries	30.7	41.2	13.7	14.4	9.0	12.4	15
Real sector	Foreign direct investment net inflows (% of GDP)	7.4	6.9	6.6	4.4	3.8	4.1	19
	Annual GDP per capita growth of selected Arab countries (in %)	3.3	2.0	3.3	0.4	2.0	1.2	17

Source: World Development Indicators, World Bank, online version and authors' calculations countries have indices below their levels of 2006. In summary, Arab countries were differently impacted upon, mostly negatively, through their stock markets, and are gaining back some of their losses at varied speeds.

Arab countries were also affected through the volume of their stock market transactions. Table 1 reports an average annual decline in the ratio of volume relative to capitalization of 7.5 % between 2008 and 2010, while Saudi Arabia and UAE experienced contractions in excess of 25 %. These volume reductions affected the liquidity of stock markets and may have resulted in a higher liquidity premium of stocks that, unfortunately, cannot be computed with the available data.

1.2 Money Supply

One of the consequences of the global financial crisis during its first year was a severe contraction of money supply. Table 1 shows that in 2008, Arab countries experienced a decline in the ratio of money and quasi-money (M2) relative to GDP, or a constant level. This monetary phenomenon no doubt had an adverse effect on economic activity in countries that were affected but was short lived for most of them given the strong increase in M2/GDP in 2009. It is also noteworthy that oil-exporting countries show more volatility in the evolution of their money supply than non-oil exporting countries, which may signal their unwillingness or incapacity to implement counter-cyclical economic policies. This inflexibility may have deleterious effects on domestic credit and consequently, on the smoothness of economic growth over the medium to long run.

1.3 Domestic Credit

As is shown in Table 1, the Arab private sector suffered a slight average annual decline in domestic credit from 2008 to 2010. This is in line with the constant level or reduction in money supply that is reported earlier. In other words, the private sector bore the brunt of the crisis through a sharp decline in stock market value and in the availability of credit, which undermined its capacity to raise funds either through the stock market or the domestic banking sector. A correlation coefficient is computed between the degree of openness (measured by exports + imports/GDP) of 6 Arab countries, and the rate of change of credit to the private sector between 2007 and 2009. It is −0.74 and indicates that countries with a high degree of openness have experienced sharper reductions in the availability of credit for their private sector, thus underscoring the higher level of financial risk faced by firms that are more exposed to globalization.

This result points to two key challenges faced by Arab economies. First, while countries that are deeply integrated globally benefit from larger world markets and experience strong growth episodes during periods of boom, they are hit harder with few mitigating mechanisms and may finally lose their capacity to reduce their degree of openness once a crisis breaks out. For such countries growth cum risk control in a globalized economy is a strategic challenge. The second challenge lies in the difficulty for domestic monetary authorities to implement counter-cyclical measures which tend to dampen economic growth and limit credit to the private sector during boom years and maintain the capacity to stimulate the economy during contractionary periods through credit expansion. The latter may be difficult to achieve if the private sector's main markets are foreign during a global crisis but can soften the adverse financial shock with perhaps little remedial effect on the declining foreign demand.

Since 2006, Domestic Credit to Government has declined slightly or remained constant for Arab economies as is shown in Table 1. Qatar caused a major change in 2009, which resulted in a significant decline of the region's average to −1.23 %. The average is just 0.22 % if Qatar is omitted. The main lesson from Table 1 is that Domestic Credit to the Public Sector grew by 0.48 % in 2008, apex year of the crisis, which was much more than in any other year before and after. A major reversal was experienced in 2009 when credit to Central Governments declined by 1.2 % for the Arab region. In other words, throughout the crisis years, Arab governments' capacity to borrow internally has declined compared to the pre-crisis period, but not significantly. In this respect Table 1 gives evidence of Government borrowing capacity to withstand the financial crisis. The correlation coefficient between selected Arab countries' degree of openness and the rate of change of domestic credit to the Public Sector is 0.07; it is not statistically different from zero. This result shows that Arab governments have a resilient capacity to borrow from domestic sources irrespective of the degree of openness of their countries. In summary, it seems that the economy's process of adjustment to the global financial crisis through domestic credit was made more at the expense of the Private Sector than of Government.

1.4 Trade and Reserves

Arab countries have suffered considerable negative impact of the global financial crisis through their current accounts. As is shown in Table 1, the average annual current account balance for all the countries has been declining steadily and does not seem to level off 3 years after the commencement of the crisis. Furthermore, the deficit has accelerated during the last 2 years, 2009 and 2010. This phenomenon affects both oil and non-oil exporting countries, although, on average oil-exporting economies such as Algeria, Kuwait, Libya and Saudi Arabia, lost 20 percentage points between 2008 and 2009. This lagged strong adverse shock is mainly explained by the large decline in export revenues and high degree of openness of most Arab countries.

The channels of transmission of the adverse impact of the global crisis are captured in the degree of openness of seven Arab countries, the evolution of oil revenues as a percentage of GDP of key Arab oil-exporters which displays an abrupt decline in 2008 and 2009, and the annual changes in tourist arrivals for oil and non-oil exporting economies. These data seem to indicate that Arab countries have highly open economies and depend too much on two sources of export revenues, oil and tourism, which are very sensitive to global demand, but have no reliable individual or collective mechanism of protection against adverse global shocks.

Table 1 displays the annual change in reserves (minus gold) of several Arab countries and inspires several observations. First, all the reported countries were affected by the crisis, with a significant average decline after 2007. Second, except for the particular case of Qatar, the average annual declining trend seems very strong, again giving evidence of the difficulty for Arab countries to reverse or remedy adverse shocks. In other words, the capacity of the region to provide a mutual insurance scheme to its members is rather limited under the current institutional arrangement. The combined effects of worsening current account balance and declining rates of change of foreign reserves signal a fall in the Arab region's external position with possible erosion of the nominal exchange rates of the national currencies and of levels of solvency of national public sectors. Finally, the strong decline in the level of reserves during the crisis gives testimony to the unpreparedness of the region's economies to manage external shocks and the systematic resort to reserve draw-downs as a palliative measure against rapid decline in export revenues and worsening current account balances. In other words, much of the global volatility is directly transmitted into domestic economies without significant mitigation. This situation calls for immediate action so that Arab countries can be better protected in the future.

1.5 The Real Sector

The impact of the global financial crisis on the real sector of Arab countries is assessed through two key variables: Foreign direct investment (FDI) net inflow since it pertains to the external sector and the Annual growth of GDP per capita in constant US Dollars, a variable with a stronger domestic focus. Table 1 shows a steady decline of FDI over the years across all the sampled countries while the crisis period reports a 40.5 % drop between 2007 (6.9 %) and the average of the years 2009–2010 (4.1 %). A significant lag occurred because the FDI ratio was almost unchanged between 2007 and 2008.

GDP per capita was also negatively influenced by the crisis considering that its average annual rate of change went from 3.3 % in 2008 to 0.4 % in 2009 for the sampled countries. The year 2010 saw a moderate improvement to 2 %, which seems to indicate a degree of resilience albeit not equally shared among countries. Generally, Arab countries have experienced modest rates of growth of GDP per capita during the period under study and lag behind various other developing regions. The average rate for 2009 and 2010 was just 1.2 % (Table 1).

Table 2 Summary of the impact of the global financial crisis on various aspects of Arab economies

Sector	Variable	Year of initial impact	Impact
Financial	Stock market index	2008	Adverse
	Volume of transactions	2009	Adverse
Money supply	M2/GDP	2008	Adverse
Domestic credit	Credit to private sector	2009	Adverse
	Credit to public sector	2008	Persistent downward trend
Trade and reserves	Net foreign assets (minus gold)	2008	Adverse
	Current account balance	2009	Reduced
	Degree of openness	2009	Adverse
	Oil revenues as % of GDP	2009	Adverse
	Number of tourist arrivals	2009	Adverse
Real sector	FDI net inflow	2009	Adverse
	Growth of GDP per capita	2009	Adverse

2 Impact of Crisis on Sub-Sahara African Countries

2.1 *Finance*

It is often argued that SSA was spared from the severity of the adverse impact of the global financial crisis. As can be seen from Table 3, the region experienced a decline in its stock market performance of −29.6 % in 2008. However, it mounted a quick recovery of 7.1 % in 2009, and 28.1 % in 2010. While the performance of the last 2 years still lags behind the pre-crisis average regional returns, this level of resilience is of key interest for non-regional investors seeking to diversify their portfolios internationally. One could note the high country-specific volatility of returns which, it is hoped, could be diversified away by a multi-country investment portfolio.

SSA stock markets have maintained a relatively constant volume of transactions throughout the 2006–2010 period, thus demonstrating a capacity to preserve their degree of liquidity even if the year 2009 saw a slight dip in the ratio of turnover to GDP. This feature is as important as the stock market return because it shows that thinness of trading in SSA countries does not get worse during periods of crisis.

Therefore, it can be concluded that the eight national stock markets reported here have shown a fair degree of sensitivity to global financial conditions through heavy declines that were contemporaneous with stock market declines in OECD and Arab countries, but have also demonstrated a large capacity to recover quickly and to maintain their degree of liquidity under various economic conditions.

Table 3 Selected average financial and economic indicators of Sub-Saharan countries

Sectors	Variables	2006	2007	2008	2009	2010	Period average (2008–2010)	Number of countries
Finance	Annual change in S&P global stock indices for selected African countries (%)	33.4	55.4	−29.6	7.1	28.1	1.9	8
	Percentage change in turnover ratio of traded stocks	15.4	13.8	17.6	11.3	22.2	17.1	8
Money supply	Rate of change in money and quasi-money (% of GDP) in selected African countries	3.4	6.8	3.3	14.2	3.2	6.9	36
Credit	Growth of domestic credit provided by banking system (Excluding Government Claims)	−0.1	0.1	0.1	0	−0.3	0	33
	Growth of claims on central Government (% GDP)	0.3	−0.1	0.3	−0.1	0.1	0.1	35
Trade and Reserves	Current account balance as a % of GDP of selected African countries	−4.6	−5.9	−8.4	−7.4	−8.5	−8.1	32
	Annual growth in exports of goods and services (%) of selected African countries	5.1	10.6	5.9	−0.8	2.6	2.6	21
	Growth of tourist arrivals in selected African countries	7.4	13.1	12.3	8.8	4.5	6.7	28
	Rate of annual change in reserves minus gold of selected African countries	43.1	34.9	16.5	25.9	3.9	15.4	34
Real sector	Foreign direct investment net inflows (% of GDP)	4.2	5.6	5.6	5.3	5.0	5.3	39
	GDP per capita annual growth for selected African countries (%)	2.8	3.3	2.0	0.7	3.0	1.9	40

Source: World Development Indicators, World Bank, online version and authors' calculations

2.2 Money Supply

The annual changes in money and quasi-money (M2) as a percentage of GDP are reported in Table 3 for 36 SSA countries. The annual averages show no clear pattern of impact of the global financial crisis on the SSA Region as a whole. The average ratio for the crisis years 2008–2010 is 6.9 % and is higher than the respective values for 2006 and 2007. Furthermore, variations from year to year of single countries do not seem to be caused by the crisis.

2.3 Domestic Credit

Domestic credit to the private sector has been largely stagnant for the period 2006–2010. In other words it was not affected by the global financial crisis in SSA. As shown in Table 3, domestic credit is not a major source of finance for private firms, even in the presence of positive economic growth. Considering that few corporations have access to market financing through stocks or bonds, it must be concluded that finance may be a major constraint for African firms, which underscores the pivotal role that foreign sources of finance could play in the region. Firms in high-growth countries such as Angola, Equatorial Guinea and Ethiopia or large economies with relatively developed financial sectors like Nigeria and South Africa share the same predicament.

A correlation is computed between the degree of openness of African economies in 2007 and the change in the private sector's access to domestic credit between 2007 and 2009. It is 0.04, which is statistically not different from 0. Considering the constant level of credit to the private sector over the period 2006–2010 reported in the preceding table, it can be concluded that openness to world trade does not lead to more borrowing for SSA firms. This situation can prevent them from taking advantage of global economic booms and hinder their corporate growth as well as the economic growth of their respective countries.

Over the period 2006–2010, the ratio of domestic credit to Central Government has hardly changed and no average annual change is significantly different from 0. As a result, the average annual change during the crisis years 2008–2010 is merely 0.1 %. Individual countries seem to have behaved in a similar manner with low variations in the internal debt of Government. This situation underscores the absence of funding of fiscal deficit from bank borrowing which may help explain the record of low inflation in most African countries over the last few years. Consequently, SSA countries whose governments do not have ready access to bond funding face sharp liquidity constraints when they have large fiscal deficits. The few remaining options include reliance on aid to fund these deficits. Overall, the global financial crisis does not seem to have had a specific impact on the capacity of African central governments to borrow from their respective banking sectors.

As a result of the constancy of domestic credit to Central Government over time, the relationship between the degree of openness of African economies in 2007 is uncorrelated with the variation of claims on the Public Sector. The correlation coefficient between the two variables is −0.05, which is not significantly different from 0.

2.4 Trade and Reserves

Most African countries have chronic and lasting current account deficits which have historically contributed to their high level of external indebtedness. The global financial crisis has caused some degree of worsening of these deficits starting in 2008. Even countries such as Angola, Botswana Lesotho and Namibia, that have recorded surpluses before the crisis were very adversely affected and seem to recover rather slowly when they do. The average annual current account deficit as a percentage of GDP was 5.25 % in 2006–2007 but fell to 8.1 % between 2008 and 2010. This represents a fall of 2.85 % of GDP, a sizable decline for poor and volatile economies.

Table 3 provides partial explanation of the worsening of SSA countries' current account deficits since 2008. Indeed, the annual rate of change of their exports was almost halved between 2007 and 2008 and became negative the following year. In just 2 years, the average annual rate of change went from 10.6 % in 2007 to −0.8 % in 2009. Overall the average annual rate of change was just 2.6 % during the crisis years 2008–2010. Every country in the sample was adversely affected through its exports. As is reported in Table 3., the same evolution occurred with respect to tourist arrivals albeit at a milder rate.

Table 3 also reports the evolution of SSA countries' annual changes in reserves (minus Gold). It shows that in 2006 and 2007, reserves grew at a healthy rate of 43.1 % and 34.9 % respectively. With the advent of the crisis the rate of growth declined to 16.5 %, a performance still better than the 3-year average during the crisis years which stood at 15.4 %. Few African countries, Eritrea and Seychelles, were immune from the crisis and maintained a high rate of growth of their reserves. It appears that the adverse shock in exports and the resulting worsening of the current account deficit were covered by most countries with slower accumulation of reserves which were partially utilized to settle international liabilities. This is a likely mechanism to cope with the scarcity of foreign exchange liquidity considering the limited access of African countries to international sources of borrowing.

2.5 The Real Sector

With a few exceptions, countries with high foreign direct investment to GDP ratios have maintained that performance while countries with low ratios have also kept that level. In other words, it is fairly difficult for a country to graduate from being a low foreign direct investment (FDI) destination to a high one – Ghana, Mozambique, and Niger –, although the reverse has proved to be possible as was seen during the crisis – Cape Verde, The Gambia, Guinea, and Sao Tome and Principe. The FDI to GDP ratio seems to have recorded an adverse impact of the global financial crisis having declined from 5.6 % in 2008, to 5.3 % in 2009 and 5.0 % in 2010. This represents an 11 % drop and constitutes a significant setback for countries that mostly have historically been marginalized from the world economy. It is noteworthy that African countries that report high FDI/GDP ratios are either small island economies – Cape Verde, Madagascar, Sao Tome and Principe, and Seychelles – or oil exporters. In the former case, even a modest investment by international standards can amount to a large percentage of the recipient country's GDP while for the latter – Congo and Niger – the spillover effects may be limited because the oil sector in Africa usually creates economic enclaves.

Table 3 reports the annual changes of SSA countries' GDP per capita. The annual growth of SSA countries' GDP per capita stood at 3.3 % in 2007, and declined gradually in 2008 and 2009 to reach 0.7 %, and then recovered in 2010 with a rate of 3.0 %. This evolution underscores SSA's vulnerability to global shocks but also its capacity to bounce back relatively fast (African Development Bank 2010). Detailed analysis shows that three types of SSA countries recorded the highest average changes in GDP per capita during the crisis years 2008–2010. The first one includes the oil-exporting countries: Angola, Congo, Equatorial Guinea and Nigeria. Small island economies such as Cape Verde, Mauritius and Sao Tome and Principe constitute the second group. The larger type of SSA countries that showed higher resilience to the crisis comprises SSA's poorest countries namely: Burkina Faso, Ethiopia, Malawi, Mozambique, Rwanda, Tanzania, Uganda and Zambia. The performance of the last groups of countries could be attributed to their low level of integration into the global economy while the oil-exporting countries may have benefitted from rising oil prices that accompanied the gradual easing of the crisis over time.

Small island countries have high degrees of openness and consequently, their economies are more correlated with the world economy. This has translated into a V-shaped evolution of the annual growth of their GDP per capita. This pattern also concerns Seychelles which scored a growth rate of 7.1 % in 2010 although its average over the period 2008–2010 is only 1.3 %.

2.6 Comparative Summary

The analysis conducted in Sect. 1 on Arab countries has revealed an adverse impact of the global crisis on virtually all aspects of their economies. There is evidence that Arab economies suffered in respect of their financial sector (stock markets and volume of transactions), money supply, domestic credit (to private and public sectors), trade and reserves (current account balance, degree of openness, oil revenues, thus exports, number of tourists arrivals and level of net foreign assets) and the real sector (FDI net inflow and Growth of GDP per capita). The size and breadth of the impact support the view postulated by the International Monetary Fund (IMF 2010) that Arab countries have historically adopted pro-cyclical economic policies, failed to enact remedial measures against economic downturns and have not implemented strategies of cross-insurance or of regional solidarity. In other words, they may be equally exposed to future global shocks given their relatively high degree of economic openness. This applies not only to their national incomes but also to the level of their national wealth.

Considering the current situation of Arab countries, a number of areas of remedial actions could be examined. The first option would include self-insurance in the form of counter-cyclical policies and cross-country insurance through regional relief funds. Both have significant risk-mitigation potential that would depend on the idiosyncratic risk of each country and the systematic risk to which all participating countries would be collectively exposed. The inter-country correlations of exports and GDP growth presented later give an idea of the efficacy of such measures. The institutional stability of such arrangements and their credibility among members would also play a role.

Diversification towards sectors that are less exposed to the volatility of the global economy could be a second solution. Naturally, its feasibility would depend on the capacity of Arab country to benefit from comparative advantage that they currently have or could build in the foreseeable future. Arguably, there is diversity in the resource, capital and labor endowments of countries of the region and success of such a policy would be determined by the national characteristics of each country, Arab countries being deprived of region-wide coordinated sectoral policies. Long term cooperation in this respect could yield substantial gains in economic growth and collective risk management.

Geographical diversification could complement and even strengthen sectoral diversification. Arab countries' global integration concerns mostly economic cooperation with OECD countries through trade and investment. This results in a type of openness that exacerbates their exposure to global shocks and threatens their income and wealth. Therefore, while geographical diversification could serve as an effective risk-mitigating measure, it needs to be achieved with regions whose economies have low correlations with Arab economies. In other words, future foreign economic expansion should target primarily non-OECD countries. In this instance, developing countries could be considered as possible candidates.

Comparison of the actual mechanism of transmission of the monetary and financial dimensions of the crisis to the respective real sectors of Arab countries and Africa may be of interest. Table 2 is an overall summary of the impact of the crisis on Arab economies. It shows that, in anticipation of the upcoming decline in exports earnings and concomitant slower growth in foreign reserves, their stock markets were adversely affected in value and in volume of transactions. Once the crisis set in in 2009, broad money supply and credit to the private sector were adjusted downward and reduced the overall liquidity of the economies, contributing to their recession. Given their poorer short term prospects and the full-blown crisis in the global economy, foreign direct investment was either delayed or curtailed in Arab countries. GDP per capita was also negatively impacted in 2009 but started a mild recovery in 2010.

Table 4 Summary of the impact of the global financial crisis on various aspects of SSA economies

Sector	Variable	Year of initial impact	Impact
Financial	Stock market index	2008	Adverse
	Volume of transactions	None	No impact
Money supply	M2/GDP	None	No impact
Domestic credit	Credit to private sector	None	No impact
	Credit to public sector	None	No impact
Trade and reserves	Net foreign assets (minus gold)	2008	Adverse
	Current account balance	2009	Adverse
	Degree of openness	None	No impact
	Annual growth of exports	2008	Adverse
	Number of tourist arrivals	2009	Adverse
Real sector	FDI net inflow	2009	Adverse
	Growth of GDP per capita	2008	Adverse

Source: World Bank's world development indicators

SSA countries have recorded a more contrasted experience with respect to the impact of the global financial crisis – see Table 4 – for the summary. While they were adversely affected through their external sectors (Current account balance, exports, tourist arrivals and net foreign assets), and consequently their real sector (FDI and Growth of GDP per capita), it is of interest to analyze areas in which they differ from Arab countries, namely where no impact of the crisis was recorded. The variables that were not affected by the global crisis include the volume of stock market transactions, money supply, domestic credit (to public and private sectors) and the degree of openness. In other words, no financial or monetary transmission of the crisis to the real sector was recorded in the case of African countries. This underscores the extent of marginalization of SSA countries from world financial and banking sectors (Benbitour 2009) and the introverted nature of these economies. This degree of isolation has one major consequence. It is possible for these countries to benefit from global economic expansion through increased exports without a concomitant rise in available funding for their economies, particularly the private sector, which seems to be the opposite for Arab countries. As a result, it is to be expected that private firms in SSA will not resort to funding from the financial sector but will rely on retained earnings, informal sources of finance and supplier credit, or accept outright abandonment of corporate growth.

Close scrutiny of the evolution of SSA economies has also revealed the following. First, they have a degree of monetization (M2/GDP) that is on average half as high as that of Arab countries. At this low level, money supply can barely constitute a channel of transmission of shocks to the economy, cash balances serving primarily for consumption and petty investment. Second, SSA countries have a higher degree of openness than Arab countries. Considering the weak link between their export performance on the one hand and money supply and domestic credit on the other hand, opportunities for financing development may be foregone. Finally, the record also shows that SSA countries have low levels of net foreign direct investment inflows (IMF 2009). In other words, foreign capital plays little role in enhancing domestic economic growth. These observations underscore the substantial contribution that Arab investment could give in the economic expansion of SSA countries. The next section will examine this issue further.

3 Investment of Arab Countries in SSA

3.1 Overview of Arab Cooperation and Investment in SSA

Arab investment in Sub-Saharan Africa has accelerated in recent years with increased interest in strengthening cooperation between the two regions and the quest for exploiting gains from Africa's growth potential in its relatively unsaturated markets. A combination of prudent macroeconomic policies, increased FDI inflows, market-friendly reforms and growth opportunities have drawn private Arab investors to SSA (Fedderke 2010). Effort is exerted from both the public and private sector on the Arab side, with key players including sovereign wealth funds (Benbitour 2009). Lessons from the 2008 economic crisis coupled with saturated Western markets, have drawn sovereign Arab funds to SSA, seeking high returns and portfolio diversification. Sovereign funds which serve both as stabilization funds and intergenerational funds particularly where oil revenues are concerned, have geared towards infrastructural investment in SSA. Arab funds rose from $1,300 Million in 2006 to $2,675 Million in 2007, a 106 % hike, with the Middle East having the highest share of the world's sovereign wealth funds by asset size; 48 % (NEPAD-OECD 2008).

Interest in infrastructural projects is explained by their high historic returns and stability of cash flows. Infrastructural development not only represents a lifeline for African countries by lubricating regional economic activities, but boosts private sector development, encouraging foreign investors to tap into new markets. The Arab Fund for Economic and Social Development (AFESD) and the Arab Bank for Economic Development in Africa (BADEA 2009) are key contributors to African infrastructural development, with public-private partnership gaining momentum in the process. Arab states have established bilateral and multilateral development institutions offering technical assistance to spur economic development, poverty alleviation, fostering an attractive investment haven and strengthening cooperation between SSA and Arab states. These institutions include; The Saudi Development Fund, BADEA, The Arab Institution for Investment Guarantee, The Islamic Development Bank, amongst others.

Key areas of Arab interest have been in telecommunications, banking and investment funds, minerals, shipping, airlines, tourism and oil (Reuters Factbox). Kuwait's Zain has invested $6 billion in 2008 to develop its telecommunications network in 15 SSA countries (Zain Company website Overview), targeted at potentially 400 million customers. Competition to invest in SSA has intensified within Arab and non-Arab firms alike and, as a result, Zain faces competition from firms such as Bharti Airtel, an Indian firm, Emirates Telecommunications Corporation and Sudatel which all are pursuing aggressive strategies. In 2010, Zain succumbed to competitive pressures and sold 100 % of Zain Africa to Bharti Airtel (Zain official company website). Libya African Portfolio's (LAP) Greencom, a Libyan holding company, acquired Uganda Telecom and Rwandatel in 2007, looking to inject substantial capital to boost its services (balancingact-africa.com).

Morocco's Attijariwafa Banking Group has extended its network within SSA, dominating the Senegalese market in 2007 via mergers and acquisitions. Its local subsidiary CBAO has risen to dominate the banking sector in Senegal along with its sister bank Credit du Senegal (cbao.sn). The Attijariwafa Banking Group aims to develop full-fledged universal banking within West Africa, offering modern services and financial solutions to all Senegalese (Oxford business Group 2007). Its subsidiaries are also dominant in Gabon, Republic of Congo, Mali (BIM SA), Côte d'Ivoire (Société Ivoirienne de Banque) and Cameroun (SCB). In shipping, the third largest container port operator DP World founded in 2005, currently in six continents is already present in Djibouti, Mozambique and South Africa and took over Dakar Port in 2007 from France's Bolloré and is looking to invest $710.7million in its facilities; 25 % more than initially agreed with the Senegalese government (Port strategy 2007). JAFZA, a part of Dubai World, agreed an $800 million deal to run a special economic zone outside of Dakar, Senegal (Jafza International Senegal).

In 2008, Dubai World's subsidiary Istithmar World Aviation acquired Djibouti's Daallo Airlines, with services now operating in East Africa and the Middle East (Gulf News). Qatar Airways and Emirates are also attempting to tap into markets dominated by African and European Airlines thereby bringing about the virtues of healthy competition to the region. New routes within SSA proposed by Qatar Airways include Kigali in Rwanda, and Kilimanjaro and Zanzibar in Tanzania, and Mombasa in Kenya (Qatar Airways press release).

OiLibya part of Greencom and managed by a Libyan sovereign fund has aggressively continued to expand in Sub-Saharan Africa. It is present in 21 SSA countries, having taken over Exxon Mobil in 2007 and acquiring all Shell's interests in Ethiopia and Djibouti (Africa today 2008). Arab firms are also investing in oil and gas exploration in Tanzania and Malawi. UAE's RAK Al Khaimah Minerals and Metal Investment Fund has acquired half of two copper mining concessions for $50 million in the Democratic Republic of Congo, pledging $200 million for cobalt and copper development (Mining Weekly 2008).

The SSA tourism industry has drawn considerable attention and interest for Arab investors. Arab private investors such as the Kharafi Group, Dubai's International Financial Advisers (IFA) have invested heavily in hotels and resorts in SSA, engaging in joint ventures and expanding their franchises.

3.2 An Export-Based Model of Optimization of International Investment

The empirical evidence discussed in Sect. 1 shows that the external sector, more specifically export revenues, constitutes one of key channels of transmission of the impact of the global financial crisis both on Arab and SSA countries. It has also shown that exports are one of the main engines of economic growth for the two regions. Therefore, any strategy aimed at mitigating the impact of global financial crises must put emphasis on minimizing the risk of export volatility through diversification (Elton et al. 2007). To this end, in what follows, a model of optimization of international investment that seeks to minimize the volatility of exports through a country's diversification in other regions is presented and some of its main implications discussed. It is assumed that a country wishes to minimize its level of export risk, measured as the variance of the rate of growth of its exports, given an expected rate of growth of its combined exports at home and in other countries where it invests.

Let,

$$x_{i,t} = \frac{E_{i,t}}{E_{i,t-1}} - 1 \tag{1}$$

$$X_t = \frac{E_t}{E_{t-1}} - 1 \tag{2}$$

$x_{i,t}$ = rate of growth of export of individual country i for period t,
X_t = rate of growth of global exports for investor country for period t.

Global (or world-wide) exports refers to the share of exports of all (S) countries that are attributed to the investor country's investments in those countries. It is assumed that each investor country considers the probabilistic distribution of each investment destination country's future exports and that the rate of growth of export revenues of every country is normally distributed.

Assume a one-period planning horizon (drop the time subscript t for ease of presentation). The rate of growth of world-wide exports of country K is:

$$X_K = W_K^T X_i = \sum_{i=1}^{S} w_i x_i \tag{3}$$

X_i is the column vector of rates of growth of exports of the S countries
w_i is the weight of individual country i in country K's world-wide exports
W is a vector of all w_i's and the superscript T indicates a transposed matrix.

To identify the optimal investment weights by a country across all investment destination countries being considered, the investor country must solve the following constrained objective function:

$$\begin{aligned} & Min \ \frac{1}{2} W_K^T V_K W_K \\ & subject \ \ to: \\ & \text{(a)} \ \ \mathrm{E}(\mathrm{X}_K) = \sum_{i=1}^{S} \mathrm{w}_i E(x_i) \\ & \text{(b)} \ \ W_{\mathrm{K}}^T \mathbf{1} = \sum_{i=1}^{S} \mathrm{w}_i = 1 \end{aligned} \tag{4}$$

V_K: Positive-definite variance-covariance matrix of the rates of growth of exports of the S countries.

1 is the column vector of ones
E (.) is the expectations operator.

The country seeks to minimize the standard deviation of its rate of growth of exports subject to an expected rate of growth of its world-wide exports that is a linear combination of the expected rates of growth of exports of all the countries multiplied by their respective optimal weights given that the total of the weights is equal to one.

The investing country can obtain reduction in the variability of its world-wide exports by diversifying its investments in other countries. This diversification effect is higher the more uncorrelated the rates of growth of exports of countries that it invests in are. We have:

$$\frac{\partial Var(X_K)}{\partial w_i} = 2w_i {\sigma_i}^2 + \sum_{j=1}^{S} \mathrm{w_j} \sigma_{ij} \tag{5}$$

$$\text{where} \quad \mathrm{Var}\ (\mathrm{X_K}) = \sum_{j=1}^{S} \sum_{j=1}^{S} \mathrm{w_i w_j} \sigma_{\mathrm{ij}}$$

$$\text{and} \quad \sigma_{\mathrm{ij}} = \sigma_{\mathrm{i}} \sigma_{\mathrm{j}} \rho_{\mathrm{ij}}$$

$\mathrm{Var}(\mathrm{X_K})$ = variance of growth of world-wide exports for country K
σ_{ij} = covariance between rates of growth of exports for countries i and j
ρ_{ij} = correlation coefficient between rates of growth of exports for countries i and j

The implication of Eq. 5 is that if a foreign country has low correlation of its export growth with the export growth of the home country, the variance of the rate of growth of the home country's global exports will be lower, ceteris paribus. Therefore, the home country will minimize its variance if it invests optimally

Table 5 Correlation matrix of annual export changes of Arab and SSA countries (2000–2010)

	Egypt	Jordan	Lebanon	Morocco	Syria	Tunisia
Egypt, Arab Rep.	1					
Jordan	−0.03	1				
Lebanon	0.46	0.16	1			
Morocco	0.38	0.26	0.04	1		
Syrian Arab Republic	0.35	0.57	0.39	0.62	1	
Tunisia	0.43	0.00	0.32	0.68	0.50	1
Average	**0.32**	**0.19**	**0.28**	**0.40**	**0.49**	**0.39**
Botswana	0.65	0.38	0.26	0.75	0.54	0.54
Cameroon	0.28	0.32	0.35	0.28	0.43	−0.08
Cote d'Ivoire	−0.40	0.40	0.37	0.03	0.41	0.05
Ethiopia	−0.07	0.45	0.33	−0.03	0.20	0.06
Gabon	0.29	−0.16	0.40	−0.11	−0.24	0.18
Gambia, The	0.21	0.01	0.15	−0.22	0.13	−0.15
Guinea	0.19	−0.57	0.33	0.15	0.10	0.44
Kenya	0.74	0.30	0.60	0.57	0.39	0.42
Lesotho	0.14	0.57	0.63	0.26	0.39	0.31
Mauritius	0.31	−0.25	0.05	0.47	0.30	0.72
Mozambique	−0.08	0.31	0.35	0.18	0.19	0.44
Namibia	0.61	0.17	0.36	−0.09	0.15	0.00
Senegal	0.77	−0.01	0.47	0.58	0.49	0.49
South Africa	0.39	0.25	−0.07	0.93	0.49	0.64
Swaziland	0.03	0.16	0.06	0.08	0.00	0.51
Tanzania	−0.12	−0.70	0.16	−0.26	−0.67	0.09
Uganda	0.41	−0.49	0.46	−0.01	0.06	−0.01
Zimbabwe	−0.60	0.17	−0.21	0.14	0.21	0.13
Average	**0.21**	**0.07**	**0.28**	**0.21**	**0.20**	**0.26**

Sources: World Bank, world development indicators and authors' calculations

(optimal weights) in countries with which it has low correlations of export growth and those foreign countries also have low correlations among themselves. This diversification is stronger the higher the share of its global investments in countries with low correlations. In other words, if a given Arab country has lower correlation of its export growth with SSA countries than with other Arab or industrialized countries, it will further reduce the variance of its global export growth by investing more in SSA.

Table 5 displays the correlation coefficients of Arab countries with other Arab countries and with SSA countries with respect to the rate of growth of exports for the period 2000–2010. It also reports the average correlation of each Arab country with all the other Arab countries on the one hand, and with all SSA countries on the other hand. Overall, with the exception of Lebanon, Arab countries have considerably higher correlations among themselves than with SSA countries. If Lebanon is excluded, the average of average correlations among Arab countries is 0.36 while the average of average correlations with SSA countries is 0.19. Therefore, SSA countries offer significantly more potential for export risk reduction to Arab investor countries that seek to diversify internationally than other Arab countries do. However, this does not apply to Lebanon that has as high an average correlation coefficient with SSA as with other Arab countries.

Table 6 reports the correlation matrix of the same countries for annual changes of GDP per capita. The results show that SSA countries are on average more correlated with Arab countries than Arab countries among themselves. The average of the average coefficients of correlation is 0.049 among Arab countries and 0.087 between Arab and SSA countries. Consequently, diversification of investments based on the correlational structure of rates of growth of GDP per capita is of limited interest when compared to correlation of rates of growth of exports. Indeed, Arab countries have much to gain by investing in SSA countries but this is best achieved through an export-based optimization model of international investment.

What are the policy implications of these findings? Arab countries can consider following three separate strategies. First, by investing more in SSA, they can expand the range of export sectors thus capturing the benefits of export diversification, exploit static comparative advantage and turn them into competitive advantage and develop areas of dynamic advantage. The accruing gains will be higher in areas that have low or negative correlation with Arab home-based export sectors. This approach would help Arab countries use their foreign direct invest in SSA as an instrument of risk mitigation against the exposure to global volatility that results from their degree of openness.

The second strategy would be to create and operate Pan-Arab investment pools dedicated to investment in SSA that individual Arab countries could buy into, thus providing a risk-sharing mechanism and an effective financial leverage tool. This pool would give Arab investors broader sectoral and geographical diversification within SSA. A third strategy for Arab countries would consist in signing trade agreements with SSA countries that are recipients of Arab foreign direct investment. These agreements would help secure preferential access of export markets for Arab subsidiaries operating in SSA and protect them from global volatility. These strategies are separate but not mutually exclusive.

3.3 *Overview of Trade Between Arab Countries and SSA*

Table 7 gives a sectoral and annual overview of trade between Arab countries and SSA and underscores four main developments. First, trade between the two regions has been growing fast and points to a large potential for both sides. Between 2005 and 2008, each region more than doubled its exports to the other. The advent of the crisis has elicited strong resilience of their bilateral trade and a strong capacity to

Table 6 Correlation matrix of annual changes in GDP per capita of Arab and SSA countries

	Algeria	Egypt	Iraq	Jordan	Lebanon	Morocco	Saudi Arabia	Syria	Tunisia	UAE
Algeria	1									
Egypt	−0.65	1								
Iraq	−0.26	0.28	1.00							
Jordan	0.09	0.39	0.49	1.00						
Lebanon	−0.26	0.33	0.39	−0.05	1.00					
Morocco	−0.05	0.00	−0.06	0.06	−0.01	1.00				
Saudi Arabia	0.35	0.22	−0.10	0.08	−0.14	−0.13	1.00			
Syria	−0.37	0.25	0.73	0.50	0.33	−0.05	−0.56	1.00		
Tunisia	0.13	0.41	0.13	0.48	0.02	0.34	0.48	−0.13	1.00	
UAE	0.48	−0.53	−0.19	−0.15	−0.63	−0.06	0.37	−0.61	0.11	1
Average within Arab	**−0.06**	**0.08**	**0.16**	**0.21**	**0.00**	**0.00**	**0.06**	**0.01**	**0.22**	**−0.19**
Angola	0.02	0.44	0.27	0.86	−0.09	−0.14	−0.04	0.51	0.22	−0.36
Benin	−0.56	0.29	−0.23	−0.13	−0.03	−0.08	−0.17	−0.20	−0.07	0.09
Botswana	0.38	−0.21	−0.10	0.19	−0.33	−0.12	0.19	−0.39	0.11	0.58
Burkina Faso	0.41	−0.29	−0.34	−0.17	−0.07	0.42	0.23	−0.38	0.06	0.04
Burundi	−0.45	0.25	0.66	0.29	0.45	0.20	−0.57	0.69	−0.19	−0.44
Cameroon	0.19	−0.34	−0.23	−0.06	−0.34	0.08	−0.04	−0.49	0.20	0.71
Cape Verde	−0.15	0.49	−0.36	0.29	−0.38	−0.11	0.23	−0.01	0.10	−0.33
Central African Republic	−0.73	0.65	0.62	0.35	0.19	−0.27	−0.22	0.71	−0.07	−0.52
Chad	0.73	−0.55	0.36	0.32	−0.11	0.09	0.21	0.07	0.26	0.43
Congo, Dem. Rep.	0.36	0.17	0.19	0.40	0.39	0.18	0.15	0.25	0.21	−0.46
Congo, Rep.	−0.32	−0.03	0.17	−0.37	−0.15	−0.14	0.08	0.09	−0.60	−0.02
Cote d'Ivoire	−0.20	0.34	0.48	0.17	0.72	0.22	−0.16	0.61	0.06	−0.81
Equatorial Guinea	0.11	−0.39	0.17	0.16	−0.01	0.25	−0.35	0.12	0.21	0.26
Eritrea	0.09	−0.39	0.08	−0.05	0.10	0.29	−0.64	0.45	−0.13	−0.35
Ethiopia	−0.47	0.61	0.80	0.52	0.38	−0.02	−0.01	0.75	0.27	−0.54
Gabon	0.14	0.31	−0.03	0.31	0.30	0.05	0.21	0.02	0.41	−0.40
Gambia, The	−0.15	0.24	0.11	−0.27	0.52	0.21	0.35	−0.28	0.55	0.02

Ghana	−0.10	0.61	0.22	0.42	0.44	0.11	0.36	0.10	0.26	−0.47
Guinea-Bissau	−0.43	0.63	0.12	−0.03	0.06	−0.26	0.57	−0.07	0.35	−0.13
Kenya	0.00	0.37	0.28	0.48	0.03	0.17	0.10	0.36	0.58	−0.35
Mali	0.01	−0.28	−0.50	−0.18	−0.26	0.58	−0.21	−0.24	0.08	0.02
Mauritius	−0.36	0.54	0.27	0.03	0.23	−0.38	0.41	−0.18	0.35	0.21
Mozambique	0.05	−0.20	0.14	0.31	0.06	0.58	−0.56	0.46	0.00	−0.35
Namibia	0.33	0.09	0.58	0.59	0.04	0.05	0.28	0.13	0.48	0.31
Niger	−0.01	0.19	−0.26	0.14	0.07	0.47	0.11	−0.19	0.11	−0.26
Nigeria	0.37	0.12	0.18	−0.01	0.30	0.13	0.66	−0.27	0.62	0.15
Rwanda	−0.01	0.07	0.42	0.61	−0.05	0.10	−0.18	0.49	−0.25	−0.19
Senegal	0.54	−0.04	−0.04	0.24	0.00	0.10	0.65	−0.31	0.72	0.23
Seychelles	−0.36	0.52	0.10	0.21	−0.13	−0.41	0.04	0.30	0.09	−0.36
South Africa	0.23	0.33	0.20	0.85	−0.33	−0.08	0.31	0.13	0.48	0.12
Tanzania	0.56	−0.08	0.34	0.66	0.21	0.11	0.09	0.30	0.20	−0.14
Togo	0.16	0.05	0.17	0.12	0.34	0.25	−0.19	0.26	−0.09	−0.38
Uganda	−0.09	0.32	0.16	0.53	0.12	0.42	−0.34	0.43	0.10	−0.45
Zambia	−0.17	0.39	0.17	−0.08	0.47	0.22	0.17	0.12	0.24	−0.53
Zimbabwe	−0.50	0.05	0.24	−0.40	0.14	−0.12	−0.38	0.35	−0.23	−0.30
Average Arab with SSA	**−0.01**	**0.15**	**0.15**	**0.21**	**0.09**	**0.09**	**0.04**	**0.13**	**0.16**	**−0.14**

Sources: World Bank, world development indicators and authors' calculations

Table 7 Statistics of merchandise exports between Arab countries and SSA (in $000s)

Exporter region: Arab States	**Importer region: SSA**						
PRODUCT	**2005**	**2006**	**2007**	**2008**	**2009**	**2010**	**2011**
Food and live animals	653,302	976,976	1,342,731	1,355,848	1,679,081	2,187,545	2,239,987
Beverages and tobacco	49,640	61,246	91,539	107,182	132,146	146,625	152,802
Crude materials, inedible, except fuels	113,675	129,615	161,631	395,314	369,051	393,218	435,688
Mineral fuels, lubricants and related materials	6,646,956	10,413,697	11,251,638	14,074,506	9,649,994	9,935,828	13,622,976
Animal and vegetable oils, fats and waxes	35,315	39,497	52,559	106,997	83,100	121,253	124,271
Chemicals and related products, n.e.s.	1,083,291	1,510,992	1,952,572	2,358,817	2,115,128	2,725,068	3,248,327
Manufactured goods	1,130,540	1,181,398	1,566,264	2,147,088	2,022,829	2,199,046	2,987,456
Machinery and transport equipment	1,980,876	2,349,469	3,107,289	4,037,848	3,810,590	3,479,398	3,760,618
Miscellaneous manufactured articles	617,194	640,804	789,062	882,192	1,014,391	940,726	962,639
Commodities and transactions, n.e.s.	132,092	154,046	128,567	520,325	246,152	873,837	1,429,962
Total	12,442,882	17,457,739	20,443,851	25,986,118	21,122,462	23,002,544	28,964,726
Exporter region: SSA	**Importer region: Arab States**						
PRODUCT	**2005**	**2006**	**2007**	**2008**	**2009**	**2010**	**2011**
Food and live animals	845,326	1,008,671	1,120,862	1,590,684	2,032,772	2,483,612	2,498,068
Beverages and tobacco	181,307	179,475	208,661	203,412	290,321	324,027	273,907
Crude materials, inedible, except fuels	481,204	593,797	673,344	850,633	716,051	762,605	966,818
Mineral fuels, lubricants and related materials	374,858	456,400	457,600	517,678	635,666	1,059,462	644,046
Animal and vegetable oils, fats and waxes	8,399	9,372	16,547	38,556	28,787	40,592	41,384
Chemicals and related products, n.e.s.	190,699	239,461	255,842	274,018	272,745	321,030	416,308
Manufactured goods	631,412	877,132	1,582,146	2,825,853	1,202,411	1,792,668	1,314,019
Machinery and transport equipment	462,540	766,975	844,714	1,025,937	957,414	966,971	858,612
Miscellaneous manufactured articles	101,181	148,447	139,536	131,668	140,809	189,726	150,629
Commodities and transactions, n.e.s.	483,654	539,865	1,098,277	1,322,754	1,291,569	2,249,563	1,357,739
Total	3,760,579	4,819,598	6,397,529	8,781,192	7,568,546	10,190,255	8,521,530

Source: UNCTAD, UNCTADstats

bounce back rapidly as evidenced by the V-shape evolution of exports during the crisis. For Arab countries the recovery of exports has been faster with SSA than with the global market. The scope for larger and deeper product diversification of trade is highlighted by the participation of every category of product in the overall trade activity. Finally, the steady growth of bilateral exports of each region seems to indicate that, with more cooperation, a higher trend and less variability could be achieved, thus benefitting everyone.

4 Conclusion

There is evidence that the global financial crisis had an adverse impact on Arab countries in respect of their financial sector, money supply and domestic credit, trade and reserves, and their real sector. The evidence also supports the view that Arab countries have historically adopted pro-cyclical economic policies and failed to enact measures that would protect them against downturns either at the individual level through counter-cyclical policies, or collective level by way of cross-insurance or establishment of regional relief funds. The high degree of openness of the Arab region exposes it to volatility of its exports and vulnerability to future shocks to which countries do not seem to respond with remedial measures. Sectoral diversification could be pursued through development of new areas of comparative advantage to enhance international competitiveness and lower their risk exposure. A second and perhaps related approach is to seek further geographical diversification, especially by way of investment in foreign countries whose export revenues have low correlation with those of Arab countries. In this respect, SSA countries could be an attractive destination for Arab direct investment.

The impact of the global financial crisis on SSA countries was different because their external and real sectors suffered while their money supply and domestic credit were unaffected. This underscores the extent of marginalization of SSA with respect to funding available to the private sector, and the low level of foreign direct investment, both constituting severe constraints on future economic growth opportunities. The weak link between export performance and funding of the private sector and the need of highly liquid Arab countries for further geographical investment diversification provide an opportunity for economic collaboration between the two regions. Arab countries would benefit from significant reduction in their global risk exposure as well as the growth potential of SSA and more availability of its commodities. SSA countries would attract higher foreign direct investment, access larger foreign export markets and secure Arab funding that is not too correlated with the economic performance of their traditional export markets located in industrialized countries. Over the last few years, a number of private, bilateral and multilateral Arab investors have increasingly invested in SSA, raising the outlays and broadening the sectoral distribution of their investments. This welcome development for SSA countries is on the rise and including more African countries. It is also one key benefit of regional integration especially if policies are coordinated or formulated at the regional level.

The proposed export-based investment optimization model is aimed at defining the combination of international and domestic investments that provide the lowest variance of export growth rates at each level of expected rate of growth of global exports. Variance reduction is more pronounced the lower the degree of correlation among destination countries. The empirical evidence shows that, on average, rates of growth of exports of SSA countries have coefficients of correlation with their Arab counterparts that are almost half as low as is the case between Arab countries. The present study has provided detailed insights into the impact of the financial crisis on the two regions and ways to improve their economic management and outcomes. It has also opened new areas of inquiry that could shed further light on appropriate growth strategies and ways to design and implement them.

Appendix: List of Arab and Sub-Saharan African Countries Included in the Study

List of Arab countries
Algeria
Bahrain
Djibouti
Egypt, Arab Rep.
Iraq
Jordan
Kuwait
Lebanon
Libya
Mauritania
Morocco
Oman
Qatar
Saudi Arabia
Sudan
Syrian Arab Republic
Tunisia
United Arab Emirates

(continued)

List of Sub-Saharan African countries
Angola
Benin
Botswana
Burkina Faso
Burundi
Cameroon
Cape Verde
Central African Republic
Chad
Congo, Republic
Côte d'Ivoire
Equatorial Guinea
Eritrea
Ethiopia
Gabon
Gambia, The
Ghana
Guinea
Guinea Bissau
Kenya
Lesotho
Madagascar
Malawi
Mali
Mauritius
Mozambique
Namibia
Niger
Nigeria
Rwanda
Sao Tome and Principe
Senegal
Seychelles
South Africa
Swaziland
Tanzania
Togo
Uganda
Zambia
Zimbabwe

References

African Development Bank (2010) African Economic outlook. Development Centre of the Organisation for Economic Co-operation and Development, Paris
Africa today website: www.africatoday.com
Arab Bank for Economic Development in Africa (2009) Annual Report 2009
Benbitour A (2009) The means to encourage Arab investment in Africa. BADEA research papers
Elton E, Gruber M, Brown S, Goetzman W (2007) Modern portfolio theory and investment analysis, 7th edn. Wiley, Hoboken, New Jersey, USA
Fedderke J (2010) The Afro-Arab cooperation in the field of investment. BADEA research papers
International Monetary Fund (2009) Regional economic outlook: Sub-Saharan Africa. International Monetary Fund, Washington, DC
International Monetary Fund (2010) Regional economic outlook: Middle East and Central Asia May 2010. International Monetary Fund, Washington, DC
International Monetary Fund (2011) Regional economic outlook: Sub-Saharan Africa: sustaining the expansion. International Monetary Fund, Washington, DC
Mining Weekly: www.miningweekly.com/page/africa
NEPAD-OECD Africa Investment Initiative (2008) Emerging public and sovereign fund investors in Africa's infrastructure: challenges and perspective
Oxford Business Group (2007) The report: emerging Morocco 2007. Oxford Business Group, Saudi Arabia
Port Strategy (2007) Dakar Dealings. http://www.portstrategy.com/news101/insight-and-opinion/post-script/dakar_dealings

Policy Recipe for Fostering Regional Integration Through Infrastructure Development and Coordination in West Africa

Mariama Deen-Swarray, Bamidele Adekunle, and Gbadebo Odularu

Abstract Regional integration is vital for the building of markets, the creation of robust and diverse economies as well as increasing opportunities for growth and attracting investment finance. It is the outcome of cooperative arrangement and processes, the implementation of intergovernmental treaties and market-led processes, which produces the platform for economies in a region to become more closely interconnected (African Development Bank 2010). Studies have shown that more than half of total trade worldwide takes place through regional trade blocs and figures show that trade under this system grew from 43 % to 60 % between 2001 and 2005 (OECD 2005). In order to achieve the laudable objectives of regional integration, transportation development and coordination has a vital role to play as a formidable force for catalyzing intra-regional trade among member states. As a vital component of investment climate, it provides market access to people and goods, thereby reducing cost of doing business.

Against this background, the poor and inadequate state of transportation network in West Africa undermines the rapid progress of its regional development initiatives. Some of the problems being faced by the transportation sector in West

A different variant of this article entitled 'Infrastructure Development and Intra-Regional Trade: A Case of ECOWAS' was published in the Journal of West Africa Integration (JWAI). These two versions are different because the version in JWAI was based on gravity model.

M. Deen-Swarray (✉)
Research ICT Africa, Cape Town, South Africa
e-mail: mdeen-swarray@researchictafrica.net

B. Adekunle
University of Guelph, Guelph, Canada

Ryerson University, Toronto, Canada
e-mail: badekunl@uoguelph.ca

G. Odularu
Forum for Agricultural Research in Africa (FARA), 12 Ameda Street, Roman Ridge, Accra, Ghana
e-mail: godularu@live.com; gbadeski@gmail.com

D. Seck (ed.), *Regional Economic Integration in West Africa*, Advances in African Economic, Social and Political Development, DOI 10.1007/978-3-319-01282-7_2,

Africa are: poor linkages among transport modes in West Africa which causes long delays and raise costs of doing business; landlocked countries are not well connected to the regional transportation networks; and inefficiency of transport services due to protected transportation market. This partly explains why intra-West African trade stands at less than 10 % of its regional GDP. In view of this, this study discusses the evolution of the four transport modes – ports, roads, airports and railways – but focuses more on roads as the most important mode of transportation in the region. Finally, while adopting both quantitative and qualitative analytical approaches, this article presents a transportation development and coordination model for West Africa and also proposes the policy options to be adopted in order to optimize transportation for regional integration in West Africa.

Keywords Regional integration • Infrastructure • ECOWAS • Policy coordination and coherence

1 Introduction

Regional integration models in Africa are recording more progresses than ever before as the continent experienced unprecedented growth in the last two decade (UNCTAD 2013, Odularu 2005). Studies have shown that more than half of total trade worldwide takes place through these regional trade blocs and figures show that trade under this system grew from 43 % to 60 % between 2001 and 2005 (OECD Report 2005). Improving the state of transportation is a crucial pre-requisite for trade, business and investment promotion, social and economic development and ensuring the regional and international competitiveness of a country. High quality and efficient transportation capacity can foster regional integration as it will facilitate the movement of persons, goods and services across borders, making information easily accessible and at the same time allowing the region to develop a stronger base for trade negotiations with the international market. It also strengthens the region's comparative advantage. Nordas and Piermartini (2004) argued that the quality of transport infrastructure may now be considered a more important determinant of trade than in previous years.

Regional integration initiatives in West Africa aim at promoting regional cooperation and ensuring that trade and other activities are easily facilitated among countries within these regional alliances. The ECOWAS[1] founded in 1975 is the West African regional body set up to promote economic integration within West Africa, with particular emphasis on industry, commerce, transport,

[1] Other sub-regional blocs within the ECOWAS include the Mano River Union (MRU), the West African Economic and Monetary Union (UEMOA), West African Monetary Zone (WAMZ) and the Community of Sahel-Saharan States (CEN-SAD) to which some of the ECOWAS members belong.

telecommunications, natural resources and agriculture to name a few (Odularu 2007). This regional bloc comprises 15 countries, with varying political, economic and social characteristics (Odularu 2006b). The ECOWAS Commission, through its mandate, endeavors to implement policies and embark on programmes and development projects that will facilitate the process of regional integration. Some of these projects include intra-regional road construction and telecommunication facilities. These are important facilities for promoting trade, which is a vital aspect of the regional integration process.

The ECOWAS has further demonstrated its acknowledgement of the importance of transportation development and coordination in fostering regional integration through the establishment of a Transport and Telecommunication Department within the Secretariat. The focus is on developing road, rail, maritime, river and air transport infrastructure in order to facilitate transport and transit within the region. The overall objectives of the transport division within this department as stated by the ECOWAS Commission are to "improve regional transport system", "provide efficient and cost effective transport system", "minimize delays by removing non-tariff barriers" and "promote intra-community trade" (ECOWAS). The telecommunications division aims to "establish a single liberalised telecommunications market within the ECOWAS sub-region", "implement the adopted Telecommunications Harmonisation Model", "fast track the implementation of GSM Roaming", "promote the use of Information and Communication Technologies (ICTs) for development", "evaluate and update the convergence criteria for Harmonisation of Telecommunications Policies", "develop a Regional Information Communication Technology infrastructure" and "facilitate the exchange of information and experiences between West African Telecommunications Regulators" (ECOWAS).

Although, ECOWAS has all these novel plans and intentions, evidence on ground indicates otherwise. The road network is not efficient or well linked. Telecommunication is better, but there are a lot of issues that need to be addressed. The cost of doing business is unnecessarily expensive because of bribes collected by customs and immigration officers, and touts along the West African corridors (Adekunle 2010). All these problems constitute obstacles to intra-regional trade because they are non-tariff barriers (NTB) to trade (Odularu 2006a).

The high cost of doing business can deter efforts to encouraging intra-regional trade as countries will look for better options and partners with which they can trade at preferable terms. Trade costs incurred as a direct or indirect result of poor quality infrastructure can take different forms. This article presents the evolution of the four transport modes – ports, roads, airports and railways – but focuses more on roads as the most important mode of transportation in the region. Finally, while adopting both quantitative and qualitative analytical approaches, this chapter presents a transportation development and coordination model for West Africa and proposes the policy options to be adopted in order to optimize transportation for regional integration in West Africa.

1.1 Statement of the Problem

Evidences abounds on how lack of efficient transportation system in the West African region affects productivity, trade and development. These include, but are not limited to insufficient poor road networks and lack of adequate alternative means of transportation. Sequel to this, the volume of trade among neighboring countries in the region is relatively low. In fact, trend in exports over an 8 year period, shows that Sierra Leone exports most of its products to western countries, with only about less than 10 % directed towards countries in the ECOWAS sub-region.

West African Trade Hub (WATH) studies and reports have revealed that delivery trucks are often damaged as a result of bad roads, thereby increasing the time spent on maintenance and reducing the productive capital rate of return. This proves to be a hindrance to the linking of isolated producers, in most cases smallholder farmers, to local and regional markets (Grigoriou 2007). There is the high possibility that delivery vans can deviate from their normal routes to avoid extremely bad roads which may result in certain communities being deprived the goods and services they need at a relatively less expensive price. More often, they will have to obtain these same products from a secondary or black market at much more inflated prices. Such scenarios not only hinder trade, but also contribute to poverty.

Apart from minimal intra-regional trade, uncertainty about delivery time and the state in which products are delivered as a result of poor quality of transportation is also a contributing factor to the cost of trade in Africa. Furthermore, delays have been shown to have a greater impact on developing countries where most of their exports are perishable agricultural products (Soloaga et al 2006). In addition to this predicament, alternative means of transporting goods are also expensive. Freight costs in developing countries are about on average 70 % higher than in developed nations, with Africa recording the highest, about twice the world average (UNCTAD 2003).

1.2 Objectives

The main purpose of this chapter is to examine the evolution of the four transport modes with more emphasis on roads transportation. The specific objectives of the study are:

- To assess the trend of growth and development in ECOWAS countries between 1990 and 2010.
- To analyse the evolution in the transportation modes in West Africa.
- To develop evidence-based policy options to be adopted in order to optimize transportation for regional integration in West Africa

1.3 Structure of chapter

Following this introductory section, the rest of the paper is organized as follows. Section 2 focuses on a review of the relevant literature surrounding the topic, whilst Section 3 discusses the relevant issues on the background to this study. Section 4 provides summary and concluding remarks as well as some policy recommendations.

2 Literature Review

This section reviews both theoretical and empirical literature on the importance of infrastructure to trade and the effect on regional trade integration. We did the review in such a way that the gap in literature is identified and our contribution to knowledge is visible.

Africa is a continent that is physically and institutionally challenged in terms of adequate provision of infrastructure. This unfortunate situation affects growth on this continent because different studies have continued to emphasize the role of infrastructure on economic development (Perkins et al. 2005; Ndulu et al. 2005). Jimenez (1995) and Barro (1990) assert that expenditure on infrastructure raises the marginal product of other capital expenditure within the economy. Investing in infrastructure, though vital, can be very costly and this is supported by the findings of a study carried out by Rosenstien-Rodan (1943).

Morrison and Schwartz (1996) confirm that a decrease in infrastructure investment reduces the productivity growth impacts of public infrastructure. In constructing a model for the technology and behavior of firms and applying it to state-level data for the manufacturing sector in the U.S.A., they find that investment in infrastructure results in a significant return to manufacturing firms, increasing their productivity. According to Bonaglia et al. (2010), infrastructure investment contributes positively to total factor productivity growth, output and cost reduction, with investment in transportation being the most productive. An empirical study by Pereira and Sagales (1999) further supports the need for infrastructure investment, suggesting that public investment has a positive effect on private investment, employment, and output at both aggregate and regional level.

Lack of adequate infrastructure in a country might be a major bottleneck for achieving sustainable growth and poverty reduction (Sahoo and Dash 2009). It is believed that properly designed infrastructural development programs can result in a more inclusive growth process that benefits poorer groups and communities in remote areas (Bhattacharyay 2010). Provision of appropriate and adequate infrastructure can boost investment and enhance trade within and across borders (Sahoo and Dash 2009). Furthermore, infrastructural development can contribute to overall economic development through creating and stimulating production facilities and economic activities. It can reduce trade and transaction costs, and create an enabling environment for competitiveness, employment and public goods creation (Egert et al. 2009; Sahoo and Dash 2009).

The cost of trading between any two countries can be greatly augmented by the time it takes to search for information, to enter into and enforce agreements, transporting the goods or products once they have been acquired and the time it may take for the other party to receive them (Nordas and Piermartini 2004). Understanding and having insight into the business environment in a country of interest might reduce these costs. Having institutions in place that are fully operational and easily accessible as well as having standard communication facilities is expected to enhance trade through the reduction of trade costs. Nordas and Piermartini (2004) state that countries that share a common language and have similar cultural characteristics will tend to understand and know more about each other and this is likely to cause such countries to trade with each other. Thus, common language and culture also make the flow of information relatively easy.

The flow of information across countries is a major determinant of the cost of searching for information on a potential trading partner. The telecommunication infrastructure is expected to play an important role in the ease of accessibility to relevant information. In the case where the state of the telephone system is undeveloped, firms are limited in their communication and this increases the transaction costs of ordering, gathering information and searching for services. Improvement in the telephone system reduces the cost of doing business and increases the level of output for individual firms in various sectors of an economy (Röller and Waverman 2001). In a study by Rauch and Trinidada (2003a), they argue that the emergence of the information economy has contributed to the reduction of search costs to a large extent. The ease of flow of electronic communication is however contingent on the trading partners having good access to telecommunication infrastructure. Nordas and Piermartini (2004) argue that "the cost of not being able to place a telephone call or access the internet may be just as important as the cost of making the call", with the former cost pertaining to the rate of penetration of telephone lines. Although information technology makes transaction and communication easy, there is still a need to physically move commodities from one point to the other and this makes distance an important variable in trade flow analysis. Distance from the primary market and high cost of transport as a result of lack of infrastructure affects the competitiveness of most African countries (Ndulu et al. 2005; Amadji and Yeat 1995). This high cost is witnessed in Africa because this continent is the most fragmented in the world with little or no connectivity among the countries. The impact of fragmentation can be reduced if quality of infrastructure available in the region is improved (Limão and Venables 2001). Improvement in the quality of infrastructure will lead to increase in trade volume and a reduction in transportation and transaction costs (Limão and Venables 2001).

Transport costs and the delivery cost of goods are very important factors in the pattern of trade flows among countries. The mode of transport that trading partners settle on can influence the time goods take to arrive at their final destination. The 2003 UNCTAD report focuses on the importance of multimodal transport services such as packaging, warehousing and transport from exporter's premises to that of the importer's. The choice made by trading partners on mode of transporting goods often depends on their geographical locations (Nordas and Piermartini 2004). Canning and Fay (1993), focusing only on transportation infrastructure for 96 countries, find high rates of return on the investment in developed and industrialized countries and moderate rates of return in underdeveloped countries. In an article on trade in ECOWAS, it is cited that it is possible for goods to be transported from Nigeria to Liberia within 2 days via sea. According to the President of the Nigeria-Ghana Chamber of Commerce, this has not been the case as ships often go through Europe or Asia before heading for the destination as a result of bureaucracy. This results in shipment from Nigeria taking about a month to get to Liberia (The Punch 2011). In other words, West Africa has one of the most expensive transportation costs in the world and some of these costs are attributed to lack of infrastructure.

Furthermore, some studies show empirically that a relationship exists between the quality of infrastructure in a particular country, the cost it imposes on trade and how adequate infrastructure can boost economic growth. Clark et al (2004), Wilson et al (2003) and Limão and Venables (2001) discover that the quality of infrastructure has a positive and significant impact on trade. Clark et al (2004) further indicate that the efficiency of the operation in a country's port can reduce the cost of freighting significantly. According to Nordas and Piermartini (2004), these studies used an overall measure of infrastructure quality or just maritime infrastructure, and expressed the need for more individual variables.

Röller and Waverman (2001) investigates the impact of telecommunications investments on economic developments using evidence from 21 OECD countries over a 20-year period and find evidence of a significant positive causal link. Canning et al. (1994) states that telephones have a positive effect on economic growth. Fink et al. (2002a) also assert that communication cost has a significant and negative impact on bilateral trade when the bilateral cost of making telephone calls is included in a gravity model. They also discover that a 10 % reduction in price of phone calls between two trading partners can increase bilateral trade by about 8 % (Fink et al 2002b).

Sanchez-Robles (1998) further show that road length and power generating capacity can explain future growth; the study indicates that physical units of infrastructure are positively and significantly correlated with growth. Public capital strongly affects growth, though the effect differs across sectors and is more relevant in the industry sector than in the agriculture, construction and services sectors (Fernandez and Montuenga-Gomez 2003). Using a panel of bilateral trade flows between 167 countries over 13 years, Grigoriou (2007) show empirically that an improvement in a domestic country's infrastructure quality would raise exports and imports by 14.5 % and 19.6 % respectively. However, the impact is found to be higher in the case of an improvement in the transit-country's infrastructure quality. In this case, export would increase by 52 %.

To a large extent, quality of infrastructure and high transaction cost can be referred to as a non-tariff barrier (NTB). In a study by the World Bank (2001), the results show that 168 of the 216 trading partners of the USA had their transport costs much higher than the tariff barriers. This is more pronounced in most countries in Sub-Saharan Africa (SSA), where the findings reveal that the transport cost incidence for exports was five times more than the tariff cost incidence. Limão and Venables (2001) carried out a study on a cross section of countries, controlling for the quality of transit-country infrastructure and they show that poor infrastructure accounts for about 40 % and 60 % of predicted transport costs for coastal and landlocked countries respectively. They further indicate that distance only accounted for a 10 % change in transport costs. Brun et al. (2005) also provide evidence of a high impact of remoteness and infrastructure on trade costs.

Other variables that may affect intra-regional trade include common border, languages and colonial histories, which have positive effect on bilateral trade (Nordas and Piermartini 2004). Carrère (2006) also suggests that SSA and ECOWAS landlocked countries will trade 28 % less than their coastal counterparts and Raballand (2003) reveals that being landlocked reduces trade by more than 80 %. This was mainly as a result of the way in which the land lock variable was represented in the study, focusing on bilateral trade between two landlocked countries. Radelet and Sachs (1999) in their study on 97 developing nations, discover that transport and insurance costs were twice as high for landlocked than for coastal countries.

In summary, Africa has various challenges in terms of regional trade integration such as the lack of capacity of staff at border posts, delays at borders, lack of adequate infrastructure, poor condition of roads, underdeveloped telecommunication and energy sectors that cause final prices of products to be inflated (East African Business Survey 2005). The role and the involvement by governments in infrastructure development cannot be overlooked. The decisions influencing infrastructure investment often comes from those in power and as Canning (1998) suggests, the trend in infrastructure stock growth in countries can be better explained by the political economy rather than by economic efficiency as governments are highly involved in infrastructure development.

Many studies in Africa cite poor infrastructure as a contributing factor to slow economic growth. However, some of the empirical studies reviewed show that infrastructure development has no significant impact on economic growth. Among these is the study by Easterly and Levine (1994), which in an attempt to explain Africa's growth tragedy using a cross-sectional regression on a list of variables, discover that infrastructure investment is not significant in explaining the trend in growth. Using a consolidated public-sector investment in transport and communications also did not find any significant impact of these variables on growth. Another study by Canning and Fay (1993), using physical measures of infrastructures such as kilometers of roads, railways per worker, electricity generating capacity per worker and telephones per worker for a cross-country sample, reveal that the variables had no significant impact on growth. Ghafoor and Yorucu (2002), finds in their study on Northern Cyprus using aggregated and disaggregated time series data from 1977 to 1998, that both the long-run and short-run elasticities of gross national product (GNP) with respect to infrastructure and human capitals are very low and in most cases statistically insignificant. The study therefore concludes that further investment in infrastructural and educational sectors will not contribute towards improving economic performance.

2.1 Summary

Polenske (1994) summarises the state of both the theoretical and the empirical literature on public infrastructure and productivity and finds that several studies show opposite conclusions in their investigation of the relationship between regional economic performance and infrastructure expenditure and views this as convincing evidence that more work needs be done on the topic. Hakfoort (1996) in reviewing the empirical literature on infrastructure and growth concludes that in general, infrastructure has a positive and significant impact on output.

The African Development Bank (1999) Annual report based on background papers, examined the importance of physical infrastructure. The report suggests that the major causes of the poor state of infrastructure are mainly structural, in particular, low economic density and geography. The challenge according to the report is to expand the quantity and quality of infrastructure in a cost – effective way. The World Bank (2000) also produced a review report on infrastructure in Africa and concludes that lagging infrastructure may be due to low demand rather than inadequate supply. The report identifies that in order to ensure sustainable institutional arrangements, it is necessary to have cross-border and regional cooperation. The report further suggests that the region has to employ sustainable incentive packages necessary to extend infrastructure access to rural areas. Rehabilitation and maintenance of existing infrastructure are seen as important in the infrastructure development process. The report also emphasizes the need for private participation, towards improving investment effectiveness and service provision.

The theoretical and empirical review of relevant and existing literature indicates that though there are varying views and findings, in general the availability and quality of infrastructure promotes trade and economic growth. This impact has not been analyzed for the ECOWAS countries, especially with respects to intra-regional trade among the 15 member countries. Thus, this article fills this gap and contribute immensely to literature.

3 Background to the Study: Regional Integration and Transportation in West Africa

3.1 Introduction

Regional integration is vital for the building of markets, the creation of robust and diverse economies as well as increasing opportunities for growth and attracting investment finance. Regional integration is also defined as the outcome of cooperative arrangement and processes, the implementation of intergovernmental treaties and market-led processes, which produces the platform for economies in a region to become more closely interconnected (AfDB 2010).

Kwaku (1995) suggests that the main force influencing the increasing number of RIAs on the African continent is the need to increase regional cooperation through the establishment of unified economic blocs. The African countries also envisage that RIAs will form the building blocks for stronger integration between countries (UNECA 2004; WTO 2005). Some express the view that regional integration will increase intra-regional trade, which will in turn spur economic growth and development through economies of scale (Kasekende and Ng'eno 2000; Mistry 2000).

With overlapping memberships in various regional bodies, there is the tendency for the capacity of these institutions to be overstretched. This can limit their technical capacity as well as the ability to exercise their enforcement powers. Adequate infrastructure might aid regional trade integration in developing countries, most especially West African countries. Africa's infrastructure need is estimated to be $93 billion annually, but only $45 billion is currently spent on it annually (World Bank 2010). This shows that there is a gap of $48 billion that needs to be spent on Africa if the continent is to catch up with the rate of development in other continents in the global village. The private sector has become more fully involved in this regard, though most of their investment is claimed to be more geared towards the information and telecommunication sector. According to the OECD (2010) report, this sector received 87 % of all investment commitments in 2008. Since infrastructural development is a catalyst and a positive externality to economic development, adequate analysis of the state of infrastructure in ECOWAS, its impacts on regional trade integration and the way forward will be the focus of this section. Specifically, we will look at infrastructure such as power, rail, road, sea/airports and telecommunications.

3.2 Transportation Infrastructure and Trade in Regional Integration

Infrastructure, as identified in the literature, plays a vital role in the development process (Perkins et al. 2005; Ndulu et al. 2005). It has the potential to improve the region's competitiveness, boost both domestic and regional trade and overall, enhance the integration of the region into the world economy. Cross-border infrastructure projects promote regional integration and contribute to regional trade and growth. These projects can however be very costly as transaction costs are high and so are the risks involved. To fund regional infrastructure projects successfully, the countries involved need to work together and coordinate well.

The disparities among African nations are obstacles that hinder the regional integration process. There is a lot of missing regional and trans-African links that pose serious threat to the success of integration (AfDB 2010). The challenge is not only the low level of physical infrastructure but also the lack of existing road and rail links and the poor connectivity to ports within the region.

With countries in the ECOWAS sub-region mainly engaged in the export of primary commodities, having a functional and efficient rail system can provide a more efficient means of transporting these goods within the region and can be comparatively cost effective. Investment in infrastructure, mainly in the transport sector, is highly likely to have a positive impact on trade that will in turn accelerate growth and development within the sub-region (Odularu 2009).

Africa's infrastructure facilities continue to lag behind that of other regions and this has been a major obstacle in achieving sustainable development (Brixiova et al 2011). The absence of well developed infrastructure has been attributed to the lack of adequate financing for such projects which are known to be very costly. According to the discoveries by Africa Infrastructure Country Diagnostic (AICD), Africa lacks the technical expertise to develop this infrastructure. There is thus a need for capacity building through proper education and the creation of an enabling environment for the development of entrepreneurs who are innovative, imaginative and are willing to take risk in the tough African business environment that is full of opportunities though at times very fragile.

Efforts towards exploring possible ways of financing infrastructure development have been ongoing at the country level. In Ghana, an external sovereign bond was used to finance such projects. The government of Nigeria is using the Private-Public Partnership to help close the infrastructure gap. One such project is the Lagos State Bus Rapid Transit, said to be the first of its kind in sub-Saharan Africa. This project is a joint venture between the Lagos Metropolitan Authority and the private sector and has succeeded in reducing traffic, cutting transport cost by about 30 % and creating a safer alternative for commuters (World Bank 2009). Another such venture is the construction of the US$385 million Lekki-Epe Toll Road in Lagos, which was the first PPP and privately funded toll project in Nigeria (AfDB 2010). It was carried out in an endeavour to upgrade the country's infrastructure in order to reduce traffic and was successfully completed in 2006.

At the continent level, the African Development Bank (AfDB) renders support to its regional member countries (RMCs) through the accessing of long-term financing which is more appropriate for infrastructure. Over US$6 billion was invested by the bank in 2009, a 177.3 % increase from the amount invested in 2008 and accounting for 52 % of the bank's portfolio (AfDB 2010). The AfDB, through the African Legal Support Facility, further supports private sector financed infrastructure projects in the region. This facility set up to provide technical advice to RMCs, seeks to ensure that the right environment with the appropriate legal and regulatory framework is in place to allow African nations enter into lucrative contracts with partners in the private sector. African countries are endowed with natural resources which are often left to be managed by the private sector, which in turn is required to make specified social contributions. It is most often the case that African economies enter such agreements without proper negotiations that would ensure they reap the utmost benefits. Private sector investments in infrastructure have increased over the years, moving from US$40 billion in 2006 to US$42 billion in 2007 (AfDB 2010).

3.3 Overview of the ECOWAS

The ECOWAS was established by the Treaty of Lagos in May 1975 to promote economic trade, cooperation and self-reliance. It is said to be the largest regional economic multi-cooperation organization in Africa, accounting for one sixth of the size and one third of the population of Africa (Odularu 2006b, 2007, 2009, 2011a, 2011b). The organization among other things, aim at ensuring regional free trade, introducing common tariff, facilitating the free movement of capital and human resources as well as promoting infrastructure development. Figure 1 shows the countries and the ecological zones in the ECOWAS region.[2]

The figure depicts that there are vast opportunities in the region because of different economic activities and agricultural production that abound. The region is also known for its mineral resources such as crude oil in Nigeria and Ghana and mineral resources in Niger.

The organization has put in place product standards and has realized free trade for industry products, removing tariff barriers. A common external tariff has been established with the rates ranging from 0 % to 20 %. As far as infrastructure goes, ECOWAS has embarked on the construction of the highway and roads that connect the region as well as focusing on aviation and railway construction. One stop border post initiatives are currently applied at borders in Ghana, Mali, Togo and Burkina Faso to assist landlocked countries in facilitating transit. Within the region, air service liberalization through the 1999 Yamoussoukro Decision have only been fully implemented by the West African Economic and Monetary Union, made up of mostly the French speaking states and Guinea-Bissau and also the Banjul Accord Group.

The characteristics of the various countries within ECOWAS make it more challenging for the successful implementation of certain infrastructure projects. Characterized by mainly small economies, fairly low population density on average and low rates of urbanization make intra-regional connectivity difficult and therefore relatively low in the sub-region. Most of the intra-regional road networks are characterized by major discontinuities. The region is also characterized by relatively high prices for the services provided by the limited existing infrastructure facilities.

The relatively small sizes of most ECOWAS member countries, makes it challenging to embark on cost-effective infrastructure development projects. Collaborating at the regional level to implement the fiber-optic submarine cable

[2] All maps in this chapter were developed with data from the Data Resource Centre, University of Guelph and developed by Dr. Gift Dumedah (McMaster University).

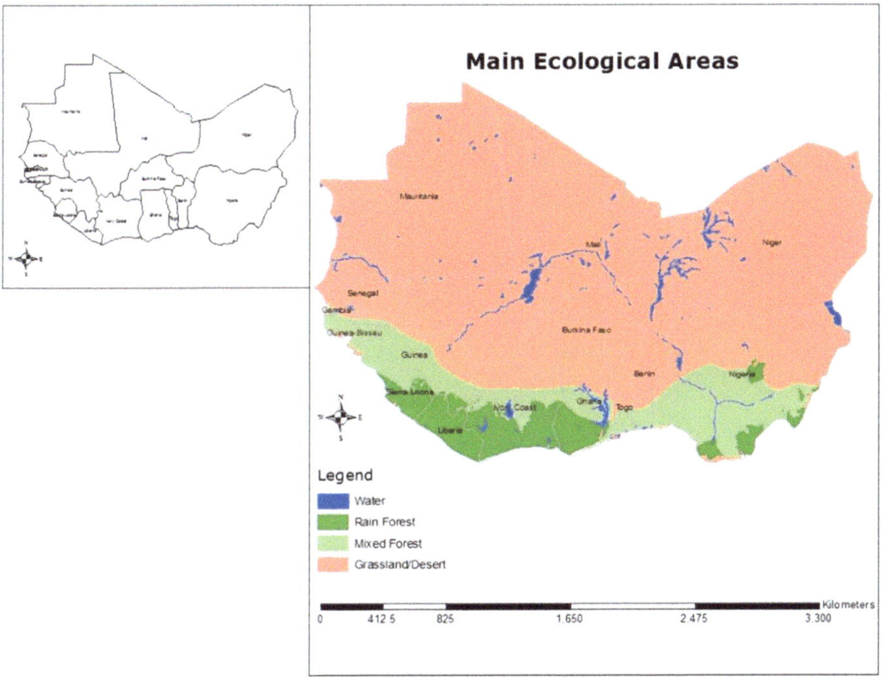

Fig. 1 ECOWAS – showing the countries and the ecological zones

will go a long way in reducing the costs associated with ICT activities. Collaboration in the various country hubs as well as the road and rail corridors is necessary to enhance the integration process. Regional integration is therefore a necessity as it can bring about low costs across all types of infrastructure.

Though there have been some improvements in the road network in the region, there are still a lot of gaps and some roads are still not in the best condition. Table 1 below shows the state of some regional roads in the ECOWAS region. It can be seen that on average, only about 45 % of such roads within ECOWAS are in good condition.

3.3.1 Trade Patterns in the Sub-Region

ECOWAS has developed a trade relation with China which has become intense with an increase in the amounts traded over the years. With ECOWAS' lack of high technology products and machinery, they have turned to China to provide these products. The West African region, on the other hand is well endowed in mineral and other natural resources, which China has very little of. As such they have engaged in a trade relationship that they envisage will be mutually beneficial. This chapter is interested in the intra-regional trade, though we acknowledge the fact that

Table 1 ECOWAS countries roads and their condition

Country	Condition		Type
	Good (%)	Fair (%)	Paved (%)
Benin	35.8	1.8	96.8
Burkina Faso	58.2	33.6	100
Cape Verde	0	0	0
Cote d'Ivoire	16.1	47.1	90.3
Gambia	0	89.4	47.4
Ghana	70.3	23.6	100
Guinea	22.2	20.7	89.1
Liberia	39.4	55.9	47.5
Mali	66.6	21.7	99.6
Niger	31.2	31	88
Nigeria	55.6	29.7	100
Senegal	39.8	15.1	99.8
Sierra Leone	19.5	58.4	33.6
Togo	49.7	0	100
ECOWAS	**45.1**	**28.4**	**92.5**

Source: AICD 2010

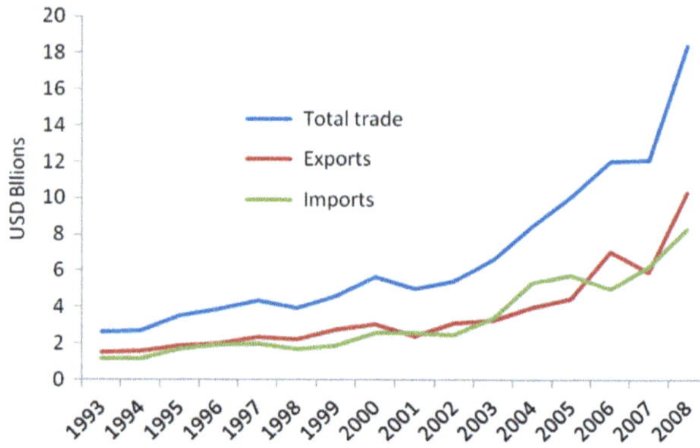

Fig. 2 Volume of trade within the ECOWAS region

lack of infrastructure might create incentive for countries to trade with countries, outside the region, that provide infrastructure through bilateral trade arrangements. In fact, the trade with China is surging and the capacity to benefit from the relationship through proper macroeconomic management is lacking though the relationship is a reality and ECOWAS governments are supposed to use compensation principle for people that are worse off (Adekunle and Gitau 2013). It is a possibility that beneficiaries will increase and transaction cost will reduce if countries within the region trade with each other. Below are graphs that depict the trade pattern within ECOWAS for the period of the study.

The trade volume within the region has continued to increase during the study period (1993–2008). This might be due to better policy implementation on the part of the ECOWAS Commission, the African Development Bank and governmental and non-governmental organizations. As seen in Fig. 2, the total trade within the

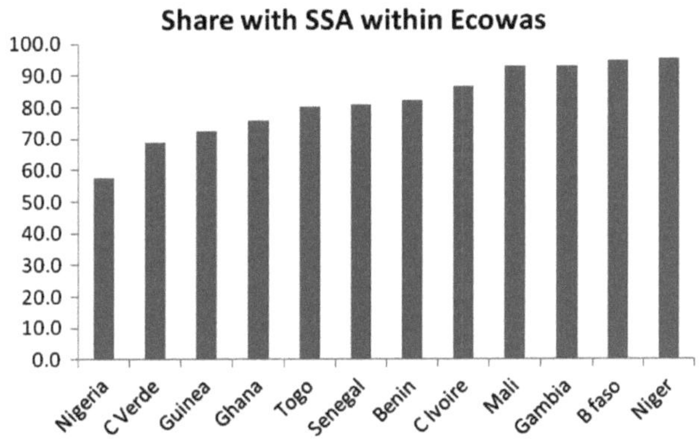

Fig. 3 Contribution of countries to ECOWAS out of total trade within SSA

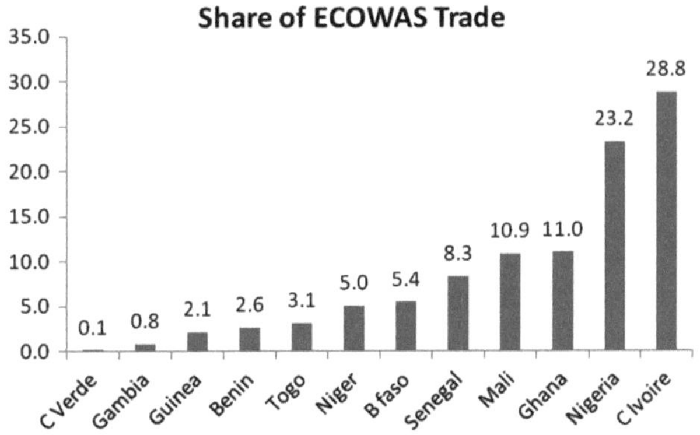

Fig. 4 Country's share of total trade within ECOWAS

region has increased from less than US$ 4 billion in 1993 to close to US$ 20 billion in 2008. In order to maintain this development there is a need for adequate infrastructure within the region.

We also examined the share of total trade in SSA accounted for by intra-ECOWAS trade for each country (except countries with no data). It was discovered that 55–90 % of the trade in SSA by West African countries were done within the region. In fact, countries such as Mali, Gambia, Burkina Faso and Niger did most of their trade activities with countries from within the region (Figure 3).

Since a lot of the ECOWAS countries trade more within the region as compared with SSA, we examined the share each country contributed to the regional trade (Fig. 4). The graph showed that Nigeria and Cote D'Ivoire accounted for 23.2 % and 28.8 % respectively. Due to the importance of these two countries, a better connectivity with other countries within the region might contribute significantly to intra-regional trade. Cape Verde had the least value of 0.1 %.

A breakdown of the total trade to imports and exports (Figure 5) indicated that the two largest countries (Nigeria and Cote D'Ivoire) export a lot to the region but they don't really import from the region. This is interesting because the other

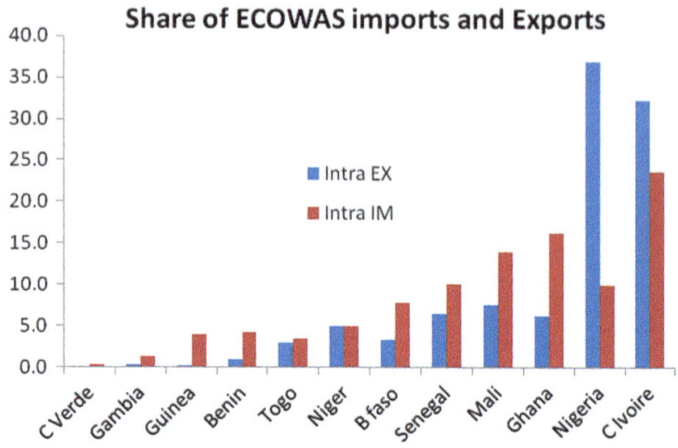

Fig. 5 Country's share of intra-regional exports and imports

countries in the region import more than they export to the region. There is a need to balance the trade flow within the region through capacity building, information dissemination and availability of adequate infrastructure.

3.3.2 Transportation in the Sub-Region

This section provides an ex-post analysis on transportation-related projects and programmes in Africa, with specific focus on West Africa.

In Africa in general and in the ECOWAS sub-region in particular, rail networks are the least developed. There have hardly been any new additions or reconstruction of railway lines since after the colonial era. According to AICD, generally, the rail roads in the region are poor and rarely used and close to non-existence. The private sector involvement in railroad construction was pronounced in Sitarail, linking Burkina Faso and Ivory Coast, was concessioned in 1995. This is the only rail network with significant cross border flow within the region. Though the rate of reform in this sub-sector picked up in the 2000s, the implementation process has proven to be slow. The 2007 statistics showed that of the 69,000 km of rail lines in Africa only 55,000 km is in operation and the majority of these are in the Southern and Northern parts of the continent (AfDB 2010).

The total road network in sub-Saharan Africa is still comparatively low at about 204 km per 1,000 km^2 of land area, with only about 25 % paved. This is way below the world average of 944 km per 1,000 km^2 of land area (AfDB 2010). Road freight is slow and expensive because of ill-maintained road networks, corruption and unnecessary paper work along the borders (Adekunle 2010). These roads are mostly in good condition and the seven major corridor in ECOWAS are almost entirely paved, though some are in poor condition. The regional corridors exclude Gambia, Sierra Leone, Liberia, Guinea Bissau and Guinea – these countries are totally neglected, and even in Nigeria there is no corridor passing through the country to Niger (as seen in AICD map – see Appendix). The present state of major corridors

Table 2 Corridors in the ECOWAS sub-region and their current state

Corridors	Good (%)	Fair (%)	Poor (%)	Paved (%)
Abidjan-Lagos	51	28	21	99
Tema-Ouagadougou-Bamako	67	31	2	100
Dakar-Bamako	48	20	32	100
Abidjan-Ouagadougou	33	23	44	100
Lome-Niamey	50	30	20	100
Cotonou-Niamey	50	8	42	99

Source: AICD 2010

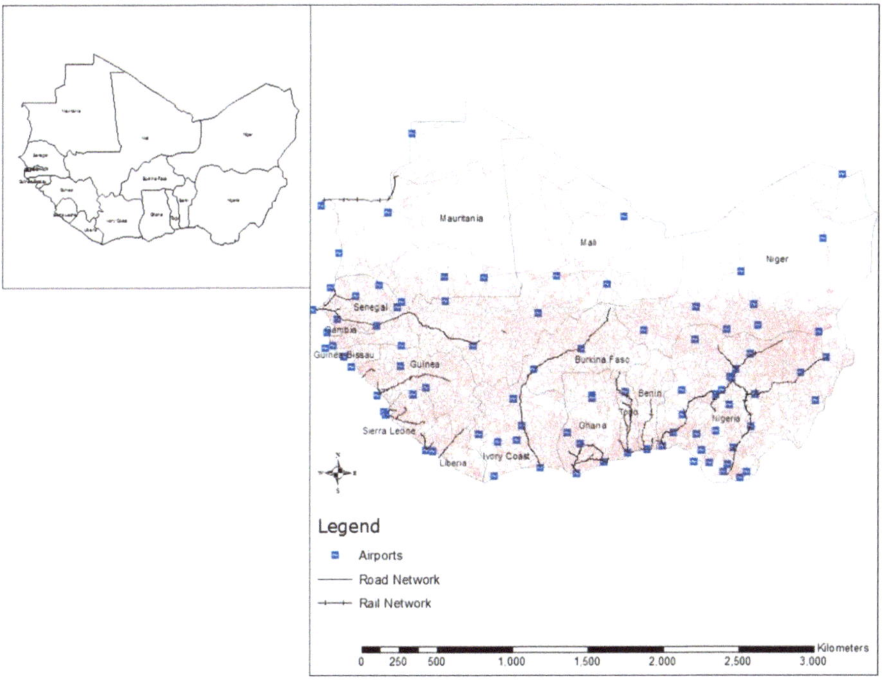

Fig. 6 Rail, roads and airports networks in ECOWAS

is presented in Table 2 and a map on the present rail, road, and airports in ECOWAS is presented in Figure 6.

With the majority of the ECOWAS countries lying along the coast, making use of the sea as a major transport route will be expected. However, there are a lot of challenges associated with the ports within the sub-region with regards to capacity, delays and bureaucracy. Ports are not of the best standards and lack the required capacity to deal with containers and goods processing. Though the ECOWAS sub-region has 25 significant ports, they are relatively small in size. The use of container transport, though in its early stage is growing with an average annual growth rate of 13.8 % in West Africa. The number of container trade handled by ports in the region increased by over 364 % between 1995 and 2005, whilst that of general cargo increased by 5.1 % during the same period (Mundy and Penfold 2008). However, the region contributes very little to total global trade.

There is little private investment in ports and with the increasing need for transshipment, it is important that this area be given the necessary attention. Within Africa, there are currently four regional hubs, two in East Africa, one in Southern Africa and one in West Africa (AfDB 2010). However, due to the civil war, Abidjan which used to play the role of the sub-regional hub has suffered some set-backs. The company Maersk currently makes use of ports in Spain and Morocco as hubs for West Africa trade. The Tema harbor in Ghana, which is one of the region's major ports, lacks the capacity to handle large numbers of containers and is currently under pressure to handle general cargo. Analysis has shown that the location of many ports within ECOWAS contributes to the lack of sufficient capacity. The location of the Apapa port in a major urban area is one such example.

Airport connectivity remains a major challenge in the sub-region. Since the collapse of the major Air Afrique Airline in 2004 and the collapse of other significant airlines within the region, coupled with stringent regulatory restrictions, inter-connections with the region have been difficult and often expensive. The air traffic within the region is mostly between Lagos and Accra (two Anglophone cities in the region), with Nigeria offering the most number of connections within the continent and the world. The major gateways to the continent, and the world in general, are however located in the Eastern and Southern parts of Africa, namely, Addis Ababa, Johannesburg and Nairobi. It is however believed that in the West, Nigeria has the potential to become its gateway but this is yet to be realized. The ECOWAS sub-region is yet to have a central air transport hub and smaller jets that can ply the West African route, linking countries to the hub.

ECOWAS countries are better in terms of accessibility to power as compared with other Sub-Saharan countries but the supply is still epileptic and expensive. There is relatively good access to signal and cables, though the services are still expensive (especially for internet access) but it's getting cheaper as a result of competition in the market. For example, there are presently more than 40 telecommunication companies in Nigeria, including MTN, Globacom and Zain (now Bharti Airtel). The fiber optic is working in the region but it is still cheaper to call US than to call some countries within the West African region, but the region is better in terms of roaming than other regions in the continent. Some of the countries in the region, namely Sierra Leone, Liberia and Guinea which had been plagued by internal conflicts are still highly dependent on satellite for communication and are yet to fully tap into the benefits of the fiber optic cable. The 2008 ICT development index (IDI) showed that of the top five countries in the African region, only one was from the West African region. These countries however still lag behind, ranking 66th–109th on a global scale. With financial assistance from the AfDB, a feasibility study for a Technology Park in Cape Verde to improve the ICT infrastructure is underway. The level of ICT concentration in the region is presented in Figures 7, 8, 9 and 10 based on 2003 data. Although some countries have gone through changes

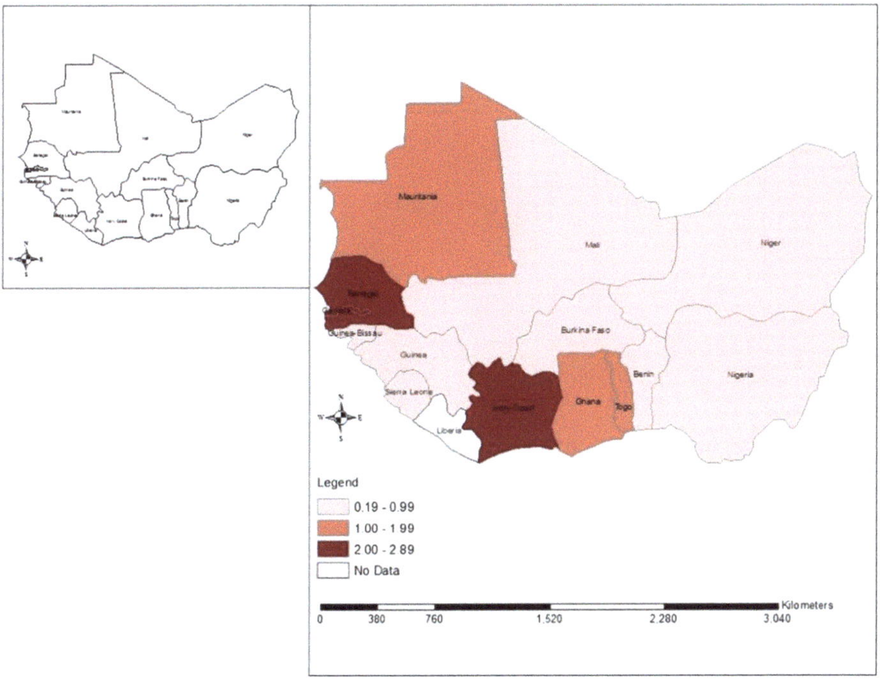

Fig. 7 Main telephone line (landlines) per 100 inhabitants

since that time, the changes are however not that different from what is shown in the maps. In fact, the accessibility to landlines has declined because of better access to mobile phones and inefficiency of the landline providers. A good example is Nigeria Telecommunication Limited (NITEL) that has not really lived up to expectations, leading to huge decline in customers subscription rates.

The ECOWAS, through funding from international donors has commissioned the construction of a 25 km Dakar toll road. This project once completed is expected to foster regional integration through an improvement of the Dakar Port. There are many other infrastructure projects being developed in Dakar to create a regional hub that is expected not only to enhance local economic activities, but also strengthen intra and inter-regional trade through the facilitation of the movement of goods and services. Efforts are also underway to reconstruct the Fulfuso-Sawla Road in Ghana that will form the major gateway from Tamale to the Upper West Region and Southern Burkina Faso. This is another project within the region that is expected to foster regional integration (AfDB Website).

The Trans-Gambia River Crossing project is also in the pipeline among the projects to be undertaken in the ECOWAS sub-region. This project will facilitate the flow of traffic between The Gambia and Senegal and also between member states of ECOWAS, through the international transport corridor between Dakar and Lagos. This is in line with the objectives of NEPAD in the area of transport that seeks to enhance regional co-operation through physical interconnections and is

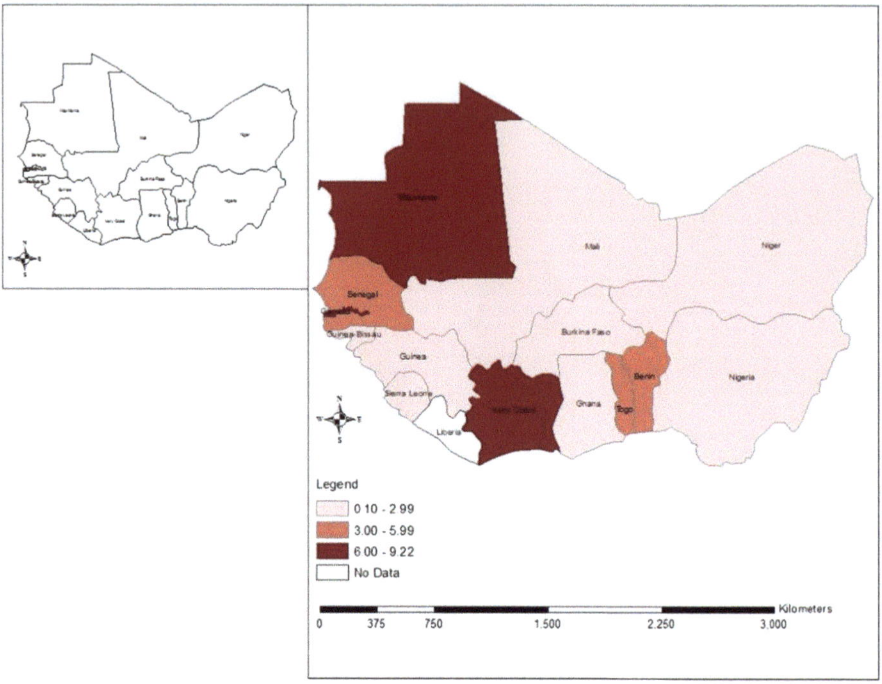

Fig. 8 Cellular subscribers per 100 inhabitants

envisaged to promote economic trade within the region. This bridge is also part of the Dakar-Gambia-Bissau-Conakry-Trans-West African Highway that is part of the ECOWAS program and is expected to close a major gap on the Coastal Trans-African Highway Cairo-Tanger-Dakar-Gambia-Bissau-Conakry-Lagos. This however remains a challenge as some of the countries within the Trans-West African Highway face national infrastructure challenges that will first need to be addressed. There is a new section of road network needed in Guinea connecting to the Boke border and one also in Liberia that will provide a link to the Ivorian border. In the case of Sierra Leone, the reconstruction of certain road networks need to be undertaken and a new road is essential in linking to the Liberian border. These are all hurdles that need to be sorted before this highway project can be fully realized. The Sierra Leone government has recently embarked on major infrastructure projects mainly in roads and this is a step that though will result in delays, will contribute to the progress of linking the region through a Trans Highway.

3.3.3 Efforts Towards Transportation Development, Coordination and Integration

As a means of mitigating the high risks and transaction costs involved in infrastructure ventures, the ECOWAS is establishing bilateral or multi-lateral special purpose

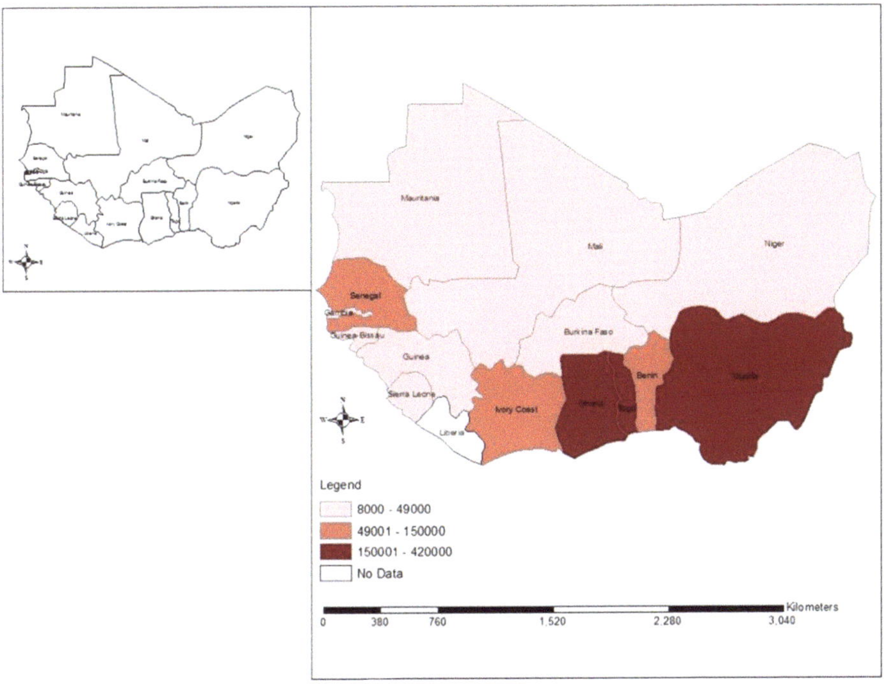

Fig. 9 Internet subscribers in ECOWAS

vehicles (SPVs), which would identify, prepare, and manage regional infrastructure projects and negotiate with private investors.

The ECOWAS sub-region works closely with the EU-Africa Partnership on Infrastructure as the project implementation body for projects designed for West Africa. This partnership aims among other things at improving economic growth, trade, regional integration and interconnectivity. The ECOWAS complements its efforts at improving physical infrastructure with that of the harmonization of legislation, regulations, and technical standards and have strategic regional bodies in place to help in facilitating trading activities.

Other organizations within the region have demonstrated their concern on the need to upgrade infrastructure within the continent. The African Development Bank in a bid to assist in the process of promoting regional infrastructure connectivity is working with several other continental initiatives. These include, the NEPAD Short-Term Action Plan (STAP), the NEPAD Medium-to-Long-Term Strategic Framework (MLTSF), the AU Infrastructure Master Plan Initiative and the Program for Infrastructure Development in Africa (PIDA).

The recently launched regional project by the International Telecommunication Union (ITU) and the European Union (EU) to facilitate the establishment of an integrated ICT market in West Africa is a commendable achievement by the regional body. The aim of ECOWAS in this regard is to adopt uniform legislative

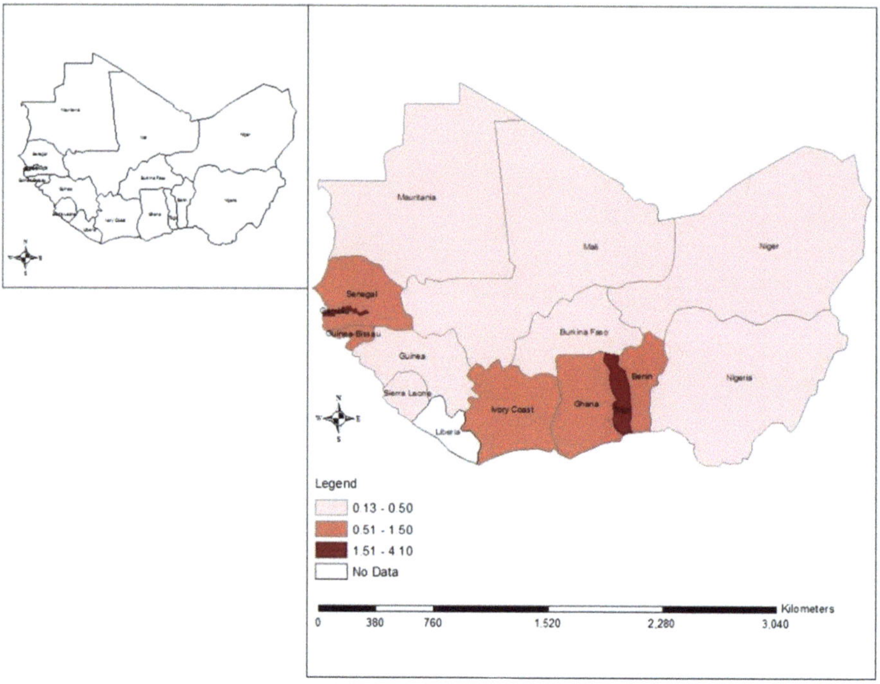

Fig. 10 Internet users per 100 inhabitants

and regulatory frameworks, have an interconnection and integration of national networks so as to have a single liberalized telecommunications market in the sub-region.

Furthermore, ECOWAS commission needs a strategic plan with appropriate policy formulation tactics and implementation assessed by monitoring and evaluation by experts rather than politicians and their loyalist. We want to see an ECOWAS with borders that aid regional trade and movement of labour – 'borderless West Africa'. It is also extremely important to have a light rail – regional light rail – that will link all the countries especially the ones on the coast. Harmonization of decision making and centralized decision making through ECOWAS commission will make project implementation across countries easier. We also hope that in a few years time we will have the equivalent of inter-state roads (US) or 400 series (Canada) in ECOWAS. The ECOWAS version can be named ECOWAS Interstate Highway (EIH) with jointly managed toll-gates – e.g. well linked road from Canada-US-Mexico (NAFTA). This is different from ECOWAS Interstate Road Transit Scheme (ISRT). The ISRT allows the movement of goods by road with customs approval in a member state that allows passage through other member states without duty, taxes and other restrictions while in transit. Trade will move in leaps if this infrastructural development is backed with mobile roam-able region and uninterrupted internet supply.

Finally, all this will happen if there is adequate data for making informed decisions and advising the policy makers. Thus, there is need for adequate collection of data on infrastructural variables within the ECOWAS commission.

4 Conclusions and Policy Recommendations

4.1 Introduction

This study has analyzed the pertinent issues relating to infrastructure development, trade and regional integration in West Africa. Within the period under study (1993–2008), the volume of trade in the sub-region rose from approximately US $4 billion to about US$20 billion, representing a 400 % increase in 15 years, which is partly an indication of desirable and workable macroeconomic policies. More specifically, 55–90 % of ECOWAS exports take place within the SSA, with Nigeria and Cote d'Ivoire recording the largest volume of about 23.2 % and 28.8 % respectively. However, on the other hand, ECOWAS member states significantly import from outside SSA. Thus, there is a dire need for a balance of trade flow within the sub-region through a policy directed towards capacity strengthening, information dissemination and expansion of infrastructural facilities.

With respect to transportation-related projects and programmes in West Africa, rail network is the least developed. In fact, the pace of rail policy reforms was accelerated in the 2000s, the implementation process has proven to be slow partly due to inadequate technical capacity in the sub-region. On the other hand, major roads are mostly in good conditions and the seven major corridors in ECOWAS are almost entirely paved, though some are in poor conditions (Adekunle 2010). It is important to note that within about three decades of existence of ECOWAS, major countries like Gambia, Sierra Leone, Liberia, Guinea Bissau and Guinea do not have regional corridors of trade. Thus, there is a need to urgently implement policies which will be targeted at the maintenance and expansion of ECOWAS corridors of trade.

Though majority of ECOWAS member states are located along the coastlines, and also have 25 large sea-ports (by African standards), they hardly utilize the sea as a major transport route. This is partly due to the lack of required capacity to process goods and manage containers. This is evident in the fact that ECOWAS as a regional bloc contributes very little to total African and global container traffic (about 1 % in terms of number of container trade handled; and about 2 % with respect to general cargo). Thus, the regional government needs to initiate policies and programmes which are targeted at developing the sea-port sub-sector of the infrastructure industry.

The airline sub-sector suffered a drastic setback since the collapse of the major Air Afrique Airline in 2004. Though Nigeria has the potential to serve as the airline hub for the sub-region, it is yet to realize this partly due to lack of willpower. Sub-regional coordinated policies should therefore be pursued in order to have a central air transport hub, in which smaller jets can ply the West African routes, and also linking various cities to the central hub.

Though ECOWAS countries are partly connected to electricity when compared to their counterparts in SSA, the supply is still largely epileptic and expensive. With respect to telecommunications, West African countries lag behind, ranking between 66th and 109th on a global scale. Thus, West Africa still needs to implement policies and programmes which will be targeted at providing affordable power supply, telecommunication services, internet access and other ICT facilities.

In summary, the qualitative and ex-post analysis indicate that West Africa has witnessed some developments but there is still a lack of institutional framework that creates incentives for infrastructural development in the region (Odularu 2006a, 2009, 2011a).

4.2 Policy Recipe for Fostering Regional Integration Through Infrastructure Development and Coordination in West Africa

- Regional infrastructure development policies should be strategically mainstreamed into West Africa's regional integration plans so that infrastructure policies respond and adapt to the needs of regional integration policies and not the other way round. Further, regional integration and transportation policies should be systematically harmonised at national and regional levels.
- West African governments should ensure that infrastructure and investment policy frameworks effectively promote the regional integration efforts. This could be achieved by (i) providing monetary and fiscal incentives for transportation development initiatives that promote regional integration; (ii) strengthening relevant institutions for transportation development.
- Infrastructure development policies should provide opportunities and alternatives to West African businesses and also promote the use of relevant institutions and tools (e.g. risk management instruments, ICT-based market information systems, et cetera.) that foster regional integration.
- There is a dire need for regular policy dialogues among all actors/stakeholders to facilitate building up consensus level on bottlenecks to more coherent infrastructure and regional integration policies without overlooking the political economy of regional integration.
- Joint venture initiatives between public and private sector, such as public-private partnerships (PPP), should be supported in order to leverage infrastructure and regional integration programmes for regional development.
- Funding for infrastructure initiatives should be made contingent upon evidence of the participation of all relevant stakeholders (private sector, non-state actors, et cetera) in the design of CAADP compacts and investment plans.
- The successful promotion and sustainable development of the sector in West Africa require strong policy and institutional support.

Appendix: Major Corridors in ECOWAS

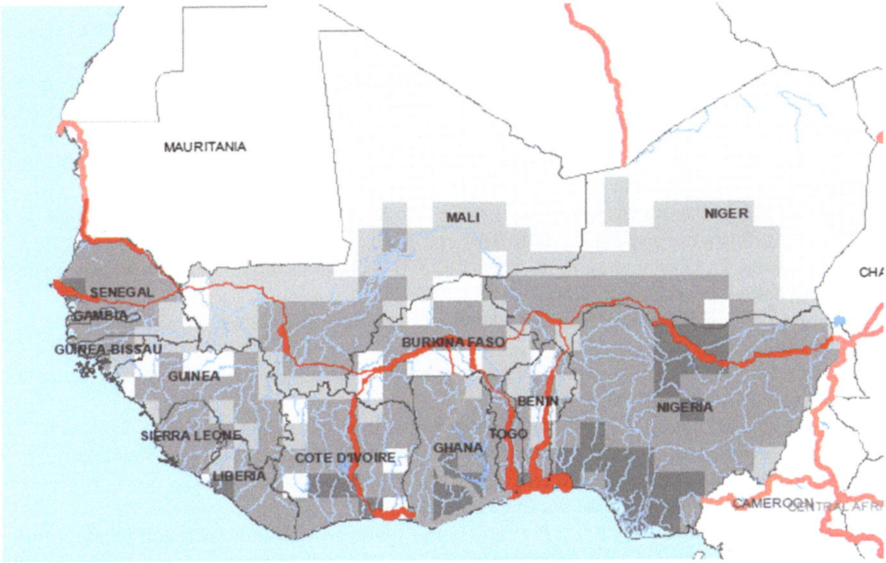

A map showing the major corridors in ECOWAS (Source AICD 2010)

Acknowledgements We thank ECOWAS-EPAU for providing the funding for this study. We also appreciate the contributions of Glen Filson, Carlyle Farrell, Caiphas Chekwoti, Diery Seck, Ciliaka Gitau, and Gift Dumedah.

References

Adekunle B (2010) Joint border post at ECOWAS borders. Nigerian Tribune, http://www.tribune.com.ng/index.php/opinion/2370-joint-border-post-at-ecowas-borders.html. Accessed 11 Mar 2010

Adekunle B, Gitau M (2013) Illusion or reality: understanding the trade flow between China and Sub-Saharan Africa. Journal of African Business 14(2):117–126

African Development Bank (1999) African development report 1999: Infrastructure development in Africa. Oxford University Press, New York, pp 25

African Development Bank (2010) Infrastructure deficit and opportunities in Africa. Economic Brief, AfDB 1Sept 2010

African Development Bank. Website http://www.afdb.org

Africa Infrastructure Country Diagnostic (AICD) (2010) Report: a time for transformation. AICD website – http://www.infrastructureafrica.org

AICD (2010) Africa's infrastructure: a time for transformation, Africa Infrastructure Country Diagnostic, Report, Forster, V. and Briceno-Garmendra, C. (eds.), World Bank, Washington DC
Amadji A, Yeat AJ (1995) Have transport costs contributed to the relative decline of sub-Saharan African exports?: some preliminary empirical evidence. World Bank policy research paper 1559, The World Bank, Washington, DC
Barro RJ (1990) Government spending in a simple model of endogenous growth. J Polit Econ 98 (5):S102–S125
Bhattacharyay BN (2010) Estimating demand for infrastructure in energy, transport, telecommunications, water and sanitation in Asia and the Pacific: 2010–2020; ADBI working paper series
Bonaglia F, La Ferrara E, Marcellino M (2000) Public capital and economic performance: evidence from Italy, (Giornale Degli Economist e Annali di Economia) GDE, Bocconi University 59(2): 221–244
Brixiova Z, Mutambatsere E, Ambert C, Etienne D (2011) Closing Africa's infrastructure gap: innovative financing and risks. AfDB Afr Econ Brief 2:1
Brun JF, Carrere C, Guillaumont P, de Melo J (2005) Has distance died? Evidence from a panel gravity model. World Bank Econ Rev 19(1):99–120
Canning F (1998) A database of world stocks of infrastructure 1950–1995. World Bank Econ Rev 12(3):529–547
Canning D, Fay M (1993) The effects of transportation networks on economic growth. Columbia University Mimeo, New York
Canning D, Fay M, Perotti R (1994) Infrastructure and growth. In: Baldassarri M, Paganaetto M, Phelps ES (eds) International differences – growth rates. St. Martin's Press, New York
Carrêre C (2006) Revisiting the effects of regional trade agreements on trade flows with proper specification of the gravity model. Eur Econ Rev 50/2:223–247
Clark X, Dollar D, Micco A (2004) Port efficiency, maritime transport costs and bilateral trade, NBER working paper, 10353, March 2004
East African Business Council (2005) A study on non-tariff barriers and development of a business climate index in the East Africa region, Report Prepared by GTZ & Daima Associates, Arusha
Easterly W, Levine R (1994) Africa's growth tragedy. In: Plenary session of African Research Consortium (AERC) meeting, Nairobi, May 1994
Economic Community of West Africa States (ECOWAS) website: http://www.comm.ecowas.int/dept/stand.php?id=f_f1_brief&lang=en
Egert B, Kozluk TJ, Sutherland D (2009) Infrastructure and growth: empirical evidence, vol 685, Working paper. OECD Economics Department, Paris
Fernandez M, Montuenga-Gomez VM (2003) The effects of public capital on the growth in Spanish productivity. Contemp Econ Policy 21(3):383–393
Fink C, Mattoo A, Neagu CI (2002a) Trade in international maritime services: how much does policy matter? World Bank Econ Rev 16(1):81–108
Fink C, Mattoo A, Neagu CI (2002b) Assessing the role of communication costs in international trade. World Bank working paper #2929. The World Bank, Washington, DC
Ghafoor A, Yorucu V (2002) Public expenditure and productivity puzzle: the case of Northern Cyprus. Middle East Tech Univ Stud Dev 29(1–2):69–85
Grigoriou C (2007) Landlockedness, infrastructure and trade: new estimates for Central Asian countries. The World Bank, Development Research Group, Trade Team, Washington, DC
Hakfoort J (1996) Public capital, private sector productivity and economic growth: a macroeconomic perspective. In: Batten D, Karlsson C (eds) Infrastructure and the complexity of economic development. Springer-Verlag, New York, pp 61–72
Jimenez E (1995) Human and physical infrastructure: public investment and pricing policies in developing countries. In: Behrman J, Srinivasan TN (eds) Handbook of development economics, vol 3B. Elsevier Science, Amsterdam
Kasekende L, Ng'eno NK (2000) Regional integration and economic integration in Eastern and Southern Africa. In: Oyejide AE, Collier IP (eds) Regional integration and trade liberalisation

in Sub-Saharan Africa: framework, issues and methodological perspectives, vol 1, Macmillan Press Ltd., London
Kwaku D (1995) The African economic community: problems and prospects. Afr Today 42 (4):1–35
Limão N, Venables AJ (2001) Infrastructure, geographical disadvantage, transport costs and trade. World Bank Econ Rev 15(3):451–479
Mistry PS (2000) Africa's record of regional cooperation and integration. Afr Aff 99:553–557
Morrison CJ, Schwartz AE (1996) State infrastructure and productive performance. Am Econ Rev 86(5):1095–1111
Mundy M, Penfold A (2008) Beyond the bottlenecks: ports in Sub-Saharan Africa, Background paper 8, Africa Infrastructure Diagnostic
Ndulu B, Niekerk LK, Reinikka R (2005) Infrastructure, regional integration and growth in Sub-Saharan Africa. In: Teunissen JJ, Akkerman A (eds) Africa in the world economy – the national regional and international challenges. The Hague, Fondad
Nordas HK, Piermartini R (2004) The global textile and clothing industry post the agreement on textiles and clothing WTO discussion paper. ERSD-2004-04
Odularu GO (2005) The challenges of globalisation and regional integration: lessons from Africa. Being a paper presented at the international conference on 'NEPAD and the future of economic policy in Africa,' at the United Nations African Institute for Economic Development and Planning (IDEP), Dakar
Odularu GO (2006a) Trade facilitation as a tool for promoting regional development in Africa. Nig Inst Int Aff Nig Forum 27(3–4):126–136
Odularu GO (2006b) International conference on ECOWAS milestones in regional integration, NIIA Conference Room, 23–24 May 2006
Odularu GO (2007) The cooperation between the EU and ECOWAS', Centre for European Integration Studies (ZEI), Bonn University, Bonn. Accessible at www.zei.de/dowload/zei_dp/dp_c176koesler_zimmek.pdf
Odularu GO (2009) Export diversification as a promotion strategy for intra-ECOWAS trade expansion. Afr J Bus Manage 3 (2): 032–038. Available online at http://www.academicjournals.org/AJBM
Odularu GO (2011a) An analysis of ECOWAS – EU agricultural trade flows. A post-doctoral dissertation published by LAP Lambert Academic Publishing, Berlin. http://www.bod.de/index.php?id=296&objk_id=628166
Odularu GO (2011b) Market access policy interventions for enhancing ECOWAS-EU agri-trade relations. Pac J Sci Technol (PJST) 12(2): 260–273, November 2011 (Fall). Visit http://www.akamaiuniversity.us/PJST12_2_260.pdf
OECD (2005) Regional integration agreements, OECD Publication, Paris. Online Access http://www.oecd.org/dataoecd/39/37/1923431.pdf
OECD (2010) Infrastructure in Africa, Policy Brief (2) October, 2010. pp 1–4. Available online at: http://www.un.org/africa/osaa/reports/2010_Infrastructurebrief.pdf
Pereira AM, Sagales OR (1999) Public capital formation and regional development in Spain. Rev Dev Econ 3(3):281–294
Perkins P, Fedderke J, Luiz J (2005) An analysis of economic infrastructure investment in South Africa. South Afr J Econ 73(2):211–228
Polenske K (1994) Roundtable discussion: critical issues in infrastructure in developing countries. Proc World Bank Annu Conf Dev Econ 1993:476–480
Raballand G (2003) Determinants of the negative impact of being landlocked on trade: an empirical investigation through the central Asian case. Comp Econ Stud 45:520–536
Radelet S, Sachs JD (1999) Shipping costs, manufactured exports, and economic growth. Mimeo, HIID, Cambridge
Rauch JE & Trindade V (2003a) Information, international substitutability and globalisation. Am Econ Rev 93(3):775–791

Rauch JE & Trindade V (2003b) Ethnic Chinese networks in international trade. Rev Econ Stat 84 (1):116–130
Röller LH, Waverman L (2001) Telecommunications infrastructure and economic development: a simultaneous approach. Am Econ Rev 91(4):909–923
Rosenstein-Rodan P (1943) Problems of industrialisation of Eastern and South-Eastern Europe. Econ J 53:202–211
Sahoo P, Dash RK (2009) Infrastructure development and economic growth in India. J Asia Pac Econ 14(4):351–365
Sanchez-Robles B (1998) The role of infrastructure investment in development: some macroeconomic considerations. Int J Transp Econ 25(2):113–136
Soloaga I, Wilson JS, Mejia A (2006) Moving forward faster: trade facilitation reform and Mexican competitiveness World Bank policy research working paper 3953, June 2006
The Punch www.punchng.com/AddComments.aspx?.../Articl.aspx?...aspx&theartic=Art20110508228915 ECOWAS trade: exporters task FG over cargo vessels; By Agency Reporter; 8 May 2011
UNCTAD (2003) Review of maritime transport, 2003. UNCTAD, Geneva
UNCTAD (2013) Intra-Africa trade: unlocking private sector dynamism. UNCTAD Economic Development in Africa Report, UNCTAD, Geneva
UNECA (2004) Assessing regional integration in Africa. United Nations Economic Commission for Africa, Addis Ababa
Wilson JS, Mann CL and Otsuki T (2003) Trade facilitation and capacity building: global perspective unpublished manuscript, World Bank, Washington, DC
World Bank (2000) Can Africa claim the 21st century. The World Bank, Washington, DC
World Bank (2001) Global economic prospects and the developing countries 2002: making trade work for the poor. The World Bank, Washington, DC
World Bank (2009) Global economic prospects
World Bank (2010) World development indicators
World Bank (2010) World Bank indicator. International Bank for Reconstruction and Development, The World Bank, Washington, DC. http://data.worldbank.org/sites/default/files/frontmatter.pdf
WTO (2005) Quantitative economics in WTO dispute settlement: thematic essays, WTO report 2005, 171–211, Geneva

Part II
Regional Macroeconomic Policy

Policy Coordination Framework for the Proposed Monetary Union in ECOWAS

Akpan H. Ekpo and Elijah Udoh

Abstract There is no doubt that regional economic integration and eventual monetary union would be generally beneficial to the economies of West Africa. Each country in the sub-region conceptualizes and implements its own monetary, fiscal and exchange rate policies, among others. There have been attempts in recent years by some countries to design such policies in line with efforts to meet both primary and secondary criteria for convergence. However, these policies seem not to be properly coordinated. They remain country specific and focused thus defeating the essence of moving towards a monetary union.

This paper attempts to shows analytically that stability can be achieved through monetary union but at a cost; loss of ability to exploit monetary policy to boost output. However, effective risk-sharing mechanisms and economic policy coordination within a holistic framework would smooth the process towards a successful monetary union.

Keywords Monetary union • ECOWAS • Policy coordination

1 Introduction

Since the European Monetary Union Euro experiment of 1999, there has been increasing interest in monetary Union and common currency areas. The Economic Community of West African States (ECOWAS) was established in 1975 with the

---

Paper presented at the 3rd Annual Conference on "Regional Integration in Africa (ACRIA 3)" held in Dakar, Senegal, July 4–5, 2012, organized by CREPOL

A.H. Ekpo (✉) • E. Udoh
West African Institute for Financial and Economic Management (WAIFEM), Lagos, Nigeria
e-mail: ahekpo@waifem-cbp.org; eudoh@waifem-cbp.org

D. Seck (ed.), *Regional Economic Integration in West Africa*, Advances in African Economic, Social and Political Development, DOI 10.1007/978-3-319-01282-7_3,

central goal of monetary and economic integration in West Africa. ECOWAS Monetary Cooperation Programme (EMCP) was established in 1987 with the intention to form one monetary zone and one common currency. The ECOWAS zone has two main blocs, namely Francophone and Anglophone countries. The Francophone countries established a monetary union in 1948 known as the WAEMU and adopted a common currency called CFA franc. The CFA zone maintain a fixed exchange rate with the CFA franc tie to the French franc at fixed parity, which was altered only once in 1994. Five non-WAEMU countries, in particular Nigeria, Ghana, the Gambia, Guinea and Sierra Leone, are in the process of forming the second monetary union to be known as the West African Monetary Zone (WAMZ) and adopting a common currency. Although the formation of a full-fledged WAMZ and a single-currency area has suffered many delays because the WAMZ member states failed to achieve the convergence criteria, it is believed that by forming a common currency, the zone can benefit immensely from enhanced trade, investment, fiscal discipline, economic growth and price stability.

In recent times, the ECOWAS countries, those within the proposed WAMZ in particular, have embarked on series of macroeconomic reforms to improve macroeconomic management of their domestic economies to attain the convergence criteria for monetary union and a common currency area. However, these reforms are not coordinated. A coordinated approach to policy is required to guide member states towards the attainment of the convergence criteria for the monetary union and thereafter for the smooth operation of the monetary union.

The main aim of this paper is to propose an economic policy coordination framework for the intended West African monetary union and common currency area. The experience of the European Monetary union has shown the economic policy coordination is essential for the success and sustainability of the monetary Union. The paper is organized thus: following the introduction, Sect. 2 reviews the literature on monetary union and optimum currency area while Sect. 3 presents the theoretical model. Section 4 focuses on the historical and institutional background of economic integration in West Africa. In Sect. 5, the experience of European Union with economic policy coordination is discussed while Sect. 6 summarizes useful lessons for the proposed ECOWAS monetary union. Concluding remarks are provided in Sect. 7.

2 Literature Review

The traditional literature on monetary union and optimal currency areas discusses the costs of forfeiting monetary policy autonomy and the corresponding importance of alternative adjustment mechanisms for external imbalances. In his pioneering study, Mundell (1961) emphasized labour mobility, as a crucial adjustment mechanism for idiosyncratic shocks, and therefore a key precondition for forming an optimum currency area (OCA). Price and wage flexibility were also seen as important for coping with idiosyncratic demand shocks. Because shocks were more likely to be similar among highly integrated economies, McKinnon (1963) suggested the degree of openness as a key indicator in forming an OCA.

Completing the trilogy of classic OCA studies, Kenen (1969) introduced product diversification as an element of an OCA emphasizing that regions with a highly diversified production base should be better equipped to maintain a currency union than regions with low diversification because the latter were more vulnerable to asymmetric disturbances. In addition, he pointed out fiscal integration among regions as a mitigating factor because of the implied risk sharing.

More recent literature extended the basic economic insights from the classical OCA approach to incorporate new dimensions, including the effectiveness and credibility of monetary policy (Beetsma and Bovenberg 1999), the centrality of shock correlations (Alesina et al. 2002), and the endogeneity of OCA adequacy.

While it is generally understood that a higher correlation of shocks between countries makes monetary union more beneficial, Melitz (1991) shows that even if countries face identical shocks, they might still need different policy responses given different initial economic positions and country-specific transmission mechanisms.

Because OCA criteria are endogenous to the creation of a monetary union, a number of studies have suggested that monetary integration may be self-validating. Frankel and Rose (1997) argue that openness (degree of integration) and income correlation are linked because the correlation of business cycles across countries depends on trade integration. Frankel (1999) notes that the endogeneity of OCA criteria means that some parameters such as openness and income correlation are not irrevocably fixed, but instead they can change over time in response to countries' fundamental policies and to exogenous factors.

Mongelli (2002) qualifies their claim, showing that the endogeneity of OCA criteria depends on the pre-existing degree of convergence. De Grauwe and Mongelli (2004) focus on the endogeneity of economic integration, financial integration, symmetry of shocks and labour market flexibility. Blanchard and Wolfers (2000) point out the endogeneity of labour market institutions and Issing (2001) emphasizes the endogeneity of political integration.

Debrun et al. (2005) integrate traditional arguments against monetary union with potential benefits by modelling explicitly the substitutability between monetary integration and domestic institutional reforms. The DMP model compares the costs of sharing a single monetary policy in terms of foregone stabilization with the benefits of the policy coordination brought about by fixed exchange rates. They establish the relevance of asymmetries in institutional quality and in the credibility of monetary commitments to macroeconomic stability. In contrast to the OCA literature, they emphasize positive "monetary externalities" associated with larger monetary unions because of the greater gains from monetary coordination and from a more effective separation between monetary and fiscal powers.[1]

---

[1] See Beetsma and Giulodori (2010) for comprehensive review of recent research on Optimum currency Area and monetary integration.

Economic and monetary integration of ECOWAS countries has been the subject of an extensive literature. Cham (2009) shows that the WAMZ has not fulfil the necessary conditions for macroeconomic convergence as well as the criteria for optimal currency area. This implies that policies must be geared towards reforming the economies of the respective countries in the WAMZ to satisfy the basic criteria for convergence and optimal currency area without which it would be counterproductive to adopt a single currency for the zone.

Taking the argument further, Masson and Pattillo (2001) and Debrun et al. (2002, 2005, 2008) develop a multi-country model of monetary union using a simple theoretical framework calibrated to reflect some of the prominent feature of African economies and political institutions, which are often ignored in the traditional EMU models. Using this model, Debrun et al. (2002, 2005) assess the proposed ECOWAS monetary unions and conclude that it would not be in the interests of other ECOWAS countries, unless it were accompanied by effective discipline over Nigeria's fiscal policies.

Debrun et al. (2010) probe the issue of a wider monetary integration in sub-Saharan Africa. The cost-benefit analysis of monetary integration indicates that the proposed monetary union would bring net losers and net gainers. They conclude that the potential gains of strengthening domestic macroeconomic frameworks do not significantly differ from those associated with monetary integration, thereby reducing the attractiveness of joining the proposed monetary unions.

Asonuma et al. (2012) using the DMP framework simulate the welfare effects of monetary integration on members of common monetary area (CMA). While the CMA taken as a whole benefits from the monetary union, some individual countries experience welfare losses.

3 Theoretical Model

In recent empirical literature on monetary union and optimum currency area, the Debrun et al. (2005) (here after DMP) model has received wide applicability. The reason for interest in this model is twofold. First, it emphasizes the role of commitment problems in macroeconomic policy, an aspect which is particularly relevant in Africa, where credible institutional fixes such as central bank independence and fiscal rules are harder to implement than in other regions. Second, it allows for analytical solutions while addressing at the same time the interaction between monetary and fiscal policies and international policy coordination (Debrun et al. 2008).

DMP assumes an n-good, n-country economic area that is small relative to the rest of the world. Countries differ in terms of size, economic governance, budget flows and terms-of-trade disturbances.

The underlying economic structure is built around a static new-classical Phillips Curve augmented with a distortionary tax and a negative externality capturing competitive devaluations in trading partners and one-period budget constraint without public debt (see Eqs. 1 and 2).

$$y_i = y_N + c\left(\pi_i - \pi_i^e - \tau_i\right) - \sum_{k \neq i,\, k=1}^{n} \theta_{i,k} c\left(\pi_k - \pi_k^e\right) + \varepsilon_i, i = 1, \ldots, n \quad (1)$$

$$g_i = \overline{\rho}_i + \mu \pi_i + \tau_i - \delta_i \quad (2)$$

Where $\theta_{i,k}$ represent the marginal effect of a monetary policy action in country k on output in country i. ε_i is the term of trade shock, g is socially beneficial government expenditure in percentage of output, δ is funds diverted from socially beneficial government expenditure in percentage of output, π is the inflation rate in country i, T is tax revenue in percent of output, y is logarithm of output and ρ is permanent non-tax revenue from natural resource endowment in percentage of output.

National monetary policies in one country affect economic activity of other countries in the region negatively. For instance, an expansionary monetary policy by one country introduces a form of 'beggar-thy-neighbour' by reducing output of other countries in the region. On the contrary, fiscal expansions have no direct spillover effects.

In the benchmark case of flexible exchange rates with politically dependent central banks, monetary and fiscal policies are determined jointly by minimizing deviations of the effective tax rate, public expenditure and inflation from specific objectives.

$$U_i^G = \frac{1}{2}\left\{-a(\pi_i - \widetilde{\pi}(\varepsilon_i))^2 - b\tau_i^2 - \gamma(g_i - \widetilde{g}_i)^2\right\} + y_i \quad (3)$$

Equation 3 implies that the marginal benefit of output gain is constant whereas deviations of inflation, taxes and expenditure from ideal levels (denoted by a tilde) are increasingly costly.

These objectives are non-negative constants except for inflation, which fluctuates to partly accommodate Phillips curve (supply shocks). This captures the preferred trade-off between the variability of inflation and that of output.

$$\pi(\varepsilon_i) = -\eta \varepsilon_i, \text{so that } \pi(0) = 0 \text{ and } \pi'_{\varepsilon_i} < 0 \quad (4)$$

A negative (positive) output shock thus induces the policymaker to tolerate positive (negative) inflation. Finally, governments prefer output expansions to contractions. Technically the marginal utility of an increase in output is constant and equal to 1 for simplicity.

Equilibrium policies deviate systematically from the first best, reflecting the government proclivity for using monetary policy to boost activity beyond its potential and the inflationary impact of the waste of tax money levied through distortionary instruments. In other words, instead of pursuing a policy of commitment to full structural reforms which may be costly in the short term but beneficial in the longer term, the authority may opt for inflationary tax which would face less opposition and counterproductive in the long run.

A vast literature suggests that the solution to this inflationary bias lies in the delegation of monetary policy to an agency (an independent central bank) whose motivations differ from the policymakers' objective (DMP 2008). The main drawback of the independent central bank model is that independence could be threatened when the incentive to engineer a monetary expansion overwhelms the cost of reverting to pure discretion (McCallum 1995). In other words, central bank independence can only tame inflationary bias if the costs of removing such independence are large enough.

Another solution to the inflationary bias problem, when national reform is impossible or incredible is the formation of a regional monetary union. In a monetary union, monetary policy is formulated by a regional/supranational central bank, whose actions maximize a weighted average of individual governments' utility functions,

$$U^{RCB} = \sum_{i=1}^{n} \omega_i U_i^G \tag{5}$$

With $\omega_i > 0, \forall_i$ and $\sum_{i=1}^{n} \omega_i = 1$

The Phillips curve faced by the supranational central bank for each member of the monetary union (M) becomes:

$$y_i = y_N + c\left(1 - \theta_i^M\right)\left(\pi_M - \pi_M^e\right) - c\tau_i - \sum_{k \notin M}^{n} \theta_{i,k} c\left(\pi_k - \pi_k^e\right) + \varepsilon_i, \forall i \in M, \tag{6}$$

With $\theta_i^M = \sum_{k \in M} \theta_{i,k}$

The time consistent policy mix yields the following solution for common monetary policy inflation rate:

$$\pi_{MU}^* = \frac{\gamma\mu b}{\Lambda}\tilde{g}_{G,A} + \frac{\gamma(1+\mu) + b - \theta_A(b+\gamma)}{\Lambda}c - \frac{\eta a(b+\gamma)}{\Lambda}\varepsilon_A \tag{7}$$

θ_A captures the extent of the monetary policy externalities internalized through participation in the monetary union. A higher θ_A will ensure that average equilibrium inflation in the union is lower. θ_A is determined by the size of the union and the intensity of intra-regional trade linkages. All things being equal, the model implies that a large group of high-inflation countries with strong regional trade linkages would expect to gain more from monetary unification than a small group of low-inflation countries with limited regional trade. DMP model, in a nutshell, demonstrates that centralized monetary policy brings about lower inflation across the union but it is less effective at stimulating output in each individual country because there is no gain to expect from a depreciation of the national currency against trading partners in the region. The major cost of unification lies in the inadequacy of the regional monetary policy in the face of country-specific shocks. Hence, pointing to the importance of countercyclical fiscal policies, effective transfer and risk-sharing mechanisms.

3.1 The Challenge of Fiscal Policy Coordination

The DMP model assumes away fiscal policy yet this aspect is important if monetary union is to be effective. However, regional fiscal policy coordination is difficult to implement; each country prefers dealing with fiscal policy rather than surrender it to a regional group. Apart from the seeming loss of sovereignty, the characteristics of countries are dissimilar across, for example, countries may be at different stages of economic development. Furthermore, priorities of countries differ. Within each country, it is rather difficult to coordinate fiscal policy. Theoretically, macroeconomic management implies the coordination of fiscal and monetary policy by the finance arm of government and the central bank. However, in practice, even in countries with central bank independence, the coordination is generally not smooth and more often the pressure comes from the fiscal side of the equation. Where there are huge deficits, the implementation of monetary policy becomes challenging. Table 3 below shows that all the countries in the WAMZ were unable to satisfy the deficit/GDP criteria for convergence indicating the presence of fiscal dominance. It is, therefore, apparent that regional fiscal policy coordination is crucial for the 'success' of a monetary union. But to formulate and implement such a policy remain an onerous task (Ekpo and Afangideh 2010a; Ekpo and Afangideh 2010b; Ekpo 2011).

4 Monetary Integration in West Africa

4.1 Historical and Institutional Arrangements

Countries in West Africa have been experiencing one form of economic integration or the other since the colonial era. The colonial administrations (French, British, Portuguese, Spanish, etc) tried to integrate the colonies into their economies as suppliers of raw materials and consumers of their finished products and even replaced the local currencies (e.g. cowries) with their currencies (British pounds sterling, French franc, Portuguese real and Spanish silver dollars).

In the 1970s, three economic groupings emerged: the first, established in 1972, was West African Economic community (presently known as West African

Economic and Monetary Union (WAEMU) or UEMOA (French acronym)). The second was ECOWAS founded in 1975 and the last was Mano River Union founded in 1976.

Over the years, the francophone countries have maintained their WAEMU backed by France and later the European Union. ECOWAS has been less successful in achieving its primary goals of greater economic and monetary integration due to some factors including, the low level intra-regional trade, unsatisfactory implementation of the trade liberalization scheme, parallel monetary arrangements and lack of political will (WAMI 2004).

In 1999, five of the non-WAEMU ECOWAS countries opted to start the process that would launch a second monetary union to be named WAMZ. Initially scheduled to be actualised in 2003, the WAMZ programme has been extended more than twice, to 2005, 2009 and now 2015 as a result of the poor performance of the member countries on the macroeconomic convergence criteria.

To complement efforts at economic integration and foster the realisation of improved economic growth and welfare of the citizens of the member countries, ECOWAS monetary Cooperation Programme was launched in 1987. The main goal of EMCP was the introduction of the ECOWAS common currency within 5 years of its implementation. This terminal date has since been revised several times and it is now pending the full-fledged operation of the WAMZ and common currency.

Some of the institutional and policy measures implemented in pursuit of the ECOWAS monetary Cooperation Programme include the following:

(a) Establishment of the West African Monetary Agency (WAMA) in 1995
(b) Trade and exchange controls
(c) Exchange Rate Alignment
(d) Market-oriented monetary controls
(e) Payments system improvement
(f) Design of an ECOWAS Exchange Rate Mechanism (EERM)

4.2 Macroeconomic Convergence

According to European Union Commission (1990, pp. 4–28), monetary union requires virtually complete convergence of economic variables. The well-functioning of a monetary union is not limited to macroeconomic convergence of its member countries alone, but it demands the convergence in policy preferences, or at least agreement on the policy objectives and therefore on the weighting of targets and choice of instruments of economic policy.

Some scholars, like De Grauwe (2006), have argued vehemently that political and fiscal convergence is critical for a sustainable monetary convergence process. They argue that political union would allow for the establishment of the systems of fiscal transfers which could help deal with asymmetric shocks and create mechanisms for mitigating cases of moral hazard arising from these transfers. The success of the German political and monetary unification and failure of previous monetary convergence projects like the Latin and Scandinavian monetary unions support De Grauwe's argument.[2] In the contemporary era, the Euro Sovereign Debt Crisis in Euro Zone further supports the need for political and fiscal convergence as the basis for successful monetary convergence.

Given that meeting the macroeconomic convergence criteria is very crucial for entry into monetary union, and a guarantee of its smooth functioning, member countries must attain and comply with certain target requirements that need to be satisfied before and after launching the monetary union.

For West Africa, these criteria have been classified into two groups: the primary and secondary criteria. The primary criteria are four, namely:

- Criterion on single digit inflation rate
- Criterion on Budget deficit as a percentage of GDP
- Criterion on central bank financing of government deficit
- Criterion on Gross reserves/import cover

The secondary criteria, though important, are not necessarily required to be achieved before launching the monetary union. Examples include:

- Ratio of tax revenue to GDP target
- Wage bill criterion
- Criterion of public investment financed from tax revenue
- Interest rate criterion
- Stock of domestic arrears criterion

ECOWAS countries are still currently far from achieving the criteria. Tables 1, 2 and 3 show the macroeconomic performances of ECOWAS member states in pursuit of the convergence criteria. Most of the countries in the CFA zone met the central bank financing criterion but not the fiscal deficit and foreign reserve criteria. The non-WAEMU countries did not satisfy most of the criteria either.

The failure of the countries within the sub-region to comply with the convergence criteria should be thoroughly investigated. Perhaps one of the biggest flaws that have marked the failure of most monetary union process is lack of commitment to the convergence rules. Fiscal discipline and political will are required on the part of the integrating countries to reap the benefits of common currency area.

Unlike monetary policy, fiscal policy is infinitely more complex, involving many trade-offs among competing interests. At the national level policy is constrained tightly by various pressure groups and political priorities (Devereux and Wilson 1989). Thus, international pressure to comply with convergence rules is inevitably overwhelmed by domestic considerations. For instance, the Maastricht rules that bound the Euro countries together were almost immediately broken by

[2] Latin Monetary Union existed from 1865 until 1927, with Belgium, France, Italy and Switzerland as members and later joined by Bulgaria, Greece, Romania, San Marino, Serbia, Spain and Venezuela. The Scandinavian monetary union existed between 1873 and 1914 with membership comprising Denmark, Sweden and Norway (Jacimovic 2012).

Table 1 ECOWAS countries position with respect to the convergence criteria, 2005–2009 averages (inflation rate)

WAEMU	Inflation rate (in percent)
Benin	4.1
Burkina Faso	4.4
Cote d'Ivoire	3.1
Mali	4.1
Niger	4.7
Senegal	2.9
Togo	4.1
Average	3.9
Non-WAEMU:	
Guinea	11.5
Nigeria	10.9
Ghana	14.5
Guinea-Bissau	3.7
Cape Verde	3.6
Sierra Leone	11.9
The Gambia	4.3
Average	8.6
ECOWAS average	6.3
Target for end-2009	≤ 5

Source: African Development Indicators 2011

France and Germany in response to domestic economic and political pressures.[3] If compliance posed a challenge to European countries with more developed political and economic institutions, there is no reason to expect faster progress towards convergence from Africa.

5 The European Experience with Economic Policy Coordination

In the context of the European Union, economic policy coordination is explicitly mentioned in the Treaty of Maastricht, Articles 103(1) and 103(3) as a common objective of member countries. According to the economic coordination framework, the European Central Bank (ECB) takes charge of designing and implementing single monetary policy while other economic policies notably budgetary and structural policies as well as labour market and wage determination remain the responsibility of individual national governments.

The European Economic and Monetary Union (EMU) also has a comprehensive system of coordination procedures. Within the system, interactions among policy actors, including monetary and fiscal actors and the European Commission as

[3] Adherence to the convergence criteria is more strictly enforced these days following the Euro zone debt crisis.

Table 2 ECOWAS countries position with respect to the convergence criteria, 2005–2010 averages (other indicators)

WAIFEM countries	Central bank financing/ total revenue	(Budget deficit)/GDP (fiscal balance/GDP)	Foreign reserve (months of import cover)
The Gambia	10.6	0.8	4.7
Ghana	2.9	10.4	3.1
Guinea	15.0	4.6	1.6
Liberia	–	(0.7)	2.0
Nigeria	–	1.7	15.8
Sierra Leone	8.6	6.5	4.9
CFA countries			
Benin	1.3	3.3	9.2
Burkina Faso	2.0	9.0	5.7
Cote d'Ivoire	2.5	1.4	3.1
Guinea Bissau	6.2	11.4	6.6
Mali	1.6	5.4	5.2
Niger	2.1	5.8	3.8
Senegal	–	5.9	3.7
Togo	4.4	2.1	4.0
Others			
Cape Verde	–	8.4	3.5
Target	≤10 %	≤4 %	≥6 %

Source: Central banks, WAMA, World Bank and regional economic outlook

Table 3 Fiscal deficit (excluding grants) as % of GDP in the WAMZ

Country	2005	2006	2007	2008	2009	2010
The Gambia	−7.4	−2.7	−1.0	−3.3	−8.6	−8.5
Ghana	−6.9	−7.0	−9.5	−10.6	−7.0	−8.2
Guinea	0.0	−0.3	0.4	−1.2	−6.5	−14.5
Nigeria	1.2	1.3	−0.6	−0.2	−3.3	−5.8
Liberia	−0.5	12.4	12.4	−2.3	1.1	6.8
Sierra Leone	−1.4	−1.6	−0.8	−3.4	−3.0	14.1

Source: WAMI's data base

representative of the common interest are well spelt out. Methods used in policy coordination vary from information exchange, discussion of best practices, policy dialogues and peer review to policy rules and objectives as well as other jointly determined actions, when appropriate.

In the process of policy coordination the principle of subsidiarity and differences in national preferences are respected. The degree and mechanisms for coordination differ according to how persuasive the economic justification for coordination in the particular policy area is. Relatively strong forms of coordination are applied where spill-overs are obvious. For instance, the severity of the danger posed by fiscal risk justifies close rule-based coordination of macroeconomic matters regarding budgetary policies. In structural policy field, weak coordination in the form of information exchange, peer review and discussion of best practices, are adopted. Nonetheless, to provide a level playing field, some structural policies like those relating to labour, product and capital markets are subjected to relatively stronger forms of coordination (see Table 4).

The broad economic policy guidelines (BEPGs) serve as the central guidance for economic policy coordination process in the EMU. BEPGs aim at presenting integrated broad recommendations for policy actors on macroeconomic and structural policies; and providing benchmarks for ex-post assessment in the context of multilateral surveillance. Unfortunately, the BEPGs are not legally binding. Compliance is voluntary and based on political will and peer pressure.

The annual coordination process starts and ends with the BEPGs. The coordination process starts in June with the adoption of BEPGs by the ECOFIN to provide inputs in the budgets' preparations, employment guidelines, macroeconomic dialogues and economic reforms in product and capital markets. Between October and December, member states submit updates on stability and convergence programmes as well as progress report on economic reforms. These are assessed by European Commission and ECOFIN in January. Between December and February, Employment Council adopts the Employment Guidelines. By March, member states are expected to submit their National Action Plans and Macroeconomic dialogue begins at technical level and at political level in May. Adoption of the BEPGs by ECOFIN takes place in June and the cycle continues.

It should be noted that economic policy coordination process is a learning-by-doing process and through regular review and information obtained from Implementation Reports subsequent BEPGs have been re-shaped in line with future focus and needs.

There are limitations associated with this model of coordination. First, it is based on one-size-fits-all approach that a sound economic policy can be determined for all countries at all times. Second, the fiscal criteria for convergence (such as deficit as percent of GDP of 3 %, debt ratio of 60 % and a fiscal balance of near zero) are not derived from explicit principles and objectives of economic policy. Third, it reduces the interaction between monetary and structural policies to a one-way relationship from structural policies to monetary policy ignoring the fact that monetary policy can be instrumental in providing the proper incentives for structural reform.

The Eurogroup tasked with the responsibility for economic policy coordination has not been given sufficient decision power. Hence despite some progress in statistical information, it has not been able to establish collective vision of the global economic situation of the Eurozone (Jacquet and Pisani-Ferry 2000).

The introduction of the Euro in 1999 offered great economic attraction in terms of countries credit rating and trade gains. Countries with lower credit ratings were able to borrow money hiding behind the superior rating of the stronger member states. In addition, the currency prevented competitive devaluation among member states. Thus, the attractive economic gains from admittance to the Eurozone without sufficient enforcement mechanism for nations failing to meet the convergence criteria created strong incentive for nations to lie their ways into the Eurozone. For instance, Eurostat reported that Greece's 2003 budget deficit was actually 4.6 %

Table 4 Forms of economic policy coordination in EMU

	Policies	Form of coordination	Mode of co-ordination	Actors involved	Procedures
Single policy	**Monetary policy**	Single policy (euro area)	Single institution	ECB	
	Exchange rate	Single policy (euro area)	Coordination in the council	Council ECB Eurogroup Commission	
	Competition policy	Single policy	Implementation by the commission	Member states Commission Council	
Close co-ordination	**Budgetary policy (balances)**	Treaty rules Commonly agreed rules and objectives	Coordination in the council	Member states Commission Council	Excessive deficit procedure, stability and growth pact, Broad Economic Policy Guidelines (BEPGs)
		Information exchange Peer review	Joint fora	Eurogroup	
	Structural policies	Rules Joint decisions Council directives Peer review	Coordination in the council	Member states Council Commission	
Weak co-ordination	**Policy-mix**	Dialogue Information exchange	Joint fora	ECB Commission Council Eurogroup Social partners	

(continued)

Table 4 (continued)

Policies	Form of coordination	Mode of co-ordination	Actors involved	Procedures
Budgetary policy (quality of public finances)	Commonly agreed objectives	Coordination in the council	Member states	BEPGs, stability and growth pact
			Commission	
			Council	
			Eurogroup	
Wage developments	Dialogue	Joint fora	Social partners	Macroeconomic dialogue (Cologne process), BEPGs
	Information exchange		Commission	
			Council	
			ECB	
Labour market policies	Information exchange	Coordination in the council	Member states	Employment guidelines (Luxemburg process), BEPGs
	Discussion of best practices		Commission	
			Council	
	Guidelines		Social partners	
	Peer review			
Product and capital market policies	Information exchange	Coordination in the council	Member states	Reports on economic reform (Cardiff process) BEPGs
	Discussion of best practices		Commission	
			Council	
	Guidelines peer review			
External representation and communication	Agreement on a common understanding	Joint fora	ECB	
			Eurogroup	
			Commission	

Source: Culled from *Europapers*, "Coordination of economic policies in the EU: a presentation of key features of the main procedures," European Commission: Directorate-General for Economic and Financial Affairs, July 2002 of GDP, rather than the 1.7 % of GDP previously reported (European Commission 2004).

This example demonstrates the risk involved in the monetary unification. The monetary unification strips national governments of the natural macroeconomic stabilization weapon (monetary policy) and leaves them with the singular option of a national fiscal policy. Though the Maastricht Treaty organizes a common surveillance of national fiscal policies, with ceilings for budgets and public debts, lack of proper communication and cooperation from the union members engender uncertainty and wrong prediction of national policies with dire consequences like the Greece's case. Hence, Sachs and Sala-i-Martin (1991) have suggested that the monetary union is a risky programme if not accompanied by the development of a federal fiscal system.

6 Lessons for the Proposed ECOWAS Monetary Union

In designing the policy coordination framework for the proposed ECOWAS monetary union, the following should be learned from the European experience. First, in order to strengthen the coordination process, members of the proposed MU need to gradually develop an economic policy philosophy that goes beyond mere procedures and criteria. It will make economic policy system of the MU transparent and reduce uncertainty on the future orientations of monetary and fiscal policies in the union. It is equally important to evolve principles that guide economic policy decision and market expectations.

Second, the formulation of these principles should be entrusted to a group of qualified experts and unquestionable personalities. The final outcome of series of debates and discussions will form a draft economic policy charter. The economic policy charter should amongst other things include: (i) assignment principles for responding to economic shocks; (ii) rules of conduct for fiscal policy behaviour that would make clear how the budget is managed over the cycle and how governments envisage to respond to unexpected revenue windfalls (shortfalls).

Third, coordination requires more transparency and predictability in economic decision makers not necessarily change of their decisions according to the common good. The quality of policy-mix can be greatly improved with transparency and predictability of each decision maker orientations and reactions to shocks. To achieve greater transparency and predictability, progress must be made in the following areas:

- The quality and homogeneity of statistical information must be improved
- Qualitative advances with respect to infra-annual information on public finances are required for national budgets to be monitored effectively
- The common central bank policy needs to be clarified. For instance, inflation target should be more precise and when undershooting or overshooting occurs it must be corrected with much vigour.
- Member states should adopt contingent fiscal policy principles.

Fourth, a collective executive body should be formed to organize the executive function needed to define and implement economic policy orientations or joint decisions according to the guidelines. The executive body would associate national finance ministers and would make fiscal policy recommendations to the monetary union member states. This collective executive body must be able to adopt strategic economic policy guidelines, white papers on structural reform, as well as specific economic policy resolutions or recommendations. It must also be able to take a position on international policy coordination and exchange rate issues.

Fifth, there should be better interaction between the monetary union procedures and national decisions. For instance, national public finance programmes should be collated at the regional level to enable a review of the aggregate union fiscal prospects and policy stance before the national programmes are scrutinised.

7 Conclusion

The paper examined monetary unification and the role of economic policy coordination. From the theoretical exposition, monetary unification has substantial benefits in terms of lower inflation rate and macroeconomic stability. However, these gains come with the sacrifice of the ability to implement national monetary policies to counter country-specific output shocks. Drawing from the experience of European monetary union, the paper argues that with appropriate economic policy coordination framework, monetary unification can become a win-win situation with benefits accruing to the entire monetary zone. The lesson for the ECOWAS countries is that monetary unification is not a substitute for domestic economic reforms. The structural reforms must take place first to provide the infrastructure for a more fruitful unification.

However, the key to a desirable holistic policy coordination framework is in examining the fiscal side of the equation. Coordination implies that each country's deviation from fiscal target is checked to maximize the welfare of the entire monetary zone. Regional fiscal policy coordination is necessary if monetary union is to be successful. A regional fiscal coordination framework could serve as a catalyst and political economy driver of useful public financial management reforms to ensure fiscal discipline and improve service delivery in Monetary Union member countries. Whether countries are willing to allow for such coordination is the big question?.

Appendix

■ ECOWAS countries position with respect to the convergence criteria, 2005–2010 (overall budget deficit)

	(Budget deficit)/GDP (Fiscal balance/GDP) ≤4 %						
WAIFEM countries	2005	2006	2007	2008	2009	2010	Average
The Gambia	(8.4)	2.7	1.0	2.7	4.0	2.9	0.8
Ghana	6.9	12.9	14.5	19.50	4.30	4.10	10.4
Guinea	1.6	2.0	0.9	1.7	7.5	14.0	4.6
Liberia	0.9	(3.0)	3.4	2.0	(1.1)	(6.6)	(0.7)
Nigeria	1.3	0.6	1.2	0.20	3.30	3.80	1.7
Sierra leone	9.5	8.5	5.0	7.1	2.7	6.1	6.5
CFA countries							
Benin	4.6	2.5	1.8	3.5	4.9	2.5	3.3
Burkina Faso	9.1	10.5	12.1	8.3	6.2	7.5	9.0
Cote d'Ivoire	2.7	1.5	1.4	2.2	(0.9)	1.6	1.4
Guinea Bissau	24.2	18.7	13.7	12.2	(1.8)	1.1	11.4
Mali	7.3	7.9	5.6	2.8	5.1	3.8	5.4
Niger	9.6	6.4	6.7	4.2	5.7	2.4	5.8
Senegal	4.7	6.8	7.1	7.2	4.9	4.6	5.9
Togo	4.1	4.0	2.3	2.3	0.6	(0.6)	2.1
Others							
Cape Verde	11.0	10.4	3.6	6.5	6.8	12.0	8.4

■ ECOWAS countries position with respect to the convergence criteria, 2005–2010 (foreign reserve/imports)

	Foreign reserve(months of imports cover) ≥6 %						
WAIFEM countries	2005	2006	2007	2008	2009	2010	Average
The Gambia	3.8	4.7	4.9	3.4	5.2	6	4.7
Ghana	3.4	3.3	3	1.8	3.2	3.7	3.1
Guinea	0.9	1.4	1.1	1	3.1	1.9	1.6
Liberia	0.8	1.6	2.2	0.9	2.4	4.3	2.0
Nigeria	10	22.9	21.6	15.9	16.3	7.8	15.8
Sierra leone	4.5	4.5	4.5	4.4	7.0	4.6	4.9
CFA countries							
Benin	7.7	10.5	12.2	7.7	7.8		9.2
Burkina Faso	3.8	4.3	7.3	5.1	7.8		5.7
Cote d'Ivoire	2.2	3	3.4	3	3.9		3.1
Guinea Bissau	6.4	6	7.2	6.8	6.6		6.6
Mali	5.5	5.6	5.6	3.7	5.6		5.2
Niger	2.9	4.3	4.2	4.3	3.3		3.8
Senegal	3.9	3.9	3.9	2.7	4.3		3.7
Togo	1.9	3.4	3.9	4.8	5.9		4.0
Others							
Cape Verde	3.2	3.8	4.4	2.7	2.8	4.2	3.5

∎ ECOWAS countries position with respect to the convergence criteria, 2005–2010 (central bank financing/total revenue)

	Central bank financing/total revenue ≤10 %						
WAIFEM countries	2005	2005	2005	2005	2005	2005	2005
The Gambia	0.0	0.0	0.0	0.0	0.0	0.0	0.0
Ghana	0.0	0.0	0.0	0.0	0.0	0.0	0.0
Guinea	(8.8)	(8.8)	(8.8)	(8.8)	(8.8)	(8.8)	(8.8)
Liberia	0.0	0.0	0.0	0.0	0.0	0.0	0.0
Nigeria	0.0	0.0	0.0	0.0	0.0	0.0	0.0
Sierra leone	0.0	0.0	0.0	0.0	0.0	0.0	0.0
CFA countries							
Benin	0.0	0.0	0.0	0.0	0.0	0.0	0.0
Burkina Faso	0.0	0.0	0.0	0.0	0.0	0.0	0.0
Cote d'Ivoire	0.0	0.0	0.0	0.0	0.0	0.0	0.0
Guinea Bissau	0.0	0.0	0.0	0.0	0.0	0.0	0.0
Mali	0.0	0.0	0.0	0.0	0.0	0.0	0.0
Niger	0.0	0.0	0.0	0.0	0.0	0.0	0.0
Senegal	0.0	0.0	0.0	0.0	0.0	0.0	0.0
Togo	0.0	0.0	0.0	0.0	0.0	0.0	0.0
Others							
Cape Verde	0.0	0.0	0.0	0.0	0.0	0.0	0.0

References

African Development Indicators (2011) The World Bank, Washington, DC

Alesina A, Barro RJ, Tenreyro S (2002) Optimal currency areas, NBER working paper no 9072. National Bureau of Economic Research, Cambridge

Asonuma T, Debrun X, Masson PR (2012) Welfare effects of monetary integration: the common monetary area and beyond, IMF working paper no 136. International Monetary Fund, Washington

Beetsma R, Bovenberg AL (1999) Does monetary unification lead to excessive debt accumulation? J Public Econ 74:299–325

Beetsma R, Giuliodori M (2010) The macroeconomic costs and benefits of the EMU and other monetary unions: an overview of recent research. J Econ Lit 48:603–641

Blanchard O, Wolfers J (2000) The role of shocks and institutions in the rise of European unemployment: the aggregate evidence. Working Paper 7282, NBER, Cambridge

Cham T (2009) Is WAMZ an optimun currency area (OCA)? West Afr J Monetary Econ Integr 9(2):96–120

De Grauwe P, Mongelli FP (2004) Endogeneities of optimal currency areas. mimeo, European Central Bank

De Grauwe P (2006) What have we learnt about monetary integration since the Maastricht treaty? J Common Mark Stud 44(4):711–730

Debrun X, Masson PR, Pattillo C (2002) Monetary union in West Africa: who might gain, who might lose and why?, IMF working paper no 226. International Monetary Fund, Washington

Debrun X, Masson PR, Pattillo C (2005) Monetary union in West Africa: who might gain who might lose and why? Can J Econ 38:451–481

Debrun X, Masson PR, Pattillo C (2008) Modelling policy options for Nigeria: fiscal responsibility, monetary credibility and regional integration. In: Collier P, Pattillo C, Soludo C (eds)

Economic policy operations for a prosperous Nigeria. Palgrave-Macmillan, Basingstoke, pp 93–120, Chapter 4
Debrun X, Masson PR, Pattillo C (2010) Should African monetary unions be expanded? An empirical investigation of the scope for monetary integration in Sub-Saharan Africa, IMF working paper no 157. International Monetary Fund, Washington
Devereux M, Wilson TA (1989) International co-ordination of macroeconomic policies: a review. Can Public Policy Anal Polit XV:S20–S34
Ekpo AH (2011) Fiscal policy coordination in West Africa countries: illustration from Nigeria. CREPOL conference, Abuja, July
Ekpo AH, Afangideh UJ (2010a) Fiscal operations in the West African sub-region: implications for regional economic integration. In: International conference on financial and monetary integration in West Africa, Accra, June
Ekpo AH, Afangideh UJ (2010b) Implications of economic and financial integration for monetary management in Nigeria. West Afr Financ Econ Rev 2(2):1–21
European Commission (2004) Report by Eurostat on the revision of the Greek government deficit and debt figures. Downloaded from: http://epp.eurostat.ec.europa.eu/cache/ITY_PUBLIC/GREECE/EN/GREECE-EN.PDF
European Union Commission (1990) One market, one money. Eur Econ 44:4–28
Frankel JA (1999) No single currency regime is right for all countries or at all times, NBER working paper no 7339. National Bureau of Economic Research, Cambridge
Frankel JA, Rose A (1997) A panel project on purchasing power parity: mean reversion within and between countries. J Int Econ 40:209–224
Issing O (2001) Economic and monetary union in Europe: political priority versus economic integration?. Paper for the 2001 conference of the European society for history of economic thought, Darmstadt, Germany
Jacimovic A (2012) The impact of large scale financial and monetary integration on the global financial system stability. Unpublished MSc thesis, Gothenburg University and University of Warwick
Jacquet P, Pisani-Ferry J (2000) Economic policy coordination in the Eurozone: what has been achieved? What should be done? an abridged and updated version of report prepared as part of a EU-commissioned project on "Challenges for EU external economic policy in the next decade" led by the Sussex European Institute, Centre on European Political Economy
Kenen P (1969) The theory of optimum currency areas: an eclectic view. In: Mundell RA, Swoboda AK (eds) Monetary problems in the international economy. University of Chicago Press, Chicago
Masson PR, Pattillo C (2001) Monetary union in West Africa (ECOWAS): is it desirable and how could it be achieved? Occasional paper no 204. International Monetary Fund, Washington
McCallum B (1995) National borders matter: Canada-USA regional trade pattern. Am Econ Rev 85(3):615–623
McKinnon R (1963) Optimum currency area. Am Econ Rev 53:717–725
Melitz J (1991) Brussels on a single money. Open Econ Rev 2:323–336
Mongelli F (2002) New views on the optimum currency area theory: what is EMU telling US, ECB working paper no 138. European Central Bank, Frankfurt
Mundell R (1961) A theory of optimum currency area. Am Econ Rev 51:657–665
Sachs J, Sala-i-Martin X (1991) Fiscal federalism and optimum currency areas: evidence for Europe from the United States, NBER working paper no 3855. National Bureau of Economic Research, Cambridge
West African Monetary Institute (2004) Regional economic and monetary integration in West Africa. WAMI, Accra

Do African Monetary Arrangements Make Sense? Evidence Based on Structural Symmetry

Francis M. Kemegue and Ousmane Seck

Abstract Complete monetary unification in Africa is theoretically supported by the possibility of ex-post endogeneity of meeting optimum currency areas(OCA) criteria. Such endogeneity, if true, should already be reflected in decades-old existing African monetary unions, created without members meeting OCA criteria. This study redefines endogenous OCA criteria of regional arrangements as steady improvement in OCA criteria calculated for members relative to third countries and investigates such endogeneity benefits by analyzing the structural symmetry of business cycles between countries in a three-step process. First we test classical business cycles for increased similarity, using a sample of 60 countries with no a priori on the connection between those countries. Second, we analyze the transmission of deviation cycles among mix of countries using a vector autoregressive model. Finally, we check the strength of the bond among countries by looking at the connection between pairs of series of deviation cycles. We find that business cycles of countries in existing African monetary areas have not grown more homogenous, and that the bond among members of existing unions in Africa has mostly grown weaker than that between these same individual countries and their major trade partners.

Keywords Monetary union • African development • Business cycle synchronization

F.M. Kemegue (✉)
Department of Economics, University of Pretoria and Framingham State University, Pretoria 0002, RSA
e-mail: fkemegue@framingham.edu

O. Seck
College of Business Administration, University of Texas El Paso, El Paso 79968, USA
e-mail: oseck@utep.edu

D. Seck (ed.), *Regional Economic Integration in West Africa*, Advances in African Economic, Social and Political Development, DOI 10.1007/978-3-319-01282-7_4,

1 Introduction

The launch of the European Union sparked interest in the creation and expansion of monetary unions across the world, and inspired the African Union to set the creation and expansion of Regional Economic Communities (REC) to be the intermediate phase towards a single African currency area. The Economic Community of West African States (ECOWAS), was to build a single currency zone by 2025 (Honohan and Lane 2000; Carmignani 2003; Masson and Pattillo 2005). Other currency areas were to emerge from REC in Eastern Africa, and in Southern Africa. Ultimately the regional currency zones were to be merged.

This large monetary unification project essentially absorbs long standing monetary zones: the West African Economic and Monetary Union (WAEMU), the Central African Economic and Monetary Union (CAEMU) and the Common Monetary Area (CMA) of Southern Africa. The essence of the support to the ideal for a larger monetary area in Africa resides in that heterogeneous countries stand a better chance of becoming more integrated over time. The three existing currency areas have similar original characteristics in that they were set up for easy currency management among heterogeneous members of colonial empires. However, attempts to expand these original monetary zones have largely failed, leading researchers to reflect on the chances of success of larger monetary areas grouping additional heterogeneous countries (Masson and Pattillo 2001; Masson and Pattillo 2005; Bayoumi and Ostry 1997) and the reasons for the survival of existing zones (Yehoue 2006). Existing currency areas in Africa are of a particular interest here because their creation did not follow proper economic integration; rather most countries inherited their membership from colonial legacy. The concept of endogeneity behind a viable larger monetary unification project assumes that the post-independence years should have witnessed substantial increase in trade, increased capital and migration flows and better economic bonds among monetary integrated economies.[1] The fate of the three currency areas have been subject to some analyses that widely follows two theoretical directions. The first is centered around tests of optimality based on whether potential members of a monetary union meet certains targets on certains macroeconomic variables such as inflation, budget deficit, etc. (Fielding et al. 2004; Carmignani 2003; Karras 2007; Agbeyegbe 2008; Bangake 2008; Tapsoba 2009). The second perspective is that of endogeneity of the optimality currency areas, that is a subtle inquiry of whether the bond in terms of criteria for optimal currency areas got stronger with time among countries joined by something other than OCA criteria (Khamfula and Huizinga 2004; Buigut and Valev 2005; Houssa 2008). The current debate on monetary unification in Africa does not dispute the heterogeneity of countries, but alludes more to the endogeneity

[1] An extensive discussion of the migration, trade and capital flows can be found in Masson and Pattillo (2005) and Masson (2006).

idea. It is commonly reported that trade intensity has not substantially increased in Africa, and business cycles are not known to be synchronized (Masson and Pattillo 2005; ?). To this effect, of the extensive literature on monetary areas in Africa (Guillaume and Stasavage 2000; Carrere 2004; Masson and Pattillo 2005; Masson 2006; Buigut and Valev 2005; Wang et al. 2007; Khamfula and Huizinga 2004; Tapsoba 2009, Carmignani 2009), the strand relevant to the current debate on the optimality or the opportunity of currency unions is the limited number of projects that specifically address the endogeneity issue. Despite the hurdle of lack of infrastructures and low level of formal trade among countries in Africa, studies that address the endogeneity idea get to the conclusion that OCA criteria endogenously increase over time (Fabrizio Carmignani 2009; Tapsoba 2009), thus marginally validating the endogeneity hypothesis. However, these projects measure endogeneity exclusively as a function of an increasing value of a coefficient computed with characteristics of member countries. Intuitively such coefficient should be increasing because of the fact that most macroeconomic measures do increase over time.

This paper considers the endogeneity hypothesis to implicitly suggest that over time the bond between members to a monetary union gets stronger than the bond between members and third countries. It is not simply the absolute idea of connection that should increase (which can just be a matter of increased globalization) but the bond relative to third countries that has to get stronger. Studies on currency unions in Africa usually apply a set of OCA criteria to potential and current members of a union without comparison of the strength of the same criteria between the concerned countries and with third countries. Tapsoba (2009) and Carmignani (2009) for example only compare their results of absolute intensity of integration to that of advanced nations in terms of magnitude. This paper attempts to fill this void by using business cycles to take an a-priori-less approach to the bond between countries in a three step process. We first test for symmetry on classical cycles in a sample of 60 countries, which is a non parametric approach to comparing classical cycles different from the dating executed in Carmignani (2009). Then we check for transmission of deviation cycles among countries in two ways: we look at the significance of their relationship in a vector autoregressive model that captures asynchronous relationships, and check the strength of their bonds in paired measures of correlation. This paper improves on current research first, by redefining endogeneity benefits as increased relative benefits compared to third countries, thus allows the possibility of transmission among countries that are not members to a monetary union, and comparing the bond between union and non-union members, and second by using a distribution free approach to the comparison of detrended data. This provides a clear and more robust, alternative explanation to the significance and the strength of monetary unions in Africa. We find that the structure of business cycles of members of existing unions in Africa have either not changed or have changed to become not similar over time. We also find that the bonds between these countries and their trade partners have grown stronger than the bond among the countries members of existing unions.

The rest of the paper is organized as follows: in Sect. 2 we review the literature on currency areas in Africa as it pertains to structural symmetry and to the endogeneity of the benefits of currency areas, then we detail the methodology used in this paper (Sect. 3). Section 4 presents the results and Sect. 5 concludes the paper.

2 Structural Symmetry and Currency Areas in Africa

The three currency areas under study were originally instruments of management of colonies. There creation was not guided by OCA criteria. The WAEMU and the CAEMC are made almost entirely of countries that were former French colonies in the Franc Zone (CFA zone) whereas the CMA regroups countries of the Rand Monetary Area in southern Africa. These zones have existed for decades and are expected to be joined by other monetary areas in the larger African monetary integration project. Nonetheless, the issues that theoretically associate these existing zones to the larger monetary project are multiple. There is the relationship between the originality of their creation and the heterogeneity of their structures, the importance of similarities of economic structures to the sustainability of a monetary union, and the methodology to quantify the endogeneity benefits and the similarities of their business cycles.

2.1 *Originality of Their Creation and Heterogeneity of the Structures of Countries in the Existing Currency Zones*

The CFA zone was created in 1948 with France guaranteeing the convertibility of the currency issued by its former colonies in exchange of a pooling of currency reserves into an account located at the French treasury. The CFA zone also allowed these former colonies to experience lower inflation rates on average than other African countries, stable exchange rates provided by the peg to the French Franc (currently to the Euro), and easy currency management through a common central bank. The monetary arrangements were parts of many other trade and military arrangements linking France to its former African colonies. The benefits of the CFA includes lower inflation, which might have come at the expense of slower growth (Devarajan and de Melo 1987; devarajan and rodrik 1991).

The CMA zone predates the CFA zone in that at the creation of the South African Reserve Bank in 1921, the South African currency was used in all the current members of the CMA (Iyabo et al. 2007) creating a de-facto currency area. However, the currency area was formalized in 1974 with the creation of the Rand Monetary Area to which Botswana withdrew in 1975. The current standing agreement is the Multilateral Monetary Agreement of 1986, which Namibia joined in 1992. Members (Namibia, Lesotho and Swaziland also known as NLS countries) issue their own currency pegged to the South African Rand, and the agreement is supposed to fairly support the economy of all participating nations. There is an intricate connection between the CMA and the South African Customs Union (SACU)as the revenues from SACU managed by South Africa are an important source of funding for CMA participating countries. Nonetheless, the currency issued by the smaller NLS nations is legal tender only in their countries whereas the South African rand is legal tender all over the area.

In summary, the creation of the three monetary areas were not inspired by OCA criteria, and appears in its most reasonable description as an easy currency management tool among heterogeneous countries. Nevertheless, suggesting endogeneity of benefits supposes that country members of a union would have grown to be somewhat similar over time.

2.2 The Importance of the Similarity of Economic Structures

Checking OCA criteria, has almost always involved similarity of some measure of economic activity. However, talking about business cycles for developing countries leads to at least three problems. The measurement of cycles, their comparison across countries and the paucity of data measuring economic activity. Notwithstanding intuitions alluding to benefits of diversity in currency unions, such as the power of fiscal federalism in absorbing regional shocks (Eichengreen et al. 1990) checking the validity of currency areas has included verifications of similarity of economic structures.

The first problem associated to business cycles in Africa, is the difficult measurement of business cycles for developing countries. It is still somewhat of an esoteric issue as the unavailability of high frequency data makes it difficult to effectively ascertain the extraction of cycles from low frequency time-series. Empirical approaches to extracting cycles involve the use of filters as the HP filter(Carmignani) and the BK filter (Tapsoba) but despite Uhlig 2001 proposal on adjusting the parameter in the HP filter there are still doubts on whether the extracted series from annual data may still be cycles. Thus this paper prefers to consider the comparison of extracted series simply as comparison of economic structures. The second involves comparing extracted cycles from developing countries to the cycles in advanced nations. Such enterprise is rendered difficult by the difference between developed and developing countries on the features of short-run macroeconomic fluctuations. There are shorter business cycles with diverse stylized facts across developing countries as opposed to the uniform developed countries (Rand and Tarp 2002). Nevertheless, the idea behind the similarity of cycles and its importance for monetary integration resides in the applicability of a single policy for countries in a zone. We thus extract similar items from data of the same frequency across countries in our data. It is the idea that guides (Buigut and Valev 2005) study of the difficult applicability of a monetary union in East Africa based on asymmetry of structural shocks. Bayoumi and

Eichengreen (1997) also carry the idea of similarity in the analysis of the extent of intra-regional trade, the correlation and size of real disturbances across countries in reflecting existing monetary arrangements following OCA criteria. They also conclude that the expansion of existing monetary areas may not be suitable. There are existing attempts comparing cycles from Sub Saharan Africa and the European Union (Nyembwe and Kholodilin 2005) that show a relationship between the two continents and also show the existence of a lagged impact for shocks affecting European countries.

The third problem related to analyzing economic fluctuations from African data is the lack of alternative variable to measure economic activity that makes authors implement various methodologies in extracting cycles essentially from GDP data. Notwithstanding all empirical problems with measurement and paucity, extracting cycles or just detrending data, follows the same strategy as in advanced countries. The use of filter is common. The HP filter is used in Carmignani (2009) whereas Tapsoba (2009) prefers the BK filter. The BK filter emerged from Baxter and Kouparitsas (2005) use of Leamer's (1983) Extreme Bounds Analysis to investigate the determinants of business cycles co-movements between countries. This approach applies band-pass filter to data in order to detach business-cycle components of the data. Other strategies involve Mark et al. (2007) who proposes a new multivariate measure of business cycle synchronicity and a multivariate measure of cycle co-movement that takes into consideration deviations between cycle amplitudes. Ayhan Kose et al. (2008) also use a Bayesian dynamic latent factor model to assess the common and country-specific factors in the G7's major macroeconomic aggregates and further determine the relative significance of the common and country-specific factors in accounting for co-movements in each observable aggregate for three different periods of time.

In this paper we empirically follow the tradition, but marginally depart from considering the detrended series extracted from filters to be cycles, and rather consider the analysis to be a comparison of structures of the economies. We also use the BK filter to extract the detrended series because it combines high and low pass filters.

2.3 Empirical Review of the Approach to the Similarity of Cycles in Africa

The seminal approach to testing the endogeneity of currency unions in Frankel and Rose (1996) and Rose (2000) used panel data to show that the intensity of cross country bilateral trade increases the bilateral correlation measure of economic activity; In essence they show that currency unions increase a measure of co-movement of economic activity. However, panel data calculations often suffers the criticism of pooling poor and rich countries in large datasets. Under that light, most subsequent studies have borrowed the seminal idea but have gone the time series route that have often involved checking the connection between a measure of synchronicity and a different measure of regional economic activity (Tapsoba 2009; Carmignani 2009). However, simple time series often fail to capture the behavior of the multiplicity of stakeholders in a currency union process. Simple time series also fail to capture changing behavior of participants over time. Therefore, more dynamic frameworks have also been used; It is the case of studies (Houssa 2008; Moneta and Ruffer 2009; Eickmeier 2007; Ayhan Kose et al. 2008) that use dynamic factor models to investigate business cycle synchronization in Africa. Houssa (2008) analyzes the costs associated with a monetary union in West Africa by considering variations in aggregate supply and aggregate demand shocks across countries using a method based on dynamic factor models. Despite the apparent novelty of factor models, they also suffer the criticism of considering backward looking aggregated factor to be the benchmark of their analysis. Houssa (2008) reveals that West African countries could hardly adjust to supply shocks in the event they formed a currency union. Moneta and Ruffer (2009) look at the degree and character of synchronization of business cycles in East Asia using a dynamic common factor model for output growth. Moneta and Ruffer (2009) finds evidence of robust export synchronization as well as the importance of external factors such as the yen-US dollar exchange rate and the oil price in determining the synchronizing activity. Some other studies focus on factors explaining synchronization: (Tapsoba 2009) finds that bilateral trade integration increases synchronization of business cycles among African countries and Carmignani (2009) checks whether the measure of synchronization in the CAEMU increases over time.

The approach in the paper is closer to that of Carmignani (2009) as we differentiate between classical cycles and deviation cycles extracted using a filter. We resort to aggregated values only as a way of summarizing the obtained results. We clearly differ from Carmignani (2009) in the ways of comparing classical cycles, and in the way of analyzing deviation cycles. We do not only capture co-movements of deviation cycles in a different way, but we also compare the strength of the bond of each country with union members to the bond of the same country with non-union members allowing a more intuitive conception of the idea of endogeneity of benefits which properly should be in relative terms.

3 Methodology

Two approaches to dealing with cycles are commonly used (Savva et al. 2010; Carmignani 2009; Darvas and Szapáry 2008). The first approach is the analysis of classical cycles obtained from log GDP data whereas deviation cycles, the second approach, are obtained from extracting cyclical components from GDP data with the use of a filter. Additionally many recent papers do extract measure of cyclical behavior of economic activity from other data such as unemployment or industrial production (Frankel and Rose 1996). Given the paucity of African data we decide to follow

(Carmignani 2009) to use the two different concepts of cycles but, as indicated earlier, with a totally different approach to analyzing classical and deviation cycles. Two reasons guide our approach. The first reason is that extracted cycles may be suitable as measure of structural differences but may not be perceived as good measures of business cycles. The second is that we redefine endogeneity to be measured as benefit relative to third countries. Thus we perform three different procedures. The first procedure, the triples test allows us to compare classical symmetry whereas the two other procedures are used to analyze deviation cycles.

3.1 Comparing Classical Structural Symmetry

On the classical symmetry, we perform univariate test on log difference real GDP using the Triples test proposed by Randles et al. (1980) and used in Razzak (2001). The test consists of creating from the time series of size *N*, all possible sets of X_i, X_j, X_k combinations of three observations (a set of triples) and computing a statistic η from a function *f* defined respectively as follows:

with $1 \leq i, j, k \leq N$.

$$f(X_i, X_j, X_k) = \frac{\left[sign\left(\left(X_i + X_j - 2 \times X_k\right) + sign\left(\left(X_i + X_k - 2 \times X_j\right) + sign\left(\left(X_k + X_j - 2 \times X_i\right)\right]\right.\right.\right.}{3}$$

Where $sign(u) = -1, 0, 1$; respectively if u is $< 0, = 0, > 0$ respectively, and $\binom{N}{3}$ is the number of triples. The *f* function only takes values of $-1/3$ for left triples, 0, and 1/3 for right triples. And

$$\eta = \binom{N}{3}^{(-1)} \sum_{i<j<k} f(X_i, X_j, X_k)$$

so that

$$\eta = \frac{[(number\ \ of\ \ right\ \ triples) - (number\ \ of\ \ left\ \ triples)]}{3\binom{N}{3}}$$

When the distribution is symmetric, $E(\eta) = 0$. Otherwise $E(\eta) \neq 0$ when the distribution is asymmetric. We test symmetry versus asymmetry as $H_0 : \eta = 0$ versus $H_A : \eta \neq 0$. Under the null hypothesis, the statistic is asymptotically normal with mean zero and standard errors $\frac{\sigma_N}{N^5}$ (see Randles et al. 1980, p. 169 for the proofs and the expression of the standard errors).

3.2 Comparing Deviation Cycles

The analysis of deviation cycles consists of performing bivariate tests of comovements in two different manners. A vector autoregressive model that allows asynchronous relationships, and comparison of bonds using a measure of correlation between the data series. An initial step in our methodology is to disentangle the cyclical component of the real GDP series from their trend. We employ the Hodrick-Prescott filter, which is robust when using annual data. One major constraint for African countries is that only annual GDP data are available. Fortunately despite the esoteric character of extracting cycles from annual data, similar attempts are carried out in Carmignani (2003) and Tapsoba (2009). We follow Ravn and Uhlig (2002) in adjusting parameters for annual frequency of data in the HP filter. Then we apply our two ways of testing transmission or comovement of the cyclical components of GDP from country j to country i using the following model:

$$\Delta y_i = \alpha + \beta \Delta y_j + \varepsilon$$

where Δy_j is the change in the cyclical component of the GDP of country j. In the above equation, the transmission of business cycles is between countries i and j.

For the vector autoregressive model we take the time to test already detrended data for unit roots, proper lag length selections and the direction of the transmission. Allowing asynchronous relationship between country cycles in a vector autoregressive model gives an insight on the possible transmission between the country. We suspect that this methodology might yield very marginally conclusive results as we believe that the considered economies are mostly extraverted. That is why we find useful to resort to the second procedure.

The last procedure consist of extracting a measure of the strength of the bond between each pair of country in the dataset for comparison. One measure close to the Pearson's correlation coefficient can be specified as

$$r_{XY} = \frac{S_{XY}(\omega)}{\sqrt{S_X(\omega) S_Y(\omega)}}$$

squaring the correlation coefficient gives

$$r_{XY}^2 = \frac{(S_{XY}(\omega))^2}{S_X(\omega) S_Y(\omega)}$$

which can be easily extracted from a fitting of paired XY data in a regression line.

For easy summary we compare the average measures of bonds of connection within a monetary union between members and the major trade partners and also build intensity of comovement of countries with their co-union members. For each country X connected with union members and third countries $Y \neq X$. For each union member X, the intensity of comovement measure $comov_X$ and β is obtained as follows.

$$comov_X = \frac{\sum_{Y=union} (measure_{XY})}{\sum_{Z=third} (measure_{XZ})}$$

3.3 The Data

We apply the three procedures above to annual GDP data of about 38 African countries and 15 of their major trade partners for the period between 1970 and 2010. The choice of GDP follows (Carmignani 2009; Tapsoba 2009) as most consistent measure of economic activity. The data is collected from the World bank's world development Indicators, UN statistics and the IMF's International Financial Statistics.

4 Results

The obtained cycles do show up and down movement as expected (Figs. 1, 2 and 3), The largest economies in the currency areas present the largest amplitudes of economic fluctuations. That is Cote D'ivoire in the WAEMU, South Africa in the CMA and finally Cameroon and Gabon in the CAEMU. To this effect, the pre-1990 fluctuations in Gabon data can be attributed to oil price variations. Tables 1, 2 and 3 display the test of symmetry performed on classical cyclical components of the series. We see that of the three zones the WAEMU groups countries with series that have been structurally similar over the whole period considered. It is therefore difficult to argue that being in a union have guided the structures of these economies to be similar over time; rather the data shows that these economies have always been similar. For counterfactual we include Ghana and Nigeria in the table, and it appears that although Ghana seems different in structure compared to the other considered economies, Nigeria looks similar. It results that the expansion of the WAEMU to Nigeria would likely result in optimal monetary policy. Table 2, that shows results for CMA countries paints a slightly different picture. All countries seem to be somehow different in the full dataset, but have clearly grown to be similar over the last two considered decades. This is the scenario for endogeneity of benefits to monetary integration, leading to the conclusion that monetary policy currently implemented in the area would likely tend to being optimal. Table 3

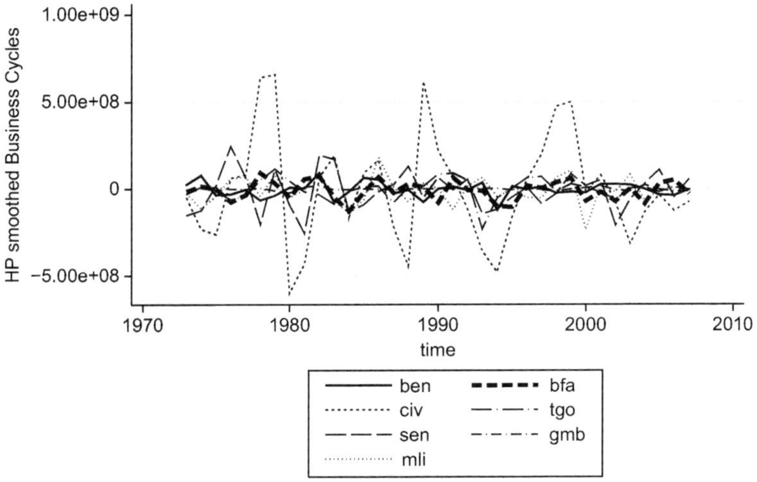

Fig. 1 Detrended series WAEMU

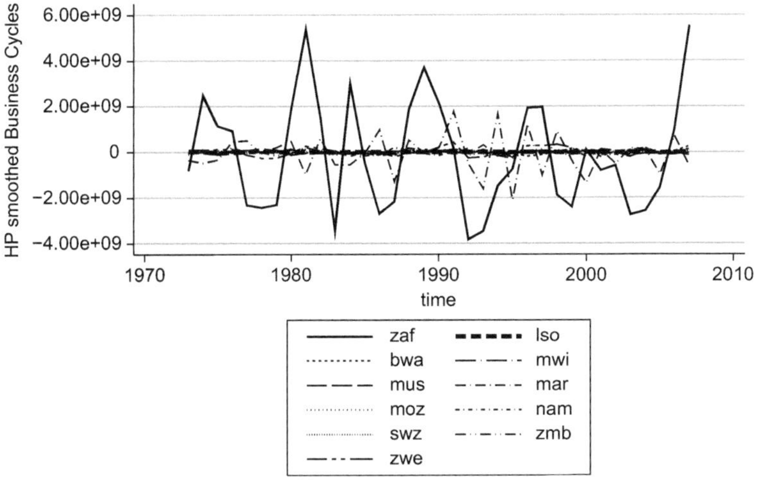

Fig. 2 Detrended series CMA

shows the results for the CAEMU area which appears to group the most structurally disparate set of countries. The countries seem to have started out similar in the dataset (just like in the WAEMU) but have apparently grown to be progressively dissimilar over the last two decades. This is the opposite picture to the one that paints endogeneity of benefits. It is noteworthy to consider that most of the CAEMU countries are oil producing countries and for that matter are likely to have more extraverted economies.

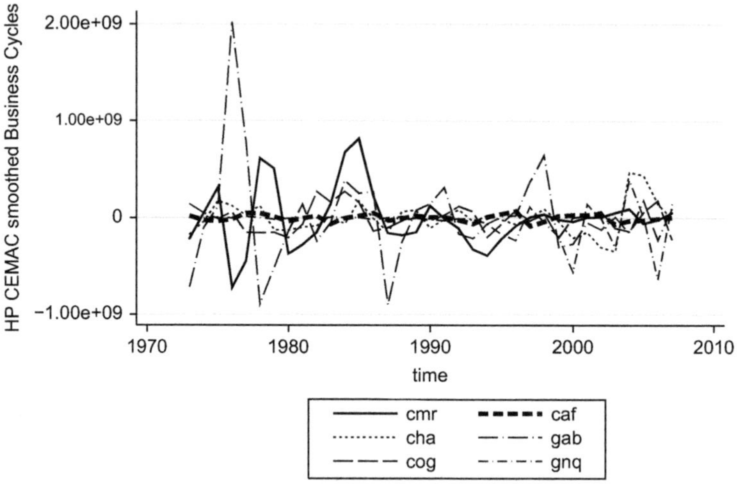

Fig. 3 Detrended series CAEMU

Table 1 Business cycles components triples test results for WAEMU countries

WAEMU 2	Full period	70–80	80–90	90–2000
Benin	Symmetric	Symmetric	Symmetric	Symmetric
Burkina Faso	Symmetric	Symmetric	Symmetric	Symmetric
Côte d'Ivoire	Symmetric	Symmetric	Symmetric	Symmetric
Gambia	Symmetric	Symmetric	Symmetric	Symmetric
Mali	Symmetric	Symmetric	Symmetric	Symmetric
Senegal	Symmetric	Symmetric	Symmetric	Symmetric
Togo	Symmetric	Symmetric	Symmetric	Symmetric
Ghana	Not symmetric	Not symmetric	Symmetric	Not symmetric
Nigeria	Symmetric	Symmetric	Symmetric	Symmetric
Niger	Symmetric	Symmetric	Symmetric	Symmetric

Table 2 Business cycles components triples test results for CMA countries

CMA	Full Period	70–80	80–90	90–2000
Lesotho	Symmetric	Symmetric	Symmetric	Symmetric
Botswana	Symmetric	Not symmetric	Symmetric	Symmetric
Malawi	Symmetric	Symmetric	Symmetric	Symmetric
Namibia	Symmetric	Not symmetric	Symmetric	Symmetric
South Africa	Not symmetric	Symmetric	Symmetric	Symmetric
Swaziland	Not symmetric	Symmetric	Symmetric	Symmetric

We then attempt to get an idea of the connection of the countries in a parametric fashion using a vector autoregressive model. The objective here is not to establish causation in the transmission, but to capture a simple pattern of synchronous and asynchronous connections between the detrended series. Specifically because they

Table 3 Business cycles components triples test results for CAEMU countries

CAEMU	Full period	70–80	80–90	90–2000
Cameroon	Symmetric	Symmetric	Symmetric	Not symmetric
Central African Republic	Not symmetric	Symmetric	Symmetric	Not symmetric
Chad	Symmetric	Symmetric	Symmetric	Symmetric
Congo	Symmetric	Symmetric	Symmetric	Symmetric
Equatorial Guinea	Not symmetric	Symmetric	Symmetric	Not symmetric
Gabon	Symmetric	Symmetric	Not symmetric	Symmetric

Table 4 Stationarity of CDEAO countries cycles

	Zt	p
Benin	−5.96	0.00
BurkFaso	−6.50	0.00
CotedIvoire	−3.20	0.02
GuinBis	−4.93	0.00
Mali	−2.79	0.06
Senegal	−2.36	0.15
Togo	0.24	0.97

Table 5 Lag order selection tests of WAEMU countries cycles

	Lag	LL	LR	df	p	FPE	AIC	HQIC	SBIC
r1	0.00	−3388.85	.b	.b	.b	2.e + 109	271.67	271.76	272.01
r2	1.00	−3347.47	82.76	49.00	0.00	5.e + 109	272.28	273.03	275.01
r3	2.00	−3239.68	215.57	49.00	0.00	1.e + 108	267.57	268.99	272.69
r4	3.00	−1371.19	3736.99	49.00	0.00	2.4e + 47	122.02	124.10	129.52
r5	4.00	2496.80	7735.98	49.00	0.00		−185.74	−183.38	−177.21
r6	5.00	2511.56	29.51	49.00	0.99		−186.92	−184.56	−178.39
r7	6.00	2545.08	67.04	49.00	0.04		−189.61	−187.24	−181.07
r8	7.00	2530.75	−28.66	49.00			−188.46	−186.09	−179.93
r9	8.00	2504.47	−52.56	49.00			−186.36	−183.99	−177.83
r10	9.00	2563.56	118.17	49.00	0.00		−191.08	−188.72	−182.55
r11	10.00	2527.31	−72.49	49.00			−188.19	−185.82	−179.65

are detrended, the series appear not to contain unit root when the value of the augmented Dickey Fuller is actually calculable (Tables 4, 7 and 10). The lag length selection test (Tables 5, 8 and 11) criteria get to different conclusions; Given the relative equivalence of the criteria and for parsimony we decide to use the Mckinon P value, the Likelihood Ratio and the FPE to provide some informal validity to our lag length selection and include up to four lags in all regressions. We find that, in general, economic structures of smaller countries are easily explained contemporaneously and asynchronously by the structures of many of the countries in the region. This is specifically the case of Guinea Bissau (GNB) in the WAEMU and the Central African Republic (CAF) in the CAEMU. We also find from the VAR that there seems to be more similarity in the cycles of mostly oil producing countries in the CAEMU than in the more diverse WAEMU (Tables 6 and 12) . The magnitude

Table 6 VAR WAEMU

	ben	bfa	civ	gnb	mli	sen	tgo
L.ben	−0.407***	0.527	8.286***	−0.153*	−0.184	0.0284	−0.318***
L2.ben	−0.0850	1.001	0.788	−1.137***	2.553**	0.159	−1.480***
L3.ben	0.0775	0.00313	−6.948***	−0.426***	−0.172	1.710***	0.585***
L4.ben	0.377*	−1.104	−8.145***	0.225	−2.933***	−0.250	2.016***
L.bfa	0.245*	−0.678	−2.651***	0.470***	−0.528	0.419***	0.855***
L2.bfa	0.639***	−1.613	−1.260	0.765**	−2.337***	−0.563**	0.566***
L3.bfa	−0.151	0.111	5.731***	−0.345**	1.107***	0.856***	0.177***
L4.bfa	1.338***	−1.081	−14.63***	0.629**	−2.500***	−0.309	1.058***
L.civ	−0.0360**	−0.0479	0.822***	0.0302	−0.138**	0.186***	0.179***
L2.civ	0.128***	−0.0861	−2.296***	0.0102	−0.274***	−0.409***	0.0508***
L3.civ	−0.0382	0.194	1.404***	−0.102*	0.528***	0.129***	−0.253***
L4.civ	0.000288	−0.0494	−0.0126	0.0936***	−0.0614	−0.136***	0.0913***
L.gnb	−0.0414	−0.255	−4.834***	−0.883***	0.635	−1.656***	0.405***
L2.gnb	0.292**	0.834	−0.0711	−0.180	2.228***	−1.677***	0.0333
L3.gnb	0.144	0.0675	2.451***	0.486**	0.403	−3.689***	−0.754***
L4.gnb	−0.898**	1.889	11.75***	−1.175**	5.642***	−0.198	−3.078***
L.mli	−0.238	0.691	−0.155	−0.674***	0.770	0.161	−0.641***
L2.mli	−0.295***	0.941**	1.036**	−0.0958	0.387	0.987***	0.259***
L3.mli	−0.0264	−0.148	−4.156***	0.186**	−1.242***	−1.182***	0.0778***
L4.mli	−0.537**	1.319	5.108***	−0.794**	2.547***	0.203	−1.372***
L.sen	−0.142*	0.495	2.693***	−0.0496	1.123***	−0.340***	−0.866***
L2.sen	−0.451***	0.305	4.295***	−0.109	0.840***	−0.417***	−0.500***
L3.sen	−0.0512	0.509	2.453***	−0.0923	0.920***	0.177***	−0.405***
L4.sen	−0.247***	−0.287*	−1.014***	0.0968**	−0.159	−0.213***	0.0320***
L.tgo	−0.455**	1.015	8.923***	−0.864***	1.463**	1.894***	−0.0489
L2.tgo	0.718***	−0.462	−13.03***	0.296	−2.219***	0.496***	1.065***
L3.tgo	−0.555***	−0.179	0.127	−0.220**	−0.922***	0.476***	0.275***
L4.tgo	−0.185*	0.388	0.588	−0.651***	0.475	0.268**	−0.214***
_cons	−3771178.9*	−9783825.3	−38516238.1***	−7605889.4**	−7804200.5	−2930695.2	−1718373.7**

* $p < 0.05$; ** $p < 0.01$; *** $p < 0.001$

Table 7 Stationarity of SADEC countries cycles

	Zt	p
Botswana	−5.298856	5.506e-06
Lesotho	−4.1779204	.00071796
Namibia	−1.8862569	.33855366
South Africa	−.95087358	.77075796
Swaziland	−6.760437	2.801e-09

Table 8 Lag order selection tests of CMA countries cycles

	Lag	LL	LR	df	p	FPE	AIC	HQIC	SBIC
r1	0.00	−2462.94	.b	.b	.b	3.8e + 79	197.44	197.50	197.68
r2	1.00	−2445.52	34.84	25.00	0.09	7.4e + 79	198.04	198.45	199.50
r3	2.00	−2421.60	47.84	25.00	0.00	1.1e + 80	198.13	198.87	200.81
r4	3.00	−2399.56	44.07	25.00	0.01	3.2e + 80	198.36	199.45	202.27
r5	4.00	−1807.43	1184.25	25.00	0.00	8.7e + 61	152.99	154.41	158.11
r6	5.00	1754.32	7123.51	25.00	0.00		−130.35	−128.66	−124.25
r7	6.00	1779.18	49.71	25.00	0.00		−132.33	−130.64	−126.24
r8	7.00	1816.63	74.90	25.00	0.00		−135.33	−133.64	−129.24
r9	8.00	1789.24	−54.78	25.00			−133.14	−131.45	−127.04
r10	9.00	1793.52	8.56	25.00	1.00		−133.48	−131.79	−127.39
r11	10.00	1801.04	15.05	25.00	0.94		−134.08	−132.39	−127.99

Table 9 VAR CMA

	bwa	lso	nam	zaf	swz
L.bwa	0.347	−0.0421	−0.0155	2.686	0.0472
L2.bwa	−0.517**	−0.0420	0.0677	−1.722	−0.0684*
L3.bwa	−0.0763	−0.0490	−0.0687	2.726	−0.00444
L4.bwa	0.171	−0.0321	0.444*	−6.158	−0.0606
L.lso	−2.046	−0.477**	0.798	−31.76	−0.207
L2.lso	−1.237	−0.471***	1.113	−5.763	−0.256
L3.lso	0.238	−0.418***	1.332	18.66	0.274*
L4.lso	−2.922***	0.0854	0.910	−37.46	−0.384**
L.nam	−0.338*	−0.0417	−0.120	9.909*	−0.0463
L2.nam	−0.0937	−0.0744**	0.0755	10.31*	−0.0309
L3.nam	−0.123	−0.0435	0.0484	4.423	−0.0143
L4.nam	−0.619***	0.0127	−0.193	2.354	−0.0955**
L.zaf	0.00466	0.000902	−0.0145	0.0665	−0.00193
L2.zaf	0.0183*	−0.000893	−0.00290	−0.223	0.00153
L3.zaf	−0.00465	−0.00272**	0.0158*	−0.254	−0.00311*
L4.zaf	0.00344	0.00162	−0.0111	−0.237	−0.00309*
L.swz	1.823*	−0.0312	2.187**	12.43	0.653***
L2.swz	0.328	0.246*	0.0809	−46.55*	−0.509***
L3.swz	0.426	0.518***	−2.210*	21.81	0.611***
L4.swz	1.298	0.156	0.714	−4.984	−0.118
_cons	−13621566.3	−6821351.5**	−1462900.8	−107494212.6	−6986700.5**

*$p < 0.05$; **$p < 0.01$; ***$p < 0.001$

Table 10 Stationarity of CEMAC countries cycles

	Zt	p
Cameroon	−2.09	0.25
Burundi	−2.36	0.15
Chad	−2.95	0.04
France	−1.41	0.58
CentrAfrRp	−1.26	0.65
Congo	−0.85	0.81
EquGuin	−2.43	0.13

Table 11 Lag order selection tests of CAEMU countries cycles

	Lag	LL	LR	df	p	FPE	AIC	HQIC	SBIC
r1	0.00	−3030.02	.b	.b	.b	1.2e + 98	242.88	242.96	243.17
r2	1.00	−2998.69	62.66	36.00	0.00	1.9e + 98	243.26	243.82	245.30
r3	2.00	−2942.03	113.32	36.00	0.00	6.7e + 97	241.60	242.66	245.41
r4	3.00	−2858.93	166.20	36.00	0.00	1.3e + 97	237.83	239.38	243.39
r5	4.00	1990.18	9698.22	36.00	0.00		−147.21	−145.19	−139.90
r6	5.00	2000.28	20.20	36.00	0.98		−148.02	−145.99	−140.71
r7	6.00	2001.10	1.66	36.00	1.00		−148.09	−146.06	−140.78
r8	7.00	1998.31	−5.59	36.00			−147.86	−145.84	−140.55
r9	8.00	1959.42	−77.77	36.00			−144.75	−142.73	−137.44
r10	9.00	1988.65	58.45	36.00	0.01		−147.09	−145.06	−139.78
r11	10.00	1982.91	−11.48	36.00			−146.63	−144.60	−139.32

of the relationship between countries is quite small, but nonetheless significant. This may just be due to the fact that the countries are exposed to similar external shocks as oil producing countries. The results from the WAEMU are a little shocking given the more advanced state of economic integration among those countries. It seems that the difference in trade profile (oil exporters, agricultural product exporters) plays a role here and again countries may just be affected by different external shocks. The VAR results including CMA zone countries are equally shocking with very little significant connection among countries, and again apparently exports economies with very little intra zone trade (Table 9). In the CMA it is a difficult call, significant explanations of cycles of other countries are relatively rare. We get that the increased similarity in structure observed in our non parametric test may not be construed for transmission. These economies may be influenced by external factors. That is why we investigate the strength of their connection among each other compared to their connection with their trade partners in our next step.

As explained in the methodology section, we compute some measures of relationship between the structures of pairs of countries and compare the values of these measures between countries in the monetary area and between countries in the area and their major trade partners. Tables 13, 14, 15, 16, 17 and 18 show the attempt to extract the strength of co-movement in the cycles of countries. The general pattern

Table 12 VAR CAEMU

	cmr	caf	cha	cog	gnq	gab
L.cmr	0.790***	0.0756***	0.137*	0.121	0.0532	0.0471
L2.cmr	−0.924***	−0.0435 *	−0.240*	−0.181	−0.131	−0.874***
L3.cmr	0.549*	0.0222	−0.0672	0.268	0.0517	0.271
L4.cmr	−0.0271	0.0227	0.0573	−0.181	0.178*	−0.555***
L.caf	2.204	−0.653***	−1.230	−1.053	1.134	5.243***
L2.caf	1.885	−0.570***	1.197	−0.722	2.977***	6.952***
L3.caf	−2.279	−1.110***	2.479***	−2.199**	2.744***	2.045*
L4.caf	−0.517	−0.418*	0.0795	−1.495	−0.127	11.74***
L.cha	0.112	−0.0527 *	0.198	−0.170	0.142	0.590***
L2.cha	−0.817**	−0.0415	−0.391**	−0.0328	−0.665***	−0.0906
L3.cha	0.141	0.176***	−0.483***	−0.348*	−0.141	1.471***
L4.cha	−0.950*	0.0935*	−0.835***	0.378	−0.511**	−2.235***
L.cog	0.510	−0.0766 *	−0.194	0.399	0.216	0.981***
L2.cog	0.114	−0.0985 **	−0.169	−0.375*	0.0781	0.463*
L3.cog	0.296	0.0168	0.159	−0.158	0.213	1.077***
L4.cog	−0.890**	0.0365	0.563***	−0.142	−0.172	0.0230
L.gnq	0.398	0.0903*	−0.259	0.408	−0.386*	−0.222
L2.gnq	0.538*	0.00882	0.291*	0.0339	0.0993	−1.073***
L3.gnq	0.240	−0.0708 **	0.633***	0.218	0.876***	−0.0711
L4.gnq	−0.142	−0.0737	0.366	−0.0123	0.319	1.075***
L.gab	0.352***	0.0552***	0.103*	−0.0516	0.224***	0.300***
L2.gab	−0.0566	−0.0268	0.0745	−0.0867	−0.00463	−0.889***
L3.gab	0.116	−0.0101	−0.0730	0.000805	0.0135	0.311***
L4.gab	0.315***	0.0197**	0.0566	−0.0903 *	0.131***	−0.195***
_cons	11401435.0	2243350.9	−9162614.7	21599424.2	−39570631.5**	−31114340.4

*$p < 0.05$; **$p < 0.01$; ***$p < 0.001$

Table 13 Regressions of ECOWAS countries cycles

	Benin	BurkFaso	CotedIvoire	GuinBis	Mali	Senegal	Togo	Nigeria	South Africa
Benin	1.00	0.10	0.17	0.01	0.02	0.03	0.05	0.07	0.06
BurkFaso	0.10	1.00	0.00	0.02	0.18	0.09	0.11	0.07	0.09
CotedIvoire	0.17	0.00	1.00	0.06	0.09	0.24	0.23	0.22	0.28
GuinBis	0.01	0.02	0.06	1.00	0.15	0.14	0.16	0.17	0.15
Mali	0.02	0.18	0.09	0.15	1.00	0.80	0.80	0.57	0.70
Senegal	0.03	0.09	0.24	0.14	0.80	1.00	0.89	0.69	0.84
Togo	0.05	0.11	0.23	0.16	0.80	0.89	1.00	0.76	0.96
Canada	0.00	0.06	0.03	0.02	0.06	0.09	0.13	0.18	0.14
China	0.01	0.08	0.03	0.05	0.36	0.36	0.51	0.30	0.50
France	0.00	0.03	0.12	0.08	0.20	0.29	0.22	0.27	0.23
Germany	0.06	0.10	0.22	0.13	0.71	0.79	0.93	0.76	0.90
Nigeria	0.07	0.07	0.22	0.17	0.57	0.69	0.76	1.00	0.74
UK	0.03	0.10	0.22	0.14	0.76	0.86	0.97	0.74	0.95
South Africa	0.06	0.09	0.28	0.15	0.70	0.84	0.96	0.74	1.00

Table 14 WAEMU intensity of comovement

	WAEMU all	WAEMU Weight	Non-WAEMU Weight	WAEMU Relative Intensity	Average WAEMU	Average Non-CEMAC
ben	0.12	0.36	0.64	0.56	0.02	0.03
bfa	0.36	0.90	0.10	8.69	0.05	0.01
civ	0.43	0.67	0.33	2.06	0.06	0.03
gmb	0.08	0.22	0.78	0.29	0.01	0.04
mli	0.32	0.64	0.36	1.75	0.05	0.03
sen	0.13	0.56	0.44	1.25	0.02	0.01
tgo	0.25	0.31	0.69	0.44	0.04	0.08

Table 15 Comovement of CMA and trade partners countries cycles

	lso	bwa	mwi	moz	nam	zaf	swz	zmb	zwe
lso	1.00	0.00	0.00	0.02	0.06	0.02	0.10	0.00	0.05
bwa	0.00	1.00	0.00	0.02	0.03	0.03	0.04	0.01	0.01
mwi	0.00	0.00	1.00	0.01	0.00	0.00	0.01	0.06	0.03
moz	0.02	0.02	0.01	1.00	0.00	0.22	0.05	0.15	0.26
nam	0.06	0.03	0.00	0.00	1.00	0.04	0.10	0.00	0.01
zaf	0.02	0.03	0.00	0.22	0.04	1.00	0.14	0.12	0.11
swz	0.10	0.04	0.01	0.05	0.10	0.14	1.00	0.05	0.02
zmb	0.00	0.01	0.06	0.15	0.00	0.12	0.05	1.00	0.06
zwe	0.05	0.01	0.03	0.26	0.01	0.11	0.02	0.06	1.00
bra	0.00	0.04	0.06	0.02	0.08	0.12	0.01	0.00	0.00
chn	0.02	0.01	0.01	0.00	0.03	0.11	0.00	0.02	0.01
hkg	0.01	0.01	0.00	0.01	0.20	0.23	0.01	0.08	0.03
nld	0.03	0.11	0.07	0.01	0.01	0.16	0.04	0.00	0.00
rus	0.02	0.03	0.01	0.00	0.08	0.15	0.05	0.00	0.00
gbr	0.10	0.21	0.01	0.00	0.00	0.07	0.00	0.03	0.06
bel	0.02	0.23	0.03	0.02	0.11	0.28	0.02	0.00	0.00
can	0.01	0.10	0.01	0.01	0.00	0.26	0.03	0.00	0.04
fra	0.12	0.27	0.00	0.00	0.02	0.13	0.00	0.02	0.01
deu	0.07	0.10	0.01	0.00	0.02	0.04	0.01	0.04	0.00
ind	0.06	0.02	0.00	0.00	0.00	0.17	0.08	0.00	0.01
ita	0.02	0.11	0.00	0.01	0.06	0.30	0.01	0.00	0.00
jpn	0.12	0.07	0.03	0.02	0.00	0.08	0.00	0.00	0.00
prt	0.05	0.21	0.02	0.04	0.04	0.05	0.01	0.00	0.04
kor	0.03	0.00	0.00	0.08	0.02	0.09	0.01	0.00	0.03
tur	0.00	0.02	0.11	0.00	0.07	0.02	0.09	0.09	0.02
usa	0.11	0.11	0.00	0.00	0.00	0.06	0.00	0.01	0.10

is that of a different story depending on the monetary area. In the WAEMU, most countries have a higher intensity of comovement with their union members whereas the CMA, about all of the countries comove better with their union members. The story is different in the CAEMU where most countries comove with their major trade partners.

Table 16 CMA intensity of comovement

	CMA all	CMA Weight	Non-CMA Weight	CMA Relative Intensity	Average CMA	Average Non-CMA
Lesotho	0.26	0.24	0.76	0.32	0.03	0.05
Botswana	0.14	0.08	0.92	0.09	0.02	0.10
Malawi	0.12	0.24	0.76	0.32	0.01	0.02
Mozambic	0.73	0.76	0.24	3.12	0.08	0.01
Namibia	0.25	0.25	0.75	0.33	0.03	0.04
South Africa	0.67	0.23	0.77	0.29	0.07	0.14
Swaziland	0.50	0.58	0.42	1.37	0.06	0.02
Zambia	0.46	0.61	0.39	1.56	0.05	0.02
Zimbabwe	0.55	0.61	0.39	1.57	0.06	0.02

Table 17 Regressions of CEMAC countries cycles

	Cameroon	CentrAfrRp	Chad	Congo	EquGuin	Nigeria	South Africa
Cameroon	1.00	0.72	0.02	0.56	0.36	0.39	0.53
CentrAfrRp	0.72	1.00	0.01	0.61	0.44	0.51	0.74
Chad	0.02	0.01	1.00	0.22	0.28	0.43	0.23
Congo	0.56	0.61	0.22	1.00	0.63	0.76	0.80
EquGuin	0.36	0.44	0.28	0.63	1.00	0.60	0.67
Canada	0.45	0.55	0.17	0.91	0.56	0.74	0.81
China	0.40	0.66	0.19	0.54	0.58	0.59	0.77
France	0.44	0.45	0.28	0.79	0.71	0.76	0.82
Germany	0.56	0.75	0.20	0.77	0.58	0.84	0.97
Nigeria	0.39	0.51	0.43	0.76	0.60	1.00	0.87
UK	0.53	0.76	0.23	0.78	0.67	0.86	0.99
South Africa	0.53	0.74	0.23	0.80	0.67	0.87	1.00

Table 18 CEMAC intensity of comovement from coefficients of determination

	Total all	CEMAC Weight	Non-CEMAC Weight	CEMAC Relative Intensity	Average Non-CEMAC	Average CEMAC
Cameroon	0.49	0.26	0.74	0.36	0.02	0.02
Central African Republic	0.97	0.07	0.93	0.08	0.05	0.01
Chad	0.74	0.25	0.75	0.33	0.03	0.03
Congo	0.70	0.11	0.89	0.12	0.04	0.01
Equatorial Guinea	0.33	0.53	0.47	1.13	0.01	0.03
Gabon	0.45	0.38	0.62	0.62	0.02	0.03

5 Conclusion

In this paper we set to review the idea of endogeneity of the benefits of currency unions usually advanced for the relevance of monetary unions in Africa. We used detrended data following the real business cycles literature, and compared the movements of these series across countries that are part of the various monetary arrangements. Comparing similarly extracted movement across a group of countries gave us room for checking the relevance of strength of connection among the countries part of monetary zones relative to third countries. We first perform a non parametric comparison of these series using the Triples Test, then we attempt to parametrically capture the relationships among the series and compare this relationship to that with third countries. We find that among countries currently members of monetary unions, The CMA zone has experienced increased similarity of the series whereas, the WAEMU and the CAEMU have either always been similar or have grown dissimilar over time. We also find that the links in terms of macroeconomic fluctuations are substantially low. These countries have stronger links with their major trade partners. This observation seems to be equally valid across all of the years considered. This mixed results lets us think that in absence of conditions for optimal currency area, endogenous benefits to monetary unions are not guaranteed. The fact that most countries may be affected mostly by external shocks casts a serious doubt on the abilities of these countries to make a common front during international negotiations.

Our conclusion is that African Union should exert caution towards monetary union by ensuring proper trade integration among countries before monetary integration. The experience of existing monetary unions show that increased ties shall not be automatically expected after monetary unions.

The approach in this paper was to compare detrended data which for advanced countries are considered to be business cycles, however such cycles are not the only criteria justifying monetary unions. Devarajan and Rodrik (1991), Devarajan and de Melo (1987) and the deliberately European perspective in Cobham and Robson (1994) give other reasons for the existence of some of the currency areas. This paper present a perspective to the issue of economic integration. further research shall look into trade networks discussed in Meissner and Oomes (2009), or the transmission of interest rates discussed in Frankel et al. (2004). In essence a full traditional perspective of why currency unions would be beneficial would not only include the transmission of growth (Baxter and Kouparitsas 2005; Baxter and Stockman 1989; Diebold and Rudebusch 1996), but also of trade and interest rates.

References

Agbeyegbe TD (2008) On the feasibility of a monetary union in the Southern Africa Development Community. Int J Finance Econ 13(2):150–157

Ayhan Kose M, Otrok C, Whiteman CH (2008) Understanding the evolution of world business cycles. J Int Econ 75(1):110–130

Bangake C (2008) Exchange rate volatility and optimum currency area: evidence from Africa. Econ Bull 6(12):1–10
Baxter M, Kouparitsas MA (2005) Determinants of business cycle comovement: a robust analysis. J Monet Econ 52(1):113–157
Baxter M, Stockman AC (1989) Business cycles and the exchange-rate regime: some international evidence. J Monet Econ 23(3):377–400
Bayoumi T, Eichengreen B (1997a) Ever closer to heaven? An optimum-currency-area index for European countries. Eur Econ Rev 41(3–5): 761–770. Paper and proceedings of the eleventh annual congress of the European economic association.
Bayoumi T, Ostry JD (1997b) Macroeconomic shocks and trade flows within Sub-Saharan Africa: implications for optimum currency arrangements. J Afr Econ 6(3):412–444
Buigut SK, Valev NT (2005) Is the proposed East African monetary union an optimal currency area? A structural vector autoregression analysis. World Dev 33(12):2119–2133
Carrere C (2004) African regional agreements: impact on trade with or without currency unions. J Afr Econ 13(2):199–239
Carmignani F (2003) The road to regional integration in Africa: macroeconomic convergence and performance in COMESA. Working papers no 67, University of Milano-Bicocca, Department of Economics, December 2003
Carmignani F (2009) Endogenous optimal currency areas: the case of the central African economic and monetary community. Discussion papers series 390, School of Economics, University of Queensland, 2009
Cobham D, Robson P (1994) Monetary integration in Africa: a deliberately European perspective. World Dev 22(3):285–299
Darvas Z, Szapáry G (2008) Business cycle synchronization in the enlarged EU. Open Econ Rev 19(1):1–19
Devarajan S, de Melo J (1987) Evaluating participation in African monetary unions: a statistical analysis of the CFA zones. World Dev 15(4):483–496
Devarajan S, Rodrik D (1991) Do the benefits of fixed exchange rates outweigh their costs? The franc zone in Africa. Policy research working paper series 777, The World Bank, October 1991
Diebold FX, Rudebusch GD (1996) Measuring business cycles: a modern perspective. The Rev Econ Stat 78(1):67–77
Eichengreen B, Obstfeld M, Spaventa L (1990) One money for Europe? Lessons from the us currency union. Econ Policy 5(10):117–187
Eickmeier S (2007) Business cycle transmission from the US to Germany–A structural factor approach. Eur Econ Rev 51(3):521–551
Fielding D, Lee K, Shields K (2004) The characteristics of macroeconomic shocks in the CFA franc zone. Working papers UNU-WIDER research paper, World Institute for Development Economic Research (UNU-WIDER), 2004
Frankel JA, Rose AK (1996) The endogeneity of the optimum currency area criteria. Working paper 5700, National Bureau of Economic Research, August 1996
Frankel J, Schmukler SL, Serven L (2004) Global transmission of interest rates: monetary independence and currency regime. J Int Money Finance 23(5):701–733
Guillaume DM, Stasavage D (2000) Improving policy credibility: is there a case for African monetary unions? World Dev 28(8):1391–1407
Honohan P, Lane PR (2000) Will the Euro trigger more monetary unions in Africa? Policy research working paper series 2393, The World Bank, July 2000
Houssa R (2008) Monetary union in West Africa and asymmetric shocks: a dynamic structural factor model approach. J Dev Econ 85(1–2):319–347
Karras G (2007) Is Africa an optimum currency area? A comparison of macroeconomic costs and benefits. J Afr Econ 16(2):234–258
Khamfula Y, Huizinga H (2004) The Southern African development community: suitable for a monetary union? J Dev Econ 73(2):699–714
Leamer EE (1983) Let's take the con out of econometrics. Am Econ Rev 73(1):31–43

Masha I, Shirono K, Harris L, Jian-Ye Wang. The common monetary area in Southern Africa: shocks, adjustment, and policy challenges. IMF working papers 07/158, International Monetary Fund, July 2007

Masson PR (2006) New monetary unions in Africa. Economie internationale 107:87–105

Masson PR, Pattillo CA (2001) Monetary union in West Africa (ECOWAS). IMF occasional papers 204, International Monetary Fund, February 2001

Masson PR, Pattillo CA (2005) The monetary geography of Africa. Brookings Institution Press, Washington, DC

Meissner CM, Oomes N (2009) Why do countries peg the way they peg? The determinants of anchor currency choice. J Int Money Finance 28(3):522–547

Mink M, Jacobs J, de Haan J (2007) Measuring synchronicity and co-movement of business cycles with an application to the Euro area. CESifo working paper series CESifo working paper no, CESifo Group Munich, 2007

Moneta F, Ruffer R (2009) Business cycle synchronisation in East Asia. J Asian Econ 20(1):1–12. Fabio Moneta and Rasmus Ruffer

Nyembwe A, Kholodilin K (2005) North–south asymmetric relationships: does the EMU business cycle affect small African economies. Technical report, ULB working paper 2005–32, 2005

Rand J, Tarp F (2002) Business cycles in developing countries: are they different? World Dev 30 (12):2071–2088

Randles RH, Fligner MA, Policello GE, Wolfe DA (1980) An asymptotically distribution-free test for symmetry versus asymmetry. J Am Stat Assoc 75:168–172

Ravn MO, Uhlig H (2002) On adjusting the Hodrick-Prescott filter for the frequency of observations. Open Access publications from University College London http://discovery.ucl.ac.u, University College London, May 2002

Razzak WA (2001) Business cycle asymmetries: international evidence. Rev Econ Dyn 4 (1):230–243

Rose AK (2000) One money, one market: the effect of common currencies on trade. Econ Policy 15(30):7–46

Savva CS, Neanidis KC, Osborn DR (2010) Business cycle synchronization of the Euro area with the new and negotiating member countries. Int J Finance Econ 15(3):288–306

Tapsoba S (2009) Trade intensity and business cycle synchronicity in Africa. J Afr Econ 18(2):287–318

Wang J, Masha I, Shirono K, Harris L (2007) The common monetary area in Southern Africa: shocks, adjustment, and policy challenges. International Monetary Fund working paper 158, IMF

Yehoue ÉB (2006) The CFA arrangements: more than just an aid substitute? Écon Int 107:107–133

Real Exchange Rate Volatility and Export Performance in the West African Monetary Zone (WAMZ)

Abu Bakarr Tarawalie, Christian Regobeth K. Ahortor, and Marshall Umo

Abstract The aim of this paper is to empirically investigate the impact of exchange-rate volatility on export performance in the WAMZ (the WAMZ countries include The Gambia, Ghana, Guinea, Liberia, Nigeria and Sierra Leone) countries using quarterly data for the period 1990–2010. The paper utilizes the Engel-Granger Dynamic OLS (DOLS) estimation technique to establish a cointegrating relationship among the model variables, while Generalized Autoregressive Conditional Heteroskedasticity (GARCH) approach is employed in modelling the real exchange rate volatility. In conformity with theoretical considerations, the results indicate that exchange-rate volatility exerts a significant negative effect upon export in Liberia, Nigeria and Sierra Leone, while a positive relationship is established in the case of The Gambia. However its impact on Ghana and Guinea is found to be insignificant during the review period. While real effective exchange rate impacts export performance negatively in the The Gambia, Ghana and Nigeria, its impact in Guinea and Liberia is positive. In Sierra Leone, the relationship between real effective exchange rate and export performance is positive in the long run but negative in the short run. A key lesson arising from this study is that trade policy actions aimed at export promotion are likely to generate uncertain results, at best, if policymakers in the WAMZ countries ignore the stability as well as the level of the real exchange rate. Thus, to improve export performance in the WAMZ, policies which will ensure stability of the real exchange rate should be pursued.

A Paper Presented at the Third Annual Conference on Regional Integration in Africa, Dakar, Senegal July 4–5, 2012

A. Bakarr Tarawalie • C.R.K. Ahortor (✉)
Research and Statistics Department, West African Monetary Institute, Gulf House, Tetteh Quarshie Interchange, PMB CT 75, Accra, Ghana
e-mail: cahortor@wami-imao.org

M. Umo
Financial Integration Department, West African Monetary Institute, Gulf House, Tetteh Quarshie Interchange, PMB CT 75, Accra, Ghana

D. Seck (ed.), *Regional Economic Integration in West Africa*, Advances in African Economic, Social and Political Development, DOI 10.1007/978-3-319-01282-7_5,

Keywords Exchange rate volatility • Exports • Dynamic OLS estimation • West African Monetary Zone

1 Introduction

There has been a widespread concern among trade economists and policymakers over the high degree of exchange rate volatility and its impact on export performance. Exchange rate volatility is a statistical measure of the tendency of the exchange rate to rise or fall sharply within a short period and is important in understanding foreign exchange market behaviour. Exchange rate volatility creates uncertainty in macroeconomic policy formulation, investment decisions and international trade flows. However, the relationship between exchange rate volatility and export flows has been studied in a large number of theoretical and empirical papers. From a theoretical point of view, the effect of exchange rate volatility on international trade is not unambiguous. This is because an increase in exchange rate risk has a substitution and an income effect. On the one hand, the substitution effect leads traders to substitute away from foreign trade towards domestic trade. It may be argued that a rise in exchange rate volatility increases the uncertainty of profits on contracts denominated in a foreign currency because this risk leads risk-averse and risk-neutral agents to redirect their activity from higher risk foreign markets to the lower risk home market. On the other hand, the income effect leads to increased trade activity, since higher exchange rate volatility and thus higher risk represents greater opportunity for profit which may lead to an increase in trade.

After the collapse of the Bretton Woods system of fixed exchange rates in 1973, the WAMZ countries amongst several countries adopted floating exchange rates system in order to reduce protectionist tendencies and promote trade as well as to gain overall macroeconomic independence, by bearing the burden of adjustment vis-à-vis imbalances in the current and capital accounts of the balance of payments. The transition to floating exchange rates and the nature and magnitude of the relationship between exchange rate volatility and trade flows has been a subject of major concern to economists. Like many developing countries, the WAMZ countries depend on the rest of the world and the level of interdependence has increased in the last decade. These countries are vulnerable to any adverse changes in other economies and changes over which they do not exercise any control. They have increasingly liberalized their trade frontiers leading to lower barriers to trade, for both goods and services. This has increased trade and intensified international competition. Exchange rate volatility may have important effects on trade flows, on direct investments, on output and so on. On the one hand, an overvaluation of the exchange rate should lead to a deterioration of the economic situation. An overvalued currency brings about resource shifts in favor of the non-tradable sectors, which reduces growth (see for example, De Grauwe (1983), Marston (1988), for a detailed analysis). On the other hand, an undervaluation of the exchange rate should lead to an improvement in economic performance.

The WAMZ countries consider exchange rate as a key macroeconomic policy instrument that enhances the country's competitiveness as well as export promotion and economic growth. The Central Banks of the WAMZ countries exchange rate policies aim at providing an environment that promotes exchange rate stability and assists the government's objective of accomplishing export led growth. In line with this, the adoption of outward-looking trade policies ensured export growth that lead to long-term economic growth. The increased liberalization of trade and foreign exchange controls, exports promotion policies and multilateral trade agreements have led to greater penetration of WAMZ countries exporters to the international markets.

The empirical literature is inconclusive regarding the effect of exchange rate volatility on export growth. On the one hand, increasing exchange rate volatility, which is a major source of exchange risks, has significant and negative implications for the volume of trade flows and a country's balance of payments (Walters and De Beer 1999; Bah and Amusa 2003; Vergil 2002). On the other hand, some studies provide evidence supporting a positive relationship between exchange rate volatility and trade flows (see, for example, De Grauwe 1988; Asseery and Peel 1991; Chowdhury 1993; among others). De Grauwe (1988) for instance argues that if exporters are sufficiently risk-averse, then an increase in exchange rate volatility results in an increase in expected marginal utility of export revenue that serves as an incentive to exporters to increase their exports in order to maximise their revenues. This lack of consensus amongst policymakers is reflected in the different exchange rate regimes that countries have pursued over time.

A major concern of policy makers following the collapse of the Bretton Wood System is the consequence of exchange rate volatility, which is a prominent feature of the floating exchange rate. Exchange rate volatility makes firms to add risk premium to the cost of traded goods leading to higher prices and lower external trade. This has important implications for trade and growth prospects of countries. Most African countries adopted economic reform programmes in the 1980s with exchange rate liberalization as a major component. Exchange rates in the WAMZ have been volatile since the adoption of the flexible exchange rate. For instance, real exchange rate volatility declined from 53.0 % in 1991 to 45.6 % in 2008. Correspondingly, export growth rose from 4.4 % to 9.7 % during the same period. The perceived correspondence between exchange rate volatility and export performance in the WAMZ raises some pertinent questions. Is there any relationship between exchange rate volatility and export performance? If yes, what is the effect of exchange rate volatility on export in the WAMZ countries and what is the magnitude of this effect?

The objective of this paper is to empirically investigate the effect of real exchange rate volatility on exports performance in the WAMZ countries. The knowledge of the degree to which exchange rate volatility affects export is important for the design of both exchange rate and trade policies. For instance, if exchange rate volatility leads to a reduction in exports, trade adjustment programmes that emphasized export expansion could be unsuccessful if exchange rate is volatile. To achieve this objective the paper utilizes the Engel-Granger

Dynamic OLS (DOLS) estimation technique. In addition, in measuring real exchange rate volatility, the Generalized Autoregressive Conditional Heteroskedasticity (GARCH) approach was employed.

The rest of the paper is organized as follows: following the introduction, Sect. 5.2 consists of an overview of the linkage between the real exchange rate volatility and exports from the theoretical aspects as well as empirical evidence. Section 5.3 provides an overview on real exchange rate volatility and export performance in the WAMZ. In Sect. 5.4, an econometric model is specified for exports, which embodies the exchange rate volatility as one of the main explanatory variables. The sources of data sets are presented in this section. Section 5.5 presents the estimation techniques, and the empirical results, while Sect. 5.6 presents the concluding remarks and policy implications.

2 Literature Review

2.1 Real Exchange Rate Volatility and Exports: A Theoretical Perspective

The breakdown of the Bretton Woods exchange rate regime in 1973, and the subsequent emergence of more flexible exchange rate arrangements, triggered a lot of concern about increased exchange rate risk and its impact on exports. Most studies found fairly systematic evidence on the increased volatility of real exchange rates in both developing and developed countries alike. Effects of exchange rate volatility on trade flows are analysed in terms of risk or uncertainty. Exporters are either very risk-averse or less risk-averse and therefore would react differently to changes in real exchange rates. Hooper and Kohlhagen (1978) and IMF (1984) postulate that if agents are risk-averse, an increase in exchange rate volatility induces them to reduce the volume of trade and reallocate production towards domestic markets.

De Grauwe (1988) argues that a rise in real exchange rate fluctuations can either have a positive or a negative effect on the volume of trade as it depends on the substitution and income effects. The substitution effect leads risk-averse agents to decrease export activities as the expected marginal utility of export revenues decreases. The less risk-averse group views the increase in exchange rate volatility in terms of greater risk. More real exchange rate volatility would prompt this category of exporters to reduce exports and divert resources to other sectors. On the other hand, the income effect causes risk-averse agents to increase exports to avoid severe fall in revenues. If agents are sufficiently risk-averse, an increase in risk associated with higher exchange rate volatility raises the expected utility of export revenue and induces exporters to export more to avoid a possibility of a reduction in their revenues. If the income effect offsets the substitution effect, there will be a positive link between exchange rate volatility and trade. Alternatively, an increase in risk will have a negative impact on trade. Earlier models based on the case of an exporter that takes production decisions before knowing the realization of exchange rates and cannot hedge this source of risk predicted that an increase in volatility negatively affects a risk-averse exporter (Clark (1973)). Under these assumptions, exports would increase with exchange rate volatility the greater the income effect and be depressed if the substitution effect outweighs the income effect. Ultimately, the effect of real exchange rate volatility on exports is ambiguous (Fountas and Aristotelous 1999a, b; Cote 1994).

Franke (1991) and Sercu and Vanhulle (1992) have shown that exchange rate variability can affect trade volume positively. Higher risk present greater opportunity for profits and, thus exchange rate volatility, to the extent that it increases risk, will increase trade. Thus, an increase in exchange rate variability will improve export performance as firms will exercise the option to export and thus increase the volume of trade. Pindyck (1982) has also shown that, under certain conditions, increased price variability can result in increased average investment and output as the firm adjusts to take advantage of high prices and to minimize the impact of low prices. Brada and Mendez (1988), from a political economy perspective, are of the opinion that movement in exchange rates can insulate the Balance of Payments from external shocks, thereby reducing the use of restrictions on trade and capital controls to attain equilibrium. The effect of this is that international trade is encouraged, even in the face of increasing exchange rate volatility.

Cote (1994), on the other hand, states that exchange rate volatility depresses trade. This occurs because markets may be imperfect particularly in less developed countries and also because hedging may not only be imperfect but also very costly as a basis for averting exchange risk. Thus, according to the risk-aversion hypothesis, exports may be negatively correlated with exchange rate volatility. In addition, Arize et al. (2000), Hooper and Kohlhagen (1978) argue that higher exchange rate volatility will depress trade volume through a rise in adjustment costs like irreversible investment due to higher uncertainty and risks. Chit (2008) posited that where hedging opportunities are non- existent or extremely expensive, risk adverse firms that must first decide on their export volumes before any uncertainty in exchange rate is resolved will nearly always experience a negative relationship between exchange rate volatility and exports.

2.2 Real Exchange Rate Volatility and Exports: Empirical Evidence

The absence of a consensus from the point of view of theory has motivated many researchers over the years to undertake empirical studies on the subject matter. However, differences in country coverage, sample periods, models and estimation techniques, which have evolved over time with the advancement in econometrics, have made it impossible to establish a consensus and truly systematic relationship between exchange rate volatility and exports.

Chowdhury (1993) investigated the impact of exchange rate volatility on the trade flows of the G-7 countries in context of a multivariate error-correction model. They found that the exchange rate volatility had a significant negative impact on the volume of exports in each of the G-7 countries. In a related study, Mahmood and Vixathep (2002) investigated the impact of exchange rate volatility on exports in four East Asians countries (Hong Kong, South Korea, Singapore, and Thailand). Their results indicated that exchange rate volatility has negative impacts on exports in both the short and long runs. Using an error-correction approach, Caballero and Corbo (1989) investigated the effect of real exchange rate uncertainty on exports for six developing countries (Chile, Colombia, Peru, Philippines, Thailand and Turkey). Their study found that real exchange rate uncertainty did reduce exports in the short-run and the results were substantially magnified in the long-run. In a related study, Samanta (1998) adopted a cointegration technique in examining the implications of exchange rate volatility for India's export. The results showed that over the period 1953–1989, exchange rate risk had a significant adverse impact on exports. The results are similar to those obtained by Hassan and Tufte (1998) for Bangladeshi's aggregate exports over the period 1977–1992.

Qian and Virangis (1994) also examine the impact of exchange rate volatility on trade in six advanced countries, using ARCH to approximate volatility and monthly data from 1973 to 1990. Their results show a negative link between exchange rate volatility and export volumes for Australia, Canada, and Japan, while for United Kingdom, Sweden, and Netherlands there is a positive relationship. Also De Vitta and Abbott (2004) observe that short-term volatility in exchange rate does not affect UK exports to the EU both at the aggregate and sectoral levels. However, there are significant negative effects of long-term volatility on UK exports to the EU. The negative link is attributed to the difficulty to hedge against long-run fluctuations. A study by Alam (2011) using Autoregressive Distributed Lags (ARDL) technique shows that real exports are cointegrated with foreign economic activity, real effective exchange rate and volatility of real effective exchange rate in Pakistan. Real effective exchange rate and its volatility are found to have separate significant negative coefficients, implying that volatility adversely affected the Pakistan's aggregate exports from 1979 to 2005.

Ghura and Greenes (1993) employed a panel data technique in exploring the effect of exchange rate volatility on the trade flows of sub-Sahara African countries. Gauging exchange rate volatility by the coefficient of variation and utilizing data covering the period 1972–1987, the study found that exchange rate volatility had a significantly negative and robust impact on trade flows. Using quarterly observations over a 20-year period in a vector co-integration model, Aliyu (2008) provided evidence of an inverse relationship between these variables. Specifically, the study revealed that volatility in the Naira exchange rate led to a 3.65 % decrease in Nigeria's non oil exports. Bah and Amusi (2003) used ARCH and GARCH models to examine the effect of real exchange rate volatility on South African exports to the U.S. for the period 1990:1–2000:4. The findings are that Rand's real exchange rate variability exerts a significant and negative impact on exports both in the long and short runs.

Other studies have found positive relationship between real exchange rate volatility and export performance. The studies by Cushman (1986), De Grauwe (1988), and Bini-Smaghi (1991), using time series data, for a group of industrialized economies found significant evidence in support of a positive relationship. Todani and Munyama (2005) employed ARDL bounds testing procedure on quarterly data for the period 1984–2004 to examine the impact of exchange rate variability on aggregate South African exports to the rest of the world as well as on goods, services and gold exports. They employed the moving average standard deviation and GARCH (1, 1) as measures of variability. The results indicate the existence of a significant positive relationship. By adopting the Johansen co-integration approach over a thirty three (33) year period between 1970 and 2003, Yusuf and Edom (2007), showed that depreciating the official exchange rate led to an increase in the export of round wood and sawn wood in Nigeria. Using annual data from 1970 to 1997 on a sample of 104 (developed and developing) countries, and employing a gravity model that took endogeneity into account, Rose (2000) found that volatility had an insignificant effect on trade. Tenreyro (2004), however, cast some doubt on the robustness of Rose's results.

The aforementioned surveys conclude that, from a theoretical perspective, there is no unambiguous response in the level of trade to an increase in exchange rate volatility because differing results can arise from plausible alternative assumptions and modeling strategies. The same ambiguity pervades much of the empirical literature, which may reflect the lack of clear-cut theoretical results as well as the difficulty in arriving at an appropriate proxy for exchange rate risk. The theoretical underpinnings are premised on the attitude of the exporters to risks, opportunities to hedge exchange rate risks, market structure, and adjustment costs. It is our view therefore that the relationship between exchange rate volatility and exports is analytically indeterminate. For this reason, the direction and size of the impact of exchange rate uncertainty on exports in the West African Monetary Zone (WAMZ) must be empirically studied before any valid conclusions are drawn. Understanding the direction and magnitude of the impact of exchange rate volatility on trade in the WAMZ is, no doubt, an important issue in the integration process.

3 Real Exchange Rate Volatility and Export Performance in the WAMZ

This section discusses the behaviour of real exchange rate volatility and export performance in the WAMZ. Specifically, it reviews the trends in real exchange rate volatility and their possible effects on export performance in the Zone.

3.1 The Gambia

As an open economy, The Gambia considers the exchange rate as an important policy instrument for export promotion and economic growth. The current exchange rate policy of the Central Bank of the Gambia is aimed at providing an environment that promotes exchange rate stability and assists the government's objective of accomplishing export-led growth. The Gambian economy operated a fixed exchange rate between 1965 and 1985, during which time the dalasi was pegged to the pound sterling. However, following the waves of a Structural Adjustment Programme, the country adopted a floating (market determined) exchange rate in 1986, which resulted in a 28 % drop in the real effective exchange rate (REER). After the change over to a floating exchange rate regime, the REER stayed within ± 10 % band of its period average from 1986 to 2000, during which period a moderate nominal appreciation of the dalasi was offset by a negative inflation differential with partner countries.

The Gambia has long been a trade hub and re-export centre for neighbouring countries due to its relatively low import taxes, well-functioning port and customs services, and limited administrative barriers. Furthermore, the increased liberalization of trade and foreign exchange controls following the implementation of the Economic Recovery Programme in 1985 boosted the country's export sector. About 80 % of Gambian merchandise exports consist of re-exports. Groundnuts remain the country's main cash crop, engaging over 80 % of the population.

Figure 5.1 shows that the real exchange rate was volatile during the period 1990–2010. It is evident from the figure that volatility had a linear upward trend during the study period, while exports-GDP ratio trended downwards. Between 1990 and 1994, real exchange rate volatility was trending upwards depicting a period of real exchange rate depreciation. During this period, there was an increase in the export-GDP ratio, indicating that the high volatility (depreciation of the real exchange rate) probably improved export performance in the Gambia. However, between 1995 and 2001, the country experienced episodes of low volatility, reflecting real exchange rate appreciation. This period also coincided with a decline in export-GDP ratio, implying that the low volatility probably caused a decline in export performance. The figure also revealed that between 2002 and 2006, the country experienced high episode of real exchange rate volatility as the real exchange rate depreciated. This period coincided with rapid depreciation of the dalasi. However, since 2007, the volatility eased off as the real exchange rate experienced mild appreciation. Despite the increased volatility of the real exchange rate since 2002, export performance remained relatively stable. However, exports-GDP ratio was above its trend between 2003 and 2010. In summary, a closer observation indicates that the periods when volatility was above its long-term trend coincided with those periods when exports-GDP ratio was also above its long-term trend, and vice versa.

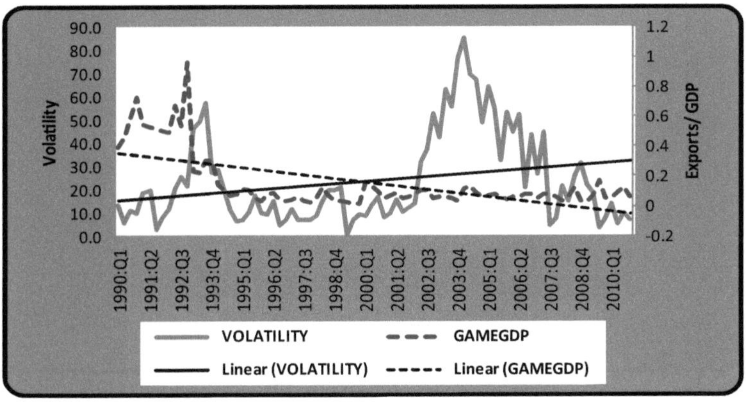

Fig. 5.1 Trends in volatility and export-GDP ratio in the Gambia, 1990:Q1-2010:Q4 (Source: Authors' compilation)

3.2 Ghana

The Ghanaian economy adopted a fixed exchange rate regime in the management of its exchange rate between 1970 and 1982. During this period, the Ghanaian cedi was pegged to the main convertible currencies, notably the British pound and the American dollar. The country however launched an Economic Recovery Programme (ERP), aimed at the rationalisation of exchange rate to stimulate exports, and "getting the prices right" in order to redirect resources towards the more productive sectors of the economy. During this period, the government made series of devaluations of the cedi between 1983 and 1986. The country adopted a managed floating exchange rate in 1986, and in September of the same year, the government adopted an auction market approach in order to accelerate the adjustment of the exchange rate and to achieve the objective of trade liberalization, leaving it partially to market forces to determine the exchange rate.

A review of Fig. 5.2 indicates that the real exchange rate had witnessed episodes of volatility during the study period. Between 1990 and 1992, the country's real exchange rate was marked with a period of high volatility, which was characterized by a decline in export-GDP ratio, depicting that real depreciation caused a decline in export performance. Furthermore, between 1993 and 1997, the real exchange rate volatility was below its trend line, representing period of real exchange rate appreciation. During this period, Ghana's export-GDP increased and was above its trend. However since 2001, the real exchange rate volatility trended downward, while export-GDP ratio increased between 2000 and 2005, and thereafter declined gradually. This revealed that, while real exchange rate was appreciating, export-GDP initially increased and declined after 2005.

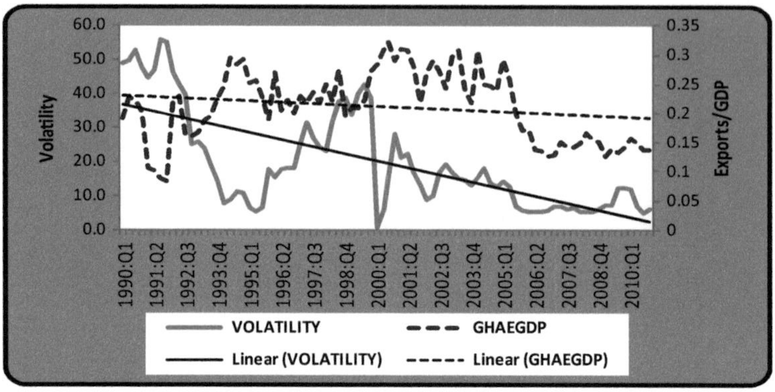

Fig. 5.2 Trends in volatility and export-GDP ratio in Ghana, 1990:Q1-2010:Q4 (Source: Authors' compilation)

3.3 Guinea

Three phases of exchange rate management can be identified in the evolution of the real exchange rate in Guinea. After achieving independence, the country abandoned the CFA Franc and adopted the Guinean franc between 1960 and 1975. A new currency, the Guinean Syli (GS) was introduced on June 11, 1975 and pegged at the rate of GS 24.68 per SDR. The currency became increasingly overvalued, and, by mid-1985, its rate exceeded GS 280 per SDR in the parallel market. With a view to attracting foreign exchange to official channels, the government created a second tier for foreign exchange in October 1985. In 1986, the Syli was replaced by the Guinean franc (GF) at GF 300 per U.S. dollar in the official market and GF 340 per U.S. dollar in the second tier, in which the exchange rate was set at weekly auctions for foreign exchange organized by the central bank. In October 1994, the authorities adopted a flexible exchange rate regime and introduced an interbank market for foreign exchange. During 2000–2002, the shortage of foreign exchange in the official market forced the central bank to move from weekly to monthly auctions in an effort to increase the volume offered at each auction. Between late 2002 and mid-July 2004, the authorities pegged the official exchange rate against the U.S. dollar and increasingly used the auction mechanism as an administrative vehicle to allocate foreign exchange. Since 2005, the central bank abandoned the official foreign exchange auction mechanism and liberalized the foreign exchange market. Since 2005, the official exchange rate has been determined weekly by a reference rate calculated as an arithmetic average of rates quoted by deposit banks and authorized non-bank foreign exchange bureaus.

Given these developments, the country experienced series of volatility in its real effective exchange rate (Fig. 5.3). Between 1990 and 2000, real exchange rate volatility was below its trend line denoting a real appreciation. In terms of export performance, export-GDP ratio increased above its trend line between 1990 and 1992, but decreased between 1993 and 1998. However, the country experienced

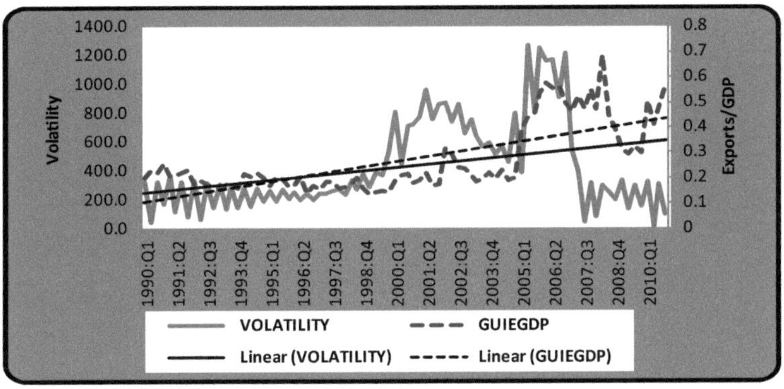

Fig. 5.3 Trends in volatility and export-GDP ratio in Guinea, 1990:Q1-2010:Q4 (Source: Authors' design)

episodes of real depreciation between 2000 and 2007, with volatility far above its trend line. During this period, export-GDP ratio increased gradually. It is also evident from Fig. 5.3 that, while volatility declined sharply in 2007 and thereafter remained below its trend line, export-GDP ratio remained high, indicating that real appreciation probably leads to an increase in export performance during the study period.

3.4 *Liberia*

Liberia has a dual currency (two legal tender) system involving the Liberian national currency (Liberian dollar) and the United States dollar. The country is operating a managed float, where there is no predetermined path and the authorities only intervene to even out any large fluctuations in the exchange rate. The Liberian dollar depreciated gradually in 2009, reflecting attempts by the Central Bank to balance the available foreign exchange against a sustained current-account deficit.

A close look at Fig. 5.4 reveals that real exchange rate volatility in Liberia experienced a decreasing trend during the study period. Between 2002 and 2003, real exchange rate volatility was above its trend line and during this period, export-GDP ratio also fluctuated around its trend line. However, between 2004 and 2008, real exchange rate volatility was below its trend line representing a real appreciation, while export-GDP growth was above its trend line for most of the period. Intuitively, while there was real appreciation of the exchange rate, export-GDP ratio increased, on average, during this period. Between 2009 and 2010, real exchange rate volatility stabilized and was above its trend line. At the same time, export-GDP ratio also declined and was below its trend line except in the last quarter of 2009 which saw a sharp rise in export-GDP ratio above its trend line.

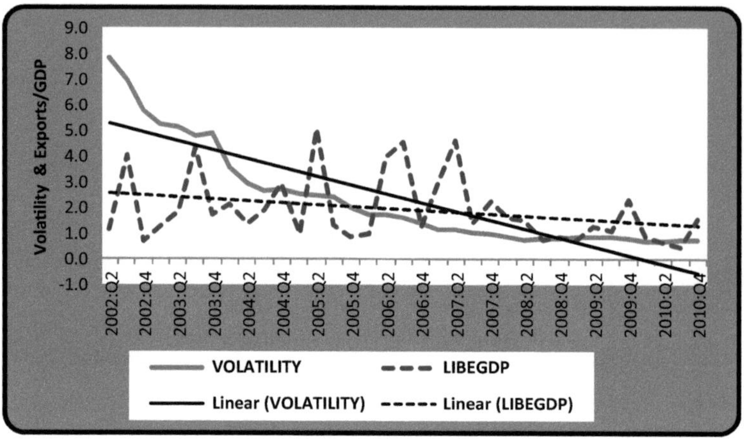

Fig. 5.4 Trends in volatility and export-GDP ratio in Liberia, 2002:Q2-2010:Q4 (Source: Authors' compilation)

3.5 *Nigeria*

The country's foreign exchange rate was fairly stable from 1980 to 1985. Prior to the policy reforms in 1986, and especially during the 196Os, Nigeria was known mainly as an exporter of primary agricultural commodities and, to a relatively small extent, as an exporter of one or two solid minerals. In 1986, the government adopted the Structural Adjustment Programme (SAP) as a strategy to achieve sustainable growth path, through structural and sectoral policy reforms. One of the cardinal points of this policy was the floating nominal exchange rate policy. As the naira was allowed to float, the nominal exchange rate movement became more pronounced, contributing to stronger movements in the exchange rate during this period. The introduction of the SAP in 1986 depreciated the naira. From 1986 to date, Nigeria's exchange rate management has gone through various stages of policy reforms. The first move started with the introduction of Second-Tier Foreign Exchange Market (SPEM) which was launched on September 26, 1986. At its commencement, a dual exchange rate system for allocation of foreign exchange was adopted. There was a policy reversal in 1994 when the naira exchange rate was again pegged.

Another era of liberalization in the foreign exchange market began in 1995 when the Autonomous Foreign Exchange Market (AFEM) was introduced. During this period, the Central Bank of Nigeria (CBN) sold foreign exchange to end-users through selected authorized dealers at market-determined exchange rate. The country also introduced, an Inter-Bank Foreign Exchange Market (IFEM) on October 25, 1999, but this was replaced by the Dutch Auction System (DAS) in 2002. This success was capped with further liberalization of the foreign exchange market in 2006 with the introduction of Wholesale Dutch Auction System (WDAS) to deepen the market and further close the market premium.

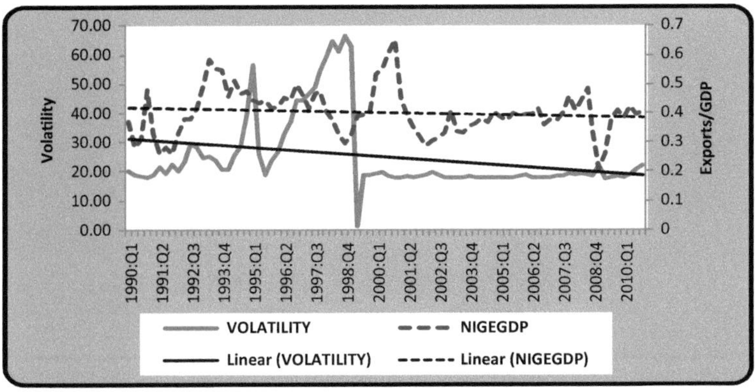

Fig. 5.5 Trends in volatility and export-GDP ratio in Nigeria, 1990:Q1-2010:Q4 (Source: Authors' compilation)

Despite the successful implementation of these different exchange rate regimes, a cursory examination of Fig. 5.5 revealed that the real exchange rate experienced high volatility between 1990 and 1999, with the real exchange rate depreciating during this period. On average, export-GDP ratio increased during the same period. However, since 2000, the real exchange rate was relatively stable, fluctuating marginally. Despite the relative stability in the real exchange rate, export-GDP ratio has been below its trend line in recent years, suggesting that the non-oil export sector in Nigeria has been performing below average in recent times.

3.6 Sierra Leone

As in the case of many developing countries, Sierra Leone continued the use of the fixed exchange rate regime after the collapse of the Bretton Woods System in the early 1970s. However, with the experience of persistent deficit in the balance of payments, series of exchange rate adjustments were adopted in the 1980s. In 1986, Sierra Leone adopted a floating exchange rate system following the introduction of SAP. During this period, the government revalued the leone from Le53 = $1 to Le23 = $1. The adoption of the floating exchange rate was aimed at increasing the competitiveness of the country's export, while maintaining a stable exchange rate with minimal volatility. In April 1991, a managed float was introduced as the previous fixed regime resulted in overvaluation of the currency. Under the managed float, the exchange rate was determined by market forces with periodic intervention by the Bank of Sierra Leone. This is being done through a weekly foreign exchange auction by the central bank.

Notwithstanding this development, Fig. 5.6 reveals that the real exchange rate witnessed periods of volatility. It is evident from the figure that between 1990 and 1995 real exchange rate volatility was declining, while export-GDP ratio was above

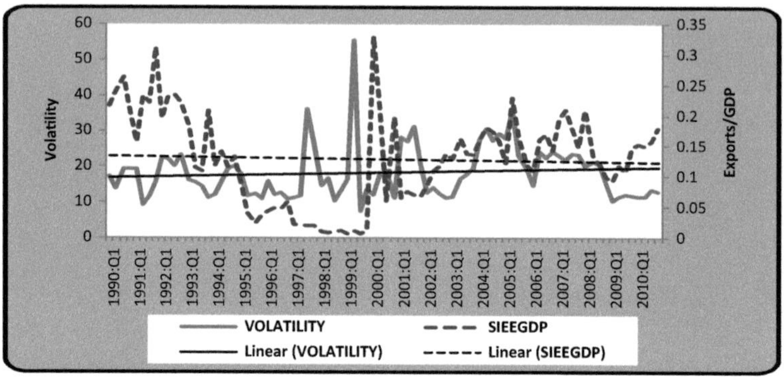

Fig. 5.6 Trends in volatility and export-GDP ratio in Sierra Leone, 1990:Q1-2010:Q4 (Source: Authors' compilation)

its trend line. This reveals that in the presence of real appreciation of the exchange rate, the country experienced improved export performance. In addition, between 1997 and 1999, the real exchange rate depreciated, causing volatility to increase, while export-GDP ratio declined gradually. The figure also shows that since 2003, both exchange rate volatility and export-GDP ratio remained above their trend lines, denoting that depreciation of the exchange rate improved the country's export performance.

4 Theoretical Framework and Methodology

4.1 Export Function

In a simple Keynesian framework, export is modelled as a function of real exchange rate, terms of trade and income of the rest of the world. Thus, the basic export demand function can be specified as

$$EXP = f(RER, TOT, YROW) \tag{5.1}$$

Where *EXP* is defined as the ratio of export to GDP, *RER* = real effective exchange rate, TOT = terms of trade, and *YROW* = income in the rest of the world. Real exchange rate appreciation (lower real exchange rate) means loss of international competitiveness and, hence, a fall in demand for export, while a depreciation implies competitiveness gains and, therefore, a rise in demand for exports. It means that for a higher real exchange rate, the export of a home country is more competitive in comparison with the foreign country and lead to more exports. The terms of trade variable is the relative price of exports to price of imports. Thus, a rise in TOT implies favourable terms of trade which should induce more exports from the home country, and vice versa. All other things being equal, a rise in the income of the rest of the world would induce and increase demand for the home country's exports.

From opportunistic perspective, exchange rate fluctuations/volatility can influence export supply of a country. Further, any export performance model of a country must take into consideration both demand and supply side factors. Thus, Eq. 5.1 can be restated as

$$EXP = f(RER, TOT, YROW, VOL) \tag{5.2}$$

Where VOL is defined as real effective exchange rate volatility, while other variables are as defined earlier. The literature suggests that exchange rate volatility may have positive or negative impact on exports performance. The empirical modelling of export performance necessitates the introduction of a stochastic term into the export function. Thus, Eq. 5.2 can be re-specified as

$$EXP_t = \beta_0 + \beta_1 RER_t + \beta_2 TOT_t + \beta_3 YROW_t + \beta_4 VOL_t + \varepsilon_t \tag{5.3}$$

Equation 5.3 is the empirical model to be estimated in this study. A priori, the coefficients are likely to have the following signs: $\beta_1 > 0$, $\beta_2 > 0$, $\beta_3 </> 0$, $\beta_4 </> 0$.

4.2 A GARCH Model of Exchange Rate Volatility

Real exchange rate fluctuations have been modelled differently in the literature. Some studies used moving average standard deviation while others used GARCH based measure of volatility. This study adopts the GARCH approach of modelling volatility. Among the various GARCH models in the literature, this study adopts GARCH (1, 1) model due to its parsimony and ability to capture volatility in most time series. The mean equation of the GARCH (1, 1) model is specified as follows[1]:

$$RER_t = \alpha_0 + \alpha_1 RES_t + \alpha_2 IMP_t + \varepsilon_t \tag{5.4}$$

Where *RES* is defined as international reserves and *IMP* represents imports. Generally the nominal exchange rate is explained by the reserve position of a country. Also, in developing countries, increase in imports usually put direct pressure on the nominal exchange rate. Changes in the nominal exchange rate affects the real exchange rate, hence, the mean equation is specified to reflect the key determinants of the real exchange rate.

---

[1] Other specifications of the mean equation including autoregressive formulation were tried but did not perform well.

The variance equation of the GARCH (1, 1) is specified as

$$VOL_t = \sigma_t^2 = \bar{\omega} + \alpha\varepsilon_{t-1}^2 + \beta\sigma_{t-1}^2 \tag{5.5}$$

Where σ_t^2 is the one-period ahead forecast variance (time variant conditional variance of the real effective exchange rate) based on past information. It represents volatility of the real effective exchange rate; $\omega \equiv$ constant term; $\varepsilon_{t-1}^2 \equiv$ news about volatility from the previous period, measured as the lag of the squared residual from the mean equation (ARCH term) in Eq. 5.4; and $\sigma_{t-1}^2 \equiv$ last period's forecast variance (GARCH term), α and β are the parameters estimated.

Equation 5.5 is the regression equation of our interest and gives the conditional variance, which is a function of three terms – the mean (constant); news about the volatility from the previous period measured as a lag of the squared residual from Eq. 5.5, ε_{t-1}^2, also known as the ARCH term; and the last period's forecast variance, σ_{t-1}^2, the GARCH term.

4.3 *Estimation Techniques*

The study begins the empirical analysis by first examining the time series properties of the variables in logarithmic forms using Augmented Dickey-Fuller (ADF) unit root test and Kwiatkowski-Phillips-Schmidt-Shin (KPSS) stationarity test. The ADF tests the null hypothesis that there is a unit root and a rejection of the null implies the series is stationary. The KPSS, on the other hand, tests the null that there is stationarity where a rejection implies the series is not stationary. The KPSS has been developed to complement the ADF unit root test which has been found to have weak power in rejecting the null. Where the two tests produce conflicting results, it is taken that the series is not stationary and further processing is undertaken.

For non-stationary series, the study conducts conitegration test on the I (1) variables to see if their linear combination is stationary before combining them with stationary series to determine cointegration of the variables in the model. The study adopts a single equation residual-based cointegration approach using Dynamic OLS (DOLS) estimation technique which has been noted to have been producing more efficient estimates than the Static OLS (SOLS) estimation technique. Where cointegration exists, Engle-Granger Representation theorem is invoked for the specification of the error-correction model. In the absence of cointegration, the study estimates a long-run model or a short-run model depending on the stationarity status of the model variables. Given that volatility is not observable, the study employed the GARCH (1, 1) approach to measure the volatility of the real effective exchange rate.

4.4 Data Type and Sources

The study makes use of secondary quarterly series for the period 1990Q1 to 2010Q4 obtained from International Financial Statistics and Direction of Trade Statistics of the IMF. However the reference period in the case of Liberia was 2002Q1 to 2010Q4, due to the unavailability of data. The quarterly GDP data were obtained through interpolation of annual time series data using Eviews 7.0. This was done using the low frequency to high frequency method and the quadratic match sum for each observation of the low frequency series. Data were obtained on export, domestic GDP, foreign income, terms of trade and real effective exchange rate. Equation 5.6 gives a measure of the real effective exchange rate:

$$RER_t = \sum_{i=1}^{n} \left[w_{it} \left(\frac{e_{it} * p_{it}}{P_{dt}} \right) \right] \tag{5.6}$$

where RER_t is real effective exchange rate, W_{it} is the ith trading partner trade weight, e_{it} is the bilateral nominal exchange rate (period average) defined as amount of local currency per unit of foreign currency for country i, and the prices for non-tradeable and tradeable goods measured by domestic consumer price index (P_{dt}) and trading partner's consumer price index (P_{it}), respectively.

5 Presentation and Analysis of Results

5.1 Estimation Results for the Gambia

5.1.1 Unit Root Test Results

From Table 5.1, all the variables are integrated of order one (I(1)) except volatility (GAMVOL) which is integrated of order zero (I(0)). For GAMEXP at log level, both ADF and KPSS tests were consistent in accepting and rejecting the null hypotheses, respectively. The log difference of GAMEXP was found to be stationary by both tests, hence log of GAMEXP is an I(1) variable. For GAMRER at log level, the ADF says it has a unit root, while the KPSS suggests it is stationary. With these conflicting results, the study went on to find the stationarity status of the log difference of GAMRER, which was confirmed by both tests. This implies that GAMRER at log level was integrated of order one. Both the ADF and KPSS were consistent in rejecting the stationarity of GAMTOT at log level but accepting it at log difference. Thus, log of GAMTOT was integrated of order one. GAMVOL at log level was found to be stationary by both tests. For GDPOECD, the ADF results contradicted that of the KPSS in that while the ADF rejected the null of non stationarity, the KPSS also rejected the null of stationarity. Examining the log

Table 5.1 Unit root test results for the Gambia

Variable	ADF Test Null: not stationary	KPSS Null: stationary	Remark on order of integration
LOG(GAMEXP)	−2.273161 (*−2.586103*)	0.608380** (*0.463000*)	I(1)
D(LOG(GAMEXP))	−11.42354*** (*−2.586103*)	0.1606632 (*0.463000*)	
LOG(GAMRER)	−1.995907 (*−3.159372*)	0.140177 (*0.146000*)	I(1)
D(LOG(GAMRER)	−6.037608*** (*−3.159372*)	0.108206 (*0.146000*)	
LOG(GAMTOT)	−2.437374 (*−2.586351*)	1.003004***(*0.463000*)	I(1)
D(LOG(GAMTOT)	−10.02231*** (*−2.586351*)	0.195518 (*0.463000*)	
LOG(GAMVOL)	−4.116470*** (*−2.585626*)	0.231075 (*0.463000*)	I(0)
LOG(GDPOECD)	−3.733144** (*−2.585861*)	0.197146** (*0.146000*)	I(1)
D(LOG(GDPOECD)	−3.175628** (*−2.585861*)	0.133485 (*0.463000*)	

Source: Computed by the Authors
Figures in parentheses are 5 % critical values for the respective tests
***1 % significance; **5 % significance

Table 5.2 Engle-Granger dynamic OLS cointegration test results for the I(1) variables only

Statistic	Value calculated	Probability value
Engle-Granger tau-statistic	−4.453718	0.0295
Engle-Granger z-statistic	−32.59284	0.0225

Source: Computed by the Authors
Null hypothesis: There is no cointegration (rejected at 5 %)

difference of GDPOECD, both tests were in agreement on its stationarity. This implies the log of GDPOECD is integrated of order one. Non-stationarity of only some of the model variables necessitated carrying out cointegration test at two stages. The results of these tests are reported in the next section.

5.1.2 Cointegration Test Results

At the first stage, cointegration test was conducted only on the I(1) variables. Table 5.2 indicates that the null of no cointegration among the model variables was rejected at 5 % significance level. Both Engle-Granger tau and z-tests of DOLS confirmed the presence of cointegration. Given that the four non-stationary variables are cointegrated, the study proceeded to the second stage of the cointegation process where all the model variables were tested jointly. The results of this second stage are reported in Table 5.3.

Both Engle-Granger tau- and z-tests show that all the variables in the export model for the Gambia were cointegrated at 1 % level of significance. The associated cointegrating relationship (which gives the long run regression estimates) is reported in Table 5.4. The cointegrating vector for GAMEXP, GAMRER, GAMTOT, GAMVOL and GDPOECD is [1, 0, −1.4, −0.3, −2.8]. The results suggest that, in the long run, volatility did have significant positive impact on export performance in the Gambia. The coefficient estimate indicates that a

Table 5.3 Engle-Granger dynamic OLS cointegration test on both I(1) and I(0) variables

Statistic	Value calculated	Probability value
Engle-Granger tau-statistic	−5.509163	0.0045
Engle-Granger z-statistic	−44.76453	0.0036

Source: Computed by the Authors
Null hypothesis: There is no cointegration (rejected at 1 %)

Table 5.4 Cointegration equation for both I(1) and I(0) variables
Dynamic OLS Estimation: Dependent Variable is LOG (GAMEXP)

Variable	Coefficient	Std. error	t-Statistic	Prob.
LOG(GAMRER)	−0.161671	0.396285	−0.407967	0.6847
LOG(GAMTOT)	1.396767	0.107464	12.99755	0.0000
LOG(GAMVOL)	0.292080	0.077580	3.764871	0.0004
LOG(GDPOECD)	2.814031	1.148462	2.450262	0.0170
C	−30.15592	12.05551	−2.501422	0.0149
R-squared	0.953923		Sum squared resid	3.337475
Adjusted R-squared	0.942404		Long-run variance	0.108728
S.E. of regression	0.228359		Durbin-Watson stat	0.931778

Source: Computed by the Authors

one-percentage increase in real exchange rate volatility causes exports to increase by 0.3 %. This corroborates the positive relationship observed in Fig. 5.1 between volatility and exports. Overall, Gambian's exports, though primary commodities, were responsive to the real exchange rate volatility induced mainly by the rapid depreciation of the dalasi.

Real effective exchange rate did not have any explanation for variations in the Gambia's exports during the study period. The negative coefficient of the real exchange rate captures more of the real exchange rate appreciation that occurred during the period. The appreciation did not hurt exports largely because Gambian exports are mainly groundnuts whose price is given in the international market. Terms of trade had a significant positive impact on the Gambia's export performance, implying favourable terms of trade encouraged exports in the Gambia, and vice versa. A one-percentage increase in the terms of trade (improvement) induces a 1.4-percentage-point increase in exports-GDP ratio. Similarly, a percentage increase in the income of the rest of the world induces a 2.8-percentage-point increase in Gambia's exports. This result confirms the a priori expectation of the study. Overall, income of the rest of the world and the terms of trade were the key variables that had more-than-proportionate long-run impacts on export performance in the Gambia during the long run.

5.1.3 Short-Run Dynamic Model Results

Having established cointegration among the model variables, the study proceeded to estimate an error-correction model of exports for the Gambia. The parsimonious error-correction model results are reported in Table 5.5. The diagnostic tests of

Table 5.5 Parsimonious error-correction model results
Dependent Variable is D(LOG(GAMEXP))

Variable	Coefficient	Std. error		t-Statistic	Prob.
C	0.005950	0.022007		0.270370	0.7876
D(LOG (GAMTOT))	0.976695	0.039900		24.47860	0.0000
D(LOG(VOL2 (−2)))	0.098893	0.029246		3.381487	0.0011
ECT	−0.407334	0.108193		−3.764874	0.0003
R-squared	0.893005	B-G LM test	0.385252 (0.6816)	F-statistic	214.2206
Adjusted R-squared	0.888837	ARCH Test	0.526341 (0.4703)	Prob(F-statistic)	0.000000
S.E. of regression	0.197656	RESET Test	0.560555 (0.4563)	Durbin-Watson stat	1.907009

Source: Computed by the Authors

serial correlation, heteroscedasticity and linear misspecification indicate non violation of the assumptions underlying the OLS estimation technique. The significant coefficient estimates show that changes in the terms of trade and volatility were the key factors driving exports in the short run. The coefficient of the error-correction term is statistically significant and correctly signed. The magnitude of the coefficient indicates that about 41.0 % of any previous disequilibrium in the long-run export relationship is corrected in the current quarter.

5.2 *Estimation Results for Ghana*

5.2.1 Unit Root Test Results

Table 5.6 shows that three of the variables are integrated of order one (I(1)), while the other two are integrated of zero (I(0)). The ADF and KPSS tests were inconsistent on the stationarity status of GHAEXP. While the ADF statistics indicate non-rejection of the null unit root hypothesis, the KPSS fails to reject the null stationary hypothesis. The log difference of GHAEXP was found to be stationary by both tests, hence, log of GHAEXP is an I(1) variable. GHARER at log level has a unit root according to both the ADF and KPSS tests. The log difference of GHARER is stationary according both tests, implying that log level of GHARER is I(1). Terms of trade and volatility variables are integrated of order zero according to both tests. The unit root test results suggest that cointegration test is carried out in two stages: first on the I(1) variables alone and secondly on all the model variables provided cointegration holds in the first stage.

Table 5.6 Unit root test results for Ghana

Variable	ADF Test Null: not stationary	KPSS Null: stationary	Remark on order of integration
LOG(GHAEXP)	−2.683038 (*−2.896779*)	0.295016 (*0.463000*)	I(1)
D(LOG(GHAEXP))	−10.05487*** (*−2.896779*)	0.129680 (*0.463000*)	
LOG(GHARER)	−2.349147 (*−2.585861*)	0.805478***(*0.463000*)	I(1)
D(LOG(GHARER))	−5.679596*** (*−2.585861*)	0.108206 (*0.463000*)	
LOG(GHATOT)	−3.688133** (*−3.161982*)	0.083326 (*0.146000*)	I(0)
LOG(GHAVOL)	−4.583605*** (*−3.158974*)	0.069334 (*0.146000*)	I(0)
LOG(GDPOECD)	−3.733144** (*−2.585861*)	0.197146** (*0.146000*)	I(1)
D(LOG(GDPOECD))	−3.175628** (*−2.585861*)	0.133485 (*0.463000*)	

Source: Computed by the Authors
Figures in parentheses are 10 % critical values for the respective tests
***1 % significance; **5 % significance

Table 5.7 Engle-Granger dynamic OLS cointegration test on I(1) variables

Statistic	Value calculated	Probability value
Engle-Granger tau-statistic	−2.859286	0.3171
Engle-Granger z-statistic	−17.21210	0.1996

Source: Computed by the Authors
Null hypothesis: There is no cointegration (not rejected at the 5 % significance level)

5.2.2 Cointegration Test Results

The first stage cointegration test was carried out on the log levels of GHAEXP, GHARER and GDPOECD which are integrated of order one using dynamic OLS cointegration technique. The results are presented in Table 5.7.

The Engle-Granger tau- and z-tests produced statistics that are smaller than their critical values, thus, giving rise to high probability values. This means that the null hypothesis of no cointegration cannot be rejected at the 5 % level of significance. Once the I(1) variables are not cointegrated, the study could not proceed to the second phase of the cointegration test. To avoid spurious regression, a short-run export model was estimated for Ghana.

5.2.3 Short-Run Model

It must be noted that estimating a short-run export model with the variables in log forms means estimating export growth performance for Ghana. The parsimonious short-run model results are reported in Table 5.8. The model passed all the diagnostic tests of serial correlation, heteroscedasticity and misspecification. The test result for significance of the complete regression as captured by the F-statistic shows that the model variables significantly jointly explain variations in export growth, although the explanatory power of the model is small (14.0 %).

Table 5.8 Export growth model results for Ghana
Dependent Variable is D(LOG(GHAEXP))

Variable	Coefficient	Std. error		t-Statistic	Prob.
C	0.098253	0.286799		0.342587	0.7329
LOG(GHATOT)	0.222325	0.106184		2.093777	0.0396
LOG(VOL2)	0.024051	0.030855		0.779479	0.4381
D(LOG(GDPOECD))	5.028241	3.748866		1.341270	0.1838
D(LOG(GHARER (−1)))	−0.837108	0.405958		−2.062055	0.0426
R-squared	0.138826	B-G LM test	0.825109 (0.4422)	F-statistic	2.450331
Adjusted R-squared	0.082170	ARCH Test	0.137931 (0.7113)	Prob(F-statistic)	0.041041
S.E. of regression	0.183708	RESET Test	1.153568 (0.2862)	Durbin-Watson stat	2.090802

Source: Computed by the Authors

From Table 5.8, the impact of real exchange rate volatility on export growth in Ghana is not statistically significant at the conventional level. The terms of trade was found to have a significant positive contemporaneous effect on export growth with an indication that a one-percentage increase in the terms of trade would cause exports growth to increase by 0.22 %. The growth rate in the rest of the world appears not to have any significant impact on export growth in Ghana during the study period. Though the coefficient was positive, it was statistically insignificant. The real exchange rate is found to have a significant dynamic negative impact on export growth.

5.3 *Estimation Results for Guinea*

5.3.1 Unit Root Test Results

The unit root results for Guinea are reported in Table 5.9. All the model variables are integrated of order one. Both the ADF and the KPSS tests are consistent on the non-stationarity of the variables at log level. The log differences of the variables are stationary according to both tests. This implies that cointegration can be done on all the variables at a time.

5.3.2 Cointegration Test Results

The cointegration test results on all the model variables using dynamic OLS technique are presented in Table 5.10. Engle-Granger tau- and z-statistics are not statistically significant, suggesting that the null hypothesis of no cointegration

Table 5.9 Unit root test results for Guinea

Variable	ADF Test Null: not stationary	KPSS Null: stationary	Remark on order of integration
LOG(GUIEXP)	−2.873972 (*−3.158974*)	0.217555*** (*0.146000*)	I(1)
D(LOG(GUIEXP))	−11.08966*** (*−3.158974*)	0.032561 (*0.146000*)	
LOG(GUIRER)	−1.262411 (*−2.588902*)	0.980317*** (*0.463000*)	I(1)
D(LOG(GUIRER))	−6.838337*** (*−2.588902*)	0.147401 (*0.463000*)	
LOG(GUITOT)	−1.954886 (*−2.585861*)	0.685300** (*0.463000*)	I(1)
D(LOG(GUITOT))	−13.22110*** (*−2.585861*)	0.051375 (*0.463000*)	
LOG(GUIVOL)	−1.495534 (*−2.588902*)	0.833625*** (*0.463000*)	I(1)
D(LOG(GUIVOL))	−9.122163*** (*−2.588902*)	0.223725 (*0.463000*)	
LOG(GDPOECD)	−3.733144** (*−2.585861*)	0.197146** (*0.463000*)	I(1)
D(LOG(GDPOECD))	−3.175628** (*−2.585861*)	0.133485 (*0.463000*)	

Source: Computed by the Authors
Figures in parentheses are 10 % critical values for the respective tests
***1 % significance; **5 % significance

Table 5.10 Engle-Granger dynamic OLS cointegration test on all variables

Statistic	Value calculated	Probability value
Engle-Granger tau-statistic	−2.650358	0.7628
Engle-Granger z-statistic	−14.36633	0.7040

Source: Computed by the authors
Null hypothesis: There is no cointegration (not rejected at the 5 % significance level)

cannot be rejected at 5 % significance level. This implies that there is no long-run relationship among the variables. Hence, the Engle-Granger Representation Theorem cannot be invoked for the specification of an error-correction model. The study, therefore, estimated a short-run model for Guinea.

5.3.3 Short-Run Dynamic Model

The results of the parsimonious short-run export model are presented in Table 5.11. The diagnostic tests (Breusch-Godfrey Serial Correlation LM Test, ARCH Heteroscedasticity Test and Ramsey RESET Test) indicate that the estimated model did not suffer from problems of serial correlation, heteroscedasticity and model misspecification. The F-test shows that the explanatory variables jointly

Table 5.11 Short-run (export growth) model results for Guinea
Dependent Variable is D(LOG(GUIEXP))

Variable	Coefficient	Std. error		t-Statistic	Prob.
C	0.000275	0.020993		0.013122	0.9896
D(LOG(GDPOECD))	2.448431	2.807699		0.872042	0.3859
D(LOG(GUIRER))	0.341741	0.238463		1.433097	0.1559
D(LOG(GUITOT))	0.678305	0.078253		8.668119	0.0000
D(LOG(VOL2(−2)))	−0.019124	0.018205		−1.050427	0.2969
R-squared	0.526379	B-G LM test	0.316777 (0.7295)	F-statistic	21.11643
Adjusted R-squared	0.501451	ARCH Test	0.108529 (0.7427)	Prob(F-statistic)	0.000000
S.E. of regression	0.134375	RESET Test	0.001170 (0.9728)	Durbin-Watson stat	2.081791

Source: Computed by the Authors

explain variations in export growth at 1 % significance level. The explanatory power of the model shows that 53 % of the variation in the dependent variable is accounted for by the independent variables. Although the coefficient of volatility carries a negative sign, it is not statistically significant. This means that volatility did not affect export growth in Guinea over the study period. The growth of income of the rest of the world and real exchange rate depreciation did not significantly impact on export growth during the period. However, the terms of trade had significant positive impact on export growth. The magnitude of its coefficient implies a one-percentage increase in the terms of trade induces 0.67 % rise in export growth.

5.4 *Estimation Results for Liberia*

5.4.1 Unit Root Test Results

Table 5.12 reports the ADF and KPSS stationarity test results. Apart from GDPOECD, all the variables in the model are integrated of order zero. For Liberia, the variables have only 36 quarterly observations due to missing data during the war period. The number of observations is not sufficient to carry out KPSS test since it goes with asymptotic critical values, hence, stationarity status of the variables are determined solely by the ADF test statistics. Accordingly, all the variables are found to be stationary except GPDOECD.

5.4.2 Dynamic Long-Run Model

Given the foregoing unit root test results, GDPOECD is the only I(1) variable and, therefore, cannot combine with any other I(1) variable in the cointegration process. The study first attempted including its first log difference in the regression model

Table 5.12 Unit root test/stationarity test results for Liberia

Variable	ADF Test Null: not stationary	KPSS Null: stationary	Remark on order of integration
LOG(LIBEXP)	−5.544743*** (*−3.204699*)	0.143792 (*0.146000*)	I(0)
LOG(LIBRER)	−2.139776*** (*−1.609798*)	0.728819** (*0.463000*)	I(0)
LOG(LIBTOT)	−5.543640*** (*−3.204699*)	0.171756** (*0.146000*)	I(0)
LOG(LIBVOL)	−2.888219*** (*−1.610747*)	0.674004** (*0.463000*)	I(0)
LOG(GDPOECD)	−3.733144** (*−2.585861*)	0.197146** (*0.146000*)	I(1)
D(LOG (GDPOECD))	−3.175628** (*−2.585861*)	0.133485 (*0.463000*)	

Source: Computed by the Authors
Figures in parentheses are 5 % critical values for the respective tests
***1 % significance; **5 % significance

but the result was not encouraging. Thus, for Liberia, the study estimated a long-run export model excluding GDPOECD. The parsimonious dynamic long-run model results are presented in Table 5.13.

The model did not suffer from problems of serial correlation, heteroscedasticity and model misspecification as the three key diagnostic tests returned insignificant F-statistics. Statistically, all the variables in the parsimonious model jointly explain variations in exports for Liberia during the study period as the F-statistic of testing the significance of the complete regression is significant at 1 %. Overall, the model explains 97 % of the total variations in exports.

The results showed that volatility and terms of trade are found to have significant effects on exports, while the coefficient of the real effective exchange rate was found to be insignificant. A one-percentage increase in volatility induces 0.19 % decrease in exports. The terms of trade have both significant positive contemporaneous effect and negative dynamic effect on exports. The net impact of the terms of trade on Liberia's exports was positive, indicating that a percentage increase in the terms of trade induces 0.61 % increase in exports. Also, there was significant export inertia as the two previous quarters' exports have explanation for the current level of exports. Here, a percentage increase in previous exports value will cause the current level of exports to rise by 0.32 %.

5.5 *Estimation Results for Nigeria*

5.5.1 Unit Root Test Results

The stationarity test results are reported in Table 5.14 which shows that NIGEXP, NIGTOT and NIGVOL are integrated of order zero; whilst NIGEGDP and GDPOECD are integrated of order one. Apart from GDPOECD, both the ADF and KPSS tests were consistent on the stationarity of the variables.

Table 5.13 Long-run export model results for Liberia
Dependent Variable is LOG(LIBEXP)

Variable	Coefficient	Std. error		t-Statistic	Prob.
C	−2.483966	1.127551		−2.202975	0.0363
LOG(LIBEXP (−1))	0.401261	0.188384		2.130023	0.0424
LOG(LIBEXP (−2))	−0.078684	0.040861		−1.925656	0.0647
LOG(LIBTOT)	0.987738	0.041059		24.05640	0.0000
LOG(LIBTOT (−1))	−0.378379	0.181635		−2.083186	0.0468
LOG(LIBVOL (−1))	−0.188325	0.073740		−2.553906	0.0166
LOG(LIBRER (−2))	0.379796	0.331804		1.144641	0.2624
R-squared	0.965850	B-G LM test	2.332151 (0.1178)	F-statistic	127.2702
Adjusted R-squared	0.958261	ARCH Test	1.127626 (0.2965)	Prob(F-statistic)	0.000000
S.E. of regression	0.133712	RESET Test	0.178692 (0.6760)	Durbin-Watson stat	2.184667

Source: Computed by the Authors

Table 5.14 Unit root test results for Nigeria

Variable	ADF TEST Null: not stationary	KPSS Null: stationary	Remark on order of integration
LOG(NIGEXP)	−4.332414*** (*−2.897223*)	0.141249 (*0.463000*)	I(0)
LOG(NIGRER)	−1.819486 (*−2.896779*)	0.270662 (*0.463000*)	I(1)
D(LOG(NIGRER))	−7.632208*** (*−2.896779*)	0.049419 (*0.463000*)	
LOG(NIGTOT)	−3.467957** (*−2.897223*)	0.180623 (*0.463000*)	I(0)
LOG(NIGVOL)	−5.767781*** (*−2.896779*)	0.400430 (*0.463000*)	I(0)
LOG(GDPOECD)	−3.733144** (*−2.585861*)	0.197146** (*0.146000*)	I(1)
D(LOG(GDPOECD))	−3.175628** (*−2.585861*)	0.133485 (*0.463000*)	

Source: Computed by the Authors
Figures in parentheses are 5 % critical values for the respective tests
***1 % significance, **5 % significance

5.5.2 Cointegration Test Results

Given the I(1) variables, cointegration test was carried out on them first before they were combined with the I(0) variables. The dynamic OLS cointegration test shows that NIGRER and GDPOECD are not cointegrated as the Engle-Granger tau- and z-statistics are not significant at the 5 % level. Thus, the second phase of the cointegration process was truncated; implying error-correction model could not be formulated (Table 5.15).

Table 5.15 Engle-Granger dynamic OLS cointegration test on I(1) variables

Statistic	Value calculated	Probability value
Engle-Granger tau-statistic	−2.042030	0.5095
Engle-Granger z-statistic	−8.037317	0.4758

Source: Computed by the Authors
Null hypothesis: There is no cointegration (not rejected at the 5 % significance level)

Table 5.16 Dynamic model results for Nigeria
Dependent variable is LOG(NIGEGDP)

Variable	Coefficient	Std. error		t-Statistic	Prob.
C	−0.802580	0.305904		−2.623634	0.0106
LOG(NIGEGDP(-1))	0.746139	0.071735		10.40137	0.0000
D(LOG(GDPOECD))	5.490079	2.975989		1.844791	0.0692
LOG(NIGTOT)	0.526474	0.070262		7.493003	0.0000
LOG(NIGTOT(-1))	−0.325805	0.108231		−3.010269	0.0036
LOG(NIGTOT(-2))	−0.112378	0.068245		−1.646684	0.1040
LOG(VOL2(-1))	0.036271	0.026007		1.394652	0.1674
D(LOG(NIGRER)) (-2)	−0.227625	0.122322		−1.860865	0.0668
R-squared	0.802562	B-G LM test	0.083473 (0.9200)	F-statistic	36.58389
Adjusted R-squared	0.780624	ARCH test	5.308405 (0.0239)	Prob(F-statistic)	0.000000
S.E. of regression	0.095297	RESET test	5.247451 (0.250)	Durbin-Watson stat	1.908514

Source: Computed by the Authors

5.5.3 The Dynamic Model

The study estimated a dynamic model with log difference of NIGRER as depreciation/appreciation and log difference of GDPOECD as the income growth in the rest of the world. The results of the parsimonious dynamic model are reported in Table 5.16. Breusch-Godfrey Serial Correlation LM Test shows that the error terms are not serial correlation but the ARCH Heteroscedasticity Test indicates a presence of heteroscedasticity. The study therefore proceeded to run White Heteroskedasticity robust model whose results are reported in Table 5.17.

Comparing the two Tables 5.16 and 5.17, it is clear that the robust estimation improved the efficiency of the estimator as growth in the rest of the world income which was significant at 10 % in the initial model became insignificant in the robust model, while volatility and real exchange rate lagged 2 which were not initially significant became significant. Hence, the discussion will focus on the results in Table 5.17. According to the F-test on the complete regression, the variables in the robust parsimonious model jointly explain variations in exports with an explanatory power of 80 %.

The magnitude of the coefficient of volatility shows that a percentage increase in volatility induces 0.04 % decrease in exports. This significant negative impact of

Table 5.17 White heteroskedasticity-consistent standard errors and covariance model
Dependent variable is LOG(NIGEGDP)

Variable	Coefficient	Std. error		t-Statistic	Prob.
C	−0.802580	0.407502		−1.969512	0.0527
LOG(NIGEGDP(-1))	0.746139	0.101186		7.373916	0.0000
D(LOG(GDPOECD))	5.490079	4.049605		1.355707	0.1794
LOG(NIGTOT)	0.526474	0.086978		6.052962	0.0000
LOG(NIGTOT(-1))	−0.325805	0.135560		−2.403392	0.0188
LOG(NIGTOT(-2))	−0.112378	0.061584		−1.824779	0.0722
LOG(VOL2(-1))	0.036271	0.018787		1.930599	0.0575
D(LOG(NIGRER)) (-2)	−0.227625	0.090258		−2.521933	0.0139
R-squared	0.802562	B-G LM test	–	F-statistic	36.58389
Adjusted R-squared	0.780624	ARCH test	–	Prob(F-statistic)	0.000000
S.E. of regression	0.095297	RESET test	–	Durbin-Watson stat	1.908514

Source: Computed by the Authors

volatility reflects risk-averse nature of Nigerian exporters. Real exchange rate depreciation had negative dynamic impact on exports with a percentage increase in real appreciation causing exports to decline by 0.23 %. The terms of trade had a positive contemporaneous but a negative dynamic effects on exports. The net impact of the terms of trade on exports was positive with a percentage increase in the terms of trade causing exports to increase by 0.09 %. A percentage rise in the past level of exports increases the current level of exports by 0.75 % points, implying export performance inertia in Nigeria.

5.6 *Estimation Results for Sierra Leone*

5.6.1 Unit Root Test Results

The results presented in Table 5.18 indicate that SIEEXP, SIERER and GDPOECD at log levels are integrated of order one, whilst SIETOT and SIEVOL at log levels are integrated of order zero. Both the ADF and KPSS test are consistent on the stationarity status of SIEEGDP, SIETOT and SIEVOL. The KPSS suggests that SIERER may be integrated of order two since it rejects the stationarity of the first log difference of SIERER at 5 % level. However, the strength of the ADF statistic shows that SIERER should be taken as an I(1) variable.

5.6.2 Cointegration Test Results

The first phase of the cointegration process focused on testing for cointegration among the three I(1) variables. The results are reported in Table 5.19. Engle-Granger tau- and z-statistics are significant at 10 % level, hence, the rejection of

Table 5.18 Unit root test results for Sierra Leone

Variable	ADF Test Null: not stationary	KPSS Null: stationary	Remark on order of integration
LOG(SIEEXP)	−2.548074 (*−2.896779*)	0.233941*** (*0.463000*)	I(1)
D(LOG(SIEEXP))	−8.670562*** (*−2.896779*)	0.066738 (*0.463000*)	
LOG(SIERER)	−2.891621 (*−3.464865*)	0.216325*** (*0.146000*)	I(1)
D(LOG(SIERER))	−10.12544*** (*−3.464865*)	0.162213** (*0.146000*)	
LOG(SIETOT)	−2.933631** (*−2.896779*)	0.238824 (*0.463000*)	I(0)
LOG(SIEVOL)	−5.563861*** (*−2.896779*)	0.191582 (*0.463000*)	I(0)
LOG(GDPOECD)	−3.733144** (*−2.585861*)	0.197146** (*0.146000*)	I(1)
D(LOG(GDPOECD))	−3.175628** (*−2.585861*)	0.133485 (*0.463000*)	

Source: Computed by the Authors
Figures in parentheses are 10 % critical values for the respective tests
***1 % significance; **5 % significance

the null hypothesis that there is no cointegration. The study proceeded with the second phase of the cointegration process by testing for cointegration among all the model variables. The results of this second test are presented in Table 5.20.

The Engle-Granger tau- and z-tests revealed the presence of cointegration among all the model variables at 5 % level of significance. The cointegration relationship among the variables is reported in Table 5.21. The related cointegrating vector is $[1, -1.6, -1.1, -1.1, 0, 0]$ for variable combination SIEEXP, GDPOECD, SIERER, SIETOT, SIEVOL and DUMMY. Thus, in the long run, volatility though negative, does not affect export performance. As in many other cases, the non-significance of volatility impact could be explained by the nature of the country's export, which are mostly primary commodities.

The income in the rest of the world, real effective exchange rate and terms of trade all had significant positive long-run impacts on export performance in Sierra Leone, which are consistent with the stated a priori expectations. A percentage increase in the income of the rest of the world induces a 2.1 % increase in exports from Sierra Leone. A one-percentage point increases in real effective exchange rate and terms of trade cause exports to increase by 1.1 and 1.1 %, respectively. Dummy capturing the civil war period in Sierra Leone has a negative but insignificant coefficient, implying the civil war tended to have a dampening effect on export performance in Sierra Leone but the impact has not been borne out by the data.

5.6.3 Short-Run Dynamic Model

The presence of cointegration calls for estimation of the error-correction model whose results are reported in Table 5.22. The diagnostic test results show that the parsimonious error-correction model did not suffer the problems of serial correlation, heteroscedaticity, and linear misspecification. All the explanatory variables jointly explain variations in export growth as indicated by the significant F-statistic

Table 5.19 Engle-Granger dynamic OLS cointegration test on I(1) variables

Statisitic	Value calculated	Probability value
Engle-Granger tau-statistic	−3.595634	0.0868
Engle-Granger z-statistic	−21.80733	0.0834

Source: Computed by the Authors
Null hypothesis: There is no cointegration (rejected at 10 % significance level)

Table 5.20 Engle-Granger dynamic OLS cointegration test on both I(1) and I(0) variables

Statistic	Value calculated	Probability value
Engle-Granger tau-statistic	−4.637704	0.0445
Engle-Granger z-statistic	−35.52098	0.0307

Source: Computed by the Authors
Null hypothesis: There is no cointegration (rejected at 5 % significance level)

at 1 %. The explanatory power of the model is 90 %. Overall, the estimated coefficients are worthy of discussion.

Volatility had a dynamic negative impact on export growth with a percentage increase inducing 0.19 percentage point decrease in export growth, while income growth in the rest of world had a positive impact on export growth over the study period. The terms of trade had both a contemporaneous and a dynamic effect on export growth, but the overall impact was found to be positive, indicating that a one percentage point increase in terms of trade would improve export performance by 0.78 %. In addition, real effective exchange rate was found to have a negative impact on export performance during the review period. There was export inertia as captured by significant effect of past export growth on current level. The magnitude of the coefficient estimate of the error-correction term shows that 37.0 % of any previous disequilibrium in the long-run export relationship will be corrected in the current period.

6 Conclusion and Policy Recommendations

This study investigates the effect of real exchange rate volatility on exports performance in the WAMZ countries within a single equation residual-based cointegration approach using Dynamic OLS (DOLS) estimation technique with quarterly data for the period 1990–2010. The study also employs the GARCH (1, 1) approach to measure the volatility of the real effective exchange rate. The results of the cointegration analysis reveal the existence of cointegration in the case of The Gambia and Sierra Leone, while no cointegration is established for Ghana, Guinea and Nigeria. The variables in the case of Liberia are found to be integrated of order zero, i.e. I(0) series, so no cointegration test is applied.

The empirical findings indicate that real effective exchange rate volatility has a significant negative impact on export performance in Liberia, Nigeria and Sierra

Table 5.21 Cointegration relationship among the I(1) and I(0) variables
Dynamic OLS Estimation: Dependent Variable is LOG(SIEEXP)

Variable	Coefficient	Std. error	t-Statistic	Prob.
LOG(GDPOECD)	1.584142	0.624446	2.536876	0.0138
LOG(SIERER)	1.079503	0.504418	2.140096	0.0364
LOG(SIETOT)	1.147853	0.074911	15.32287	0.0000
LOG(VOL2)	−0.040485	0.182072	−0.222356	0.8248
DUMMY	−0.239165	0.178828	−1.337400	0.1861
C	−24.86272	7.042972	−3.530146	0.0008
R-squared	0.957691		Sum squared resid	3.321404
Adjusted R-squared	0.943588		Long-run variance	0.118525
S.E. of regression	0.235280		Durbin-Watson stat	0.990083

Source: Computed by the Authors

Table 5.22 Error-correction model results for Sierra Leone
Dependent Variable is D(LOG(SIEEXP))

Variable	Coefficient	Std. error		t-Statistic	Prob.
C	−0.030582	0.027842		−1.098381	0.2756
D(LOG(SIEEXP(−2)))	0.183439	0.095339		1.924075	0.0582
D(LOG(GDPOECD))	6.603415	3.674514		1.797085	0.0765
D(LOG(SIERER))	−0.643909	0.238760		−2.696892	0.0087
D(LOG(SIETOT))	0.917087	0.043338		21.16151	0.0000
D(LOG(VOL2(−2)))	−0.185458	0.053515		−3.465548	0.0009
D(LOG(SIETOT(−2)))	−0.133498	0.094925		−1.406353	0.1639
ECT(−1)	−0.373941	0.093543		−3.997542	0.0002
R-squared	0.898224	B-G LM test	0.029869 (0.9706)	F-statistic	92.03721
Adjusted R-squared	0.888465	ARCH Test	0.005151 (0.9430)	Prob(F-statistic)	0.000000
S.E. of regression	0.179862	RESET Test	1.708664 (0.1953)	Durbin-Watson stat	1.997669

Source: Computed by the Authors

Leone, while significant positive long- and short-run impacts are established in the case of The Gambia. However, its impacts in Ghana and Guinea are found to be insignificant. The results are consistent with the three strands in the literature: volatility-harming-exports hypothesis as found in Grobar (1993), Gonzaga and Terra (1997), Sekkat and Varoudakis (1998), Ogun (1998), Adubi and Okumadewa (1999), Sorsa (1999) and Darrat and Hakin (2000); volatility-promoting-export hypothesis as contained in studies like Franke (1991) and Secru and Vanhall (1992); as well as volatility-not-affecting-exports hypothesis as articulated in Kohlhagen (1978), Bailey and Tavlas (1988), and Holly (1995).

The results also reveal a positive relationship between terms of trade and export performance for all the countries, indicating that improvement in terms of trade triggers increases in export performance in the WAMZ countries. Furthermore, income from the rest of the world impacts positively on export performance in the WAMZ countries, although it is found to be insignificant in the case of Ghana, Guinea and Nigeria. It is also found that real effective exchange rate has a negative impact on export performance in the case of The Gambia, Ghana and Nigeria, while a positive relationship is established in the case of Guinea and Liberia. However, while a positive relationship is revealed in the long run in the case of Sierra Leone, its impact is negative in the short run.

6.1 Recommendations

Given that a negative relationship was established between real effective exchange rate volatility and export performance in the case of Liberia, Nigeria and Sierra Leone, export performance can be improved if governments in these countries undertake policies aimed at maintaining a stable real effective exchange rate. This can be achieved by pursuing simultaneously disinflationary policies and nominal exchange rate stability.

Also, in order to ease the impact of real effective exchange volatility, the authorities in Liberia, Nigeria and Sierra Leone are encouraged to implement policies aimed at diversifying the pattern of their exports, which would improve economic fundamentals and help bring about sustained growth in export earnings. The countries are also encouraged to continue implementing viable fiscal and monetary policies as well as structural reforms that would contribute to the decline in per unit cost of production and the improvement in international competitiveness of exports.

Given that a positive relationship was established between exchange rate volatility and export performance for The Gambia, however, the authorities are urged to implement measures aimed at stabilizing the exchange rate. Excessive depreciation of the exchange rate may impact negatively on other macroeconomic variables, which in turn may dampen the positive impact on export growth.

Despite the insignificant impact of real effective exchange rate volatility on export performance in Ghana and Guinea, excessive volatility may adversely affect other macroeconomic variables in these economies through other channels. Therefore, a stabilization policy aimed at mitigating excessive exchange rate volatility is an appropriate strategy to promote macroeconomic stability in these countries.

The Authorities of the WAMZ countries are urged to initiate policies to boost local production to satisfy local consumption, in a bid to reduce demand pressures on their respective exchange rates. This will help stabilize their exchange rates while increasing production capacity, boosting stock of export goods, growth and income. The study also reveals a positive relationship between terms of trade and export performance for the WAMZ countries. Thus, the Authorities are urged to consolidate the gains from high export prices by improving the quality (value addition) and volume of exportables, as well as maintaining stability in both domestic prices and exchange rate.

Another lesson from the findings is that trade policy actions aimed at promoting exports are likely to generate uncertain results, at best, if policymakers in the WAMZ countries ignore the stability as well as the level of the real exchange rate. In other words, if policymakers wish to boost exports, policies that will ensure stability of the exchange rate should be pursued.

Overall, the WAMZ countries are encouraged to maintain the real exchange rate at its appropriate level that will achieve both internal and external equilibrium. Keeping it at competitive levels and avoiding excessive volatility is crucial for enhancing export performance and economic growth. Thus, monitoring real exchange rate movements would serve as a useful tool for central banks to ensure macroeconomic stability and growth.

References

Adubi AA, Okumadewa F (1999) Price exchange rate volatility and Nigeria's trade flows: a dynamic analysis. AERC Research paper No.87, African Economic Research Consortium, Nairobi, Kenya

Alam S (2011) Exchange rate volatility and Pakistan's bilateral imports from major sources: an application of ARDL approach. Int J Econ Finance 3(2):245–254

Aliyu SUR (2008) Real exchange rate misalignment: An application of behavioral equilibrium exchange rate (BEER) to Nigeria. MPRA Paper, No. 10343, http://mpra.ub.uni-muenchen.de/10343/1/MPRA_paper_10343.pdf

Al-Mahmood BS, Vixathep S (2002) Exchange rate volatility and exports from East Asian countries to Japan and US (Manuscript), University of Japan

Arize CA, Osang T, Slottje JD (2000) Exchange rate volatility and foreign trade: evidence from Thirteen LDCs. J Bus Econ Stat 18(1):10–17

Asseery A, Peel DA (1991) The effects of exchange rate volatility on exports. Econ Lett 37:173–177

Bah I, Amusa HA (2003) Real exchange rate volatility and foreign trade: evidence from South Africa's exports to the United States. Afr Finance J 5(2):1–20

Bailey MJ, Tavlas GS (1988) Trade and investment under floating rates: the U.S. experience. Cato J Fall:421–449

Bini-Smaghi L (1991) Exchange rate variability and trade: why is it so difficult to find any empirical relationship? Appl Econ 23:927–935

Brada JC, Méndez JA (1988) Exchange rate risk, exchange rate regime and the volume of international trade. KYKLOS 41:263–280

Caballero RJ, Corbo IV (1989) The effect of real exchange rate uncertainty on exports: empirical evidence. The World Bank Econ Rev 3:263–278

Chit MM (2008) Exchange rate volatility and exports: evidence from ASEAN-China free trade area. J Chin Econ Bus Stud 6(3):261–277

Chowdhury AR (1993) Does exchange rate volatility depress trade flows? Evidence from error correction models. Rev Econ Stat 76:700–706

Clark PB (1973) Uncertainty, exchange risk, and the level of international trade. West Econ J 11:302–313

Cote A (1994) Exchange rate volatility and trade: a survey, working paper 94–5, Bank of Canada

Cushman DO (1986) Has exchange risk depressed international trade? The impact of third-country exchange risk. J Int Money Finance 5:361–379

Darrat A, Hakin S (2000) Price linkages, efficiency, and integration of emerging stock markets in the Middle East. J Econ Dev 93:703–738

de Grauwe P (1983) Symptoms of an overvalued currency: the case of the Belgium Franc. In: International economic adjustment: small countries and the European Monetary System, Blackwell, Oxford, pp 99–116

de Grauwe P (1988) Exchange rate variability and the slowdown in growth of international trade. IMF Staff Papers 35:63–84

De Vita G, Abbot A (2004) The impact of exchange rate volatility in UK exports to European union, IMF working paper, WP/98/107

Fountas S, Aristotelous K (1999a) Has the European monetary system led to more exports? Evidence from bilateral exports in the European monetary system. Econ Lett 62(3):357–63

Fountas S, Aristotelous K (1999b) The impact of the exchange rate regime on exports: evidence from the European monetary system, working paper no 38, National University of Ireland, June

Franke G (1991) Exchange rate volatility and international trading strategy. J Int Money Finance 10(2):292–307

Ghura G, Greene T (1993) The real exchange rate and macroeconomic performance in Sub-Saharan Africa. J Dev Econ 42:155–174

Gonzaga G, Terra MC (1997) Equilibrium real exchange rate, volatility, and stabilization. J Econ Dev 54:77–100

Grobar LM (1993) The effect of real exchange rate uncertainty on LDC manufactured exports. J Dev Econ 41:367–376

Hassan MK, Tufte DR (1998) Exchange rate volatility and aggregate export growth in Bangladesh. Appl Econ 30(2):189–201

Holly S (1995) Exchange rate uncertainty and export performance: supply and demand effects. Scott J Polit Econ 42:381–391

Hooper P, Kohlhagen SW (1978) The effect of exchange rate uncertainty on the prices and volume of international trade. J Int Econ 8:483–511

IMF (1984) Exchange rate volatility and world trade, occasional paper no 28, July, International Monetary Fund, Washington, DC

Kohlhagen SM (1978) The behavior of foreign exchange markets – a critical survey of the empirical literature. New York University, Series in Finance and Economics, New York

Marston RC (1988) Exchange rate policy reconsidered. In: Feldstein M (ed), International economic cooperation. University of Chicago Press, Chicago, pp 79–136 (1990)

Ogun O (1998) Real exchange rate movements and export growth: Nigeria, 1960–1990. Research Paper 82, African Economic Research Consortium

Pindyck R (1982) Adjustment costs, demand uncertainty, and the behavior of the firm. Am Econ Rev 72:415–427

Qain Y, Varangis P (1994) Does exchange rate volatility hinder exports growth? Empir Econ 19:371–396

Rose A (2000) One money, one market: estimating the effect of common currency on trade. Econ Policy 30:7–45

Samanta S (1998) Exchange rate uncertainty and foreign trade for a developing country: an empirical analysis. Indian Econ J 45:51–65

Sekkat K, Varoudakis A (1998) Exchange-rate management and manufactured exports in Sub-Saharan Africa. OECD Development Centre Working Papers 134, OECD Publishing. http://www.oecd-ilibrary.org/development/exchange-rate-management-and-manufactured-exports-in-sub-saharan-africa_211147404816

Sercu P, Vanhulle C (1992) Exchange rate volatility, international trade, and the value of exporting firm. J Bank Finance 16(1):152–182

Sorsa P (1999) Algeria – the real exchange rate, export diversification, and trade protection. IMF Working Paper, WP/99/49

Tenreyro S (2004) On the trade impact of nominal exchange rate volatility. Working Paper 03-2 Federal Reserve, http://www.bos.frb.org/economic/wp/wp2003/wp032.pdf

Todani KR, Munyama TV (2005) Exchange rate volatility and exports in South Africa. Annual Forum: Trade and uneven development: opportunity and challenges. http://www.tips.org.za/files/773.pdf
Vergil H (2002) Exchange rate volatility in Turkey and its effect on trade flows. J Econ Soc Res 4 (1):83–99
Walters S, De Beer B (1999) An indicator of South Africa's external competitiveness. S Afr Quart Bull 213:54–67
Yususf A, Edom C (2007) Determinants of timber exports in Nigeria: an error correction modeling approach. MPRA Paper No. 2608, http://mpra.ub.uni-muenchen.de/2608/

Tax Effort in ECOWAS Countries

Mohamed Ben Omar Ndiaye and Robert Dauda Korsu

Abstract Tax revenue mobilization is essential in the fiscal operations of every economy. The Economic Community of West African States (ECOWAS) therefore has a criterion on tax revenue under the convergence criteria of the ECOWAS Monetary Cooperation Programme (EMCP), which states that tax ratio (as a percentage of GDP) should be at least 20 %. Despite the different tax reforms in the various member states the satisfaction of this criterion remains a challenging one. The objective of this study is therefore to investigate the determinants of tax revenue and construct an index of tax effort in the various economies of the ECOWAS region. Such investigation provides information on those countries that are operating their tax systems below capacity and those that are operating above their tax potential given the nature of the economies, with a view to providing guiding principles for fiscal policy operations.

The methodology involved the estimation of stochastic frontier tax functions for direct tax, indirect tax, trade tax and total tax (with and without natural resource related tax) for all the ECOWAS countries with the inclusion of five non-ECOWAS sub-Saharan African countries in the estimation, over the period 2000–2010. The tax efforts of these countries were determined from the stochastic frontier estimations over the period 2000–2010.

The results of the stochastic frontier tax functions show that literacy rate has a positive effect on all the categories of tax considered, financial depth has a positive effect on indirect tax and trade tax, agricultural share of GDP has a negative effect on direct and indirect tax, and openness of the economies to import and GDP per capita have positive effects on trade tax.

The results of the tax effort estimation show that all the ECOWAS countries are below their tax capacities though with differences in magnitude across tax type and countries. Moreover, Guinea Bissau in the UEMOA and Nigeria in WAMZ had high tax efforts (more than 75 % over the period 2000–2010), when natural resource

M.B.O. Ndiaye (✉) • R.D. Korsu
West African Monetary Agency (WAMA), 11/13 ECOWAS Street, Freetown, Sierra Leone
e-mail: bendiaye@yahoo.com; rdkorsu@yahoo.co.uk

D. Seck (ed.), *Regional Economic Integration in West Africa*, Advances in African Economic, Social and Political Development, DOI 10.1007/978-3-319-01282-7_6,

related taxes are included in total tax revenue but the exclusion of natural resource related taxes from total tax revenue reduced the tax efforts of these countries to 25 % and 7 % respectively for Nigeria and Guinea Bissau over the period 2000–2010. Other countries which were high tax effort countries with the inclusion of natural resource related taxes remained high tax effort countries with the exclusion of natural resource related taxes.

ECOWAS Countries therefore need to put further effort to raise tax revenue. Moreover, there is more potential to raise indirect tax and trade tax revenue than direct tax revenue and Senegal and Ghana could be used as models for reforming indirect taxes since they have relatively high tax efforts on these taxes.

Keywords Tax Efforts • Stochastic Frontier • ECOWAS

1 Introduction

Countries focus on domestic resource mobilization with a view to spending for development purpose and a key component of domestic resource mobilization is tax revenue generation. The tax performance of a country is therefore an important issue for consideration in both developed and developing economies. With this recognition, tax reforms have been undertaken by many developing economies in the last decade, with a view to enhancing tax revenue, among others. These reforms are also common in the ECOWAS region.

In the ECOWAS region, tax revenue occupies an important aspect of revenue generation. Hence, among the secondary convergence criteria of the ECOWAS Monetary Cooperation Programme (EMCP) is the criterion on Tax Revenue performance, which states that member countries should have tax revenue to be at least 20 % of GDP. Despite various tax reforms in member countries, the satisfaction of this criterion remains a challenging issue.[1] Over the period 2001–2004 only Gambia and Ghana met this criterion (Both countries met it with 22.4 % in 2004) before the rebasing of Ghana's GDP. After the rebasing of Ghana's GDP only Gambia met this criterion.[2] Over the period 2005–2009 only Cape Verde and Ghana consistently met the criterion, with an average of 22.7 % for Cape Verde and 24.4 % for Ghana (before the rebasing of Ghana's GDP). After the rebasing of Ghana's GDP, only Cape Verde satisfied this criterion during this period. During this period, Liberia satisfied the criterion in 2009 with 23.2 %. Over the period 2001–2009, UEMOA's best performance on this criterion was 16.1 % (in 2009) and the best performance of WAMZ was 19.1 % (in 2001) while the best performance of ECOWAS was 17.3 % (in 2001).

[1] Appendix Table 8 shows the trend of the performance on the ECOWAS convergence criterion on tax revenue (% of GDP).

[2] In 2010, Ghana re-based its GDP to 2006, and the report of that activity revealed that Ghana's GDP was underestimated from 2006 to 2010. Based on the new figures, Ghana is classified as a lower middle income country instead of a low income country.

In 2010, tax performance in ECOWAS countries was weak, only Cape Verde and Liberia satisfied the ECOWAS convergence criterion in respect of tax revenue performance with tax-GDP ratio of 20.9 % and 24.7 % respectively. At the zone level, the performance in 2010 was similar to the country scenarios. Performance in the UEMOA zone was 16.2 % while in the WAMZ it was lower at 10.5 %. ECOWAS registered 12.5 %. The lowest levels of tax revenue performance in 2010 were registered in Guinea Bissau (6.1 % of GDP), Sierra Leone (11.1 % of GDP) and Burkina Faso (12.0 % of GDP). Apart from Cape Verde, a relatively high performance was recorded in Senegal (19.4 % of GDP), Gambia (18.6 % of GDP) and Benin (18.4 % of GDP).

There is a heavy reliance on international trade taxes in ECOWAS countries, which erodes long term external competitiveness. User charges and property and income taxes contribute an infinitesimal proportion of total revenues in most of the countries. Taxes on wealth, bequest, land and property exist in theory but have been rendered ineffective by design problems or lack of interest in its administration or a combination of both while personal income and corporate taxes are levied on narrow bases at high rates which are often sub-optimal. Direct taxes represent a small proportion of tax revenue (about 30 %) and international trade taxes constitute the largest proportion of total tax less direct tax.

The poor performance on the tax revenue criterion implies that ECOWAS countries have limitations in their revenue collection mechanisms. But it remains unclear whether this limitation is predicated on low capacity to generate tax revenue (below maximum capacity) or by unwillingness to use already-achieved maximum tax capacity to fund public investments that can generate more revenue. An understanding of this issue can guide the various countries with respect to the appropriate mix of fiscal policy measures, particularly in countries with high fiscal deficit. If a country experiences fiscal deficit and is making maximum use of its taxable capacity, fiscal deficit has to be reduced for such an economy through expenditure rationalisation. However, if a country is operating below its taxable capacity, it would require the country to undertake tax reforms that would increase tax revenue in an effort to scale down budget deficit. Moreover, under these scenarios, knowledge of the determinants of tax revenue is important for revenue mobilisation.

The tax performance of a country is measured in both the static and dynamic approaches (Begun 2007). The static approach gives the potential for a given country to increase its tax revenue at a given point in time (which could be compared with other countries). This is referred to as tax effort while the tax buoyancy provides the idea of a dynamic index, which measures the response of the tax system with respect to the base, which is typically taken to be GDP, although other bases could also be used, (as in consumption for sales taxes and imports for tariff). In order to determine how close a country is to its tax potential, the idea of tax effort, the static concept is singled out for attention. The objective of the study is therefore to investigate the determinants of tax ratio (percentage of GDP) and construct an index of tax effort in the various economies of the ECOWAS region. This would provide information on those countries that are operating their tax system below their capacity and those that are operating above the maximum capacity, with a view to providing recommendations in respect of the appropriate fiscal policy drive.

The paper is organized as follows: Following the introductory section is Section 2 which deals with literature review. Section 3 is methodology, Section 4 is empirical results and Section 5 is conclusion and recommendations.

2 Literature Review

2.1 Theoretical Concept

The concept of tax effort was first introduced by Lotz and Morss (1967) with interest in studying international tax ratio and was also applied empirically by Bahl (1971). It has gone through some amendments following the works of Stotsky and WoldeMariam (1997).

Tax effort measures the extent to which a country has utilised its taxable capacity and it is a static measure of tax performance since it reveals information on the taxable capacity of a country in relation to actual tax performance at every point in time (for example, every year). It is obtained from a model based concept, whereby the actual tax ratio is divided by a predicted value of tax ratio. Thus, the predicted tax ratio is the measure of taxable capacity. Hence, the accuracy of the tax effort of a country depends to a large extent on the accuracy of the model used to explain the tax ratio.

The concept of tax effort is related to a country's effectiveness in mobilizing internal resources. It concerns not only its tax policy but also all economic policy measures that may influence the level of public revenue. It helps to assess the degree to which a country can exploit its tax potential. Thus, a tax effort higher than one (or 100 %) may lead to the conclusion that the country has difficulty to mobilize additional resources because it largely exploits its tax potential. However, a tax effort that is lower than one indicates an under exploited tax capacity.

The tax effort phenomenon helps to distinguish the share of tax revenue determined by structural factors from the share determined by economic policy and other factors. The structural factors which public authorities cannot exploit in the short term are the tax potential or the public revenue potential. However, monetary, budgetary and exchange rate policy measures that are likely to influence the level of effective public resources, do define the actual tax effort.

2.2 Empirical Literature

The literature on tax effort as a way of assessing the tax performance across different countries is huge. In spite of the fact that panel data technique deals with the concept of average while stochastic frontier tax function deals with the concept of maximum most studies have focused on the application of panel data technique and very few have applied the stochastic frontier approach. The reason for this might partly be due to the wide applications of panel data in various applied studies in comparison to stochastic frontier techniques. A recent study that used the concept of stochastic frontier is Pessino and Fenochietto (2010) for 96 developed and developing countries.

In the determination of the determinants of tax ratio, which precedes the estimation of the tax effort of a country, most studies have used total tax share in GNP or GDP as the dependent variable while a few have used total tax share as well as direct tax and indirect tax share in GNP or GDP.

The explanatory variables have taken different combinations in the literature, often chosen based on data availability. Common in the literature is agricultural share in GDP, which has often been found to have a negative effect though not significant in some studies. For example, Shin (1969) and Piancastelli (2001) found agricultural share of GDP to have a negative and significant effect on total tax revenue share in GDP while ALm and Martinez-Vazquez (2003) found a negative but insignificant effect of agricultural share in GDP in a panel of developed and developing countries. Instead of agricultural share of GDP, some studies have used manufacturing, industry or service share of GDP and the results are not uniform, though a positive effect seems to be common among the studies that used this variable as an explanatory variable. Trade/export/import share in GDP, and M2/GDP ratio have been found to have positive and significant effect on total tax share in GDP by many studies- for example, Bahl (2003) and Ahsan and Wu (2005). Per capita income have also been a factor with positive effect on tax revenue in empirical studies though not found to be significant in some studies, a few studies have also found it to have a negative effect (for example, ALm and Martinez-Vazquez (2003)). A number of other explanatory variables have been used in the literature. However, all of them have not been used simultaneously in one study. These explanatory variables include: population growth, external debt stock GDP ratio, inflation rate, urban population as a share of total population, a corruption index and a measure of income inequality (for example, the Gini coefficient).

The study departs from previous studies in the literature by focusing on the ECOWAS region and considers the tax efforts for direct, indirect, trade and total tax, whereby tax effort for total tax is considered with and without natural resource related tax.

3 Methodology

3.1 The Stochastic Frontier Tax Function

The tax efforts of the ECOWAS countries is estimated using the stochastic frontier tax function, which is basically an application of the stochastic frontier production function, as it is the most recent technique in estimating tax efforts in a cross-section time-series context, compared to the fixed and random effects techniques which have also been applied in the empirical literature.

The stochastic frontier production function was first developed by Aigner et al. (1977) for measuring technical efficiency. The ith individual specific stochastic output frontier production function at time t is written as:

$$Yit = \exp(\beta 0 + \beta Xit + Vit - Uit) \quad \mathrm{i} = 1, 2, 3 \ldots\ldots\ldots\ldots \mathrm{N} : \mathrm{t} = 1, 2, 3 \ldots\ldots\ldots \mathrm{T} \tag{1}$$

Where Y is the output variable, X is the vector of input variables, β is a vector of parameters, V is the disturbance term which is stochastic and can be positive or negative, U is the inefficiency term and is also a random variable with non-negative truncation. U follows a normal distribution with mean μ and variance σu^2, V follows a normal distribution with zero mean and variance σv^2 and U and V are statistically independent. The technical efficiency level of individual i at time t is the ratio of the actual to potential output (Kumbhakar and Lovell 2000).

In the context of stochastic frontier tax function, Y_{it} which is an output in the frontier production function is a tax ratio (percentage of GDP), the vector X which represents the inputs in production are the determinants of tax ratio.

The counterpart of technical efficiency in the stochastic frontier production function under stochastic frontier tax function is tax effort, which is obtained as the ratio of actual tax revenue to the stochastic frontier tax revenue (which is the tax capacity) and is between zero and one. Hence for a stochastic frontier tax function estimated for N countries over T periods the tax effort of country i in period t ($TAXEFF_{it}$) is given by Eq. 2.

$$\boldsymbol{TAXEFFit} = \frac{Yit}{\exp(\beta 0 + \beta Xit + Vit)} = \frac{\exp(\beta 0 + \beta Xit + Vit - Uit)}{\exp(\beta 0 + \beta Xit + Vit)} = \exp(-Uit) \tag{2}$$

In accordance with the tax effort literature, for example, Pessino and Fenochietto (2010), Hudson and Teera (2004), Tanzi (1978) and Bahl (1971), the reduced form equation of tax ratio takes the vector X in Eq. 2 to compose of the following variables, GDP per capita (GDPPC), openness of the economy (OPNM), the share of agriculture in GDP (AGS), Proportion of total population that lives in the urban sector (URB), financial depth (M2/GDP ratio), inflation rate (INF) and literacy rate (LIR). There are other variables which can be included in the vector X. But empirical studies do not include all possible determinants (for example, income distribution which is measured by the Gini coefficient and a measure of corruption). Because of availability of data on these variables for most of the countries, we did not consider all the theoretical determinants in the stochastic frontier estimation.

Per Capita GDP is used as a proxy for the level of development of a country. The expected sign of the coefficient associated with this variable is positive on the basis that the more developed a country is the easier it is for the country to apply high technology driven techniques to collect taxes and this increases tax revenue.

Openness of an economy to international trade is expected to have a positive effect on tax revenue as a result of the increase in trade volume engendered by liberalization, which in turn increases international trade tax revenue owing to increase in the base.

The share of agriculture in GDP is expected to have a negative effect on tax revenue. This is predicated on the fact that it is difficult to tax this sector given the nature of their operations in developing economies, often rural based with weak access to the banking system.

The coefficient associated with the share of urban population in total population is expected to be positive. This stems from the fact that the demand for government services increases with increase in urban population and many public sector activities are concentrated in the cities. Hence, higher tax revenue are expected to be collected in order to satisfy the increase in demand for public services. This implies that governments increase their commitment to tax collection efforts when there is a growing demand for their services, precipitated in part by growing urban population.

Increase in the degree of monetization of an economy increases tax revenue because it becomes easier to collect tax revenue. Hence, the coefficient of broad money as a ratio to GDP, which is a measure of the depth of the financial system, is expected to be positive. The coefficient of the rate of inflation is expected to be negative precipitated on the fact that high rates of inflation acts as a sign of poor macroeconomic policy, which reduces investment and hence tax revenue. The coefficient associated with literacy rate is positive. This is because people are more likely to know the reasons for paying tax in a more educated society than a less educated society and this has positive effect on tax compliance.

3.2 Estimation Technique

The estimation of the stochastic frontier tax function in Eq. 1 was done using data on the relevant variables over the period 2000–2010 for all the ECOWAS countries and some non-ECOWAS countries in sub-Sahara Africa. The inclusion of non-ECOWAS countries in the study is predicated on the fact that working with only ECOWAS countries benchmarks tax efforts to the best performing countries in ECOWAS, which could lead to overestimation of tax effort compared to benchmarking it to the best performing countries in sub-Sahara Africa. Five countries were selected from the non-ECOWAS group. The choice was dictated by considering countries with total tax ratio (percentage of GDP) being more than 20 %. In this respect, South Africa (with tax ratio of 31.2 %), Namibia (with tax ratio of 26.1 %) and Botswana (with tax ratio of 22.5 %) were considered. Two other countries, Kenya (with tax ratio of 18.3 %) and Zambia (with tax ratio of 17.0 %) which had high tax ratios relative to most ECOWAS countries, though less than the 20 % benchmark, were also included among the countries. The choice of the benchmark of 20 % was based on the fact that the macroeconomic convergence criteria for a single currency in the ECOWAS region has tax revenue GDP ratio to be at least 20 %.

The stochastic frontier tax function specified in Eq. 1 was estimated using the 15 ECOWAS and 5 non-ECOWAS sub-Sahara African countries for five various tax categories. These categories are: direct tax (dtaxr), indirect tax (itaxr), trade tax (ttaxr), total tax (the sum of direct, indirect and trade taxes excluding natural resource related tax (dittaxr)) and total tax, including natural resource related tax (ditntaxr). The estimation was done in the general-to-specific context whereby insignificant variables were dropped until the parsimonious model was obtained. We considered the tax inefficiency term to follow the Battese and Coellie (1992) half normal model and the Battese and Coellie (1992) general truncated normal model. The log-likelihood was used to determine the appropriate frontier. Based on the choice of frontier model, the tax efforts were obtained for each tax category considered, using Eq. 2.

3.3 Data Sources and Description

The data for modelling Eq. 2 is from the World Development Indicators, African Development Indicators and African Economic Outlook and the International Financial Statistics. Appendix Table 9 shows the description of the data.

4 Empirical Results

4.1 Descriptive Statistics of Variables

Table 1 shows the descriptive statistics of variables used in the estimation. A brief comparison of the revenue from the various taxes on an intra-zone and inter- zone basis is done in this sub-section. This comparison is also done for the explanatory variables.

The descriptive statistics of variables show that the average of total tax revenue (excluding natural resource related tax) as a percentage of GDP over the period 2000–2010 was 13.2 % for ECOWAS countries, 20.6 % for five the non-ECOWAS countries (Botswana, Kenya, Namibia, South Africa and Zambia) and 15.0 % for all

Table 1 Descriptive statistics of the frontier estimation variables

Variable	Obs	Mean	Std Dev	Min	Max
UEMOA					
Direct tax, % GDP	88	3.5	1	0.9	6.4
Indirect tax, % GDP	88	3.7	2.9	0	10.5
Trade tax, % of GDP	88	5	2.3	0.01	9.8
Direct, indirect, trade tax, % GDP	88	12.2	3.4	1.3	18.52
Natural resource tax, % GDP	88	1.9	2.5	0	11.93
Total Gov. Tax plus natural resource tax, %GDP	88	14.1	4	3.5	24.29
Literacy rate	88	39.2	13.5	16	65.8
Inflation	88	4.7	5	−3.5	19.4
M2 as a ratio of GDP	88	0.3	0.1	0.1	0.4
Openness	88	37.8	13	21.2	97
Agricultural share of GDP	88	32.8	9.3	11.91	54.84
Urban population, % total population	88	32.9	10.6	16	49.9
GDP per capita PPP U.S. $(2005)	88	322	151.1	150.71	628.2
WAMZ					
Direct tax, % GDP	66	4.5	1.8	1.9	11.33
Indirect tax, % GDP	66	4.3	2.8	1.1	10.7
Trade tax, % of GDP	66	4.6	2.9	0.3	11.2
Direct, indirect, trade tax, % GDP	66	13.4	5.3	4.6	27.7
Natural resource tax, % GDP	66	4.6	9.9	0	35.2
Total Govt. Tax plus natural resource tax, %GDP	66	17.9	7.9	9	41.5
Literacy rate	66	52.1	16.5	29.5	78.9
Inflation	66	12.9	8.1	−2.8	40.5
Openness	66	43.4	18.5	20.5	99.1
M2 as a ratio of GDP	66	0.2	0.1	0.1	0.43
Agricultural share of GDP	66	37.8	16.4	19.67	75.52
Urban population, % total population	66	46	9.1	31	61.4
GDP per capita PPP US$ (2005)	66	310	102.6	135.4	540.3
Cape Verde					
Direct tax, % GDP	11	6.7	0.3	6.1	7.1
Indirect tax, % GDP	11	7.4	3.5	3	11.3
Trade tax, % of GDP	11	6	1.7	4.7	8.7
Direct, indirect, trade tax, % GDP	11	20.1	2	16.7	22.8
Natural resource tax, % GDP	11	1.3	0.2	1.1	1.8
Total Govt. Tax plus natural resource tax, %GDP	11	21.4	1.9	18.5	24.2
Literacy rate	11	77.4	2.1	73.8	79.5
Inflation	11	5.8	8.1	−2.3	21.7
Openness	11	59.2	7.1	50	73
M2 as a ratio of GDP	11	0.8	0.1	0.6	0.88
Agricultural share of GDP	11	9.2	1.9	6.8	12.6
Urban population, % total population	11	57.3	2.5	53.4	61.1
GDP per capita PPP US$ (2005)	11	1505.3	255.4	1215.3	1,904
ECOWAS					
Direct tax, % GDP	165	4.1	1.6	0.9	11.3
Indirect tax, % GDP	165	4.2	3	0	11.3
Trade tax, % of GDP	165	4.9	2.5	0.01	11.2

(continued)

Table 1 (continued)

Variable	Obs	Mean	Std Dev	Min	Max
Direct, indirect, trade tax, % GDP	165	13.2	4.6	1.3	27.7
Natural resource tax, % GDP	165	2.9	6.6	0	35.2
Total Govt. Tax plus natural resource tax, %GDP	165	16.1	6.2	3.5	41.5
Literacy rate	165	46.9	17.6	16	79.5
Inflation	165	8	7.7	−3.5	40.5
Openness	165	41.5	16.1	20.5	99.1
M2 as a ratio of GDP	165	0.3	0.2	0.05	0.9
Agricultural share of GDP	165	33.2	14.2	6.8	75.5
Urban population, % total population	165	39.8	12.4	16	61.4
GDP per capita PPP US$ (2005)	165	396.7	329.6	135.4	1904
Non-ECOWAS					
Direct tax, % GDP	55	8.8	3.6	2.6	15.6
Indirect tax, % GDP	55	6.1	3.1	1.5	10.7
Trade tax, % of GDP	55	5.6	4.2	0.6	16.3
Direct, indirect, trade tax, % GDP	55	20.6	6.2	10.1	34.6
Natural resource tax, % GDP	55	0.9	1.7	0	5
Total Govt. Tax plus natural resource tax, %GDP	55	21.5	5.3	13.8	34.6
Literacy rate	55	83.2	3.8	68	88.2
Inflation	55	9.8	5.5	2	26.3
Openness	55	29.6	5.6	19.5	41.7
M2 as a ratio of GDP	55	0.4	0.2	0.2	0.9
Agricultural share of GDP	55	12.5	11.7	1.5	34.6
Urban pPopulation, % total population	55	41.2	14.7	19.7	60.4
GDP per capita PPP US$(2005)	55	2078.8	1482	317.4	4219.7
All countries in the estimation					
Direct tax, % GDP	220	5.3	3.1	0.93	15.6
Indirect tax, % GDP	220	4.6	3.2	0	11.3
Trade tax, % of GDP	220	5.1	3	0.01	16.27
Direct, indirect, trade tax, % GDP	220	15.03	5.9	1.3	34.6
Natural resource tax, % GDP	220	2.4	5.8	0	35.2
Total Govt. Tax plus natural resource tax, %GDP	220	17.5	6.4	3.5	41.5
Literacy rate	220	56	22	16	88.2
Inflation	220	8.5	7.3	−3.5	40.5
Openness	220	38.5	15.1	19.5	99.1
M2 as a ratio of GDP	220	0.3	0.17	0.1	0.9
Agricultural share of GDP	220	28.1	16.3	1.5	75.5
Urban population, % total population	220	40.1	13	16	61.4
GDP per capita PPP US$(2005)	220	817.2	1075.1	135.4	4219.65

the countries combied. Within ECOWAS, UEMOA had an average tax ratio (excluding natural resource related tax) of 12.2 %, WAMZ had 13.4 % and Cape Verde had 20.1 %. Average tax ratio with the inclusion of natural resource related tax was 16.1 %, 21.5 % and 17.5 % in ECOWAS, non-ECOWAS and all the countries combined. The difference between the tax ratio with the inclusion of natural resource related taxes and that without the inclusion of natural resource related tax was 2.9 % for ECOWAS countries compared to 2.4 % for the non-ECOWAS countries, implying that natural resource related tax was higher in the ECOWAS countries than the five non-ECOWAS countries. Within the ECOWAS countries, the average tax ratio with the inclusion of natural resource related tax was 14.1 % for UEMOA countries, 17.9 % for WAMZ countries and 21.4 % for Cape Verde over the period 2000–2010, revealing that natural resource related tax was about 4.6 % of GDP in the WAMZ countries, 1.9 % in the UEMOA and 1.3 % in Cape Verde.

The average tax ratio for trade tax is higher than that of direct and indirect taxes in the ECOWAS countries. The average trade tax, indirect tax and direct tax ratios over the period 2000–2010 were 4.9 %, 4.2 % and 4.1 % respectively for the ECOWAS region, 5.6 %, 6.1 % and 8.8 % respectively for the non-ECOWAS countries. This implies that trade tax revenue was higher than indirect tax in the region and indirect tax is higher than direct tax. However, in the non-ECOWAS region, direct tax revenue was higher than indirect tax revenue while indirect tax revenue is higher than trade tax revenue. Within ECOWAS, trade tax was higher than both direct tax and indirect taxes in the UEMOA and WAMZ but not in Cape Verde, where indirect tax was higher than trade tax and direct tax. The average tax ratios for direct, indirect and trade were 3.5 %, 3.7 % and 5.0 % respectively for UEMOA, 4.5 %, 4.3 % and 4.6 % respectively for WAMZ and 6.7 %, 7.4 % and 6.0 % respectively for Cape Verde. These figure also reveal that direct tax and indirect tax ratios are higher in Cape Verde than in WAMZ and are higher in WAMZ than in UEMOA while trade tax ratio was higher in Cape Verde than in WAMZ and UEMOA but less in WAMZ than in UEMOA.

With respect to the independent variables, Table 1 shows that literacy rate, urban population proportion, M2/GDP ratio and GDP per capita were higher in the non-ECOWAS countries than the ECOWAS countries. Literacy rate, M2/GDP, urban population proportion and GDP per capita over the period 2000–2010 were 83.2 %, 0.4 %, 41.2 % and US$ 2078.8 in the five non-ECOWAS countries and 46.9 %, 0.3 %, 39.8 % and U.S. $396.7 respectively in ECOWAS. Within ECOWAS, literacy rate was higher in Cape Verde (77.4 %) than in WAMZ (52.1 %) and UEMOA (39.2 %), M2/GDP ratio was higher in Cape Verde (0.8) than in WAMZ (0.2) and UEMOA (0.3), urban proportion was higher in Cape Verde (57.3 %) than in WAMZ (46 %) and UEMOA (32.9 %) and GDP per capita was also higher in Cape Verde (US$1505.3) than in WAMZ (U.S$310) and UEMOA (U.S $322). Agricultural share of GDP was lower in the non-ECOWAS countries (12.5 %) than the ECOWAS countries (33.2 %) and within ECOWAS, WAMZ had a higher agricultural share of GDP (37.8 %) than UEMOA (32.8 %) and Cape Verde (9.2 %). Inflation rate was lower in ECOWAS (8.0 %) countries than the non-ECOWAS countries (9.8 %). The low inflation rate in ECOWAS relative to the non-ECOWAS countries could be attributed to the low inflation rate in the UEMOA (4.7 %) and Cape Verde (5.8 %) as the WAMZ had an average inflation rate of 12.9 %. Openness of the economy, which was measured as the ratio of imports to GDP (in percentage) was higher in the ECOWAS countries (41.5 %)

than the non-ECOWAS countries (29.6 %) and within ECOWAS it was higher in Cape Verde (59.2 %), than WAMZ (43.4 %) and UEMOA(37.8 %).

4.2 The Determinants of Tax Revenue

Stochastic frontiers tax functions were estimated for various forms of tax revenue. Tables 2, 3, 4, 5 and 6 show the results of the maximum likelihood estimation of the stochastic frontier tax functions. The various taxes for which the estimations were done are direct tax, indirect tax, trade tax, total government tax (the sum of direct, indirect and trade tax) and total government tax plus taxes related to natural resource rent. For each of the taxes considered, estimation was done under two scenarios: (i) by considering the inefficiency term in tax mobilization to follow the Batesse-Coelli half normal distribution (ii) by considering the inefficiency term to follow the Batesse-Coelli general truncated normal distribution.

The results show that across the various tax functions, the parameter estimates of the half normal and general truncated normal distributions are similar. The signs and significance of the variables in each of the estimated model are similar, except for the case of indirect tax where the share of agriculture is not significant in the half normal model but is significant in the truncated normal model. The Log-Likelihoods of the estimations are however higher for the truncated normal models than the half normal model except for the model which includes natural resource related tax, implying that the truncated normal models are in general better than the half normal models for the determination of tax efforts. The null hypothesis that the inefficiency term in tax mobilisation is zero cannot be rejected for both the half normal and truncated normal cases. This is the case across all the tax types considered. These test results are shown at the bottom of each of the tables (Tables 2, 3, 4, 5 and 6).

Table 2 shows the stochastic frontier tax function for direct tax. The table shows that direct tax in the countries in the estimation is determined by the share of agriculture in GDP and literacy rate. Agricultural share of GDP has negative effect on direct tax while literacy rate has a positive effect and both are significant at the 1 % level, suggesting that the higher the share of agriculture in GDP the lower is direct tax and the more literate the population is the better the direct tax mobilization process. All the other variables which were included in the initial estimation of the model were found to be insignificant.

Table 3 shows the stochastic frontier tax function for indirect tax. The result shows that indirect tax in the countries in the estimation is determined positively by the degree of monetization (financial dept) of the economy (measured as the ratio of M2 to GDP), negatively by the share of agriculture in GDP and positively by literacy rate. Thus, unlike direct tax which is determined only by the share of agriculture in GDP and literacy rate, indirect tax is also determined by the financial depth of the economies. The share of agriculture is however not significant in the half normal version of the model but given that the log likelihood is higher in the

Table 2 The stochastic frontier tax function: direct tax

	Battese Coelli half normal		Battese Coelli truncated normal	
	Coefficient	P-Value	Coefficient	P-Value
Constant	0.129	0.593	0.098	0.674
Ln(M2/GDP)	–	–	–	–
Ln (AGS)	−0.203	0.000	−0.234	0.000
Ln (GDPPC)	–	–	–	–
Ln (URB)	–	–	–	–
Ln (OPN)	–	–	–	–
Ln(LIR)	0.626	0.000	0.632	0.000
	Log likelihood = −82.55		Log likelihood = −76.56	
	Likelihood-ratio test for $\sigma u^2 = 0$		Z test for $\sigma u^2 = 0$:	
	$\chi^2 = 42.16$ (0.000)		Z = −5.73 (0.000)	

Table 3 The stochastic frontier tax function: indirect tax

	Battese Coelli half normal		Battese Coelli truncated normal	
	Coefficient	P-Value	Coefficient	P-Value
Constant	1.941	0.000	1.945	0.000
Ln(M/GDP)	0.118	0.000	0.115	0.000
Ln (AGS)	–	–	−0.002	0.000
Ln (GDPPC)	–	–	–	–
Ln(URB)	–	–	–	–
Ln (OPN)	–	–	–	–
Ln(LIR)	0.143	0.000	0.142	0.000
	Log likelihood = −190.174		Log likelihood = −187.310	
	Likelihood-ratio test for $\sigma u^2 = 0$		Z test for $\sigma u^2 = 0$:	
	$\chi^2 = 34.88$ (0.000)		Z = −2.05 (0.020)	

Table 4 The stochastic frontier tax function: trade tax

	Battese Coelli half normal		Battese Coelli truncated normal	
	Coefficient	P-Value	Coefficient	P-Value
Constant	−0.162	0.000	−0.162	0.000
Ln (M2/GDP)	0.158	0.000	0.157	0.000
Ln (AGS)	–	–	–	–
Ln (URB)	–	–	–	–
Ln (GDPPC)	0.059	0.000	0.059	0.000
Ln (OPN)	0.324	0.000	0.324	0.000
Ln (LIR)	0.316	0.000	0.315	0.000
	Log likelihood = −219.26		Log likelihood = −216.26	
	Likelihood-ratio test for $\sigma u^2 = 0$		Z test for $\sigma u^2 = 0$:	
	$\chi^2 = 88.70$ (0.000)		Z = −14.71 (0.000)	

general truncated version of the model, we attach importance to the general truncated version, suggesting that the share of agriculture in GDP is a variable that matters in the stochastic frontier tax function for indirect tax.

Table 5 The stochastic frontier tax function: total tax including natural resource related tax

	Battese Coelli half normal		Battese Coelli truncated normal	
	Coefficient	P-Value	Coefficient	P-Value
Constant	1.365	0.000	1.994	0.000
Ln (M2/GDP)	0.187	0.000	0.201	0.000
Ln (AGS)	–	–	–	–
Ln (GDPPC)	–	–	–	–
Ln (URB)	0.102	0.076	0.118	0.042
Ln (OPN)	–	–	–	–
Ln (LIR)	0.388	0.000	0.368	0.000
	Log likelihood = −14.581		Log likelihood = −19.29	
	Likelihood-ratio test for $\sigma u^2 = 0$		Z test for $\sigma u^2 = 0$:	
	$\chi^2 = 9.94$ (0.001)		Z = −5.71(0.000)	

Table 6 The stochastic frontier tax function: total tax excluding natural resource related tax

	Battese Coelli half normal		Battese Coelli truncated normal	
	Coefficient	P-Value	Coefficient	P-Value
Constant	−0.095	0.000	0.462	0.000
Ln (M2/GDP)	0.012	0.000	0.061	0.000
Ln (AGS)	–	–	–	–
Ln (GDPPC)	0.079	0.000	0.049	0.000
Ln (URB)	0.034	0.000	–	–
Ln (OPN)	0.149	0.000	0.054	0.000
Ln (LIR)	0.529	0.000	0.569	0.000
	Log likelihood = −57.15		Log likelihood = −56.74	
	Likelihood-ratio test for $\sigma u^2 = 0$		Z test for $\sigma u^2 = 0$:	
	$\chi^2 = 64.86$ (0.000)		Z = −11.478 (0.000)	

Table 4 shows the stochastic frontier tax function for trade tax. The table shows that trade tax in the countries in the estimation is determined positively by the degree of monetization (financial dept) of the economy (measured as the ratio of M2 to GDP), positively by GDP per capita (a proxy for the level of development of the economy), positively by openness of the economy to import and positively by literacy rate. Hence, while the share of agriculture in GDP is important in explaining direct tax and indirect tax it is not important in explaining trade taxes in the countries used in the estimation. Also, while GDP per capita and openness to trade are not important in explaining direct tax and indirect tax they are significant in the trade tax model. Literacy rate, which is significant in both the direct tax and indirect tax stochastic frontier models, is also significant in the model for trade tax. The ratio of M2 to GDP is also significant in the trade tax model as in the indirect tax model, unlike the direct tax model. Openness to trade has the highest elasticity with respect to trade tax, followed by literacy rate and financial dept but literacy rate has the highest elasticity in the direct and indirect tax stochastic frontiers.

Table 5 shows the stochastic frontier tax function for total tax, including natural resource related tax revenue. The table shows that total tax revenue, including natural resource related tax, from the countries in the estimation depends on financial dept, urbanization and literacy rate. While financial dept and literacy rate are significant at the 1 % level, urbanistion is significant at the 5 % level. Urbanisation is not significant in the model that excludes natural resource related tax. Moreover, GDP per capita and openness are significant in the model that excludes natural resource related tax but both are insignificant in the model that includes natural resource tax. Table 6 shows the stochastic frontier tax function for total tax, excluding natural resource related tax revenue.

4.3 Estimated Tax Effort of Countries

The tax effort of the ECOWAS countries and the other countries in the estimation were obtained from the estimated stochastic frontier tax functions as the ratio of actual tax revenue (as a percentage of GDP) to potential tax revenue (as a percentage of GDP), as in Kumbhaker and Lovell (2000) and Pessino and Fenochietto (2010). The tax efforts were obtained for various categories of taxes as well as total tax (with and without natural resource related taxes).

Table 7 shows the tax efforts of ECOWAS Countries over the period 2000–2010. The tax efforts of the countries over the period 2000–2010 show that the tax efforts of ECOWAS countries for direct tax are high though they are below the tax capacities. The exceptions to this are Guinea Bissau and Nigeria with direct tax efforts of 41 % and 53 % respectively. For the other ECOWAS countries, the direct tax efforts range from 63 % (for Togo) to 87 % (for Gambia).

In the case of indirect tax, with the exception of Senegal, Ghana and Burkina Faso with tax efforts from indirect tax being 92 %, 86 % and 67 % respectively, the tax efforts of most of the ECOWAS countries are low, ranging from 11 % (for Togo) to 55 % (for Guinea).

In the case of trade tax, the tax efforts of the ECOWAS countries are generally low, ranging from 17 % (for Nigeria) to 58 % (Sierra Leone and Gambia) with the exception of Liberia, Niger, Mali and Benin with trade tax efforts of 70 %, 78 %, 81 % and 86 % respectively. For most of the ECOWAS countries, the tax efforts from trade tax are higher than that from indirect tax. The exceptions are Ghana, Senegal, Burkina Faso, Guinea and Cape Verde.

Considering the aggregation of the three taxes (direct, indirect and trade), the tax efforts of all the ECOWAS countries were below their potential in spite of the fact that most of them had tax efforts indices which were more than 70 %, ranging from 72 % for Guinea to 86 % for Niger. Cape Verde, Sierra Leone, and Liberia had tax efforts being 61 %, 62 % and 68 % respectively while the low tax effort countries are Nigeria, Guinea Bissau, Togo and Cote D'Ivoire with tax efforts of 24 %, 35 %, 47 % and 54 % respectively. The low tax efforts of Guinea Bissau derives from its very low tax efforts on both trade and indirect tax and the same holds for Cote D'Ivoire though Cote D'Ivoire had a higher tax efforts on these two taxes than Guinea Bissau. Togo's low tax effort was mainly driven by its very low tax efforts

Table 7 Tax efforts of ECOWAS countries over the period 2000–2010

Region/ country	Country	Direct tax	Indirect tax	Trade tax	Total tax excluding natural resource related tax	Total tax including natural resource related tax
UEMOA	Benin	0.82	0.33	0.86	0.81	0.84
	Burkina Faso	0.78	0.67	0.30	0.78	0.77
	Cote D'Ivoire	0.73	0.32	0.43	0.54	0.85
	Guinea Bissao	0.53	0.13	0.31	0.35	0.78
	Mali	0.79	0.24	0.81	0.80	0.86
	Niger	0.85	0.28	0.78	0.86	0.81
	Senegal	0.77	0.92	0.27	0.84	0.82
	Togo	0.63	0.11	0.51	0.47	0.78
	Liberia	0.77	0.36	0.70	0.68	0.86
WAMZ	Nigeria	0.41	0.15	0.17	0.24	0.82
	Gambia	0.87	0.38	0.58	0.79	0.85
	Ghana	0.82	0.86	0.36	0.75	0.78
	Guinea	0.83	0.55	0.31	0.72	0.81
	Sierra Leone	0.78	0.25	0.58	0.62	0.82
Cape Verde		0.71	0.58	0.33	0.61	0.80
Non-ECOWAS	Botswana	0.28	0.25	0.46	0.41	0.84
	Kenya	0.84	0.75	0.15	0.59	0.80
	Namibia	0.90	0.56	0.75	0.88	0.82
	South Africa	0.88	0.77	0.06	0.70	0.80
	Zambia	0.87	0.21	0.66	0.65	0.82

on indirect taxes while Nigeria's low tax effort emanates from its very low tax efforts on all the three tax types considered.

For all the ECOWAS countries, when natural resource related taxes are included in tax revenue, tax efforts are high with the least being 77 % (Burkina Faso) and the highest being 86 % (Mali and Liberia). However, Nigeria is the country with the greatest difference between the two types of tax efforts (with resource related taxes and without resource related taxes). Nigeria has a total tax effort of 24 % when natural resource related tax is excluded from taxes but when it is included, it has a tax effort of 82 %, implying that more effort was placed on mobilising natural resource related tax revenue than other types of taxes during the period 2000–2010.

In the non-ECOWAS countries included in the estimation, effort on direct tax outweighs efforts on indirect and trade taxes, as observed in most ECOWAS countries, with Botswana being the exception, where trade tax effort outweighs efforts from direct and indirect taxes. Namibia had the highest tax efforts on direct tax and trade tax (being 90 % and 75 % respectively) while South Africa had the highest tax efforts on indirect tax with 77 %, followed by Kenya with 75 %. When effort on total tax is considered without including natural resources, all the countries had a relatively high tax effort though less than 100 %, ranging from 59 % (for Kenya) to 88 % (for Namibia), with the exception of Botswana with a tax effort of 41 %. With the inclusion of tax revenue from natural resources makes, the non-ECOWAS countries with high tax efforts remained high tax effort countries and Botswana moved from a low tax effort country (41 %) to a high tax effort country (84 %).

5 Conclusion and Recommendations

5.1 Conclusion

Assessment of the convergence criteria under the ECOWAS Monetary Cooperation Programme shows that satisfaction of the tax revenue performance criterion has been challenging, as in the case of some of the other criteria for the member states. The non-satisfaction of this criteria, which implies poor fiscal performance on the side of revenue generation, coupled with high government expenditure by member states has made it difficult for member states to perform well on the primary criterion on budget deficit. The primary criterion on budget deficit also has implications for the satisfaction of the criterion on inflation.

Based on the recognition of the interactions or linkages among the secondary criterion on tax revenue, the budget deficit and the rate of inflation and the poor performance of member states on tax revenue (as a percentage of GDP) WAMA found it imperative to investigate whether each of the ECOWAS countries is operating its tax generation process below or above its potential, a phenomenon known as tax effort.

The methodology involved the use of aggregate annual data over the period 2000–2010 for all the ECOWAS countries and five non-ECOWAS sub-Saharan African economies (Botswana, Kenya, Namibia, South Africa and Zambia). The empirical estimation considered tax revenue models based on Pessino and Fenochietto (2010), Hudson and Teera (2004) and earlier by Tanzi (1978) and Bahl (1971). Stochastic frontier tax functions were estimated for the following tax-GDP ratios: direct tax, indirect tax, trade tax and total tax (with and without natural resource related tax). The explanatory variable were GDP Per capita, openness of the economy to import, agricultural share of GDP, urbanisation, financial dept, literacy rate and inflation. The stochastic frontier tax functions were estimated using the general-to-specific method by arriving at the parsimonious models through the deletion of insignificant variables using both the half-normal and general truncated normal distributions for the inefficiency term of the stochastic frontier model.

The actual tax revenue ratios were divided by the predicted values, to obtain an index of tax effort for each of the countries over the period 2000–2010. These were used to determine whether a country is above or below its potential in terms of tax performance. An index that is above one means that the country is above its tax potential while an index that is below one implies that the country is below its tax potential.

The estimated stochastic frontier tax functions show that: (i) direct tax effort is explained negatively by the share of agriculture in GDP and positively by literacy rate, (ii) indirect tax effort is explained negatively by the share of agriculture in GDP, positively by financial deepening and literacy rate (iii) trade tax is explained positively by financial deepening, GDP per capita and openness of the economy and literacy rate (iv) total tax revenue is explained positively by financial deepening, GDP per capita and openness of the economy and literacy rate. When natural resource related tax is included in total tax, the proportion of urban population in total population has a positive effect on total tax revenue. Inflation rate is not found to be significant in determining any of the tax ratios considered.

The tax effort indices show that all the ECOWAS countries and the non-ECOWAS countries considered in the study were below their tax capacities in 2010 and during the period 2000–2010. However, apart from Guinea Bissau, Togo and Nigeria with tax efforts on direct tax being 21 %, 50 % and 55 % respectively, the ECOWAS countries had high tax efforts on direct tax in 2010. Moreover, the tax efforts of ECOWAS countries were higher on direct tax than on indirect tax and trade tax in 2010 and during the period 2000–2010. The tax efforts on indirect tax during the period 2000–2010 were low for most of the ECOWAS countries, with the exception of Burkina Faso, Senegal and Ghana the indirect tax efforts were below 60 % in all the ECOWAS countries. In terms trade tax in ECOWAS countries, with the exception of Benin, Mali, Niger and Liberia tax efforts were lower than 50 % in 2010 and 60 % during the period 2000–2010. When total tax excluding natural resource related tax is considered, Guinea Bissau, Nigeria, Togo and Sierra Leone had tax efforts below 50 % while Cote D'Ivoire, Niger and Cape Verde had tax efforts which are between 55 % and 65 % and the rest of the ECOWAS countries had high tax efforts in 2010 (in the range of 70 % and 97 %). The inclusion of natural resource related tax in total tax revenue changed Guinea Bissau, Nigeria, Togo and Sierra Leone from low tax effort to high tax effort countries in 2010 with the greatest change in tax effort coming from Guinea Bissau in 2010 and over the period 2000–2010, the greatest came from Nigeria.

5.2 Recommendations

Drawing from the results of the study, the following recommendations are important to the ECOWAS countries.

1. Guinea Bissau and Togo, from the UEMOA countries, and Nigeria from the WAMZ countries, should place great emphasis on administrative procedures that would enhance their direct tax revenue mobilization as these countries have low tax efforts on direct tax and they therefore have potential to raise more direct tax revenue through improved tax administration.

2. The ECOWAS countries should review their procedures for mobilizing indirect taxes to determine where leakages are with a view to strengthening compliance on indirect taxes though, Senegal and Ghana showed high effort on indirect tax mobilisation. This could be done by reviewing the method of administration of the Value Added Tax (VAT), which is usually the biggest component of indirect tax. The methods of administration of value added tax (VAT) in, Senegal and Ghana could be used as references for other countries. This is imperative given the fact that indirect taxes are far below their potential in most of the countries (the existence of low indirect tax efforts).
3. The ECOWAS countries require efforts to improve their trade tax mobilization as most of them are operating more than 40 % below their trade tax potential, though Benin, Mali, Niger and Liberia showed high tax efforts on trade tax. This is more important in Nigeria, Senegal, Burkina Faso Guinea Bissau, Guinea, Ghana and Cape Verde which were below their trade tax potential by at least 70 % over the period 2000–2010.
4. Guinea Bissau in the UEMOA and Nigeria in WAMZ had high tax efforts (more than 75 % over the period 2000–2010) when natural resource related taxes are included in total tax revenue but the exclusion of natural resource related taxes from total tax revenue reduces the tax efforts of these countries to and 25 % and 7 % respectively for Nigeria and Guinea Bissau over the period 2000–2010. This therefore suggests that these two countries require shifting of tax administration from emphasis on natural resource related taxes which is considered to be windfall relative to other tax types.
5. Each of the ECOWAS countries should continue to encourage policies that would improve the use of the financial as the depth of the financial system has positive effect on indirect and trade tax revenue.
6. The ECOWAS countries should emphasise policies that would encourage the development of the agricultural sector so that it becomes an easy-to-tax sector, in the interest of increasing direct and indirect tax revenue. This follows from the fact that the study found that agricultural share of GDP has negative effect on both direct and indirect tax revenue. This could be done by bolstering the transformation of agricultural products to industrial products.
7. As ECOWAS countries impose taxes on imports, it is important for them to maintain a policy of no non-tariff barriers to trade, except for health, social and security reasons. This is important because openness of these economies to import has a positive effect on trade tax revenue.
8. To the extent that literacy rate is found to have a positive and significant effect on all tax types considered, efforts at improving the literacy rates in the ECOWAS economies are to be sustained, as this would improve the ability of tax payers to understand when and why taxes are paid, thereby increasing compliance across all tax types.
9. The positive effect of GDP per capita on trade tax suggests that it would be essential for supply side policies which can improve the growth of the economy to be strengthened. This includes continued priority for investment in physical capital (including roads, electricity, and the health sector).

Appendix

Table 8 Tax revenue (% of GDP) performance in ECOWAS member states

	2000	2001	2002	2003	2004	2005	2006	2007	2008	2009	2010
Benin	12.8	12.6	13.7	14.4	14.6	14.5	15.4	16.9	17.2	16	18.4
Burkina Faso	11.8	9.4	9.7	10.3	11.8	11.8	12	12.5	12.1	11.8	12
Cape Verde	17.3	18.7	19.7	18.6	19.6	21.5	23.4	24.4	25.2	21.7	20.9
Cote D'Ivoire	14.3	14.6	15.8	14.5	14.2	13.9	14.4	15.5	15.6	16.4	17
The Gambia	23.3	19.2	14.1	13.8	22.4	17.2	18.8	19.4	17.6	17.5	18.6
Ghana[a]	11.6	10.6	9.6	11.7	13.1	12.7	12.4	12.2	11.6	12.1	12.8
Guinea	10.2	11.4	12	10.5	9.5	12.2	14.8	13.5	14.7	15.2	17
Guinea Bissau	11.4	10.4	8.6	9.2	7.7	11.3	11.3	5.7	5.5	6.9	6.1
Liberia	13.7	11.4	10.7	6.4	9.2	14.7	13.2	12.6	12.5	23.2	24.7
Mali	12.3	12.7	12.5	14.2	14.8	15.4	14.9	14.2	13.3	14.6	14.2
Niger	9.1	8.9	10.5	10.5	11	10.3	10.7	11.5	11.7	12.6	13.4
Nigeria	16.7	19.5	14	15.7	14.8	17.2	14.9	11.7	16.2	12	15
Senegal	17.3	16.6	16.9	16.8	17.4	18.6	19	19.5	18.3	18.9	19.4
Sierra Leone	10.8	13.4	11.4	16.7	13.7	8.1	8.5	7.8	8.7	9.8	11.1
Togo	11.0	10.5	11.5	13.9	15.7	14.6	15.4	16.2	14.9	14.7	14.3
UEMOA	**13.9**	**13.7**	**14.6**	14.4	14.8	14.7	15.1	17.3	16.7	16.1	16.2
WAMZ	**16.5**	**19.1**	**14.2**	**15.9**	**15.3**	**17.4**	**15.6**	**14.3**	**17.8**	**11.9**	**10.5**
ECOWAS	**15.6**	**17.3**	**14.3**	**15.4**	**15.1**	**16.5**	**15.5**	**15.3**	**17.4**	**13.4**	**12.5**
No. of countries	**1**	**0**	**0**	**0**	**1**	**1**	**2**	**1**	**1**	**1**	**2**

Sources: WAMA and the central banks in ECOWAS

[a]The figures are based on the rebased GDP figures

Table 9 Data description and sources

Variable	Symbol	Description	Source
GDP per capita	GDPPC	Real gross domestic product divided by total population	African Development Indicators
Openness	OPEN	Calculated as t import, divided by GDP	International Financial Statistics
Share of agriculture	AGS	Calculated as agricultural value added divided by GDP	African Development Indicators
Urbanisation	URB	Calculated as total urban population divided by total population	African Development Indicators
Monetisation	(M2/GDP)	Calculated as the ratio of broad money to nominal GDP	African Development Indicators

(continued)

Table 9 (continued)

Variable	Symbol	Description	Source
Inflation rate	INF	Calculated as the percentage change in consumer price index	WAMA Database
Nominal GDP	GDP	GDP at current price	African Development Indicators
Tax revenue	TR	Total tax revenue generated by the central and state government	WAMA Database
Real GDP	Y	GDP at constant price	African Development Indicators
Literacy rate	LIR	Calculated as 100 minus illiteracy rate	African Development Indicators
Direct tax ratio	DTAXR	Calculated as total direct tax revenue divided by GDP	African Economic Outlook
Indirect tax ratio	ITAXR	Calculated as total indirect tax revenue divided by GDP	African Economic Outlook
Trade tax ratio	TTAXR	Calculated as total trade tax revenue divided by GDP	African Economic Outlook
Total tax excluding natural resource related tax	DITTAXR	Calculated as the sum of direct, indirect and trade taxes	African Economic Outlook
Total tax including natural resource related tax	DITNTAXR	Calculated as the sum of direct, indirect and trade taxes plus natural resource related tax	African Economic Outlook

References

Ahsan SM, Wu S (2005) Tax structure and reform in China, 1979–2002. Mimeo, Department of Economics, Concordia University, Canada

Aigner DJ, Lovell KCA, Schmidt P (1977) Formulation and estimation of stochastic frontier production function models. J Econom 6:21–37

ALm J, Martinez-Vazquez J (2003) Sizing the problem of the hard-to-tax. Paper presented at the hard to tax: an international perspective conference, Andrew Young School of Policy Studies, Georgia State University, 15–16 May 2003

Bahl RW (1971) A regression approach to tax effort and tax ratio analysis. IMF Staff Pap 18:570–612

Bahl RW (2003) Reaching the hardest to tax: consequences and possibilities. Paper presented at the "Hard to tax: an international perspectives" conference, Andrew Young School of Policy Studies, Georgia State University, 15–16 May 2003

Battese G, Coelli T (1992) Frontier production functions, technical efficiency and panel data: with application to paddy farmers in India. J Prod Anal 3:153–169

Begun L (2007) A panel study on tax effort and tax buoyancy with special reference to Bangladesh. Working paper series: WP0715Bangladesh Bank

Hudson J, Teera J (2004) Tax performance: a comparative study. J Int Dev 16(6):785–802

Kumbhakar S, Lovell K (2000) Sochastic frontier analysis. Cambridge University Press, Cambridge

Lotz JR, Morss ER (1967) Measuring 'Tax Effort' in developing countries. IMF Staff Pap 14:478–499

Pessino C, Fenochietto R (2010) Determining countries' tax efforts. Hacienda Publ Esp/Rev de Econ Publ 195:61–83
Piancastelli M (2001) Measuring the tax effort of developed and developing countries: cross-country panel data analysis, 19989–95. Discussion paper: CEPR. Discussion paper no 3643
Shin K (1969) International difference in tax ratio. Rev Econ Stat 51:213–220
Stotsky JG, WoldeMariam A (1997) Tax effort in sub-Saharan Africa. IMF working paper, WP/97/107 73
Tanzi V (1978) Inflation, real tax revenues, and the case for inflationary finance: theory with an application to Argentina. IMF Staff Papers, Sept 1978

Heterogeneity of Saving-Investment Causality in Waemu Zone and Fiscal Coordination Implication

Christian Lambert Nguena

Abstract Monetary unions are characterized by contemporary institutional arrangements that entrust monetary policy to a supranational entity while fiscal policies are framed by rules imposed on the budget deficit. Limits on public deficits are usually justified by the idea that government deficits reduce national savings, which ultimately reduces domestic investment and economic growth. However, this idea that domestic savings must necessarily increase if investment increases cannot be taken for granted. Moreover, it is possible that within the union, countries reveal different saving-investment causality, which is capable of rendering considerable credibility and effectiveness of budgetary rules of government deficits systematic prohibition as a means to revitalize investment. This study raises the question of domestic savings-investment causality in the WAEMU zone. It has been determined in each country from a methodology based on co integration vector representations analyze leading to error correction. The existence of a causality heterogeneity between savings-investment in the WAEMU zone leads to consider a new model of fiscal coordination incorporating this heterogeneity, including the adoption of a new budget rule more flexible based on a structural balance without public investment.

Keywords Monetary union • Savings-investment causality • Heterogeneity • Fiscal coordination

West African Economic and Monetary Union.This paper have been improved by taking into account relevant comment from participant of the third Annual international conference for Regional Integration in West Africa (ACRIA 3) under the them: "Policy Coordination for Regional Integration in West Africa" at Dakar – Senegal, July 4–6, 2012. Special thank you also to the anonymous reviewer and Ms Carine E. Magne for editing. However the author is the only responsible of the paper contain.

C.L. Nguena (✉)
CEREG (Centre d'Etudes et de Recherche en Economie et Gestion), University of Yaounde II-Soa, Yaounde, Cameroon
e-mail: clanguena@yahoo.fr

D. Seck (ed.), *Regional Economic Integration in West Africa*, Advances in African Economic, Social and Political Development, DOI 10.1007/978-3-319-01282-7_7,

Jel Classification C51 • C59 • E62 • F43 • H50 • O40

1 Introduction

The relationship between the domestic savings and investment is one of the biggest controversies in macroeconomics. At the heart of the debate is the question of the meaning of causality which occurs between these two variables. Is it saving that causes investment or is it investment that causes savings? As the theory of natural unemployment rate was the central issue in studies of monetary policy, the question of causality between savings and domestic investment is in turn decisive for fiscal policy. Indeed, the economic significance of government deficits is commonly built around the negative effects they have on the volume of domestic savings, and finally on capital formation. Behind this interpretation of the deficits is the idea that domestic savings consistently cause domestic investment. Government deficits then correspond to a public sector dissaving, which reduces domestic savings, which in turn will reduce investment. It is this view which usually justifies the choice of austerity fiscal policies or of the inter-temporal budget balance in developing countries plagued by budget problems with important consequences in terms of their external payments. If inversely, it is investment that causes savings, policies of abstinence from both the government and the private sector are needed and can be rather deflationary consequences. What matters then is the increase in capital expenditure with multiplier effects that we know. This indicated that the appropriate fiscal policy for an economy should be drawn under the constraint of the direction of causality which exists between savings and investment, and it also requires an empirical determination of causality given the indeterminacy theory that exists in this regard.

Transposed to the specific cases of monetary unions, the interest of savings-investment causation analysis is multiplied. Indeed, interest in the study of monetary unions, specifically their effectiveness, has growing with European unification. From this unification, came out several institutional arrangements covering fiscal and monetary aspect. The monetary policy was entrusted to a supranational and independent of political pressures entity, the European Central Bank, when fiscal policy remains the responsibility of national authorities. However, the definition of a Community budgetary criterion governing the expenditure in the EU[1] more binds the hands of public authorities of different countries. A maximum has been imposed on public deficits which must not exceed 3 % of GDP. According to several authors (Palley 1996; Alexiou 2004) Indeed, the definition of the fiscal convergence criterion stated in monetary union reflects the emergence of a neoliberal consensus which suggests that only balanced budgets or surpluses are the keys to revitalize domestic investment because government deficits absorb national savings that was

[1] European Union.

intended for investment and thereby increases interest rates. Everything happens as the saving-investment causality is systematic and subject of consensus and more precisely, it would be exercised systematically from savings to investment.

Monetary union is a group of several countries with economies often structurally and/or conjunctural different sharing a common currency and strive to coordinate their policies. It is therefore likely that the degree of structural heterogeneity (productive structures, labor markets and financial structures) between countries remains long time after the unification with respect to circumstances heterogeneity that would normally fade over time (Nguena 2012). It comes as the specificity of each country may be indicative of saving-investment causality variance from one country to another within the monetary union, thereby putting into question the Community fiscal rule of government deficits systematic prohibition which is ultimately effective if all countries have similar causalities in the direction of domestic savings to domestic investment. In the presence of savings-investment heterogeneity causality, the fiscal community rule becomes like an asymmetric shock hitting member countries. Given that it allows the growth of domestic savings, it will be virtuous only in countries of the Union which has revealed causality from savings to investment. In other countries who do not reveal such causality, this rule will have recessive consequence. That is why the empirical analysis of saving-investment causality becomes important in the context of a monetary union as the WAEMU with institutional architecture relatively close to EU and which could also introduce heterogeneities that actual arrangements would have difficulty to manage.

The purpose of this paper is to analyze the causality relationship between savings and investment in the WAEMU zone. More specifically, we will (i) determine the causality direction between domestic savings and investment in each country and (ii) capture the major fiscal coordination implications in the monetary union.

The rest of the paper is organized as follows: Sect. 2 presents a brief literature review of major theoretical and empirical contributions to savings-investment relationship; Sect. 3 presents the methodology; Sect. 4 presents the data and the results obtained and Sect. 5 focus on economic policies implications.

2 Brief Literature Review

- ***Causality direction between savings and investment: The theoretical indeterminacy.***
  The savings-investment relationship is generally known in theory through the divergent viewpoints that oppose economists especially concerning the causality direction that prevails. For economists called Classics and neoclassical, savings and investment equilibrium are made by interest rate on loanable funds market. Moreover, according to traditional analyzes of the link between finance and economic development, saving is the precondition for productive investment

and economic growth, thus economic development (Gurley and Shaw 1956; Goldsmith 1969). For these authors, the main contribution of the financial system to economic growth is based on the fact that it ensures the efficient functioning of payment system, which mobilizes savings and improve its allocation to investment through positive real interest rates. The assumption of prior savings is also present in models of financial liberalization developed by McKinnon (1973) and Shaw (1973). These models estimate that we can increase the level of domestic investment by stimulating the accumulation of domestic savings through real positive interest rates and an encouragement of competition between financial institutions. Bencivenga and Smith (1991) also showed that financial intermediaries, by the allocation of savings to illiquid assets process, and by reducing premature liquidation of profitable investments, improve capital productivity, and thus stimulate economic growth.

The analysis of Keynes (1936) proposes for its part, the reversal of causality, which traditionally runs from savings to investment. This new conception of the causal link between savings and investment developed by Keynes and recovery more precisely by the post-Keynesian theories (Godley and Cripps 1985; Sodokin 2004) theoretically offers an alternative approach to the savings and financial institutions role for economic development. In a post-Keynesian perspective, “finance” precedes the “savings” in the financing process of productive investment. Through an income multiplication process initiated by investment, it ultimately creates a savings in the economy.

Blecker (1997) goes further by stating that the traditional view that savings generally tends to precede the investment can be questioned for two reasons. The first reason is that economic policies aimed systematically increasing the savings rate may depress investment in contrast, because they have the immediate effect of significantly reducing aggregate demand. The second reason is that a reinterpretation of domestic savings role in case of international capital mobility environment is relatively high. Indeed, Blecker (1997) and especially Feldstein and Horioka (1980) mainly showed that if there is international capital mobility, savings will move to regions of the globe that offer a better return than the one of domestic savings. It follows that the association between domestic saving and domestic investment will be strong when capital mobility and economic integration is low. Other authors also share the view that investment precede saving in the process of income creation and multiplication. Skott (1989) following the Keynesians considers investment as the key variable. His argument is that firms first decide the level of investment to achieve, and later, income and savings are adjusted accordingly. For Gordon (1995) as for Harcourt and Spajic (1998), causation in fact, takes place from investment to savings.

- ***Indeterminacy reinforced at the National Accounting level:***
  In open economy, there are four possible uses of goods and services produced. The national income identity expressed these four components of gross domestic product (GDP).

$$Y = C + I + G + EXn.$$

With Y the GDP, C the private consumption, I the total investment, G the government consumption and EXn is net exports of goods and services obtained by the difference between exports of goods and services and imports of the same nature. According to this equation (in fact this equality purely accounting), domestic spending which are expenditure made on national territory, is the sum of consumption, investment, government spending and net exports. This equality shows the links between production and expenditure on the national territory. By changing the positions of certain variables in the equation, we get successively:

$Y - C - G = I + EXn.$ We know that domestic savings is: $Y - C - G.$

Thus, $S = I + EXn.$
By subtracting I from the two equation sides, the national income accounting identity can be rewritten like follow:

$$S - I = EXn.$$

This presentation of the national income accounts identity shows that net exports of an economy must be equal to the difference between its savings and investment.

By disaggregating domestic savings into private savings (S^p) and public (S^g), we obtain:

$$I = S^p + S^g - Exn$$

Reasoning from this accounting identity, at the end of period, investment increases only as the two components of domestic savings increase. But it is extremely important to emphasize that this accounting identity is informational only. It teaches us only that domestic investment is equal to the sum of private and public savings net current account, not a causal relationship between variables.

The total savings in the economy is indeed the sum of budget surplus, household savings and retained earnings of private enterprises. How can we be sure that the increase in one component of domestic savings, for example, will leave other components unchanged? Indeed, an increase in taxes, while increasing public savings, will reduce disposable private income and hence private savings, thus leaving relatively unchanged the total savings; It is the neutrality of boosting investment policy funded on a prior rise in public savings which will be observed. Moreover, an increase in public savings can be sufficiently valued by the private sector which can then increase its consumption while reducing it savings, which once again, tend to leaves unchanged the volume of domestic savings.

We can multiply the examples, but the truth is evident: the relationship between these two macroeconomic variables (savings and investment) is ambiguous and complex. Solving the problem with an empirical point of view is one of the ways to resolve the indeterminacy.

- ***Causality direction between savings and investment: Divergent empirical results.***

  Although few in number, empirical work who have studied causality between savings and investment are instructive. As such, we can first retain the studies of Palley (1996) for the U.S. case and Alexiou (2004) with regard to some countries in the euro zone. Both authors argue that the empirical determination of the saving-investment causality should inform the budgetary authority on the relative superiority of one or other budgetary option including: abstinence or increased investment expenditure. Palley (1996) adopts a methodology based on the Granger test and on analysis of impulse response functions to validate the hypothesis of Keynesian "paradox of thrift" on U.S. data. His findings are that investment tends to precede the increase in savings and an increase in savings greatly reduces the investment through its negative effect on aggregate demand. Alexiou (2004) adopts a similar approach to that adopted by Palley (1996) with a slightly different in that the impulse response functions have been abandoned in favor of an analysis of variance decomposition of error forecast. It leads to results that investment generally precedes savings in euro area countries retained, but the analysis of variance decomposition results still leaves a relative heterogeneity between countries. The author then concludes that these differences in results could find explanation by exploring the structures of these countries, including differences in financial structures. Undertook to test the theoretical hypothesis that one of the channels through which financial development affects economic growth is that it favors capital accumulation through greater allocation from savings to investment. The authors wanted to bring the savings-investment causality direction issue to the levels of financial development for the Caribbean and Latin America countries. The saving-investment causality was tested by using a methodology based on the recent cointegration. However, the authors do not systematically come to the result that the level of financial development shaped the saving-investment causality in their sample.

  Studies of causation devoted to African countries do not relatively exist. Nevertheless, we have identified two of them. Elbadawi and Mwega (2000) find a causal rate of domestic savings to domestic investment in Sub-Saharan Africa using the Granger causality (1969) and aggregate data from across the region; Unlikely Agbetsiafa (2002) makes use of causality tests from vector representations error correction in countries like Ivory Coast, Nigeria, South Africa, Zambia and Kenya; Causality is everywhere from savings to investment, except in South Africa where prevails a bidirectional causality between domestic saving and investment.

From this empirical literature review, two main conclusions emerge. The first which have a more methodological importance, is that the determination of causation is generally made on a case by case basis (by country) which has conditioned the use of countries time series. The second conclusion seems in turn related to the first well; Indeed, the saving-investment causality seems to be conditioned by national structural specificities, which requires to use countries-analyzes.

3 Methodology

Methodological approaches within the studies that have analyzed empirically the savings – investment relationship are diverse and have not always addressed the important issue of causality between these two variables. First, a number of studies have used ordinary least squares on a single equation to examine the savings – investment relationship. Therefore they have unfortunately suffered of the major econometric problem of simultaneity bias, due to the fact that they have neglected the possibility of return effect. Furthermore, these studies have made direct estimation without first analyzing the time series properties of saving and investment. However, as shown by Nelson and Plosser (1982), most macroeconomic time series are non stationary in levels. Then a large number of empirical studies have used cross-sectional estimates, which made extremely difficult to apply their results to a specific country. Finally, very few of these studies have involved Africa.

This study goes beyond these methodological shortcomings by resorting exclusively to recent techniques within the time series econometrics to determine the causality direction.

Empirically, to test causality, it is common to apply the Granger causality test (1969). However, the cointegration technique promoted by Engle and Granger (1987) and Granger (1988) provides a significant contribution in conducting the causality tests. As part of our study, tests of causality based on vector representations of error correction are used for each of the WAEMU countries.

3.1 From Cointegration to Causality

The vector model with error correction requires that the series used are cointegrated. It is therefore important to first test the existence of cointegration relationships between the series (Johansen 1988) prior to estimating equations of the VECM. The starting point is a VAR representation like follow:

$$xt = \eta + \sum_{i=1}^{p-1} \Pi\, xt - i + \varepsilon t \tag{1}$$

where x is a vector $(n\ x\ 1)$ of variables that can be $I\ (0)$ or $I\ (1)$. Π is a matrix $(n\ x\ n)$ of coefficients, ε is a vector $(n\ x\ 1)$ of interference with normal properties.

If there is a cointegrating relationship between the variables *I (1),* the above equation must be change and we obtain the following vector representation with error correction VECM:

$$\Delta xt = \eta + \sum_{i=1}^{p-1} \theta i \Delta xt - 1 + \Pi xt - 1 + \varepsilon t \tag{2}$$

Where Δ is the difference operator, and θ is a matrix $(n\ x\ n)$ of coefficients. The rank, r, of the matrix Π determines the number of cointegrating relationships. If the rank of this matrix is n or equal to zero, the VAR model is estimated respectively at level or at first difference; This due to the fact that there is no cointegrating relationship between variables in the model.

However, if the matrix rank Π is less than n, then there are $(n\ x\ r)$ matrices β (cointegration parameters) and α (adjustment matrix that describes the weight with what each variable enters the equation) so that $\Pi = \alpha\beta'$ and, Eq. 2 is chosen as the model to be estimated. The matrix Π is estimated (by the method of maximum likelihood) as an unrestricted VAR undergoing test to determine whether the restrictions implied by the reduced rank of the matrix Π may be, or not, rejected.

The statistics used to determine the rank (cointegration) of the matrix Π are given by the *Trace* statistic:

$$\lambda_{trace} = -T\sum_{i=r+1}^{k} \log(1-\lambda_i), \text{for r} = 0, 1, \ldots, \text{k} - 1 \text{ and } \lambda_i \text{ the i-th eigenvalue of the matrix } \Pi,$$

T = number of observations, k = number of variables, r = matrix rank.

and the statistics *maximum eingenvalue*, which is given by:

$$\lambda_{\max} = -T\log(1-\lambda_r)$$

The statistics of Johansen (1988) follow a probability distribution (similar to a χ^2) tabulated using simulations by Johansen and Juselius (1990).

By performing the cointegration test (Johansen 1995) on internal savings *(s)* and investment *(i)* variable (in neperien logarithm), the *VECM* representation between these two variables should be written:

$$\begin{bmatrix} \Delta i_t \\ \Delta s_t \end{bmatrix} = \begin{bmatrix} \eta_1 \\ \eta_2 \end{bmatrix} + \begin{bmatrix} \sum_{i=1}^{l} \delta_{1i} & \sum_{i=1}^{m} \gamma_{1i} \\ \sum_{i=1}^{l} \delta_{2i} & \sum_{i=1}^{m} \gamma_{2i} \end{bmatrix} \begin{bmatrix} \Delta i_{t-i} \\ \Delta s_{t-i} \end{bmatrix} + \begin{bmatrix} \alpha_1 \\ \alpha_2 \end{bmatrix} [\beta_1 \quad \beta_2] \begin{bmatrix} i_{t-1} \\ s_{t-1} \end{bmatrix} + \begin{bmatrix} \varepsilon_1 \\ \varepsilon_2 \end{bmatrix} \tag{3}$$

Where α capture the adjustment speed from a state of imbalance to the long-term relationship. This imbalance is defined here as the gap that exists between lagged values of a variable of domestic saving and investment [$gap = i_{t-1} - \beta_1 - \beta_2 s_{t-1}$]. If saving and investment are cointegrated, the deviations from the long-run equilibrium has the effect in the short term, to induce changes in the evolution of one or all variables in order to force the system return to its long-run equilibrium.

The equation of cointegration between saving and investment is written:

$ECT_{t-1} = \beta_1 i_{t-1} + \beta_2 s_{t-1}$ and $ECT_{t-1} = i_{t-1} + (\beta_2/\beta_1)\ s_{t-1}$ depending on whether it was normalized to investment or $ECT_{t-1} = (\beta_1/\beta_2)\ i_{t-1} + s_{t-1}$ if we have normalized with respect to savings.

Unlike the Granger standard test (1969), this alternate methodology based on the error correction mechanism, consider the possibility that the passed value of a level variable (eg y) may help explain common variations of other variable (eg x), although past values of differentiated series y cannot. The intuition is as follows: If x and y follows a common and constant path over time, the common variations of x are partially the result of an adjustment of x in order to meet its alignment with it. This causality cannot be detected by the Granger standard test (1969) who has only identified the possibility that past changes in one variable can help explain current changes in another variable.

As for the Granger standard test, it is possible to determine causality in the opposite direction or when there is a causality in both directions. However, if the two variables are co integrated, causality exists in at least one direction. The result of total lack of causality in any direction identified by the test of Granger (1969) is switched off here; As soon as the series follow a common trend, there will always be at least one causality.

To perform the test, we rely on the representation Eq. 3 and estimated each following Eqs. 4 and 5, with i and s respectively investment and domestic savings.

$$\Delta i_t = \eta_1 + \sum_{i=1}^{l} \delta_{1i} \Delta i_{t-i} + \sum_{i=1}^{m} \gamma_{1i} \Delta s_{t-i} + \alpha_1 [\beta_1 i_{t-1} + \beta_2 s_{t-1}] + \varepsilon_{1t} \quad (4)$$

$$\Delta s_t = \eta_2 + \sum_{i=1}^{l} \delta_{2i} \Delta i_{t-i} + \sum_{i=1}^{m} \gamma_{2i} \Delta s_{t-i} + \alpha_2 [\beta_1 i_{t-1} + \beta_2 s_{t-1}] + \varepsilon_{2t} \quad (5)$$

This procedure is preferred to the standard Granger (1969) because it allows to show a temporal causality emanating from (i) the sum of independent variables coefficients in first difference and lagged ($\sum \delta$, $\sum \gamma$) et (ii) the return term α. In addition, the error correction model allows the identification of causality even though the lagged and differentiated coefficients of explanatory variables are not significant (Miller and Russek 1990).

3.2 Causality Sources and Types

There are therefore two causality sources, one from the cointegration equation if $\alpha \neq 0$ and the other from the differentiated and lagged variables coefficients. The cointegration equation (*ECT*) measures the relationship of long-term equilibrium, while the coefficients of lagged variables refer to the short-term dynamics. The significance of the coefficient associated with *ECT* highlights the existence of an error correction mechanism that leads to the variables return to their long term condition.

Given the existence of different sources of causality (short term or long term, which is impossible to perceive if we use the classic Granger causality test), we present three different tests used in the literature Recent: The short term causality test, the long-term causality test and the strong exogeneity test.

- The short term causality test.

  In the previous model Eq. 3, to test "Δs_t does not cause Δi_t at short-term", we examines the significance of the coefficients of lagged variables by testing the null hypothesis *Ho*: All $\gamma_{1i} = 0$ by using Wald test. Failure to reject the null hypothesis implies that domestic savings does not cause domestic investment in the short term.
- The long-term causality test (or weak exogeneity).

  The test of weak exogeneity which refers to the notion of long-term causality test (long-run non – causality test) is done by testing the null hypothesis H_0: $\alpha_1 = 0$, if the null hypothesis is not rejected it implies that domestic investment is "weakly exogenous" because it does not address the imbalance that can occur. If instead the null hypothesis is rejected, the change in investment is due to the influence of long-term equilibrium relationship and long-term causality is established from savings to investment. The null hypothesis is tested by using the maximum likelihood test (LR).
- The strong exogeneity test.

  Finally, we present the strong exogeneity test, which imposes strong restrictions attached by testing the significance of lagged variables (short-term dynamics) and the equation cointegration ECT. This test verifies the short term and long term causality. In particular, "Δs_t does not cause Δi_t" if the null hypothesis Ho: All $\gamma_{1i} = \alpha_1 = 0$ is not rejected. The strong exogeneity test does not distinguish short-run and long-term causality; It is a more restrictive test that indicates the global causality in the system.

In summary, the non-significance of all coefficients tested involves the "strong exogeneity" of the variable (investment or savings).

4 Data Source and Empirical Results

4.1 Data Source

We needed data of savings and investment for each UEMOA zone country on a relatively long period. Our choice of data on savings and domestic investment are due to several reasons like their availability over a long period. First, the economies of the UEMOA zone are potentially open, and can therefore benefit from significant inflows of foreign capital that takes into account savings and domestic investment. Then this is for us to take into account any savings and investment available in all these economies.

The data cover the period 1980–2010 for each country and come from the database of the World Bank (World Development Indicators 2011). After some adjustments that were necessary due to the presence of negative savings number in some countries, the logarithmic series were generated. The sample includes all seven UEMOA member countries namely Benin, Burkina Faso, Ivory Coast, Guinea Bissau, Mali, Senegal and Togo.

4.2 *Empirical Investigation Results*

4.2.1 Stationarity Tests Results

Two main unit root tests have been used and applied to the series of savings and investment in logarithm in each country. These tests are augmented Dickey-Fuller and Phillips-Perron. Visual examinations of our different series allowed us to choose the more plausible regression specification for these tests. Moreover, since these tests are sensitive to the number of lags used, they were selected based on the findings of the *AIC* and *SIC*. The stationarity tests show that for all countries, all the series are generally stationary in first difference (see Appendices).

4.2.2 Johansen Cointegration Tests Results

The results of cointegration tests using the methodology of Johansen (estimated by the method of maximum likelihood) are presented in Appendices of this document. It is from information provided by data visualization that has been chose the most plausible specifications from the five proposed by *Eviews* software to realize the cointegration test. Option 2 assumes that a lack of linear trend in the VAR and the presence of a constant in the cointegrating relationship seemed most appropriate and was finally chosen for all these countries. The appropriate number of lags was given by the *AIC* and *SIC*. The results in Annex attest the existence of a cointegrating relationship between savings and domestic investment over the period of study in Benin, Mali and Senegal; To Burkina Fasso, Ivory Coast, Guinea Bissau and Togo, no cointegration was detected.

In conclusion, the existence of cointegrating relationship between savings and investment in Benin, Mali and Senegal let us forecast at least the existence of a causal relationship between domestic saving and investment in each country.

4.2.3 Results of Short and Long Term Causality Tests

The Appendix provides estimation results in each country of the various tests of causality. For four countries (Benin, Ivory Coast, Mali and Senegal), there is long-term causality between two variables. Specifically for the Ivory Coast and Senegal, the direction of causality runs from savings to investment, while for Benin and Mali it is rather from investment to savings. The results also confirm the absence of a short-term causality between the two variables for all countries. The following table summarizes these different causality results country by country (Table 1).

Finally we can affirm that we have three groups of countries in the WAEMU zone. The first group of countries for which a causality from savings to investment is long-term; This is the Ivory Coast and Senegal. The second group consists of countries for which the reverse causality prevails (Benin and Mali) and the third group of countries for which no causality is statistically significant (Burkina Faso, Guinea Bissau and Togo).

Following these results, it appears that the increased volume of domestic savings will ultimately ensure increased investment in only two countries: Ivory Coast and Senegal. In the rest of countries, an increase in savings does not have the same virtuous effects. Due to that, it follows that the UEMOA zone countries does not all need equivalent therapies to stimulate strong and sustained economic growth.

5 Economic Policies Implications

Our empirical results show that for the two former countries (Ivory Coast and Senegal), abstinence policies of would be appropriate because they would generate a significant volume of domestic savings to finance domestic investment. It is therefore a problem of inadequate financial resources which explains the low investment and growth in these countries, including the existence of dual internal and external financial constraint. For other countries, an increase in their volume of domestic savings is not a necessary and sufficient condition to ensure capital formation and thereby ensure economic growth. Savings does not precede investment in these countries, and therefore, pro-savings policies are totally inappropriate. In these countries we should identify investment irreversibility factors in order to significantly reduce them and, ultimately increase investment spending. The strategy is to focus directly on investment, not on savings, because savings would not have neither short nor long term virtuous effect.

The UEMOA zone heterogeneity is like countries have different saving-investment dynamics and thus optimal fiscal policies that should be different. However, it should not be forgotten that these countries are members of a monetary union. It is clear from our results that the optimal budget strategies for these countries are not similar, we should not forget that fiscal policies in UEMOA zone are constrained by a standard that limits the public deficit, which can significantly reduce discretion of national authorities in countries where the optimal fiscal

Table 1 Abstract of causality test results

	Long term		Short term
Countries	*s . . .?. . . i*	*i . . .? . . .s*	*s . . .?. . . i* ou *i . . .? . . .s*
Benin		→ (+)	Absence
Burkina Faso	Absence		Absence
Ivory Coast	→ (+)		Absence
Bissau Guinea	Absence		Absence
Mali		→ (+)	Absence
Senegal	→ (+)		Absence
Togo	Absence		Absence

Source: Author calcul with World Bank data base (2011)

strategy is related directly to the investment rate. Thus, as the recent debate on the practice of a single monetary policy in a heterogeneous union tends to lead to the need to integrate the heterogeneity in the monetary standard rules, as the heterogeneity issue in the union must also be present in the fiscal arrangements design in a monetary union. If the benefits of coordination in relation to different policies are well established, what should matter is choosing the right coordination which will eventually equalize between all partner countries, costs and benefits of membership in the union.

How then to reconcile heterogeneity and optimal coordination? This can be done by reflecting on a new fiscal rule that would be more appropriate and which will have the dual advantage of combining flexibility and credibility while promoting economic catch-up in the area. A flexible fiscal rule is a rule that does not sanction the budgetary authorities frequently; But governments of the UEMOA zone are not always able to respect the current fiscal convergence criteria. Moreover, a fiscal rule is credible when it punishes appropriately. However, the fiscal rule at community level in the UEMOA zone goes against any deficit. We therefore feel that governments bind the hands while the critical development needs are felt. Therefore, questioning this criterion is important because macroeconomic costs associated with this rule are high. A ceiling on the current public deficit can be structurally depress for growth. If, as suggested by some recent theoretical and empirical work, the potential growth is influenced by government spending that contribute to productive capital formation or to increase productivity, the fiscal policies rules that lead governments to reduce this type of expenditure are doubly harmful because: they generate pro-cyclical fiscal policies variations and lower the potential growth path of the economy in every recession. Yet it is possible to design a rule on the government deficit, which avoids this serious pitfall. Like Creel et al. (2002), we advocate a *rule of nullity of the deficit*:

- *Structural*: A relevant fiscal indicator should reveal the orientation of discretionary fiscal policy. In this sense, the structural deficit, after corrections for cyclical effects on the total deficit, should be considered as an indicator of the stance of fiscal policy in the WAEMU zone.
- *Without public investment*: The second criterion indicates that the public investment expenditure is not constrained by the rule. This would give UEMOA zone

countries a substantial leeway, allowing them to implement a massive economic stimulus packages to offset the effects of the current stagnation of activity and, for countries which need it (Benin, Mali, Togo, Burkina Faso and Guinea Bissau), to catch up economically their partners by improving their public infrastructure and education supply, sources of potential growth.

Such rule would release free investment and ideally reflect the discretionary fiscal policy orientation; It would thus enjoy greater flexibility and credibility, but would face a major problem, particularly, the structural balance measure.

Appendix

1. *BENIN*

- **Stationarity test:**
  Trend and intercept

	Level		First difference		Second difference	
	ADF	CV	ADF	CV	ADF	CV
INV	1.333036	−3.587527	−1.882750	−3.603202	−10.95744	−3.603202
S	−0.021983	−3.587527	−5.205564	−3.595026	/	/

INV est I(2) et S est I(1)

- **Johansen cointégration test**
  Unrestricted Cointegration Rank Test (Trace)

Hypothesized No. of CE(s)	Eigenvalue	Trace statistic	0.05 critical value	Prob.
None	0.476314	32.81319	12.32090	0.0000
At most 1	0.459458	15.99477	4.129906	0.0001

Trace test indicates 2 cointegrating eqn(s) at the 0.05 level

- **Short term causality test**

Lags: 1

Null hypothesis	Obs	F-statistic	Probability
D(S) does not Granger Cause D(D(INV))	25	0.08756	0.77007
D(D(INV)) does not Granger Cause D(S)		0.00053	0.98177

Causality absence

- **Long term Granger causality test**

Null hypothesis	Obs	F-statistic	Probability
S does not Granger Cause INV	27	1.25565	0.27356
INV does not Granger Cause S		28.2170	1.9E-05

Investment cause savings

2. *BURKINA-FASO*

– **Stationarity test**

	Level		First difference		Second difference	
	ADF	CV	ADF	CV	ADF	CV
INV	−1.556921	−3.603202	−3.366407	−3.603202	−6.277407	−3.612199
S	−1.827521	−3.690814	−6.910576	−3.690814		

INV is I(2) when S is I(1)

– **Johansen cointégration test**
Unrestricted Cointegration Rank Test (Trace)

Hypothesized No. of CE(s)	Eigenvalue	Trace statistic	0.05 critical value	Prob.
None	0.283826	6.414474	12.32090	0.3873
At most 1	0.022276	0.405508	4.129906	0.5877

Trace test indicates no cointegration at the 0.05 level
There is no cointegration relation

– **Short term causality test**

Lags: 1			
Null hypothesis	Obs	F-statistic	Probability
D(S) does not Granger Cause D(D(INV))	17	0.00807	0.92971
D(D(INV)) does not Granger Cause D(S)		3.34621	0.08874

Causality absence

– **Granger causality test**

Lags: 1			
Null hypothesis	Obs	EF-statistic	Probability
S does not Granger Cause INV	20	0.74040	0.40151
INV does not Granger Cause S		0.06756	0.79804

Causality absence

3. *IVORY COAST*

– **Stationarity test**

	Level		First difference	
INV	−2.527338	−3.574244	−4.774915	−3.580623
S	−1.696037	−3.574244	−5.657587	−3.580623

All series are integreted in order 1

- **Johensen cointégration test**
  Unrestricted Cointegration Rank Test (Trace)

Hypothesized no. of CE(s)	Eigenvalue	Trace statistic	0.05 critical value	Prob.
None	0.166005	6.062838	12.32090	0.4284
At most 1	0.034396	0.980044	4.129906	0.3736

Trace test indicates no cointegration at the 0.05 level
There is no cointegration relation between investment and savings

- **Short term causality test**

Lags: 1

Null hypothesis	Obs	F-statistic	Probability
D(S) does not Granger Cause D(INV)	28	0.71330	0.40636
D(INV) does not Granger Cause D(S)		0.09920	0.75540

No causality

- **Granger causality test**

Lags: 1

Null hypothesis	Obs	F-statistic	Probability
S does not Granger Cause INV	29	11.5909	0.00216
INV does not Granger Cause S		0.10223	0.75173

S cause INV

4. *GUINEE-BISSAU*

- **Stationarity test**

	Level		First difference	
INV	−1.743625	−3.658446	−4.724146	−3.690814
S	−2.105865	−3.791172	−6.040698	−3.791172

All series are integreted in order 1

- **Johansen cointégration test**

Hypothesized no. of CE(s)	Eigenvalue	Trace statistic	0.05 critical value	Prob.
None	0.360295	6.255635	12.32090	0.4055
At most 1	8.37E-05	0.001172	4.129906	0.9791

Trace test indicates no cointegration at the 0.05 level
There is no cointegration

- **Short term causality test**

Null hypothesis	Obs	F-statistic	Probability
D(S) does not Granger Cause D(INV)	14	0.00014	0.99061
D(INV) does not Granger Cause D(S)		0.21735	0.65016

No causality

– **Long term causality test**

Lags: 1			
Null hypothesis	Obs	F-statistic	Probability
S does not Granger Cause INV	16	1.61813	0.22564
INV does not Granger Cause S		0.07774	0.78477

No causality

5. *MALI*

– **Stationarity test**

	Level		First difference	
INV	0.690846	−3.595026	−7.829135	−3.595026
S	0.108273	−3.603202	−4.010726	−3.622033

All series are cointegreted in order 1

– **Johansen cointégration test**

Unrestricted cointegration rank test (Trace)				
Hypothesized no. of CE(s)	Eigenvalue	Trace statistic	0.05 critical value	Prob.
None	0.636512	23.36405	12.32090	0.0005
At most 1	0.003812	0.087840	4.129906	0.8076

Trace test indicates 1 cointegrating eqn(s) at the 0.05 level
There is no cointegration relation

– **Short term causality test**

Lags: 1			
Null hypothesis	Obs	F-statistic	Probability
D(S) does not Granger Cause D(INV)	23	4.34151	0.05023
D(INV) does not Granger Cause D(S)		3.08184	0.09448

No causality

– **Granger causality test**

Lags: 1			
Null hypothesis	Obs	F-statistic	Probability
S does not Granger Cause INV	25	0.34023	0.56563
INV does not Granger Cause S		4.31284	0.04971

Investment cause savings

6. *SENEGAL*

– **Unit root Test**

	Level		First difference	
INV	−0.596670	−3.574244	−4.423356	−3.580623
S	0.392427	−3.580623	−8.214434	−3.580623

All series are integreted in first order

– **Johansen cointégration test**

Unrestricted cointegration rank test (Trace)				
Hypothesized no. of CE(s)	Eigenvalue	Trace statistic	0.05 critical value	Prob.
None	0.398607	15.28752	12.32090	0.0155
At most 1	0.036782	1.049315	4.129906	0.3551

Trace test indicates 1 cointegrating eqn(s) at the 0.05 level
There is one cointegration relation

– **Short term causality test**

Lags: 1			
Null hypothesis	Obs	F-statistic	Probability
D(S) does not Granger Cause D(INV)	28	1.29464	0.26598
D(INV) does not Granger Cause D(S)		1.15262	0.29326

No causality

– **Test de causalité de Granger**

Null hypothesis	Obs	F-statistic	Probability
S does not Granger Cause INV	29	9.90591	0.00410
INV does not Granger Cause S		0.08860	0.76833

Domestic savings granger cause domestic investment

7. *TOGO*

– **Stationarity test**

	Level		First difference	
Variable	ADF	CV	ADF	CV
INV	−2.391790	−3.603202	−5.415838	−3.612199
S	−3.664734	−3.603202		

INV is stationary in first difference and S is at level

– **Johansen cointegration test**

Unrestricted cointegration rank test (Trace)				
Hypothesized no. of CE(s)	Eigenvalue	Trace statistic	0.05 critical value	Prob.
None	0.134879	5.437904	12.32090	0.5077
At most 1	0.078446	1.960643	4.129906	0.1902

Trace test indicates no cointegration at the 0.05 level
There is no cointegration relation between INV and S

– **Short term causality test**

Lags: 1			
Null hypothesis	Obs	F-statistic	Probability
S does not Granger Cause D(INV)	24	2.23939	0.14941
D(INV) does not Granger Cause S		0.08625	0.77188

No causality

– **Granger causality test (Long term)**

Null hypothesis	Obs	F-statistic	Probability
S does not Granger Cause INV	25	2.85737	0.10508
INV does not Granger Cause S		2.22934	0.14962

No causality

References

Agbetsiafa D (2002) Capital mobility, saving and investment link: evidence from Sub-Saharan Africa. J Afr Finance Econ Dev 5(2):77–88
Alexiou C (2004) An econometric investigation into the macroeconomic relationship between saving and investment: evidence from EU region. Int Rev Appl Econ 18(1):93–102
Bencivenga V, Smith B (1991) Financial intermediation and endogenous growth. Rev Econ Stud 58(2):195–209
Blecker R (1997) Policy implications of the international saving – investment correlation. In: Pollin R (ed) The macroeconomics of saving, finance, and investment. The University of Michigan Press, Ann Arbor
Creel J, Latreille T, Le Cacheux J (2002) Le Pacte de Stabilité et les politiques budgétaires dans l'UE. Revue de l'OFCE, hors série, pp 245–272
Data available at (accessed on 19/09/2013): http://data.worldbank.org/news/WDI-2011-database-and-publication-available
Elbadawi I, Mwega F (2000) Can Africa's saving collapse be reversed? World Bank Econ Rev 14 (3):415–443
Engle RF, Granger CW (1987) Cointegration and error correction: representation, estimation, and testing. Econometrica 55:251–276
Feldstein M, Horioka C (1980) Domestic saving and international capital flows. Econ J 90:314–329
Godley W, Cripps J (1985) Macroeconomics. Oxford University Press, London

Goldsmith R (1969) Financial structure and development. Yale University Press, New Haven
Gordon D (1995) Putting the horse (back) before the cart: disentangling the macro relationship between investment and saving. In: Epstein AG, Gintis MH (eds) Macroeconomic policy after the conservative era. Cambridge University Press, Cambridge
Granger CW (1969) Investigating causal relations by econometric models and cross-spectral methods. Econometrica 37:424–438
Granger CW (1988) Some recent developments in a concept of causality. J Econom 39:199–211
Gurley JG, Shaw ES (1956) Financial intermediaries and saving – investment process. J Finance 11(2):975–994
Harcourt G, Spajic L (1998) Post-Keynesianism. Working paper, Cambridge
Johansen S (1988) Statistical analysis of cointegration vectors. J Econ Dynam Control 12:231–254. Reprinted in Engle RF, Granger CWJ (eds) (1991) Long-run economic relationships. Oxford University Press, Oxford, pp 131–152
Johansen S (1995) Likelihood-based inference in cointegrated vector autoregressive models. Oxford University Press
Johansen S, Juselius K (1990) Maximum likelihood estimation and inference on cointegration – with applications to the demand for money. Oxf Bull Econ Stat 52:169–210
Keynes JM (1936) The general theory of employment, interest and money. MacMillan, London
McKinnon R (1973) Money and capital in economic development. Brookings Institution, Washington, DC
Miller SM, Russek FS (1990) Cointegration and error-correction models: the temporal causality between Government taxes and spending. South Econ J 57(1):221–229
Nelson CR, Plosser CI (1982) Trends and random walks in macroeconomic time series: some evidence and implications. J Monet Econ 10:139–162
Nguena CL (2012) The role of foreign trade in economic growth and individual heterogeneity problem in panel data: the case of African countries. MPRA WP, http://mpra.ub.uni-muenchen.de/49559/1/MPRA_paper_49559.pdf
Palley T (1996) The saving-investment Nexus: why it matters and how it works, vol 1, Center for economic policy analysis working paper. Public Policy Department, AFL-CIO, Washington, DC, pp 613–622
Shaw E (1973) Financial deepening in economic development. Oxford University Press, New York
Skott P (1989) Conflict and effective demand in economic growth. Cambridge University Press, Cambridge
Sodokin K (2004) Epargne, système de financement et développement économique en Afrique: une alternative post-keynésienne. Communication au Colloque "Développement durable: Leçons et perspectives", du 1er au 4 juin 2004, Ouagadougou, Burkina-Faso
http://data.worldbank.org/news/WDI-2011-database-and-publication-available. Accessed 19 Sept 2013

Part III
Regional Trade

Determinants of a Successful Regional Trade Agreement in West Africa

Sam Olofin, Afees Salisu, Idris Ademuyiwa, and Joel Owuru

Abstract In this paper, we evaluate the determinants of effectiveness of the Economic Community of West African States (ECOWAS) at promoting regional trade in West Africa between 1995 and 2010. We employ the modified gravity model (GM) that allows for the inclusion of country specific and country-pair characteristics in addition to the traditional GM variables (income and distance). Our findings reveal that economic size, distance, geographical factors such as common border, landmass, landlockedness of countries and socioeconomic variables like common language, political stability and availability of infrastructure significantly influence intra-regional trade within the ECOWAS region. We also find that the *francophones* dominated region (WAEMU) is exports trade creating while the anglophones dominated region (WAMZ) is trade diverting. Therefore, for ECOWAS to be successful in terms of facilitating intra-regional trade, current efforts at forming a synergy between WAEMU and ECOWAS should take cognizance of promoting trade between members, irrespective of colonial origin.

1 Introduction

The last two decades have witnessed tremendous growth in regional trade agreements (RTAs) in different forms (ranging from free trade agreements to economic and monetary unions and economic partnership agreements) and scope (one off treaty based arrangement and management arrangements). In fact, as at 15th of January 2012, about 511 notifications of RTAs had been received by the World Trade Organisation/General Agreement on Tariff and Trade (WTO/GATT).

S. Olofin • A. Salisu • I. Ademuyiwa (✉) • J. Owuru
Department of Economics, Centre for Econometrics and Allied Research, University of Ibadan, Ibadan, Nigeria
e-mail: idris_ademuyiwa@yahoo.com

D. Seck (ed.), *Regional Economic Integration in West Africa*, Advances in African Economic, Social and Political Development, DOI 10.1007/978-3-319-01282-7_8,

Table 1 Trends in RTAs notification to GATT/WTO

Periods of notification of GATT/WTA	Period average of RTAs within the period
1951–1960	2
1961–1970	3
1971–1980	10
1981–1990	8
1991–2000	62
2001–January 2012	129

Source: Compiled and computed by authors from GATT/WTO website
The RTAs reported includes free trade agreements, economic integration agreements and custom unions. Some agreements were revised on a future date after initial notifications but were not captured above to prevent a case of double counting

Of these, almost 90 % were free trade agreements and partial scope agreements while custom unions accounted for the remaining 10 %. This represents a significant increase when compared to about 400 agreements reported by Whalley (2006). Table 1 shows the number of RTAs reported by the WTO for 10 year period averages starting from 1951.

Africa has not been spared of the proliferation of RTAs around the world. On average, each country in the continent belongs to at least four RTAs and the continent now has over 30 RTAs most of which are free trade agreements and economic integration agreements. Like other RTAs in other regions of the world, the objectives of RTAs in Africa include attainment of economic objectives like promotion of regional integration and trade; improvement of regional competitiveness; attraction of foreign direct investment (FDI) and non-economic objectives like conflict prevention and resolution and increasing the region's bargaining power in the multilateral front.

The quest to meet the aforementioned objectives has also resulted in the formation of RTAs in West Africa. Precisely, the urge to achieve a successful regional trade agreement has continued to dominate the agenda of the established economic communities in the region (Salisu et al. 2012). RTAs in the region presently include the Economic Community of West African States (ECOWAS) which consists of 15 out of the 17 West African countries and is the only free trade agreement in the region and a prospective monetary and economic union. Others are the West African Economic and Monetary Union (WAEMU) which is a monetary and currency union with eight francophone countries as members and the CFA Franc as official currency, the West African Monetary Zone (WAMZ) which is also an aspiring currency union with six Anglophone countries as members and the Mano River Union (MRU) which is a cooperative agreement. Notwithstanding their forms, they are all explicitly concerned with the promotion of intra-regional trade flows (Ogunkola 1998) and are not immune from the challenges typical to RTAs in Africa.

Africa has potentials to expand its trade (both intra-regional and extra regional trade) and increase its competitiveness so as to grow and attract the much needed foreign direct investment (FDI) through mutually beneficial RTAs. According to

Table 2 Trend in Africa's share in world exports

Years	World exports (in US Million dollars)	Africa Exports (in US Million dollars	Percentage of African exports in world exports
1980	2,035,542	121,875	6.0
1990	3,479,906	105,100	3.0
2000	6,448,571	149,402	2.3
2010	15,174,439	493,243	3.3

Source: Compiled and computed by the authors from UnctadStat (2011)

Oyejide (2003), trade-led growth can reduce rural poverty when it expands employment in small-holder agriculture and can lower urban poverty when it is associated with increased output and exports of labour-intensive manufactures. In other words, the fact that RTAs should inherently be beneficial to Africa is not in doubt as there exists a consensus as to the fact that regional integration efforts and schemes act as avenues for battling the different challenges facing the African continent as a whole. Also, increased linkages among African countries, through an expansion of intra-regional trade, can be a crucial device for creating the necessary growth spillovers and fostering the regional takeoff (Longo and Sekkat 2004). Despite these facts, the performance of RTAs in Africa especially in the attainment of the economic objectives has been relatively disappointing.[1] For instance, as reflected in Table 2, there has been no significant improvement in Africa's contribution to world exports in the past four decades.

Further, studies have revealed that the impact of RTAs on intra-African trade have been very small (see Yang and Gupta 2005) especially in comparison with its extra-regional trade (see Cassim 2001). Further, econometric analyses have also confirmed that regional integration in Africa (through various regional schemes) has been a failure (see Elbadawi 1997). Similarly, Ogunkola (1998) found intra-ECOWAS trade to be too low while according to Bundu (1995), after so many years of establishment, no significant impact has been felt on development in West Africa even though countries have adopted the different programs of ECOWAS.[2]

A peculiar problem perceived to be hindering the success of RTAs in West Africa in particular is the presence of different agreements and possible overlaps amongst them. These overlaps may result in duplication of responsibilities, potentially conflicting commitments and the waste of already scarce resources (Robert 2004). Stemming from these problems, some salient questions come to mind. They include; what factors can facilitate the effectiveness of a regional trade agreement in West Africa? Currently, how have the overlaps aforementioned affected intra-regional trade? While the closest effort at examining the consequent effect of these overlaps on trade is by Musila (2005) who focused on the intensity of trade creation

[1] Unlike Africa, the contribution of other regions like Asia has been on the increase during the same period. This is partly due to the increasing competitiveness of the region and its transition to production of value added goods via improved technology.

[2] Bundu Abass is a former Executive Secretary of ECOWAS.

and diversion in COMESA, ECCAS and ECOWAS as a whole, we are of the opinion that an inward looking analysis for some RTAs within West Africa in particular will be more insightful.

In the present study, we therefore seek to add to the existing literature in two different ways. First, we extend the gravity model (GM) to capture the determinants of an effective RTA in ECOWAS especially in order to domesticate and update the findings by Longo and Sekkat (2004) on the role of political stability, infrastructure and economic policy in intra-African trade. Second, since two sub-regions have remained prominent in ECOWAS namely WAEMU and WAMZ, we further examine the possibility of trade creation or diversion between these sub-regions within ECOWAS. Therefore, apart from the conventional specification that highlights the main determinants of bilateral trade, this study adopts a Vinerian-type gravity model specification with three dummies per FTA with a view to capture the trade creation and trade diversion effect of each RTA. We expect that the presence of trade diversion within the region will reveal a lack of synergy among the RTAs in the region and a possible factor responsible for the setbacks earlier mentioned in West Africa while the presence of a trade creation will prove otherwise.

Foreshadowing our main results, we find that economic size, distance, geographical factors such as common border, landmass, landlockedness of countries and socioeconomic variables like common language, political stability and availability of infrastructure significantly influence intra-regional trade within the ECOWAS region. We also find that the *francophones* dominated region (WAEMU) is exports trade creating while the Anglophones dominated region (WAMZ) is trade diverting. Nonetheless, the current effort to synergize WAEMU and WAMZ sub-regions is expected to enhance bilateral trade in ECOWAS.

This paper is organized as follows. Section 2 presents some background analysis and stylized facts about the trade relation of ECOWAS member countries. Relevant empirical and theoretical studies are reviewed in Sect. 3. Section 4 describes the methodology employed while Sect. 5 presents the result of estimations carried out. Section 6 concludes the paper.

2 Stylized Facts About Trade in ECOWAS

ECOWAS is a common market and therefore it trades with other regions in the continent, the other RTAs in the world and individual countries (both developed and developing). In this section, we analyze the trends in ECOWAS trade across different periods i.e. 1995–2000, 2001–2005 and 2006–2010. Thus, trends in intra-ECOWAS trade, ECOWAS trade with other regions in Africa, ECOWAS trade with developing and developed countries and the major RTAs in the world between the periods aforementioned are discussed. Further, it also compares the share of intra-ECOWAS and extra-ECOWAS trade in total trade by the region.

2.1 Trends in ECOWAS Intra-regional Trade

Intra-regional trade in ECOWAS in terms of exports, imports and consequently total trade can be described as being biased towards a number of countries.[3] Of the total exports within the region, Nigeria has the highest percentage between the periods 1995–2010 (see Table 3 in the Appendix). In fact, the country contributed about 36 % of the total exports in the period 1995–2000 and this increased to about 40 % in the period 2006–2010. The reason for Nigeria's dominance cannot be unrelated to her position as a major crude oil exportser in the region. Closely followed is Cote-d'Ivoire, which accounted for about 35 % of the total intra-ECOWAS exports in the period 1995–2000 though it decreased to about 28 % in the 2006–2010 period. Senegal also contributed a relatively high proportion of intra-ECOWAS exports while other countries in the region accounted for less than 5 % with Gambia and Guinea contributing the least.

Cote-d'Ivoire dominated intra-ECOWAS imports by receiving about 23 % of the regions imports between the period 1995 and 2000. Also significant is the proportion of imports by Ghana, Mali, Nigeria and Burkina Faso with each of them accounting for about 19 %, 12 %, 10 % and 9 % respectively. For all these countries except Burkina Faso, their intra-ECOWAS imports share for 2006–2010 reflects an increase relative to their 1995–2000 values. That a country like Nigeria does not contribute as much to total imports in the region as it does to exports confirms the earlier position on the effect of its leadership in crude oil production and reflects its retrogression in terms of commodity trade.

On the aggregate, Cote-d'Ivoire accounts for the highest percentage of intra-ECOWAS trade with almost 29 % in the periods 1995–2000 though this contribution fell to about 26 % in the 2006–2010 period. Expectedly, Nigeria by virtue of its role in intra-ECOWAS exports, seconded with a share of about 24 % of total trade between 1995 and 2000 which increased to about 26 % in the 2006–2010 period. Other drivers of intra-regional trade in ECOWAS are Ghana and Senegal which contributed about 13 % and 8 % between 2006 and 2010 respectively.

2.2 Trends in ECOWAS Trade with Developed and Developing Countries

ECOWAS trade with developed and developing countries, though biased towards the developed countries, revealed an interesting finding. Of the region's total exports, the developed countries accounted for about 68 % in the 1995–2000 period only to reduce to 63 % in the 2006–2010 period. Consequently, developing countries' share of ECOWAS exports increased from about 32 % in 1995 to 2000

[3] This section on intra-regional trade excludes four countries namely Liberia, Guinea Bissau, Sierra Leone and Cape Verde because of lack of sufficient data.

period to 37 % from 2006 to 2010. For imports, during the periods 1995–2000, the developed countries contributed almost 63 % to ECOWAS imports while the developing countries accounted for about 37 %. However, the trend changed in the period 2006–2010 when the share of developing countries increased to about 52 % and those of the developed countries reduced drastically to about 48 %. In other words, the developing countries overtook the developed countries during the period 2006–2010.

As shown in Fig. 1 below and Table 4 (in the Appendix), on the aggregate, while developed countries accounted for about 66 % of total trade with ECOWAS in the 1995–2000 period, the developing countries accounted for 34 %. This margin closed up in the period 2006–2010 as the percentage changed to 57 % and 43 % for developed and developing countries respectively. The interesting revelation here is that developing countries are perhaps making efforts to promote trade within their regions.

2.3 *Trends in ECOWAS Trade with African Regions*

Apart from intra-regional trade and trade with developed and developing countries, another stylized fact can be derived from ECOWAS members' trade with other regions in Africa. As depicted in Table 5 (in Appendix) and Fig. 2 below, Middle Africa accounted for the larger share of exports from ECOWAS for the period 1995–2000 with about 46 % of the total. Other regions like the Northern and Southern Africa also received a high percentage of ECOWAS exports of about 26 % and about 24 % respectively. In the period 2006–2010 however, this observed trend changed as Southern Africa led other regions with about 58 % of the region's total exports while Middle Africa which had hitherto gotten the highest dropped its share to get about 34 %.

For ECOWAS' imports, Southern Africa's share increased from about 48 % in the period 1995–2000 to about 54 % in 2006–2010 period while that of Northern Africa dropped from about 28 % to about 14 % in the same periods. While most of ECOWAS total trade is with the Southern and Middle Africa, this analysis revealed that ECOWAS trades only on a very small scale or magnitude with the Eastern region of the continent. The sudden rise in the trade relation between ECOWAS and Southern Africa requires specific emphasis especially starting from the turn of the decade. This is perhaps the result of aggressive initiatives by the Southern Africa continent to synergize with other regions of the continent through initiatives like NEPAD (The New Partnership for African Development).

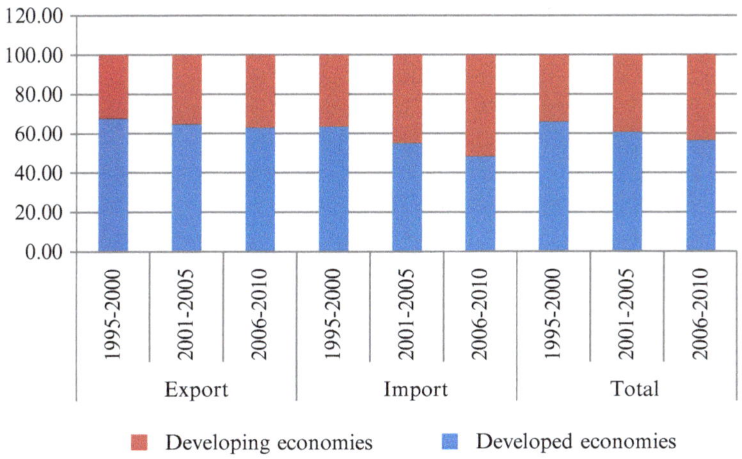

Fig. 1 Percentage share of developing and developed countries in ECOWAS' total trade (1995–2010) (Source: Graphed by the authors)

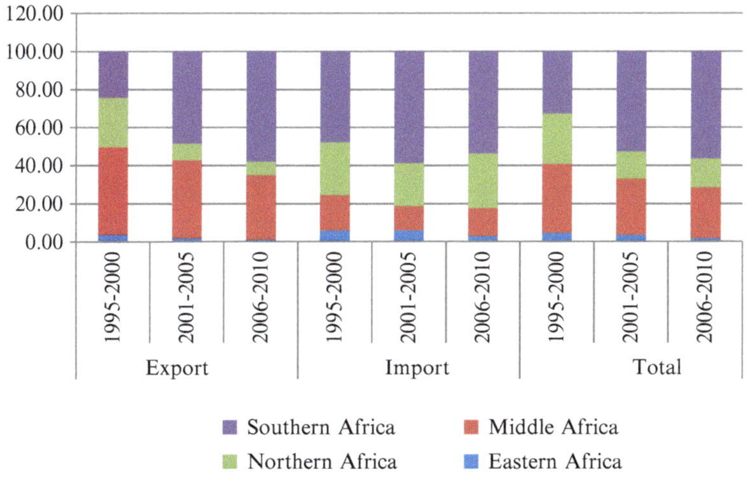

Fig. 2 Percentage share of African regions in ECOWAS' trade (1995–2010) (Source: Graphed by the authors)

2.4 Trends in ECOWAS Trade with Other Major RTAs in the World

ECOWAS trade relation with 16 of the major RTAs in the world again reflects a lopsided pattern in favor of those in Europe, America and Asia as against those situated even in Africa. In the period 1995–2000, the European Union (EU) and the Asia-Pacific Economic Cooperation (APEC) accounted for about 23 % each of

ECOWAS' total exports to RTAs while the Free Trade Area of the Americas (FTAA) and the North American Free Trade Agreement (NAFTA) received about 20 % and about 17 % respectively. Other RTAs contributed below 5 %. The same story cannot however be told when their respective contributions in the period 2006–2010 are examined. Precisely, APEC and FTAA dominated with about 22 % each and NAFTA's share of ECOWAS exports also increased to about 19 % while the share of EU dropped drastically to just 15 %. Perhaps this is a reflection of how the global financial crisis has constrained import demand for African goods by the EU countries especially in addition to their domestic crisis.

A similar trend is noticeable in the pattern of imports by ECOWAS from these RTAs. As shown in Figs. 3, 4, and 5 and Table 6 (in Appendix), the proportion of imports from EU dropped from about 38 % in the 1995–2000 period to about 26 % in the 2006–2010 period while those of APEC, FTAA and Asia-Pacific Trade Agreement (APTA) rose from about 23 %, 10 % and 7 % to about 25 %, 11 % and 15 % respectively. On aggregate, in terms of ECOWAS total trade with the major RTAs, one noticeable trend is the continuous lost of contribution by the EU and the increase in the share of APEC and FTAA. Perhaps this implies that the European market is losing its trade linkages with West Africa despite colonial affiliations while trade ties between ECOWAS and the duo of the Asian and American markets have been waxing stronger in recent times. These deductions can however be subjected to empirical validation.

2.5 Comparison of Intra-ECOWAS and Extra-ECOWAS Trade

Expectedly, the share of extra-ECOWAS trade in total trade is higher than that of intra-ECOWAS trade since ECOWAS is a small region relative to the rest of the world (which are invariably its trading partners)[4]. However, the main aim of this sub-section is to see if the share of intra-ECOWAS trade has increased significantly within the period of study. The result as depicted in Table 7 (in the Appendix) and Fig. 6 below shows that there has not been a significant increase in the share of intra-ECOWAS trade since 1995. In other words, one may infer that ECOWAS trade has been more outward looking than inward.

In conclusion, five major stylized facts can be drawn from the analysis undertaken thus far on ECOWAS trade relations. First, intra-regional trade in ECOWAS has been biased towards a number of countries namely Cote-d'Ivoire,

[4] It is important to note that the total value of intra-ECOWAS trade (both exports and imports) used here excludes those of Guinea Bissau, Liberia, Sierra Leone and Cape Verde because of lack of sufficient data. However, the results obtained are not expected to differ significantly from those in this section since this countries exert little influence on the total (precisely less than 10 % of the total).

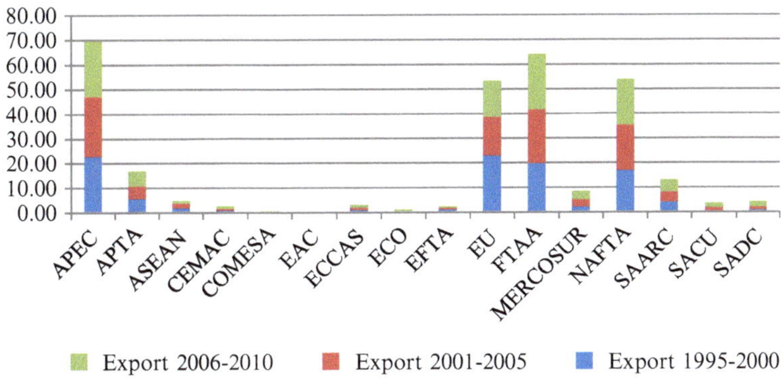

Fig. 3 Percentage share of the major RTAs in ECOWAS' exports (1995–2010) (Source: Graphed by the authors)

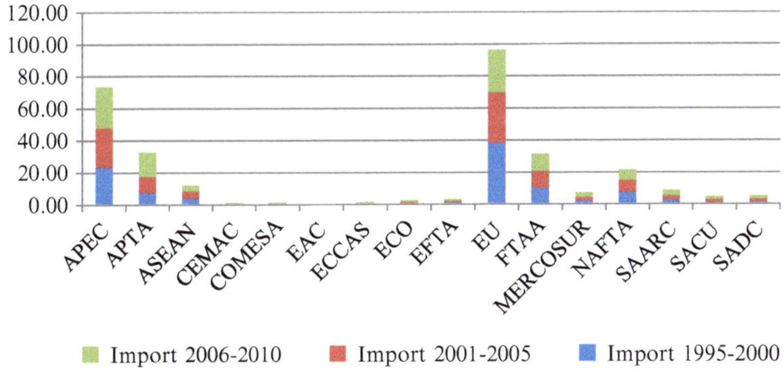

Fig. 4 Percentage share of the major RTAs in ECOWAS' imports (1995–2010) (Source: Graphed by the authors)

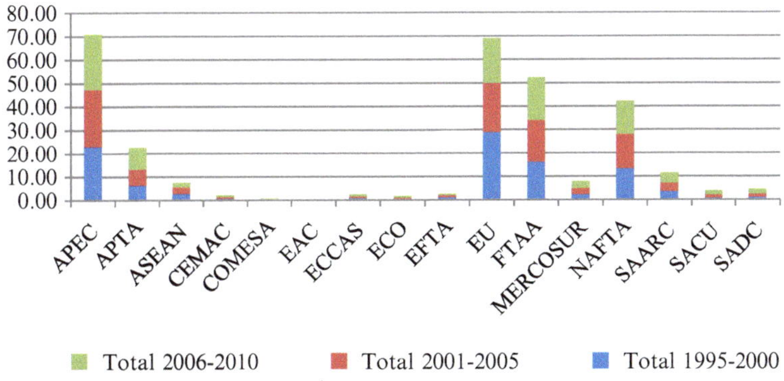

Fig. 5 Percentage share of the major RTAs in ECOWAS' total trade (1995–2010) (Source: Graphed by the authors)

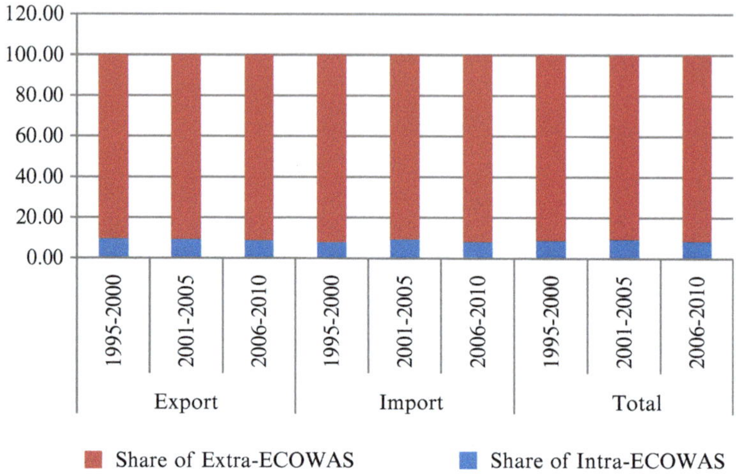

Fig. 6 Percentage share of intra-ECOWAS and extra-ECOWAS trade in total trade (1995–2010) (Source: Graphed by the authors)

Nigeria and Ghana while other countries in the region contribute relatively little to trade within the region. Secondly, in terms of ECOWAS trade with developed and developing countries, the region trades more with the developed world although the gap appears to be narrowing in recent times (i.e. from 2006 to 2010). Thirdly, the Southern African region is increasingly dominating trade with ECOWAS in terms of intra-African trade and it is followed by Middle Africa which has been losing its contribution overtime. Fourthly, out of the 16 major RTAs constituting ECOWAS' major trading partners, EU, APEC and FTAA play more significant roles. However, while the share of EU has been declining, those of APEC and FTAA have been increasing. Finally, there has been no significant increase in the ratio of intra-ECOWAS trade to its total trade (i.e. both in terms of intra and extra-ECOWAS trade).

3 Literature Review

Empirical research done in areas related to those of this study is multi-facet with different objectives. While some studies have examined trade flows, trade potentials and prospects within other regions of the world (see Filippini and Molini 2003; Papazoglou 2007; Bhattacharya and Bhattacharya 2007; Athukorala 2012 among others as noted by[5] Kepaptsoglou et al. 2010) and in Africa (see Ogunkola

[5] For the sake of intellectual transparency, it is salient to note that this section gains extensively from the brilliant work done by Kepaptsoglou et al. 2010 especially in getting access to literatures and opinions that were hitherto beyond the reach of the author.

1998; Cassim 2001; Musila 2005; Salisu et al. 2012), some have attempted to understand the determinants and predict the formation of regional trade agreements (RTAs) (see Baier and Bergstrand 2004; Egger and Larch 2006; Jayathilaka and Keembiyahetti 2009; Chen and Joshi 2010).

Also, apart from studies that have attempted to advance the methodology used in modeling international bilateral trade like Baier and Bergstrand (2004), Baier and Bergstrand (2007), Carerre (2006) Martinez-Zarzoso et al. (2009) to mention but a few, in the past decade, a relatively larger number of studies have focused on investigating the impact of RTAs on regional trade and welfare especially in terms of their tendency to divert or create trade (see Ghosh and Yamarik 2004; Musila 2005; Carrere 2006; Baier and Bergstrand 2007; Jugurnath et al. 2007; Magee 2008; Abott et al. 2008; Egger et al. 2008; Martinez-Zarzoso et al. 2009; Hur et al. 2010; Egger and Larch 2011; Foster et al. 2011) while some have examined the success factors of existing RTAs (with Vicard 2009 playing a significant role in this respect).

Owing to their policy implications and relevance to the present study, the results from some recent studies on the effect of RTAs on regional trade among member countries worth examining.[6] Nobel Laureate Jan Timbergen (1962) was one of the first to publish an empirical study in this regard. He found that the effect of RTAs on trade within the British Common Wealth members (Benelux Free Trade Agreement, FTA) to be insignificant accounting for about only a 5 % increase. Afterwards, results have been mixed, at best (Baier and Bergstrand 2007).

Recent studies across the world have come out with different results on the effects of RTAs on trade. Baier and Bergstrand (2007), in a study aimed at estimating the average treatment effect of FTAs on bilateral trade flows between the periods 1960–2000 for 96 countries found that the effect of the FTAs on trade flows is quintupled and on average an FTA approximately doubles two members' bilateral trade after 10 years. Similarly, Carrere (2006) assessed the ex-post regional trade agreement effect of seven RTAs in 130 countries for a period of 1962–1996. The result showed that the RTAs have generated a significant increase in trade though often at the expense of the rest of the world. This reflects a clear case of trade diversion.

Also, Jugurnath et al. (2007) used pooled data for a 5 year period average between 1980 and 2000 to ascertain if five different RTAs within the Asian-Pacific Region have been trade creating or trade diverting. The result revealed that while some RTAs were trade creating, others were trade diverting. Lee et al. (2009) explores the consequences of FTAs among the ASEAN +3 (China, Japan and Korea) and ASEAN +6 (China, Japan, Korea, India, Australia and New

[6] The authors deliberately selected the reviewed studies bearing in mind the fact that they adopted different methodologies. So we attempt to compare results when different methods were used.

Zealand) in terms of economic welfare, trade flows and sectorial outputs. After simulations for the period 2008–2015, the results revealed that Singapore, China and other ASEAN countries would realize a relatively large welfare gain while the impact in the European Union (EU) and North America are negligible. Egger and Larch (2006) examined the effect of the European Agreements enacted in the 1990s on the 15 EU incumbent economies and ten potential entrants located in Central and Eastern Europe. They found that the agreement resulted into a positive effect on trade in goods.

Finally, it is important to note that other studies including, but not limited to Soloaga and Winter (2001), Musila (2005), and Lee and Park (2007) have found RTAs to have positive effect on trade (see kepaptsoglou et al. 2010 for more reviews on this). As rightly noted by Kepaptsoglou et al. (2010) and Baier and Bergstrand (2007), recent evidence do not provide a clear cut evidence as to whether RTAs have been trade diverting or trade creating. Notwithstanding, recent findings have showed that making provision for the endogeneity of the RTA variables in gravity models improves the predictive power of the model and prevent the probable problem of under and over-statement of estimates. Perhaps the negligence of this by earlier studies account for the results they derived which showed that RTAs have negative effect on trade and welfare of countries and regions. It is important to note however that the issues on RTAs and bilateral trade relationship have remained inconclusive (Salisu et al. 2012).

On the determinants of a successful regional trade agreement, the results from empirical analyses (usually with the gravity model) have shown that different factors can be linked to the effectiveness of RTAs. Studies have found factors such as the trading partners Gross Domestic Product (GDP), transportation cost (usually proxied with bilateral distance), sharing of a common border, common language, GDP per capita, landmass or area, population of partners among others to be significant to bilateral trade (see Cassim 2001; Longo and Sekkat 2004; Carrere 2006; Jugurnath et al. 2007; Magee 2008; Vicard 2009; Martinez et al. 2009; Lohman 2011 amongst others).

Following Jacob Viner (1950), some studies have also attempted to divide the total effect of belonging to the same RTA or not on trade into a trade creation or trade diversion effect. The focus of such studies which include Solaoga and Winter (2001), Carrere (2006), Jugurnath et al. (2007), Magee (2008), Martinez-Zarzoso et al. (2009) among others, is to compare the magnitude of each of these integration effects so as to ascertain if RTAs are trade creating or trade diverting on the aggregate. The present study contributes to this strand of literature by adopting the Vinerian approach to estimate the effect of RTAs in ECOWAS on the region's trade.

4 Methodology

4.1 Model Specification and Estimation Technique

Although it has its origin in physics and precisely in the postulates of Sir Isaac Newton's "Law of Universal Gravitation", the gravity model has no doubt earned itself a near universal acceptance as it has been applied to a range of academic disciplines (including geography and sociology). In international economics, the gravity model has become the main tool for estimating the determinants, patterns and effects of bilateral trade since it was first adopted by Nobel Laureate Timbergen (1962) and Linnerman (1966). Particularly, the model has gained popularity with analyzing the effects of RTAs on trade and welfare in different geographical and economic regions of the world. In this respect, a gravity model involves regressing bilateral trade on a series of explanatory variables, then using dummy variables to ascertain whether this relationship is affected by the existence of RTAs (Jugurnath et al. 2007). These explanatory variables include the traditional variables of the model namely economic sizes (usually proxied with GDP) and transaction cost (usually represented with the distance between trading partners) and other variables that have been incorporated into the model overtime. According to Head (2003), the model in its conventional form can be expressed as below;

$$F_{ijt} = R_{ijt}\frac{M_i\ M_j}{D_{ij}} \tag{1}$$

Given the multiplicative form of Eq. 1, the model can be re-specified in a log-linear form after taking the natural logs as below;

$$\boldsymbol{ln} F_{ijt} = \boldsymbol{\beta}_1 \boldsymbol{ln} M_{it} + \boldsymbol{\beta}_2 \boldsymbol{ln} M_{jt} + \boldsymbol{\beta}_3 \boldsymbol{ln} D_{ijt} + \boldsymbol{\beta}_4 \boldsymbol{ln} R_{ijt} + \boldsymbol{\varepsilon}_{ijt} \tag{2}$$

Where the inclusion of the $\boldsymbol{\varepsilon}_{ijt}$ makes it estimable with OLS and F_{ijt} is bilateral trade between countries i and j and M_i and M_j are the GDPs or economic size equivalent of countries i and j respectively. D_{ij} represents bilateral distance between the two countries while R_{ij} denotes remoteness of the trading partners from the rest of the world. Other variables have been incorporated in different studies notwithstanding to augment the afore-stated variables though most of them lack theoretical justification as noted by Anderson and Van Wincoop (2003). Given the strong empirical prowess and theoretical acceptance of the gravity model for the analysis of bilateral trade flows, this study adopts the model.

In line with the main thrust of the study, two gravity models are specified and estimated. The first model is estimated with the aim of examining the determinants of an effective RTA within ECOWAS countries while the second incorporates the effects of RTAs in West Africa on trade in a procedure similar to those of Carrere (2006), Jugurnath et al. (2007) and Martinez-Zarzoso et al. (2009). It is the authors' belief that for ECOWAS to be the successful and effective regional arrangement it aspires to be, there must not be any form of trade diversion within the region. Stemming from Eq. 2 above, the first model is specified as below;

$$\begin{aligned}&\boldsymbol{ln}EXPORT_{ijt} = \boldsymbol{\alpha}_0 + \boldsymbol{\alpha}_1\boldsymbol{ln}GDP_{it} + \boldsymbol{\alpha}_2\boldsymbol{ln}GDP_{jt} + \boldsymbol{\alpha}_3\boldsymbol{ln}D_{ijt} + \boldsymbol{\alpha}_4\boldsymbol{ln}GDPPC_{it}+\\&\boldsymbol{\alpha}_5\boldsymbol{ln}GDPPC_{jt} + \boldsymbol{\alpha}_6BORDER_{ijt} + \boldsymbol{\alpha}_7LANGUAGE_{ijt} + \boldsymbol{\alpha}_8LANDLOCKED_{it}+\\&\boldsymbol{\alpha}_9LANDLOCKED_{jt} + \boldsymbol{\alpha}_{10}\boldsymbol{ln}AREA_{it} + \boldsymbol{\alpha}_{11}\boldsymbol{ln}AREA_{jt} + \boldsymbol{\alpha}_{12}\boldsymbol{ln}INFRA_{it}+\\&\boldsymbol{\alpha}_{13}\boldsymbol{ln}INFRA_{jt} + \boldsymbol{\alpha}_{14}\boldsymbol{ln}ECOPOL_{it} + \boldsymbol{\alpha}_{15}\boldsymbol{ln}ECOPOL_{jt} + \boldsymbol{\alpha}_{16}POLSTAB_{it}+\\&\boldsymbol{\alpha}_{17}POLSTAB_{jt} + V_{ijt}\end{aligned} \tag{3}$$

This specification allows for the inclusion of both country specific characteristics (like landlockedness, area, economic policy, infrastructural development and political stability) and country pair characteristics (like border and language). The dummy for landlockedness is operationalized such that it takes up the value of one if a county is landlocked and zero otherwise while the dummies for border and language take the value of one if the trading partners share a common border or common language and zero otherwise. The infrastructure variable is computed as an average of road length per capita and number of telephones per capita while the political stability variables are gotten from different indicators. The economic policy variable used is the flow of FDI into the country as this is believed to reflect, to a large extent, the level of confidence of rational investors on the economy.

Apriori expectation dictates that economic size of trading partners is positively related to trade between them so that α_1 and α_2 are expected to be positive. The distance variable is a proxy for transportation cost and therefore higher the distance is expected to mean an increase in transportation cost and consequently a reduction in bilateral trade (so $\alpha_3 < 0$). Countries with a common border and language are expected to trade more with one another base on this level of affinity, so we expect that α_6, $\alpha_7 > 0$. Landlocked countries do not readily have access to the sea and consequently transaction cost are relatively greater and trade is often debarred, hence α_8, α_9 should be negative. Availability of infrastructure and a stable economic policy is expected to promote trade and hence α_{12}, α_{13}, α_{14} and α_{15} are anticipated to be positive. Also, political instability and absence of violence is expected to foster trade so that α_{16} and α_{17} to be positive. GDP per capita is often used to proxy the level of development of trading partners. Therefore, a high level of development in either partner should result into higher trade, so we expect α_4 and α_5 to be positive. The sign of the coefficient of *area* is indeterminate as revealed by Jugurnath et al. (2007).

In order to examine the trade creation or diversion impacts of RTAs within ECOWAS, RTA dummies for WAEMU and WAMZ are added to Eq. 4 above. Therefore the resulting gravity equation can be specified as below;

$$\begin{aligned}&\boldsymbol{ln}EXPORT_{ijt} = THE\ ABOVE\ (8.3)+\\&+\alpha_{19}\sum_{k=1}^{n}RTA_{ki}\,RTA_{kj} + \alpha_{20}\sum_{k=1}^{n}RTA_{ki} + \alpha_{21}\sum_{k=1}^{n}RTA_{kj}\end{aligned} \tag{4}$$

Table 8 Interpreting static integration effects

Coefficients	Extra-bloc	Imports (α_{21})		Exports (α_{20})	
Intra-bloc	Sign	+	−	+	−
α_{19}	+	Pure TC (M)	TC + MD ($\alpha_{19} > \alpha_{21}$)or MD ($\alpha_{19} < \alpha_{21}$)	Pure TC (X)	TC + XD ($\alpha_{19} > \alpha_{20}$) or XD ($\alpha_{19} < \alpha_{20}$)
α_{19}	−	ME	MD + MC	XE	XD + XC

Source: Martinez-Zarzoso et al. (2009)

TC denotes trade creation in terms of imports (M) or in terms of exports (X), *MD and XD* denotes imports and exports diversion, respectively, *ME and XE* denotes extra-bloc imports and extra-bloc exports expansion respectively, *MC and XC* denote intra-bloc imports and extra-bloc exports contraction respectively

According to Marinez-Zarzoso et al. (2009), the gravity model represents a good counterfactual to identify the effects of an RTA, since it suggests a "normal" level of bilateral trade for a given sample and dummies are used to capture "above or below normal" levels of trade resulting from an RTA[7]. The RTA_{ki} will take the value of 1 if the exporting country is a member of the trading bloc k and 0 otherwise. Table 8 below provides cursory information about the interpretation of the RTA dummies. Positive coefficient of RTA_{ki} (i.e. $\alpha_{20} > 0$) implies that RTA_k is trade creating as it shows that members' exports to non-members are higher than the level obtainable in the absence of an agreement. In the same vein, when α_{21} is greater than zero, it implies that members' imports from non members are higher than their normal level. These are indications that RTA_k is trade creating. The integration dummy $RTA_{ki}\,RTA_{kj}$ will be one if both source and reporting countries are members of the same RTA and zero otherwise. Therefore, a positive value of α_{19} will imply that the extent to which members of the RTA_k trades with one another is higher than the level obtainable in the absence of an agreement and hence this tells us if intra-RTA trade has increased or decreased relative to those obtainable without the formation of such RTA.

Explicitly, Eq. 4 above can be re-specified as below in the context of WAEMU and WAMZ as the existing regional agreement of some forms within ECOWAS.

$$\boldsymbol{ln}\, EXPORT_{ijt} = THE\ ABOVE\ (as\ in\ 1) + \alpha_{19}\ WAEMU_{it}\ WAEMU_{jt} + \alpha_{20}\ WAEMU_{it} + \alpha_{21}\ WAEMU_{jt} + \alpha_{22}\ WAMZ_{it}\ WAMZ_{jt} + \alpha_{23}\ WAMZ_{it} + \alpha_{24}\ WAMZ_{jt} \tag{5}$$

This study makes provision for the likely impacts of efforts geared at having a synergy between ECOWAS as a whole and WAEMU. Precisely, these efforts were initiated with the signing of a cooperation agreement between the duo in

[7] The language dummy in Eq. 4 has been dropped in subsequent estimations involving RTAs to prevent a case of multicollinearity.

Ouagadougou (Burkina Faso) in 2003 and later in Abuja (Nigeria) in 2004. These agreements were aimed at developing a common plan of action on trade liberalization and macroeconomic policy convergence. In order to take account of these developments, Eq. 5 is estimated in different period variants. The first is for the period 1995–2010. The second variant covers the period before the agreements were properly internalized being from 1995 to 2004 while the third variant covers the post agreement period which is 2005–2010.

We estimate the two models noted above (i.e. Eqs. 4 and 5 where Eq. 4 is our model 1 and Eq. 5 is our model 2). We employ the Least Square Dummy Variable (LSDV) approach of fixed effects to estimate models 1 and 2. The LSDV approach is relevant in this case as earlier mentioned as it allows for the inclusion of dummy variables to capture both the country specific and country pair characteristics. Ignoring these specific effects when in fact they exist in the trade model may lead to bias result and misleading inferences (see for example, Baltagi et al. 2003; Carrere 2006).

4.2 Data Issues and Data Sources

Some of the variables used for this study are not without some debates raised in the literature. To this end some of them are examined and reasons are provided for their adoption. This study adopts bilateral exports as the dependent variable of choice primarily because previous empirical studies in Africa have found it to have a good fit (see Longo and Sekkat 2004; Musila 2005; Salisu et al. 2012). However, it is pertinent to note that opinions are mixed as Elbadawi (1997) is indifferent between the use of imports or exports and argues that both are influenced by the same factors while Jugurnath et al. (2007) noted that imports more closely proxy the effects of domestic trade.

Economic size is usually measured with GDP even though opinions differ as to whether it should be measured in terms of Purchasing Power Parity (PPP) or official exchange rate. For Cassim (2001), PPP is a better measure of relative standards and thus this study adopts the PPP version of GDP for analysis. Another concern raised is about the true exogeneity of this variable in the gravity model as both exports and imports are parts of GDP. To resolve this simultaneity problem, some studies have used instrumental variables like population to replace GDP while most studies have made no adjustment for this problem either because of absence of a good instrumental variable or because this effect is perceived as being negligible. This study follows the latter.

Bilateral distance between trading partners is often used as a proxy for transportation cost. Again, concerns have been raised about the sufficiency of this variable as a measure of transportation costs because some of these costs are actually inelastic to distance, fixed in nature or vary from country to country. Notwithstanding, distance really matters to trade in West Africa as the stylized facts in the study reveals. Hence, this study adopts the geographical distance between capital cities of trading partners.

Other control variable adopted in this study includes GDP per capita, infrastructure, political stability, border dummy, landlockedness dummy, economic policy, language, and area.[8] The inclusion of GDP per capita (which is often used to proxy factor endowment) is to test the effect of the proclaimed similarity of factor endowment on trade in ECOWAS while the addition of infrastructure, political stability and economic policy is informed by findings by Longo and Sekkat (2004). The language dummy on its part is also expected to highlight the role of colonial ties on trade in ECOWAS as the region is divided into Francophone and Anglophone countries. The data used in the study covers a period of 16 years (ranging from 1995 to 2010). Data covers 11 West African Countries (which includes Benin, Burkina Faso, Cote-d'Ivoire, Mali, Niger, Senegal, Togo, Gambia, Ghana, Guinea and Nigeria).[9]

Data used for the empirical analyses were obtained from the following sources:

1. Bilateral Exports and Imports: **UNCTADSTAT** (2011): Merchandise trade by partner and product, 1995–2010.[10]
2. GDP, GDP per capita, Infrastructure and Economic Policy and Total land area: **WDI** (2011): World Bank.
3. Bilateral distances, Common (official) language, Border: **CEPII Database**.[11]
4. Political Stability Figures: **World Governance Indicators (2011).**

5 Result Interpretation

5.1 *Results of Model 1 (for the Basic Gravity Model)*

Like most gravity models found in the literature, the overall explanatory prowess of the model is good with a coefficient of determination R^2 of about 67 %. It is not surprising therefore that most of the coefficients of the independent variables in the model are statistically significant.

[8] Variables adopted find their basis in some of the literatures reviewed in the third section above.

[9] Other countries in the ECOWAS region (i.e. Sierra Leone, Liberia, Guinea Bissau and Cape Verde) were excluded because of lack of sufficient data as most of them faced problems of social unrest for a long period. However, we are confident that their exclusion will not significantly affect the estimation results as these countries have relatively small contributions to the region.

[10] Find data at: http://unctadstat.unctad.org/ReportFolders/reportFolders.aspx

[11] Find data at: http://www.cepii.fr/anglaisgraph/bdd/distances.htm

In terms of the traditional variables of the gravity model, column two of Table 9 reveals that GDP and bilateral distance are statistically significant and correctly signed. Precisely, the elasticity coefficient of GDP for the exporting country is 1.7 implying that holding other factors constant, a 1 % increase in economic size will on the average result into about 1.7 % increase in bilateral exports in the ECOWAS region. A similar but smaller elasticity coefficient is gotten for the GDP of importing countries. While this result is greater than those obtained by Longo and Sekkat (2004) in a study on intra-African trade in which they obtained an elasticity coefficient of about 1.28 %, it is very close to the result of Salisu et al. (2012) in a study on intra-regional trade in WAEMU of about 1.78 %. Ultimately, this result implies that the larger the economic size of an exporting country in the ECOWAS region, the more exports it turns out.

For bilateral distance which is a proxy for transportation cost, it is evident from our results that holding other factors constant, a 1 % increase in transportation cost will reduce bilateral exports by about 1.5 % on the average. In short, closer trading partners have relatively higher magnitude of trade occurring between them. These results are in line with the findings of virtually all gravity models estimated in the literature as they reveal that economic size and transportation costs are important determinants of bilateral trade between countries (see Longo and Sekkat 2004; Musila 2005; Carrere 2006; Jugurnath et al. 2007; Magee 2008; Vicard 2009; Martinez-Zarzoso et al. 2009 among others). Therefore, efforts at increasing the economic size of countries in the region and reducing the cost of transportation will no doubt significantly increase intra-regional trade.

Geographical variables such as sharing a common border, landmass or area, landlockedness of countries and socioeconomic variables like common language, political stability and availability of infrastructure are found to be significant in promoting intra-regional trade within the ECOWAS region. Again, these results are in line with previous findings done for other RTAs within Africa and beyond (see Cassim 2001; Longo and Sekkat 2004; Musila 2005; Carrere 2006; Jugurnath et al. 2007; Martinez-Zarzoso et al. 2009; Lohmann 2011; Athukorala 2012; Salisu et al. 2012 for comparisons).

The coefficient of border as shown in Table 9 is significant and positive implying that sharing a common border promotes bilateral trade in the region. In fact, the result reveals that the sharing of a common border by trading partners increases bilateral exports between them by about three times (i.e. $\boldsymbol{e}^{1.06}$) compared to the absence of a common border. Similarly, the result also shows that sharing a common official language promotes bilateral exports between trading partners by more than three times (i.e. $\boldsymbol{e}^{1.32}$) relative to the absence of such. However, these developments should not be wholly seen as a good story for ECOWAS countries. For instance, the region under the auspices of ECOWAS is supposed to be a common market where there is free movement of goods, services and factors of production. Therefore, holding other factors constant, border should not be a significant factor in bilateral trade as moving goods from Senegal to Nigeria should be as easy as moving goods from Ghana to Nigeria irrespective of their official languages. In other words, the region should be border-less.

Table 9 Regression estimation results for both Model 1 and Model 2 (with its variants)

Explanatory variables	Model 1 with basic gravity variables only (for 1995–2010)	Model 2 with RTA dummies (for 1995–2010)	Model 2 with RTA dummies (for 1995–2004)	Model 2 with RTA dummies (for 2005–2010)
GDP source	1.71***	1.85***	1.79***	1.41***
	(10.85)	*(7.09)*	*(5.28)*	*(4.37)*
GDP partner	0.77***	0.97***	1.03***	0.56*
	(4.89)	*(4.43)*	*(3.61)*	*(1.94)*
GDP per capita source	−0.55***	−1.14***	−1.32***	−0.64
	(−2.84)	*(−3.92)*	*(−3.44)*	*(−1.40)*
GDP per capita partner	−0.71***	−0.78***	−0.51	−0.18
	(−3.70)	*(−3.06)*	*(−1.51)*	*(−0.43)*
Common language	1.32***	–	–	–
	(12.33)	–	–	–
Bilateral distance	−1.52***	−1.08***	−1.01***	1.28***
	(−16.59)	*(−4.54)*	*(−3.83)*	*(−5.17)*
Common border	1.07***	1.30***	1.44***	0.98***
	(7.81)	*(3.64)*	*(3.62)*	*(2.64)*
Land area source	−0.16	−0.08	−0.50	0.49
	(−1.02)	*(−0.29)*	*(−0.14)*	*(1.61)*
Land area partner	0.39***	0.08	0.06	0.36
	(2.34)	*(0.36)*	*(0.21)*	*(1.19)*
Landlocked source	−1.08***	−2.79***	−2.95***	−3.32***
	(−5.19)	*(−6.47)*	*(−5.77)*	*(−6.98)*
Landlocked partner	−1.38***	−0.89**	−0.88*	−0.36**
	(−6.60)	*(−2.03)*	*(−1.69)*	*(−1.98)*
Economic policy source	−0.06	0.08***	0.09**	−0.06
	(−1.27)	*(2.98)*	*(2.48)*	*(−1.24)*
Economic policy partner	0.02	0.01	−0.01	0.01
	(0.44)	*(0.50)*	*(−0.43)*	*(0.19)*
Political stability source	0.36***	0.20***	0.17**	0.22**
	(4.66)	*(3.01)*	*(2.04)*	*(2.24)*
Political stability partner	0.48***	0.15**	0.26***	−0.01
	(6.23)	*(2.29)*	*(2.99)*	*(−0.13)*
Infrastructure source	−0.47***	−0.12	−0.17	0.16
	(−4.80)	*(−0.77)*	*(−0.71)*	*(0.95)*
Infrastructure partner	−0.035	−0.04	−0.07	−0.04
	(−0.36)	*−0.25*	*(−0.31)*	*(−0.27)*
WAEMU dummy source	–	4.17***	4.64***	3.73**
		(2.66)	*(2.69)*	*(2.29)*
WAEMU dummy partner	–	−1.21*	−1.31	−0.84
		(−1.60)	*(−1.58)*	*(−1.06)*
WAEMU dummy Both	–	3.60***	3.80***	3.57***
		(4.33)	*(4.07)*	*(4.07)*
WAMZ Dummy source	–	4.01**	4.64**	3.64*
		(2.01)	*(2.10)*	*(1.74)*

(continued)

Table 9 (continued)

Explanatory variables	Model 1 with basic gravity variables only (for 1995–2010)	Model 2 with RTA dummies (for 1995–2010)	Model 2 with RTA dummies (for 1995–2004)	Model 2 with RTA dummies (for 2005–2010)
WAMZ dummy partner	–	1.04**	0.99	1.47**
		(1.96)	(1.60)	*(2.53)*
WAMZ dummy both	–	−1.99**	−1.93*	−2.09**
		(−2.16)	*(−1.86)*	*(2.17)*
R^2	0.66	0.75	0.72	0.80
No. of observations	1,760	1,936	1,210	726

Source: Authors' computation

The z-statistics for the coefficients are in italics and bracket below them. *, **, *** represent 1 %, 5 % and 10 % levels of statistical significance

Landmass or area of the importing country is significant and positive. This is not in line with the results obtained by Jugurnath et al. (2007) and Cassim (2001) in which the coefficients for area were significantly negative and were interpreted to mean that the more the landmass, the larger the natural resources available and thus lower the need for trade. Here, our result implies that despite a large landmass, countries in the region still imports more from their trading partners. Perhaps this is not surprising as countries with the larger landmass like Mali and Niger are desert regions devoid of adequate natural resources. Countries that are landlocked find it more laborious and expensive to trade mainly because of their lack of accessibility to markets. Therefore, the coefficients of landlockedness for both exporting and importing countries as shown in column two of Table 9 are negative and significant. We can infer that landlockedness of some countries in the region has a high negative effect on bilateral exports.

Unlike Longo and Sekkat (2004), only political stability is found to be a significant driver of bilateral trade while infrastructural developments and the level of confidence in economic policy are found to be mostly insignificant. This does not imply that these factors are not salient for an effective regional trade agreement but rather reflects the fact that their effects have been overwhelmed by political considerations and problems as is the case in the African continent as a whole. More so, countries in the region are not significantly different in terms of the level of confidence rational investors have in them, with the exemption of Nigeria and Ghana.[12] Also the state of the few available infrastructure in the region is deplorable. For instance, Kaplan (2006) noted that much of the sparse road network is in poor condition, and frequent checkpoints, one every 14 km on the road between Lagos (Nigeria) and Abidjan (Cote-d'Ivoire), shrink markets.

[12] This position is formed based on the level of FDI inflow into these countries from rational investors over the years of which Nigeria and Ghana account for about 54 % and 22 % respectively of total FDI into the countries in 2010.

5.2 Results of Model 2 (for the Gravity Model with RTAs)

Ultimately, the second specification is aimed at capturing the existence of trade creation and trade diversion within the RTAs in West Africa while its variants are aimed at examining changes in the trend at different periods. The coefficient of determination of the three period variants ranges from about 60 % to about 80 %. We focus on interpreting the coefficients of the RTA dummies since the coefficients of the traditional gravity variables do not differ significantly from those in model 1.

The first notable result is the fact that the coefficients of the regional trade dummies are not significantly different across the period variants. In other words, the signing of the agreement has not changed the trade creation or diversion tendencies of WAEMU and WAMZ countries. The Table 9 depicts these. Therefore, we interpret the result of the pooled variant of the model (i.e. the one for the period 1995–2010).

5.2.1 The WAEMU Integration Dummies

For all the period variants of the model involving RTAs estimated, the coefficients of the WAEMU dummies are similar in magnitude and signs and are mostly statistically significant. However, of more importance to our interpretations are the signs of the three WAEMU dummies. From Eq. 5 above and the results presented in Table 9, α_{19} is positive with the value of about 3.6. This implies that there is an increase in bilateral exports within WAEMU members by about 3.6 % as a result of the formation of WAEMU. Similarly α_{20} (that is meant to capture change in extra-WAEMU exports) is also positive with a value of about 4.2. This indicates that bilateral exports from WAEMU members' to non-WAEMU member have, on the average, increased by about 4.2 % relative to a situation where WAEMU does not exist. These two coefficients suggest evidence of trade creation in terms of exports for WAEMU. However, α_{21} (which represents change in extra-WEAMU imports) is negative with value -1.2. This implies that despite the increase in intra-WAEMU exports, WAEMU members' bilateral imports from non-WAEMU members in ECOWAS has, on the average, decreased by about 1.2 % as a result of their belonging to WAEMU. This result conforms to the findings by Coulibaly (2009), except that he found WAEMU's extra-RTA exports to become negative later on. However, it is important to note that his analysis was done relative to the World at large and not ECOWAS alone as in our case.

Therefore, for the period 1995–2010, our empirical result shows that while the formation or existence of WAEMU as a regional arrangement has resulted in pure trade creation in terms of exports, it has also given rise to a diversion of imports away from non-WAEMU member countries within the ECOWAS region. However, this trend has not changed even when the pre and post cooperation agreement period between ECOWAS and WAEMU is espoused. The implication of this result is that WAEMU as an RTA in the region has a positive effect on intra-ECOWAS exports since it is purely exports creating. However, the presence of an imports diversion by WAEMU may not be healthy for the region.

5.2.2 The WAMZ Integration Dummies

Like the WAEMU integration dummies, the WAMZ dummies are mostly statistically significant and similar (in terms of magnitude and sign) across the period variants for RTA models estimated. Specifically, from Eq. 5 above and the results presented in Table 9, α_{22} is negative with the value of about -1.99. This implies that there is a decrease in bilateral exports within WAMZ by about 2.0 % as a result of the formation of WAMZ. Similarly α_{23} (that captures change in extra-WAMZ exports) is also positive with a value of about 4.01. This indicates bilateral exports from WAMZ members to non-WAMZ member has, on the average, increased by about 4.0 % relative to a situation where WAMZ does not exist. These two coefficients suggest evidence of extra-WAMZ exports expansion. However, α_{24} (which represents change in extra-WAMZ imports) is positive with value of about 1.10. This implies that despite the decrease in intra-WAMZ exports, WAMZ members' bilateral imports from non-WAEMU members in ECOWAS has, on the average, increased by about 1.1 % as a result of their belonging to WAEMU. This is a case of extra-WAMZ imports expansion.

Therefore, for the period 1995–2010, our results reveal that the existence of WAMZ has resulted in both exports and imports expansion to non-WAMZ members within the ECOWAS region. However, this result does not differ even when we take cognizance of period variant RTA models and the fact that WAMZ was only established in the year 2000.[13] The implication of these is that although there seems to be a synergy between WAMZ countries and non-members in the region as evident in the extra-imports and extra-export expansion, there exists a low level of intra-WAMZ exports which remains a major concern.

Table 10 below compares the magnitude of the coefficients of the WAEMU and WAMZ RTA dummies. This is done to evaluate the differences in the trade creation or diversion tendencies between them.

The table above reiterates the afore-stated observations. Further, it shows that from the period 1995 to 2010 bilateral exports amongst WAEMU members has

[13] The results of the variants of the RTA model that span 1995 to 2004, 2005 to 2010 and the pooled for 1995 to 2010 were found to be very similar in magnitude and signs. Although WAMZ was formed in the year 2000, since the result of the variant for 2005 to 2010 does not differ from other periods, it is safe to draw the afore-stated conclusions. Moreover, WAMZ and WAEMU are used here to check the effect of the dichotomy between Francophone and Anglophone West African countries.

Table 10 Summary of the magnitude of trade creation (diversion) for WAEMU and WAMZ

RTAs	Intra-RTA trade coefficient	Extra-RTA exports coefficient	Extra-RTA imports coefficient
WAEMU	3.60	4.17	−1.21
WAMZ	−1.99	4.01	1.04
Differences	5.59	0.16	2.25

Sources: Authors' computation

increased significantly relative to bilateral exports amongst WAMZ members. However, despite the inability of WAMZ members to promote bilateral exports with one another, both RTAs have increased exports to non-members of their respective RTAs though WAEMU has the higher magnitude. For extra RTA imports, WAMZ members have increased imports to non-members from 1995 to 2010 while WAEMU members' import from non-members has reduced over the same period. It's pertinent to note that apart from the traditional gravity variables, another requisite for a successful RTA in West Africa is for each of the RTAs in the region to be trade creating in terms of both exports and imports of goods and services.

6 Policy Implications and Conclusion

The proliferation of RTAs in the World has been associated with myriad reasons but the most important for developing economies is to promote sustainable regional development and facilitate the attainment of non-economic goals like conflict prevention and resolution. Using the modified gravity model, this paper estimates the effects of both the qualitative and quantitative factors driving bilateral trade flows among ECOWAS member countries. To achieve this objective, the paper estimated the gravity model with the basic variables (i.e. distance and economic size) and other salient socio-economic factors like political stability, economic policy consistency and infrastructural development on intra-ECOWAS trade. Further, it applies the Vinerian integration effects to verify the presence of trade creation, exports diversion and imports diversion effects of the *francophones's* dominated WAEMU and the *anglophones'* dominated WAMZ on intra-ECOWAS Trade.

The results reveal that apart from socio-economic and geographical factors, others including political and institutional factors are salient to the effectiveness of intra-ECOWAS trade. Stemming from these, therefore, we provide a number of insightful recommendations to policy makers in the region. First, although some literature posit that the negative effects of geographical factors like landlockedness, bilateral distance and area on trade are beyond the control of policy makers, we think otherwise. Certain routes and ports can be dedicated to landlocked countries through their close neighbors that are opened to the sea, environmental measures like aforestation can be embarked upon to reduce the menace of desert encroachment in some countries with a large landmass like Mali and Niger while bilateral distances can be made insignificant to trade with the availability of infrastructures like good roads and railway networks that extend across borders and telecommunication services. However, our results reveal that infrastructure has not stimulated trade within the region. This may not be unconnected with the deplorable state of infrastructure in the region. Therefore, there is no gain-saying the fact that infrastructural development is critical for the success of regional trade agreement in the region.

Secondly, socio-economic factors like market size, income and economic policy have been proven by different studies (ours inclusive) to be inevitable for expansion of trade and attraction of both local and foreign investors. This is underscored by the fact that an increased market size creates business opportunities for both local and foreign investors and by extension widens the employment strength and boosts income. Unfortunately, the UNDP Human Development Index 2009 reveals that most countries within the region rank among the least successful in the world with over 50 % of the population living below the poverty line. Therefore, it is imperative for policy makers to develop human capital through health and education so as to increase employment and productivity necessary to boost income.

Thirdly, perhaps there is no other factor as significant to the success of any regional trade agreement in West Africa as political stability is. Evidently, there is hardly any country in the region that has successfully overcome problems relating to the different variants of political instability ranging from ethnic conflicts to terrorist attacks since independence. It is not surprising therefore that our result re-iterates the aforementioned. Therefore, we recommend that more concerted efforts from all stakeholders should be geared towards prevention and prompt resolution of conflict and political instability in the region. In short, it will be mild to say the visions of ECOWAS will be unattainable without political stability in the region especially since the security problem has taken a *contagion effect* dimension.

Finally, although concerns have been raised about possible institutional overlaps between WAEMU and ECOWAS as a whole and its consequent effects, our study reveals that such concerns seems valid as the effect of the overlaps is inherent in intra-ECOWAS trade. The presence of imports diversion in the *francophones* dominated region (WAEMU) and the absence of a high trade within the *anglophones* dominated region (WAMZ) is not negligible and calls for necessary attention. Therefore, efforts at forming a synergy between WAEMU and ECOWAS should take cognizance of promoting trade between them, irrespective of colonial origin, to prevent a case of intra-ECOWAS trade diversion.

Appendix: Tables

Table 3 Percentage share of ECOWAS countries in intra-regional trade (1995–2010)

Country	Periods	BEN	BFA	CIV	GHA	GMB	GIN	MLI	NER	NGA	SEN	TGO
Exports share	**1995–2000**	1.9	2.1	34.7	4.2	0.0	0.3	6.1	4.5	36.2	6.7	3.3
	2001–2005	4.1	3.5	30.8	4.3	0.0	0.4	1.9	2.5	36.9	7.9	7.7
	2006–2010	4.9	1.8	28.1	6.5	0.0	0.3	1.8	3.0	39.6	8.5	5.6
Imports share	**1995–2000**	5.2	8.7	23.0	18.5	1.2	3.6	12.4	4.5	9.8	8.7	4.5
	2001–2005	5.2	9.7	22.4	18.8	0.8	2.6	12.0	4.1	9.8	10.8	3.8
	2006–2010	6.1	8.6	24.4	20.5	0.7	1.1	13.0	4.0	12.7	7.6	1.4
Share in total	**1995–2000**	3.5	5.2	29.2	11.0	0.6	1.9	9.1	4.5	23.7	7.6	3.8
	2001–2005	4.6	6.5	26.8	11.3	0.4	1.5	6.8	3.3	23.8	9.3	5.8
	2006–2010	5.5	5.1	26.3	13.4	0.3	0.7	7.3	3.5	26.4	8.1	3.5

Source: Authors' computation from UNCTADSTAT 2011

Table 4 Percentage share of developing and developed countries in ECOWAS' total trade (1995–2010)

	Exports			Imports			Total		
Countries/periods	1995–2000	2001–2005	2006–2010	1995–2000	2001–2005	2006–2010	1995–2000	2001–2005	2006–2010
Developed economies	67.75	64.73	63.00	63.45	54.94	48.22	65.82	60.69	56.50
Developing economies	32.25	35.27	37.00	36.55	45.06	51.78	34.18	39.31	43.50

Source: Authors' computation from UNCTADSTAT 2011

Table 5 Percentage share of African regions in ECOWAS' trade (1995–2010)

	Exports			Imports			Total		
Countries/periods	1995–2000	2001–2005	2006–2010	1995–2000	2001–2005	2006–2010	1995–2000	2001–2005	2006–2010
Eastern Africa	3.67	1.85	1.03	6.12	5.94	2.92	4.55	3.51	1.74
Middle Africa	46.13	41.03	34.02	18.50	12.70	14.69	36.15	29.50	26.77
Northern Africa	26.01	8.61	7.16	27.69	22.67	28.68	26.62	14.34	15.23
Southern Africa	24.19	48.51	57.79	47.70	58.69	53.71	32.68	52.65	56.26

Source: Authors' computation from UNCTADSTAT 2011

Table 6 Percentage share of some major RTAs in ECOWAS' total trade (1995–2010)

	Exports			Imports			Total		
RTAs/Period	1995–2000	2001–2005	2006–2010	1995–2000	2001–2005	2006–2010	1995–2000	2001–2005	2006–2010
APEC	22.59	24.48	22.22	23.30	24.51	25.41	22.87	24.49	23.38
APTA	5.55	5.08	6.07	7.24	10.25	14.96	6.20	6.83	9.32
ASEAN	1.73	2.06	0.92	4.13	4.29	3.66	2.65	2.81	1.92
CEMAC	0.79	0.81	0.92	0.33	0.37	0.42	0.61	0.66	0.74
COMESA	0.24	0.12	0.13	0.24	0.39	0.39	0.24	0.21	0.22
EAC	0.02	0.02	0.01	0.05	0.08	0.06	0.03	0.04	0.03
ECCAS	0.98	0.95	1.06	0.36	0.39	0.48	0.74	0.76	0.85
ECO	0.23	0.34	0.48	0.71	0.65	1.02	0.42	0.44	0.68
EFTA	1.03	0.73	0.49	1.03	0.96	0.88	1.03	0.81	0.64
EU	22.81	15.75	14.69	38.24	31.45	26.43	28.74	21.06	18.98
FTAA	19.66	21.91	22.43	10.28	10.50	10.46	16.05	18.05	18.06
MERCOSUR	2.18	2.99	3.19	2.26	1.99	2.67	2.21	2.65	3.00
NAFTA	16.86	18.30	18.65	7.45	7.73	6.18	13.25	14.73	14.10
SAARC	4.02	4.07	4.98	2.46	2.69	3.39	3.42	3.60	4.40
SACU	0.52	1.12	1.80	0.92	1.82	1.75	0.67	1.36	1.78
SADC	0.77	1.29	1.96	1.01	1.94	1.83	0.86	1.51	1.91

Source: Authors' computation from UNCTADSTAT 2011

Table 7 Percentage share of intra-ECOWAS and extra-ECOWAS trade in total trade (1995–2010)

Periods	Exports			Imports			Total		
	1995–2000	2001–2005	2006–2010	1995–2000	2001–2005	2006–2010	1995–2000	2001–2005	2006–2010
Share of intra-ECOWAS	9.66	9.46	8.85	7.95	9.40	8.08	8.77	9.43	8.46
Share of extra-ECOWAS	90.34	90.54	91.15	92.05	90.60	91.92	91.23	90.57	91.54

Source: Author's computation from UNCTADSTAT 2011

References

Abbott P, Bentzen J, Tarp F (2008) Trade and development: lessons from Vietnam's past trade agreements. World Dev 37(2):341–353
Anderson J, Van Wincoop E (2003) Gravity with gravitas: a solution to the border puzzle. Am Econ Rev 93(1):170–192
Athukorala P (2012) Asian trade flows: trends, patterns and prospects. Jpn World Econ (forthcoming). doi:10.1016/j.japwor.2012.01.003, JAPWOR 760
Baier S, Bergstrand J (2004) Economic determinants of free trade agreements. J Int Econ 64 (1):29–63
Baier S, Bergstrand J (2007) Do free trade agreements actually increase members' international trade? J Int Econ 71(1):72–95
Baltagi D, Egger P, Pfaffermayr M (2003) A generalized design for bilateral trade flow models. Econ Lett 80:391–397
Bhattacharya S, Bhattacharyay B (2007) An empirical analysis on prospects and challenges of BIMSTEC-Japan trade integration. J f Asian Econ 18(3):509–536
Bundu A (1995) ECOWAS and the future of regional integration in West Africa. In: Lavergne R (ed) Regional integration and cooperation in West Africa: a multidimensional perspective. International Development Research Centre (IDRC), Ottawa
Carrere C (2006) Revisiting the effects of regional trade agreements on trade flows with proper specification of the gravity model. Eur Econ Rev 50:223–247
Cassim R (2001) The determinants of intra-regional trade in Southern Africa with specific references to South African and the rest of the region. DPRU working paper. Development Policy Research Unit, University of Cape Town
Chen M, Joshi S (2010) Third country effects on the formation of free trade agreements. J Int Econ 82:238–248
Coulibaly S (2009) Evaluating the trade effect of developing RTAs: a semi-parametric approach. J Econ Integr 24(4):709–743
Egger P, Larch M (2011) An assessment of Europe agreement's effect on bilateral trade GDP, and welfare. Eur Econ Rev 55:263–271
Egger H, Egger P, Greenaway D (2008) The trade structure effects of endogenous regional trade agreements. J Int Econ 74:278–298
Elbadawi I (1997) The impact of regional trade and monetary schemes on intra-Sub Saharan Africa trade. In: Ademola O, Elbadawi I, Collier P (eds) Regional integration and trade liberalization in sub-Saharan Africa. Macmillan, London, pp 210–225
Filippini C, Molini V (2003) The determinants of East Asian trade flows: a gravity equation approach. J Asian Econ 14(5):695–711
Foster N, Poeschl J, Stehrer R (2011) The impact of preferential trade agreements on margin of international trade. Econ Syst 35:84–97
Ghosh S, Yamarik S (2004) Are regional trading arrangements trade creating? An application of extreme bounds analysis. J Int Econ 63:369–395
Head K (2003) Gravity for beginners. University of British Columbia, Canada
Hur J, Alba J, Park D (2010) Effects of hub-and-spoke free trade agreement on trade: A panel data analysis. World Dev 38(8):1105–1113
Jayathilaka R, Keembiyahetti N (2009) Adverse selection effect for South Asian countries in FTA formation: an empirical study on the determinants of FTA among the bilateral trading partners. South Asia Econ J 10(1):1–30
Jugurnath B, Stewart M, Brooks R (2007) Asia/Pacific regional trade agreements: an empirical study. J Asian Econ 18:974–987
Kaplan S (2006) West African integration: a new development paradigm? The Wash Q 29(4): 81–97. The Centre for Strategic and International Studies and The Massachusetts Institute of Technology

Kepaptsoglou K, Karlaftis M, Tsamboulas D (2010) The gravity model specification for modeling international trade flows and free trade agreement effects: a 10-year review of empirical studies. Open Econ J 3:1–13

Lee H, Park I (2007) In search of optimized regional trade agreements and applications to East Asia. World Econ 30(5):783–806

Lee H, Owen R, van der Mensbrugghe D (2009) Regional integration in Asia and its effects on the EU and North America. J Asian Econ 20:240–254

Linnermann H (1966) An econometric study of international trade flows. North-Holland, Amsterdam

Lohmann J (2011) Do language barriers affect trade? Econ Lett 110:159–162

Longo R, Sekkat K (2004) Economic obstacles to expanding intra-African trade. World Dev 32 (8):1309–1321

Magee C (2008) New measures of trade creation and trade diversion. J Int Econ 75:349–362

Martinez-Zarzoso I, Felicitas N, Horsewood N (2009) Are regional trading agreements beneficial? Static and dynamic panel gravity models. North Am J Econ Finance 20:46–65

Musila J (2005) The intensity of trade creation and trade diversion in COMESA, ECCAS and ECOWAS: a comparative analysis. J Afr Econ 14(1):117–141

Ogunkola O (1998) An empirical evaluation of trade potential in the economic community of West African states, vol 84, AERC research paper. African Economic Research Consortium, Nairobi

Oyejide A (2003) Trade reforms for economic growth and poverty reduction. Dev Outreach 5 (3):4–6

Papazoglou C (2007) Greece's potential trade flows: a gravity model approach. Int Adv Econ Res 13(4):403–414

Robert R (2004) The social dimension of regional integration in ECOWAS, vol 49, Working paper. Policy Integration Department, International Labour Organisation, Geneva

Salisu A, Ademuyiwa I, Owuru J (2012) Intra-regional trade in WAEMU: an empirical study, Unpublished Manuscript

Soloaga I, Winters A (2001) How has regionalism in the 1990s affected trade? North Am J Econ Finance 12:1–29

Tinbergen J (1962) Shaping the world economy: suggestions for an international trade policy. Twentieth Century Fund Press, New York

UNCTAD Statistics (database) (2011) Bilateral exports and imports merchandise trade by partners. http://unctadstat.unctad.org/ReportFolders/reportFolders.aspx

Vicard V (2009) Determinants of successful regional trade agreements, Paris School of Economics, University Paris i Pantheon-Sorbonne & Banque de Francey

Viner J (1950) The customs union issue. Carnegie Endowment for International Peace, New York

Whalley J (2006) Recent regional agreements: why so many, why so much variance in form, why coming so fast, and where are they headed?, CESifo working paper no 1790. http://hdl.handle.net/10419/25835

World Development Indicators (database). http://data.worldbank.org/data-catalog/world-development-indicators. Washington, DC: World Bank

Yang Y, Gupta S (2005) Regional trade agreements in Africa: past performance and the way forward, IMF working paper 5:36. IMF, Geneva

Regional Integration: Comparison Between SADC and ECOWAS

Falilou Fall, Blandine Vachon, and Cosimo Winckler

Abstract As the priority over regional integration in Africa is gaining a political momentum, this paper draws an overview on commercial regional integration over the past 15 years in two Regional Economic Communities (REC), ECOWAS and SADC. Since WAEMU is part of ECOWAS, we distinguish their respective dynamics as they may sometimes differ. Evolution of intraregional trade from 1995 to 2010 is proxied by the ratio of intraregional exports over total national exports over detailed bilateral trade data. As widely recognized, intraregional trade has slowly evolved at low levels since 1995. Based on gravity equations and national data, our study disaggregates some determinants of intraregional trade. As expected, bad national infrastructures affect intraregional trade, so as sectoral economic trends such as industrial and manufacturing growth. We also study whether the existence of regional leaders has positive or negative influences over intraregional trade. Adverse effects seem not to exist as the leading economies' performance appears to be positively correlated to intraregional trade. Conversely, overall economic performance of RECs' does not systematically translate into increased intraregional trade. When differentiating exports by types of goods, differences between levels of industrialization and development of RECs become more salient. SADC appears to be less regionally integrated and is more open to global trade. Conversely, ECOWAS and WAEMU are more integrated regionally

Disclaimer This paper does *not* reflect any of the views of the French Ministry of Foreign Affairs, or those of the Ecole Nationale de la Statisique et de l'Administration Economique. The findings, interpretations, and conclusions expressed in this paper are entirely those of the authors.

F. Fall (✉)
University Paris 1, Paris, France
e-mail: falilou.fall@univ-paris1.fr

B. Vachon
ENSAE, Malakoff, France

C. Winckler
MAE, Ministry of Foreign Affairs, Paris, France

D. Seck (ed.), *Regional Economic Integration in West Africa*, Advances in African Economic, Social and Political Development, DOI 10.1007/978-3-319-01282-7_9,

but less integrated into global trade. Beyond a political processes, intraregional exports seems therefore to be a second best solution for these countries.

1 Introduction

In Africa, regional integration ranges from free trade zones such as South African Development Community[1] (SADC) to monetary unions such as the West African Economic and Monetary Union[2] (WAEMU). Arguments for promoting regional integration classically comprise increase of market sizes, economic diversification or improvement of political power in international negotiations (see Sect. 2). Although these arguments are well-known, when compared to the rest of the world, intra-African trade is dismally low. Intra-African trade represents 12 % of all exchanges made from African countries as opposed to 21 % in Latin America and 61 % in the EU. The lack of African trade integration does not mean that structures fostering regional integration are missing: one half of African countries belong to two regional organisations and a third of them belong to three. A country such as Namibia belongs, for example, to three different regional entities: a customs union, a common market and a free trade area.

Amongst the eight Regional Economic Communities (RECs) designated by the African Union as key pillars for the future African Economic Community, two appear to have the broadest economic perspectives at an African level: SADC and the ECOWAS[3] (CEDEAO). They both share comparable characteristics: although South Africa's share over Africa's GDP is very important and its level of development is higher, ECOWAS' and SADC's population are comparable, and so are their economic sizes and the relative importance of their respective economic leaders (Nigeria and South Africa). South Africa's GDP accounted for 64 % of SADC's aggregate GDP in 2010 (187.6 billion 2,000 constant USD) while Nigeria represented nearly 62 % of ECOWAS' GDP (USD 85.6 billion).

As these two regions have all chances to becoming the most important RECs in Sub-Saharan Africa (SSA), this papers aims at comparing their levels of trade regional integration, their determinants and the particular roles of their regional leaders. The important asymmetry between Nigerian and South African economies and their neighbours may as well lead to positive economic spillovers on their neighbouring countries, as to crowding out effects of weaker firms. Since WAEMU represents a deeper level of regional integration within ECOWAS, we extend our analysis and comparison to this ERC.

Using a variety of indicators and models based on gravity equations and panel data, both in random and fixed settings, our paper shows that the recent development of trade within the two RECs is submitted to two contradictory forces. A growing region will tend to diminish regional trade, whereas the growth of economic leaders will reinforce regional trade. This is true for all three RECs.

Our paper is organized as follows. Section 2 reviews regional integration literature on Africa, with a special focus on papers dealing with trade dynamics in SADC and ECOWAS. Section 3 provides details on data and indicators used for our analysis, as well as a more in-depth justification of the comparison between SADC and ECOWAS. Section 4 sets the models which we use for our regressions, taking a particular look into the hypotheses that underlie the use of particular models. Section 5 presents our results on the levels and determinants of regional integration in SADC, ECOWAS and WAEMU, while Sect. 6 explores the roles of South Africa and Nigeria in their respective RECs. Paper ends with some concluding remarks (Sect. 7).

2 Literature Review

Regional integration can be included into the field of the economic geography, which has been much developed after the seminal article by Krugman (1980; 1991). The main idea is to use a gravitational model, following Tinbergen's rule. As put by the AfDB joint report to the G20 in 2011, regional integration in Madariaga, Nicole, "Mesure et Evolution récente de l'intégration commerciale en zone Franc", Macrodev, n 1, Africa will help interconnect countries, facilitate among other things foods supply and will enhance Africa' s place in the international supply chain.

Krugman sets a model relying on economies of scale and transportation costs, and shows how the concentration of manufacturing producers in one region will foster that concentration even further. He underlines that economies of scale come with mass production and the development of transports. Otherwise, if there is only a small proportion of population involved in manufactures, the tendency for concentration will not be strong. There will be small manufactures, or towns, serving isolated and disconnected markets. Therefore, the success of regional integration hinges on initial conditions, which are not very favourable. Disconnected distribution of industry is real in Africa. Indeed, in this article, countries face a trade off between proximity to the larger market, which is profitable thanks to the home market effect, and producing to the smaller market, where competition is less harsh and wages are lower (but so is demand). For African RECs, the question remains to know if such populated areas do exist (19 African countries have fewer than five million people). There are some highly populated areas though, such as Nigeria, which has the biggest population in Africa, 170 million (seventh most populated country in the world), or the Democratic Republic of Congo (73 million, 19*th* country). They also emphasise the crucial role of infrastructures, a recurrent concern in articles on SSA (Behar and Manners 2008), which matter more with the increased completion and pressure of just in time production and management systems, without mentioning the difficult access to ICTs.

Krugman and Venables (1990) note that trade barriers, at intermediate level can make it attractive to outsource to low wage peripheries, instead of concentrating in the centre. If manufacturing sectors have fixed costs and increasing returns to scale, then intermediate trade barriers may re inforce divergence between centres and peripheries. If trade barriers are really low, then there are strong incentives to concentrate at the centre the manufacturing sector. Indeed, the fixed costs imply that prices have to be a minimum high for firms to cover them. At the periphery, the complete removal of trade barriers will decrease prices and equalise wages in the two regions, thus making it unprofitable for firms to produce there. In other words, the integration process is not monotonous, it will first make wages diverge and then converge. Anything that will impede changes in the relative wages will further concentration. This matters for regional integration since there are still many trade barriers, either as tariffs or as rules of origins, that do hinder trade and exchange among fellow members (see Flatters and Stern (2006)). If, as we find, tariffs hold up regional integration, if they are too lowered, they might totally prevent it by reinforcing concentration on leading countries.

Indeed, the vital need for regionalisation is the enhancement of harmonization and the assertion of the political will to implement all that has already been agreed upon. Less than a lack of funds or objectives, it is the absence of concrete action that hinders the development of RECs. For instance, harmonisation of Common Exterior Tariffs between ECOWAS and WAEMU has been postponed, as well as SADC's project of a custom union (Alemayehu and Haile 2002). The report underlines that, if African exports and imports have risen since the 1980s, its global share of trade has declined. Governments intend to harmonise transport related standards and regulations, eliminate obstacles to the free movements of goods and services. Trade costs are high in Africa, between 100 and 300$ per ton for a shipping delay of up to 40 days. Some countries, for instance, prefer not to register under the ECOWAS Free Trade Scheme, since rules of origin are so stringent that it cause extra trouble.

Despite these concerns, regional integration appears as the most urgent priority for African RECs (Adeaoti and Alii (2012)), as it is understood as a driving force emerging from African actors. With the tri-partite FTA agreement between SADC, COMESA and EAC in negotiations, and the endorsement of *Framework, Roadmap and architecture of the Continental Free Trade Area*, regional integration is currently being given a new impetus.

Another dimension of regional integration is the very nature of exports. Indeed, Easterly and Reshef (2009) show that East African countries do not export the same products towards their neighbours and the rest of the world. There is trade-off between quality and cost, and if quality is decisive for exports outside African country, it is the cost that matter for intra regional exports. Excluding exports of extraction products, they also dismiss the idea that exports are heavily dependent on commodity prices (seeing that they excluded from their analysis exports of extraction products such as oil or any mineral ore). They underline that exports are driven by Big Hits[4], and that these hits change over time and with the countries. According to them trade is less hampered by changes in global prices than by detrimental policies, high transportation and bureaucracy costs, low income of target markets.

Since the 1980s, Africa as a whole has halved its world market share for exports. Freund and Rocha (2011) find, like Rodrik, that remoteness and the high number of landlock countries can explain and correct the low levels of trade found in gravitational equations, thus showing that once these constraints are taken into account, African trade is not lower than in other regions. Therefore, even if African trade has a specific structure, based on different exports to intra regional partners and the others, it is not low when controlling for geographical constraints, and income levels. Low trade is also a consequence of low development. Cottet et al. (2012) also find that for WAEMU countries, traditional products (corresponding to the intensive margin of production) push exports, such as cotton and phosphate for Togo or fishing in Guinea-Bissau.

SADC has experienced a decline of its share of world trade since the mid-1980s. Conversely, intra-regional trade rose as compared to SADC global trade during the 1990s, while members became more open to trade, as seen by Behars and Edward (2011). Though SADC countries do not export much from the SACU, they import much more. Behar and Manners (2008) show that intra SADC trade is higher (more than double), than what their estimates predict for trade between a ember and a non-member. Nevertheless, Chauvin and Gaullier (2002) are skeptical about the SADC Free Trade Agreements, underlining that if a country is ex ante specialised in primary products, regionalisation will just compound that specialisation at the expense of manufacturing sectors. The loss due to regional integration would be especially true for SACU countries, who derive a huge part of their revenue from custom royalties. Besides, apart from a few countries (South Africa, Zimbabwe), which can provide SADC countries with manufactured goods, all SADC countries export mostly primary products. This absence of complementarity makes it difficult to stimulate each other's trade. For SADC trade specifically, authors present administrative trade costs as the main obstacle to trade development in SSA, as well as geographic constraints.

Moreover, Hammouda et al. (2009) have calculated that after integration in SADC countries, it will take 4 years to eliminate 50 % of the income gap between members, but that the remaining half will disappear in 24 years. Integration and convergence are not a monotonous process. They find absolute divergence, and no structural changes in the contributions of labour and capital to productivity. They also show that income distribution is diverging, disparities increasing over time in the SADC.

The Zone Franc is one of the largest monetary union after the European Union. If there are discussions about the exact multiplicative factor of intra trade induced by the monetary union in the zone, it is found that it does stimulate regional trade. Madariaga (2010) studies the openness degree of the WAEMU, and shows that it has been stagnating ever since the end of the 1990s. These countries have specialised in primary products that are less and less demanded on the global market, weakening their economy and trade. The antiquated textile or peanut industries which add this stagnation. WAEMU is more integrated than other RECs, though still much less than other non African REC such as the ASEAN. She shows that intra trade depends of the geographic situation, especially land-locked countries. Besides, if WAEMU exports are more directed outside the zone, they are mostly destined to Nigeria, a neighbouring power that does not belong to the WAEMU. In terms of exports, two countries gain a growing role over the period: Nigeria and China (see Madariaga 2010). Freund and Rocha (2011) study the reasons why there has not been a growth catch up of African RECs. In

ECOWAS states, they find a tendency to grow at similar rates, even though these countries do not have the same initial income per capita. That being said, the dispersion of income is rather narrow in the REC. So there is a tendency for convergence in WAEMU, but towards a low equilibrium. Cottet et al. (2012) try to determine the diversification process of Zone Franc countries. They show that if the growth rate of industrial exports are rather low, there are diversification processes and there differ with the countries. Yet, the newly exported products did not contribute much to the exports growth. The take into consideration innovation and sophistication by using new concentration measures. The idea is that the specialisation of the base industry matters as much as the different products exported. They analyse trade over the two periods, in terms of extensive and intensive margins, extensive margins measuring the exports of new products. New products are those exported during the second period but not the first. They are disconstructed in function of whether they represent a large share of exports or not. Exports in the Zone Franc are highly concentrated, especially for oil exporting countries. Zone Franc exports are actually among the most concentrated in the world. Even if countries do not have the same diversification processes, countries that are the more diversified are also the less concentrated, such as Cote d'Ivoire, Senegal or Togo.

3 Description of the Data

3.1 Data Origin

Our main database is the Base pour l'Analyse du Commerce International (BACI, *Base for International Trade Analysis*) from the *Centre d'Etudes Prospectives et d'Informations Internationales* (CEPII) (Gaulier and Zignago 2010).

BACI data are drawn from UNCTAD's Commodity Trade Statistics (Comtrade) database. This database contains yearly exports flows of at least 1,000 USD, in value and in volume, indicating exporting and importing country, at a six-digit code disaggregation[5] (HS6, Harmonized Commodity Description and Coding System of the World Customs Organization).

Since Comtrade is the compilation of countries' import and export declarations to the UN, this database have some caveats (missing values and frequent unequal quality of declared flows). For instance, around a third of all flows are declared only once. BACI database corrects for some of the caveats, by the use of mirror flows[6]. By doing so, BACI database covers a much larger range of countries than Comtrade database, with higher reliability (more than 239 countries or territories are covered in the BACI database for the 1995–2004 period, instead of 130 countries on average between 1994 and 2007). All SADC and ECOWAS countries are therefore covered by the BACI database.

Some limits may be, however, pointed apart from unreported trade and its corresponding selection biases. Neither BACI nor Comtrade indicate whether exports are re-exports, which may bias analysis of produced goods (see Cottet et al. (2012)). Countries who have access to the littoral will report goods transiting by havens, but will not mention goods entering the country by terrestrial means. Moreover, Comtrade data does not distinguish countries within the South African Custom Union: Botswana, Lesotho, Namibia and South Africa are therefore pooled into a single "country", SACU. This element forces our analysis to consider SACU, rather than South Africa alone, as the leading country within SADC, which may introduce some aggregation bias.

To complement information found in the BACI database, other data are added from different sources. Data for the use of gravity models were drawn from the gravity database (Head et al. 2010). Bilateral distances are population weighted and measure the distance between the two involved countries' capital. Other variables such as trade costs and growth rates are taken from World Bank's World Development Indicators.

Finally, since the HS6 level of disaggregation is too detailed to allow for a relevant sectoral analysis Hammouda et al. (2009), we have used the Broad Economic Categories (BEC) of the UN. BEC classification is built on the different transformation levels, to distinguish for export sophistication and primary use (primary, intermediate, consumption and investment).

3.2 Variables of Interest and Additional Indexes

To carry through our analysis and capture different determinants of regional integration, we use different variables and indexes in this paper.

We first estimate the ratio of intra-regional trade, which is the ratio of exports inside one's region on total exports. We estimate that indicator over the whole period and the mean ratio over periods of 5 years, in order to isolate specific evolution of our variable during the period considered, which might false the estimates over the full period.

We estimate comparative advantages, as defined by Balassa, for several type of goods of BEC classification (primary, intermediate, investment and consumption goods), and we use the "Ellison-Glaeser γ" index (see Ellison and Glaeser (1997), which measures the spatial concentration of firms by sector by comparing the actual distribution of firms or sectors with a random distribution a country's territory (here RECs are taken as the "countries").

4 Models Estimated

4.1 *The Gravitational Equation*

In order to measure regional integration, we base our estimations on the gravitational model, adding variables to account for spatial, cultural and institutional proximity between countries and regions (see Anderson and Van Wincoop 2001). As in Newton's equation, trade flows depend on the size of the two countries considered (here countries i and j) and the costs of bilateral trade, first approximated by distance:

$$M_{ij} = \frac{Y_j^{\alpha} Y_i^{\beta}}{d_{ij}^{\theta}} \tag{1}$$

M_{ij} is the annual trade between countries i and j, Y_j is country j's GDP, Y_i country i's, and d_{ij} the distance between the two of them. The terms α,β and θ represent elasticities of the importing country to import, exporting country to export and of both to the inverse of distance. This equation is a good proxy for trade *potential* between two partners.

We have considered an augmented version of that equation, including variables to measure costs such as the time needed to export a container, or other elements of proximity (language, common border). Moreover, we added growth rates to measure the general trends of the economies considered, thus the evolutions of their size over the time period considered.

Since we follow countries over a timespan of 15 years, we log-linearise our equation to fit panel data. By using logs of variables, we are able to interpret our results directly in terms of growth rates, grasping trends over the years. The basic equation therefore becomes:

$$lnM_{ijt} = \gamma + \alpha lnY_{it} + \beta lnY_{jt} - \theta lnd_{ij} + \epsilon_{ijt} \tag{2}$$

4.2 *OLS Regression on Exports Values*

We start our analysis by estimating the simple gravitational equation, using OLS estimates, and augment it progressively for robustness check. Although this type of estimates are not adapted to all samples, OLS estimates are instructive and widely used by an important part of economic literature on regional integration (see Kepaptsoglou et al. (2010)).

We create a dummy variable for each year, in order to control for time evolutions. We regress the share on the two trading partners' GDP and the log distance between the two countries. Control variables include the countries' areas, the percentage of paved roads in both countries (taken as a proxy for infrastructures) (see Behar and Manners 2008), a dummy for having a common colonizer post 1945 and another for a common legal origin of law (taken as proxies for similar institutions). There is also a dummy for contiguity, meaning direct spatial proximity and another for a shared language, which is a proxy for cultural proximity.

4.3 Panel Analysis Over the Share of Intraregional Trade

Gravitation analysis usually uses values of exports as the dependent variable. To analyze the determinants of intraregional trade, we also regress on the share of intraregional trade, which we define as follows:

$$share_{i,t} = \frac{X_{i,t,intra}}{X_{i,t,total}} \tag{3}$$

where $X_{i,intra}$ are total yearly exports (in value) of country i to countries of its REC, and $X_{i,total}$ are its total exports for the year t.

Regress on $share_{i,t}$, basing our regression equation on Eq. 4, with the idea of the gravitation equation, adding other variables to control for trade costs, infrastructures, economic dynamics and the weight of both the REC and the leader.

Since economic dynamics are taken into account with the value added to GDP (annual percentage of growth) of different sectors, we do not linearize them. Only GDPs and distances are linearized. The equation for the second estimated model is therefore:

$$\begin{aligned} share_{it} = \gamma + \alpha lnY_{i,t} + \beta lnY_{j,t} - \theta lnd_{ij} + \nu_i costs_{i,t} + \nu_j costs_{j,t} + \mu_i infrastructure_{i,t} \\ + \mu_j infrastructure_{j,t} + \eta_i dynamics_{i,t} + \eta_j dynamics_{j,t} + \phi lnY_{lead,t} + \psi lnY_{REC,t} \end{aligned} \tag{4}$$

Given that we follow specific countries, we might have important fixed effects, due to geographical, historical or cultural unobservable determinants (see Nunn 2009 To test this hypothesis, we ran several Hausman tests on the three RECs. Our sample of panel data therefore corresponds to a fixed effect and weak exogeneity frame.

4.4 Clustered OLS Over the Intraregional Share of Trade with Time Dummies

Using fixed effect estimators forbids from using constant variables over the time such as dummies or distances between countries. Consequently, we also used a third estimation model: intraregional share is also regressed with an OLS estimator, including dummies for the different years and other dummies to capture time invariant dimensions (similarly to Eq. 4). OLS regressions with time dummies allow us to capture time invariant aspects belonging to specific regions, therefore representing an alternative way of measuring of fixed effects. We therefore can control for selection biases such as effects for common legal frameworks, contiguity or common spoken languages. Moreover, we control for another source of unobserved fixed effects by clustering our data by exporting countries.

5 Descriptive Statistics

The first striking feature of intra regional trade in SSA is its low level, a feature which has been stable over time. This is true for all three regions, SADC, ECOWAS and WAEMU, when compared to other RECs of the world. Despite the existence of the African Economic Union since 1994, re affirmed in 1999 with the creation of a political entity, the African Union, devoted to the fostering of regional integration, intra African average protection rate is still high, 6.7 %. (African Economic Outlook 2013, OECD).

African RECs have low intra regional trade, around 10 % all over the period (see Fig. 1). Despite the implementation of several protocols since the beginning of the 1990s and resolutions towards bigger integration, intra regional trade remained broadly constant and weak for all three regions, far from the 50 % share of the ALENA. Whereas trade of these RECs grew during the 2000s, intra regional trade stagnated over the period. This goes against the predictions of trade economic theories. The latter does predict that regional integration, for several reasons, will increase trade among members.

5.1 SADC and ECOWAS: A Short Historical Perspective

The South African Development Community was founded in 1992, following the South African Development Co-Ordination and Co-Operation (created in 1980 by nine "Frontline States", Angola, Botswana, Lesotho, Malawi, Mozambique, Swaziland, Tanzania, Zambia, Zimbabwe). The original goal of the SADCC was to reduce members' economic dependence to apartheid South Africa. In 1992, a declaration and a treaty formalised the Co-Ordiantion Conference, and the SADCC became the SADC. South Africa joined the SADC in 1994. The SADCC had a rather market based approach to integration, which is no longer the case in the SADC' objectives. The original strategy was based on imports substitution, along with complementary regional and national programmes (which is not a market based approach). SADC's objectives also included political issues. Regional integration is one of SADC's objectives, as re stated in the SADC Trade Protocol (signed in 1996). Nevertheless, as of today, trade with the rest of the world outweighs regional trade, which represents around 10 % of all SADC's exports (in 2010, 20.4 billion of exports were intra SADC, vs. 164.95 billion to the rest of the world). That proportion remains rather constant over time, as can be seen in the

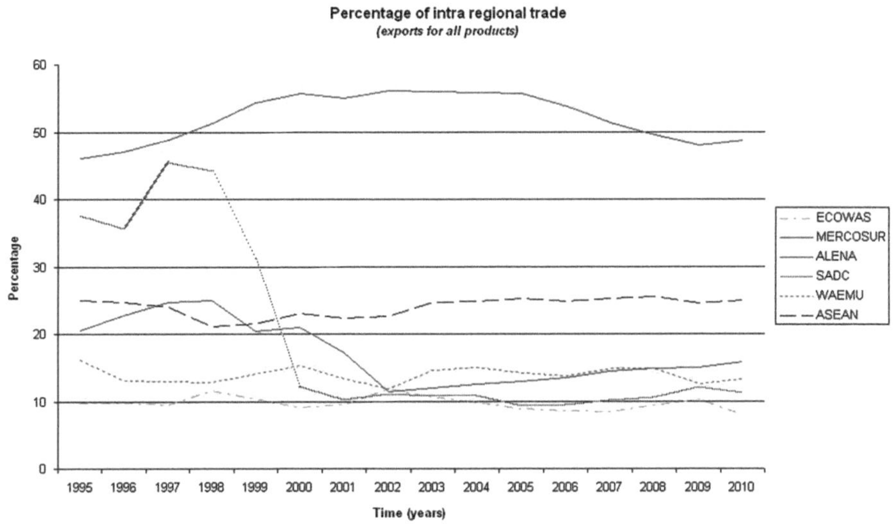

Fig. 1 Model 1:
$v_{ij} = \gamma + \alpha Y_{it} + \beta Y_{jt} - \theta d_{ij} + \delta_1 1_{intratrade} + \delta_2 1_{destination} + \delta_3 1_{origin} + \delta_{t1} 1_{1995} + \ldots + \delta_{t15} 1_{2010} + \lambda X_{ij} + \in_{ijt}$

following table, even though there have been moves from the SADC. There are some partnerships with the EU, but SADC states do not always negotiate agreements as a bloc. As a matter of fact, even between SADC members, some bilateral agreements still exist (for instance, Botswana and Malawi have an Customs Agreement in force ever since 1956). The indicative roadmap stipulates that the FTA should be turned into a Custom Union in 2020, a Common Market in 2015, a monetary union in 2016 and an Economic Union in 2018. The SADC is therefore an evolving REC.

The SADC Trade Protocole aims at creating a free trade area (FTA) and then a Custom Union. The protocole was signed in 1996, but the implementation of the FTA started only in 2000. It was effective in 2008 when SADC joined EAC and COMESA into the African Free Trade Zone. It aimed at reducing 85 % of all intra-SADC tariffs at 0 by 2008, and the rest by 2012. The SADC Free Trade Area was indeed created in 2008. Nevertheless, even if SADC global trade doubled over the period considered (see graphic), intra regional trade remained rather stagnant. Leading trade partners include the European Union, Eastern Asia (especially China) and the North American Free Trade Area. According to Maringwa (2009), there is no conclusive evidence that the SADC Trade Protocols benefits were not purely marginal. The reduction of tariffs has been accompanied by a rise in non tariff trade barriers such as rules of origin. SACU is the heart of SADC, it is 100 years old. The very presence of a custom union within the REC reflects the disparity of members' situations, and of co-operation between the countries. For instance, SACU's GDP represents around two thirds of SADC's total GDP. For the countries involved, it represents a non negligible source of revenue. According to Maringwa (2009), in Lesotho, receipts from the SACU represent 28 % of GDP and 53 % of government revenue. If sACU countries share revenues from their custom union and grow basically at the same rate, this is not true for the totality of SADC members. Between 1990 and 2005, growth rates of GDP ranged from 5.6 % (Zimbabwe) to 10 % for Angola. Both SACU and SADC have their main trading partners are outside Africa. For SACU they are the United States, the MERCOSUR, China and India. SADC's major trading partner remains the European Union.

ECOWAS is older than SADC. This group of 15 countries was created in 1975 by protocols following the African Union Treaty of Lagos, and signed a revised treaty in 1993. The revision of 1993 aimed at accelerating regional integration and increase political co-operation. The third article of the ECOWAS Treaty stipulates that: "The aims of the Community are to promote co-operation and integration, leading to the establishment of an economic union in West Africa in order to raise the living standards of its people, and to maintain and enhance economic stability ..." Regional integration therefore follows a Trade Liberalisation Scheme, similarly to the SADC Trade Protocol. Liberalisation started with unprocessed goods, handicrafts and industrial products of community origin. Condition 4 mentions that "Such goods must be subjected to import clearance procedure spelt out under Nigeria Import and Export Guideline". This explicit reference to Nigerian rules highlights the importance of Nigeria inside ECOWAS. A partnership with the European Union superimposes itself with that Trade Liberalisation Scheme.

The WAEMU was created by the treaty of Dakar in 1994 and in 1997, Guinea-Bissau became its ninth member. WAEMU is the most integrated and is part of the "Zone Franc", alongside the countries of the Economic and Monetary Community of Central Africa (CEMAC) and Comoros. The Franc CFA is pegged to the euro The Union aims at the harmonization of legal frames, the creation of a common market, multilateral monitoring of macroeconomic policies and coordination of sectoral national policies in the main fields of economic activity. Recently, WAEMU members took a further step into regional integration by deciding the creation of Union Parliament, deepening political integration.

We first use trade profiles from the World Trade Organisation (WTO, see Table 1). Global ranks are an absolute measure of trade, and ranks and shares give us the global trade positions of countries and RECS. This allows for a general and comprehensive view of how countries of the SADC and ECOWAS trade. As expected, SADC has a better rank than ECOWAS for trade in merchandises. This difference deepens when it comes to exchange of services. Inside SADC, there are more imports of services than merchandise imports, even though SADC has a better rank for merchandises. SADC imports more merchandises as compared to other countries in the world. These ranks are pushed upwards by a few countries, such as SACU or Angola. This explains partly the differences of rank between SADC and ECOWAS, since there are only a few important exporting countries in ECOWAS (Nigeria and Cote d'Ivoire) and since mean levels of development are lower in ECOWAS than in SADC. Moreover, South trade grew over the period, from 7 % in

Table 1 Mean export flow in value (trillion USD)

Region		1995–2000	2001–2004	2005–2010
ECOWAS	Total	0.027	0.0378	0.089
	Intra regional (% of total exports) (% of total exports)	0.003 (10 %)	0.004 (10.43 %)	0.008(8.5 %)
SADC	Total	41.93518	60.54317	138.246
	Intra regional	4.06461 (9.69 %)	5.749025 (9.49 %)	14.87424(10.7 %)
WAEMU	Total	1,324.366	1,524.298	2,700.318
	Intra regional	147.694 (11 %)	185.846 (12 %)	328.882 (12 %)

Source: BACI database

2006 to 16 % in 2011. From 2002 to 2006, the average annual growth rate of exports was 38 % for Sub Saharan Africa, and 22 % globally.

5.2 *A Brief Presentation of SADC and ECOWAS' Trade Evolutions*

Both regions were in a situation of trade growth over the studied period (1995–2010), with an acceleration starting in 2002. This acceleration is more important for SADC, as can be seen by the clear rupture in trend in Fig. 2 for both imports and imports. This acceleration is less pronounced when it comes to GDP. Since SADC and ECOWAS are so open to the rest of the world, FDI also determine trade patterns. This is even more accurate at the end of the period, when FDI helped countries to go through the crisis, in 2008. The rise in FDI after the crisis was not uniform across all countries. For instance, South African FDI declined of 70 %, while FDI in other countries such as Nigeria or Ghana increased. In 2011, FDI in South Africa nearly tripled, showing the rather volatile patterns followed by investors. Because of the declining demand from non African countries in the aftermath of the crisis, some countries may try to turn themselves to regional trade, for instance Nigerian investors.

The South African GDP represents the bulk of SADC's GDP, even if the share of other countries grew slightly over the years. South Africa was more affected than other SADC members by the 2008 crisis, which means that, by the end of the period, other members' share of SADC's GDP was larger (Bedossa and Letilly 2012). South Africa's growth during the 2000s is fueled mostly by gains in the terms of trade and FDI. Terms of trade improved following a rise in value of exports, due to the demand for raw materials and ore products. In other words, the region's trade patterns have undergone some evolution over our period, which means that regional trade has much evolved during these years too.

For ECOWAS, we find the same general trends, with an acceleration of trade growth in 2002, which is found both in Nigeria, the leading country of the zone, and in the other members. There is a change of trend in 2002, but after that, growth remains steady with no significant change in GDP trends. According to ECOWAS's annual rapport of 2002, the REC accounted for 65 % of West African's GDP, and for 70 % of its population. If the REC is important within the sub-region, relatively to the whole African continent, its weight is smaller, 14 % of GDP and 29 % of population. Nigeria represents 45 % of ECOWAS' GDP, and 66 % of ECOWAS exports involve Nigeria, mainly due to the rise of oil prices. The report also states that, in the aftermath of 9/11, ECOWAS underwent a contraction of its exports, because tightened security measures increased trade costs.

Another reason for the sudden rupture in trend at the beginning of the 2000s is the beginning of several partnerships, such as the US African Growth Act of 2000 (AGOA) or the European "Everything But Arms" Programme (EBA). 13 ECOWAS countries are part of the AGOA. The EBA program implies that Least Developed Countries[7] benefit from duty free and quota free (DFQF) access to the EU for all their exports. If DFQF policies were complete (only a third of LDC's exports are DFQF), the first two beneficiaries should be SADC members: Malawi, who would see a 24 % rise of exports thanks to tobacco, and Zimbabwe, with a 14 % rise of exports. The EBA program is also coupled with a Partnership Economic Agreement, aiming at the creation of a free trade zone between ECOWAS and the EU. These programmes favor trade to the EU or the US, at the expense of regional partners. Yet, they are conditional on investments for the improvement of infrastructures and trade. Three axes were evoked in 2002: easing road transports, liberalise air transport on the sub region and connect together the different rail networks. These are some of the major impediments of African regional trade: the burden of custom procedures (if not corruption) and the poor state of infrastructures. Therefore, these programmes may in the long term facilitate intra regional trade.

Both Nigeria and the rest of ECOWAS also face a sharp rise in exports and imports (see Appendix 1). Nigeria is less hit by the crisis after 2008, as compared to other members, who had started to gain more weight in ECOWAS' trade. The discrepancy between Nigeria and the other countries is much smaller. Most exports are from Nigeria, and if the gap was starting to be filled between 2003 and 3009, the crisis stopped this. In 2010, Nigerian exports were more prominent in ECOWAS than they ever were since 1995.

6 Analysis of Regional Trade Integration

6.1 Simple OLS Show That Belonging to an ERC Has a Positive Effect on Regional Trade

To show if being a member of ECOWAS, SADC or WAEMU, favors intraregional trade, we first regress on exports in values (Eq. 4, see 4.2). We only keep exchanges involving countries from the three regions, as exporters or importers and whichever their partner is. Since our aim is to estimate the effect of the leadership on trade, we include a dummy variable in our regression (this is model 1).

Outcomes of the traditional variables from the gravitation equation evolve broadly as expected: when costs of trade diminish (common language or border), exports grow. This is also true when distance decreases. That result goes against the grain of economic theory, but can be explained. Since we controlled (among all other variables) for contiguity, the distance dummy measures the impact of distance for countries that are *not* geographical neighbours. Since trade outside Africa raised dramatically over the period, it can be assumed that the farthest a country is, the more likely it is that it will be a developed one, with whom the REC has preferential trade agreements. Total value of exports grows when two countries are members of ECOWAS: it is the only region for which regional integration appears to have a significant positive impact on intraregional trade. Neither for SADC nor for WAEMU is this intra coefficient significantly positive. As a first estimate, regional integration does not therefore seem to have any significant influence on intra regional trade for SADC and ECOWAS.

To estimate the determinants of intraregional trade, we then regress intraregional share of total trade. We start with the simple gravitational equation, with intraregional share of trade as our dependent variable and we augment our model progressively. We first include variables of trade costs (approximated by distance in the classic gravitational equation). The second equation adds other cost variables, the third one includes economic dynamics measured by sectoral growth rates and, finally, the fourth and last equation includes several dummies covering the common cultural and institutional backgrounds.

Basic gravitational equations show the expected signs for all three RECs: population-weighted distances have a negative effect on intraregional share of trade and GDP exert a positive influence. The only notable exception is the negative effect of GDP of exporter in ECOWAS in the augmented equation. Other trade costs, reflected by the time export a container also show the expected signs (see Annexes F1 to F3).

Sectoral growth exerts a positive effect on intraregional share of trade in ECOWAS. Industrial growth increases intraregional trade, while growth of the manufacturing industry diminishes the share. This may be linked to structural evolutions: industrial sector grew in terms of GDP %, up to 25.24 %, whereas the manufacturing sector went down (9.26 %, see Appendix 3). The latter appears to be less profitable, a country with a growing manufacture sector would be less economically healthy than a country where the industry sector grows.

6.2 Average Evolution of Intraregional Trade Over the Years

After analysing the determinants of trade, we turn to its evolutions. All three RECs have undergone an important trade growth dynamics between 1995 and 2010. That is reflected by structural changes, exposed in Appendix 3.

To analyze them, we also partition our data into three periods and re-estimated the intraregional trade ratios for each period. By doing, so, we can determine whether the changes that did occur had an influence on intraregional trade. We follow the idea developed in Islam 1995 ("Growth Empirics, A panel data approach", Quarterly Journal of economics, vol 107, pp 407–437) that by setting-up 5 years (not over-lapping) spans, our results are less influenced by business cycle fluctuations and less likely to be serially correlated than they would be in annual data set.

For each period, we regress the mean ratio of intraregional trade on the mean of our variables of interest. We use again a fixed effect (within estimation), controlling for heteroskedasticity by clustering exporters together. Actually, since estimates are means for each period, this is equivalent to using simple OLS estimates, still controlling by cluster (Table 2).

6.2.1 Evolution of Intraregional Trade Between 1995 and 2010

SACU's GDP has a positive effect on intraregional trade, even though that effect diminishes over time. Over the period, intra-regional trade in SADC is therefore less and less dependent on the economic well-being and size of its leader. Conversely, SADC's GDP has a negative effect, which also decreases over time. To further explore intraregional dynamics we analyse variables for exporters and importers separately. The constant growth rate of trade (8 percentage points for each period), is reflected by the growing positive impact on intraregional trade of both imports, and exports growth, of the exporter. This impact start from negative coefficients for 1995–2000 to positive ones for 2005–2010. The negative impact of industry growth of the exporter augmented over the time, even if the industrial sector's size remained rather constant over time. The same effect is found for the manufacturing goods in the exporter, whereas the growth of agriculture in the importers country has a positive impact on intraregional trade.

For ECOWAS, the region's GDP has a positive effect on intra regional trade, for 2001–2004. During that period, the growth of the region's GDP augmented the share of intra regional exports from its members. On the contrary, Nigeria's GDP has a negative impact, meaning that Nigeria's growth over the period was detrimental to other ECOWAS members. The effect of imports growth in the exporting country has changed over time. On the following table, this effect appeared to be small and statistically insignificant. By deconstructing over the years, that coefficient becomes significant (to a 0.1 % level), and varies over time. Indeed, it is negative for 1995–2005 and turns positive. Therefore, an acceleration of imports has a positive

Table 2 Regression of mean intra SADC exports share on mean data

Time period	1995–2000	2001–2004	2005–2010
Exporter			
Population	0.308***	0.218***	0.330***
	(0.042)	(0.030)	(0.030)
GDP	−0.215***	−0.222***	−0.321***
	(0.030)	(0.017)	(0.021)
Mean weighted tariff rate	0.018	0.043***	0.024**
	(0.011)	(0.008)	(0.009)
Percentage of paved road	−0.013	−0.051***	−0.050***
	(0.011)	(0.008)	(0.012)
Economic trends (growth rates,% of GDP)			
Exports	−0.076*	−0.032	0.027
	(0.038)	(0.017)	(0.018)
Imports	0.013	−0.001	0.042***
	(0.018)	(0.009)	(0.008)
Industry	−0.134***	−0.193***	−0.227***
	(0.035)	(0.022)	(0.027)
Agriculture	0.103***	0.059***	0.028*
	(0.012)	(0.011)	(0.011)
Services	−0.240***	−0.119***	−0.026
	(0.036)	(0.031)	(0.034)
Manufacturing	0.209***	0.170***	0.098***
	(0.046)	(0.028)	(0.026)
Importer			
Population	0.026***	0.027***	0.024***
	(0.005)	(0.006)	(0.007)
GDP	−0.024**	−0.033***	−0.040***
	(0.008)	(0.007)	(0.008)
Mean weighted tariff rate	0.011**	0.006	0.002
	(0.004)	(0.005)	(0.005)
Percentage of paved road	−0.003	−0.006	−0.008
	(0.003)	(0.004)	(0.004)
Economic trends (growth rates,% of GDP)			
Exports	−0.005	−0.002	−0.005
	(0.004)	(0.004)	(0.005)
Imports	0.001	0.007	0.014**
	(0.003)	(0.004)	(0.005)
Industry	−0.017*	−0.008	−0.002
	(0.008)	(0.007)	(0.007)
Agriculture	0.029***	0.018***	0.019***
	(0.005)	(0.005)	(0.005)
Services	−0.009	−0.022**	−0.022**
	(0.008)	(0.007)	(0.008)
Manufacturing	0.025**	0.026**	0.024**
	(0.009)	(0.008)	(0.008)

(continued)

Table 2 (continued)

Time period	1995–2000	2001–2004	2005–2010
Regional characteristics			
GDP of leading country (SACU)	0.685***	0.456***	0.052***
	(0.125)	(0.065)	(0.015)
SADC's GDP	−0.734***	−0.477***	−0.032*
	(0.125)	(0.066)	(0.015)

Source: BACI database
Significance level: *5 %, **1 %, ***0.1 %. Standard deviations are in brackets
The coefficient for the constant are not displayed, since they do not have a specific meaning

effect on intraregional trade at the end of our period in ECOWAS as it is the case for SADC's imports. It is also during this last 5-year segment that imports registered a remarkable expansion, of 10 percentage points. The similar evolution of the estimated coefficients for exports comforts that idea (Tables 3 and 4).

For WAEMU countries, there have been some changes in the determinants of intra trade over the years. If, during the first period, the determinants of intra regional trade do not include the economic trends of the exporter (apart from the self-explanatory growth of exports), they become significant over the years. This means that, at the beginning of the 2000s, WAEMU countries export to specific countries, and there is a logic behind the choice of partners. Interestingly enough, the growth of exports of the importer has always been significant. This can be explained by the fact that the bulk of WAEMU exports are to Nigeria, which then re-exports these products to the whole world. Hammouda et al (2009) for instance report the reactions of some exporters, who prefer exporting to Lagos than Cotonou, even if Cotonou is nearer, because corruption and customs burdens are lower in Lagos. Even if the WAEMU has a common exterior tariff since 1994, WAEMU's GDP growth only affects intra regional exports positively from 2000 on.

6.2.2 Fixed Effects Analysis on Intraregional Trade Extends the Study of Integration Determinants

Following the gravitation equation literature, one would expect negative coefficients for mean costs of trade[8], since higher costs should hinder exchanges. Positive signs of coefficients on costs of imports are instructive when it comes to intraregional trade: when trade becomes too expensive for the exporter (or importer). That country will simply export more to its fellow regional members, thus increasing intra zone trade. In other words, intra zone trade can be envisaged as a second best practice, the first best being trading globally (see also Busson and Villa 1994). This result can be confirmed by the significantly negative coefficients attached to the percentage of paved roads: contrary to what would be expected, better infrastructures may boost the internal economy, but not immediately intraregional trade.

Table 3 Regression of intra ECOWAS exports ratio (mean data over 5-year periods)

Time period	1995–2000	2001–2004	2005–2010
Exporter			
Population	0.194	1.120***	−0.086
	(0.129)	(0.114)	(0.093)
GDP	0.437***	−0.896***	0.120
	(0.116)	(0.081)	(0.070)
Mean weighted tariff rate	−0.032*	0.086	−0.316***
	(0.016)	(0.045)	(0.045)
Economic trends (growth rates,% of GDP)			
Exports	−0.064***	0.198***	0.059*
	(0.017)	(0.059)	(0.025)
Imports	−0.036***	−0.316***	0.113***
	(0.009)	(0.052)	(0.022)
Industry	−0.243***	−0.351***	−0.297***
	(0.029)	(0.050)	(0.040)
Agriculture	−0.102***	0.033	0.128***
	(0.012)	(0.027)	(0.017)
Services	−0.062*	−0.008	−0.175***
	(0.029)	(0.057)	(0.023)
Manufactured goods	0.122***	−0.043	0.008
	(0.019)	(0.050)	(0.017)
Importer			
Population	−0.454***	−0.675***	0.027***
	(0.037)	(0.049)	(0.003)
GDP	0.283***	0.250***	−0.019*
	(0.018)	(0.013)	(0.008)
Percentage of paved roads	−0.025	0.305***	0.157***
	(0.026)	(0.041)	(0.024)
Mean weighted tariff rate	0.030**	−0.145***	−0.204***
	(0.011)	(0.017)	(0.036)
Percentage of paved roads	−0.099***	−0.116***	0.071***
	(0.013)	(0.007)	(0.008)
Economic trends (growth rates,% of GDP)			
Exports	0.033*	0.140***	−0.063***
	(0.014)	(0.025)	(0.013)
Imports	−0.052***	0.001	0.069***
	(0.011)	(0.008)	(0.010)
Industry	0.158***	−0.632***	−0.229***
	(0.020)	(0.079)	(0.028)
Agriculture	−0.037**	−0.109***	−0.080***
	(0.013)	(0.018)	(0.008)
Services	−0.039	0.377***	0.028***
	(0.031)	(0.040)	(0.006)
Manufactured goods	−0.117***	0.788***	0.273***
	(0.019)	(0.065)	(0.041)

(continued)

Table 3 (continued)

Time period	1995–2000	2001–2004	2005–2010
Regional characteristics			
Leading country's GDP (Nigeria)	−0.275***	−3.727***	−0.015**
	(0.043)	(0.445)	(0.006)
ECOWAS's GDP	0.060	3.923***	0.010
	(0.064)	(0.450)	(0.008)

Source: BACI database
Significance level: *5 %, **1 %, ***0.1 %. Standard deviations are in brackets
The coefficient for the constant are not displayed, since they do not have a specific meaning

That being said, these results do not apply to the WAEMU, for which signs of trade costs (for both importers and exporters) are the expected one. Trade costs (of exporting for the exporter, of importing for the importer) diminish intraregional trade. This is classical in the sense that costs are classified as "repulsive" forces in the gravitational model. These results might imply two things. Either WAEMU is less prone to intraregional trade and its regional exports act the same way as its total exports, or the presence of tariffs within the region itself make it also difficult for members to remain strictly regional. Nevertheless, for WAEMU countries, dealing with a protectionist importer will also rise the share of intraregional exports. This is significative, contrary to the two other zones, and also hint at the idea of a withdrawal on the region when trade becomes more costly.

Economic dynamics also bend regional trade, but differently depending on regions. For SADC, the growth of industry or manufacturing reduces intraregional trade significantly. Therefore, SADC developing industry causes, ceteris paribus, its members to export more with the rest of the world. Conversely, for ECOWAS states, the growing industries increase slightly and very significantly intraregional trade, whereas the growth of imports and manufacturing goods diminish the share. ECOWAS countries trade more with the rest of the world when they import more and export their manufactured products. This is all the more interesting as we have seen in the first part that ECOWAS is on the whole a less "exporting region" than the SADC. Manufactured goods can refer to craftsmanship, i.e. products that do not use much capital. In our typology, manufactured goods might necessitate machinery, but they are much less capital intensive than industrial goods. For ECOWAS, intraregional trade is more sensitive to imports than exports. Interestingly enough, the same coefficients as ECOWAS have the same sign and significantly for WAEMU, except for agricultural growth. Indeed, if agriculture grows of one basis point, intraregional trade inside WAEMU will also rise by 0.2 basis point. This might be due to the fact that WAEMU gathers important agricultural countries, especially some of the world's first cotton producers (Table 5).

Table 4 Regression of mean intra WAEMU exports share on mean data

Time period	1995–2000	2001–2004	2005–2010
Exporter			
Population	0.208*	0.119*	0.053
	(0.093)	(0.056)	(0.084)
GDP	0.205**	0.045	1.189***
	(0.063)	(0.025)	(0.040)
Mean weighted tariff rate	0.020	−0.013***	2.368***
	(0.013)	(0.002)	(0.089)
Percentage of paved roads	0.207***	0.005	−0.125***
	(0.026)	(0.005)	(0.010)
Economic trends (growth rates,% of GDP)			
Exports	−0.021**	0.015***	0.198***
	(0.007)	(0.004)	(0.033)
Imports	−0.005	−0.028***	−0.510***
	(0.011)	(0.004)	(0.020)
Industry	−0.059*	−0.030***	0.147**
	(0.026)	(0.007)	(0.042)
Agriculture	0.007	0.035***	0.102***
	(0.007)	(0.008)	(0.011)
Service	0.020	0.013*	0.075
	(0.034)	(0.006)	(0.042)
Manufactured goods	0.024	−0.005	−0.205***
	(0.017)	(0.005)	(0.011)
Importer			
population	−0.174***	−0.101***	0.026***
	(0.020)	(0.021)	(0.003)
GDP	0.134***	0.087***	−0.039***
	(0.013)	(0.009)	(0.006)
Mean weighted tariff rates	0.084***	0.009*	−0.184***
	(0.014)	(0.004)	(0.031)
Percentage of paved roads	−0.054***	−0.018***	0.104***
	(0.011)	(0.004)	(0.012)
Economic trends (growth rates,% of GDP)			
Exports	0.032**	−0.007**	−0.128***
	(0.012)	(0.002)	(0.014)
Imports	−0.037***	−0.029***	0.168***
	(0.005)	(0.002)	(0.016)
Industry	0.003	0.033***	−0.306***
	(0.012)	(0.006)	(0.035)
Agriculture	−0.030**	−0.017**	−0.030*
	(0.011)	(0.005)	(0.010)
Services	−0.017	0.003	0.099***
	(0.015)	(0.004)	(0.006)
Manufactured goods	−0.005	0.024***	0.281***
	(0.014)	(0.005)	(0.046)

(continued)

Table 4 (continued)

Time period	1995–2000	2001–2004	2005–2010
Regional characteristics			
Leading country's GDP(Cote d'Ivoire)	−0.143***	−0.055***	−0.621***
	(0.017)	(0.006)	(0.023)
WAEMU's GDP	−0.002*	0.002***	0.020**
	(0.001)	(0.000)	(0.004)

Source: BACI database
Significance level: *5 %, **1 %, ***0.1 %. Standard deviations are in brackets
Regressed directly without a constant

7 Decomposition of Trade by Products

To complement our analysis we deconstruct exports and imports by the type of good traded, something specially important for African economies which are often very concentrated. Diversification is one of the advantages that can theoretically ensue from a better regional integration. As of 2007, programmes such as EBA or AGOA did not really improve product diversification for African trade. 85 % of LDC's exports were made of 25 HS6 products (Table 6). In this section, we examine product diversification first in exports, and then we focus on intra regional exports.

7.1 Changes in Exported Goods

We calculated the mean values of trade flows gathered by types of product, and for each period.

Over the three periods, goods of extracting industries came up on the list. Products of metal and nickel are the first exported type of goods, followed by iron, which has gained importance during these 15 years, and by nickel. Inorganic chemicals disappeared from the list for 2001–2004 but then reappeared. Besides, wood products came down. These results give an indication of the soar in energy prices that occurred at the beginning of the 2000s. An explanation in the growing share of oil exports is the stabilisation of Angola, which is the second largest oil producer after Nigeria in SSA. The rise of products linked to extraction is another explanation of low intra regional trade, since these products (such as diamonds or oil) exported to countries outside the region (Table 7).

For ECOWAS, textiles products (such as silk) disappeared from the most exported goods, while lac, gum and resine augmented. Ships became more and more important too, while wood products made their entrance during the last period[9]. Wooden goods ranked directly five. Oil does not appear in the top ten ECOWAS' exports, even if Nigeria is the first oil producer of SSA. Moreover, ECOWAS counts eight "extracting" countries, versus seven for the SADC. Yet, if metals and ores are among the first traded goods in the two RECs, SADC seems to

Table 5 Fixed-effect estimation of intra-regional trade ratio, 1995–2010

	SADC	ECOWAS	WAEMU
Exporter			
population	−0.004076577***	−0.323510521***	−0.047337041
	(0.000770714)	(0.076875752)	(0.173257396)
GDP (mn _)	−0.0780***	0.0239*	0.1244**
	(0.0079)	(0.0112)	(0.0368)
Cost to export (US$ per container)	−0.000053060**	−0.000111772***	−0.000044038*
	(0.000018093)	(0.000018792)	(0.000016786)
Cost to import (US$ per container)	0.000038243***	−0.000000206	−0.000064871**
	(0.000011277)	(0.000019593)	(0.000021465)
Time to import (days)	0.0014***	0.000175	0.0013
	(0.0004)	(0.0004)	(0.0007)
Tariff rate, applied, weighted mean, all products (%)	0.000066149	0.000828936**	−0.006253384***
	(0.000242001)	(0.000310760)	(0.001104314)
Roads, paved (% of total roads)	−0.000397712***	−0.001401228***	−0.002765417***
	(0.000073010)	(0.000372886)	(0.000485987)
Economic trends: growth rates			
Imports of goods and services (annual % growth)	0.000145091	−0.001261553***	−0.001119525***
	(0.000155504)	(0.000287960)	(0.000320023)
Exports of goods and services (annual % growth)	0.000408348*	0.000852570*	0.000509422
	(0.000163308)	(0.000428083)	(0.000787135)
Industry, value added (annual % growth)	−0.000484488*	0.001074209***	0.002755541***
	(0.000239133)	(0.000311117)	(0.000469804)
Agriculture, value added (annual % growth)	0.000168517	0.000052200	0.001947368***
	(0.000144180)	(0.000272080)	(0.000479473)
Services, etc., value added (annual % growth)	−0.000054820	−0.000809020*	−0.000349384
	(0.000227935)	(0.000369008)	(0.000583473)
Manufacturing, value added (annual % growth)	−0.000617267***	−0.001645939***	−0.002324770***
	(0.000158255)	(0.000267903)	(0.000518500)
Importer			
population	0.001756369	0.056845355	−0.135976796
	(0.001909774)	(0.063222093)	(0.109809738)
GDP (mn$)	0.016425599*	−0.007198164	0.027932032
	(0.007237262)	(0.013564543)	(0.029148366)
Cost to import (US$ per container)	0.000004377	0.000007389	0.000028607**
	(0.000004377)	(0.000005764)	(0.000009780)
Tariff rate, applied, weighted mean, all products (%)	0.000014645	0.000177576	0.004325371*
	(0.000276345)	(0.000420171)	(0.001677678)
Roads, paved (% of total roads)	0.000049275	−0.000017382	−0.000462175
	(0.000096536)	(0.000262154)	(0.000541763)
Economic trends: growth rates			
Imports of goods and services (annual % growth)	−0.000075482	−0.000008970	0.001150078
	(0.000135859)	(0.000330908)	(0.000674224)
Exports of goods and services (annual % growth)	−0.000019526	−0.000130081	−0.000845026*
	(0.000117888)	(0.000240012)	(0.000417794)
Industry, value added (annual % growth)	0.000398687	0.000460876	−0.000262130
	(0.000276043)	(0.000538362)	(0.000950328)

(continued)

Table 5 (continued)

	SADC	ECOWAS	WAEMU
Agriculture, value added (annual % growth)	−0.000105833 (0.000155715)	−0.000086374 (0.000290421)	−0.000131595 (0.000522739)
Services, etc., value added (annual % growth)	−0.000426349 (0.000262965)	0.000498115 (0.000530133)	−0.000790076 (0.000887392)
Manufacturing, value added (annual % growth)	−0.000456908 (0.000250920)	−0.000610559 (0.000473686)	0.000384314 (0.000590137)
Regional characteristics			
GDP of leader ($) (resp. SACU, Cte d'Ivoire, Nigria)	0.057726088*** (0.011255715)	0.118563916*** (0.015572602)	0.023231304*** (0.004817506)
GDP of region of interest ($)	0.006594628 (0.003714945)	−0.019255406*** (0.002681746)	−0.012545219* (0.005620292)
Constant	−0.971795327*** (0.243421059)	−1.805319164*** (0.230472720)	−0.851665187* (0.347116088)

Source: BACI database
Significance level: *5 %, **1 %, ***0.1 %. Standards deviations are in commas

have more developed those exports. Besides, ECOWAS counts several oil producing countries (Niger, and Ghana, though Ghanean oil exploitation started in December 2010), while most of agriculture in ECOWAS is first subsistence agriculture.

We calculated Balassa's index of Revealed Comparative Advantages (RCA) for exports, using the world as a reference[10] (results are available by the authors). If the index is 1 for a sector in particular country, then the share of exports for that sector, as compared to total national exports corresponds to the same share in the world as a whole. In most cases, SACU has revealed comparative advantages of around one, meaning it has exactly the same specialisation as the rest of the world.

For ECOWAS, RCA indexes are much higher than one for primary goods, and are higher than for investments or even consumption goods. Indeed, most countries rely on ores and extracting activities, from oil to iron and diamonds, and on their agricultural production (such as cashew nuts for Guinea at the beginning of the period). Both types of products are classified as primary. For instance, inside ECOWAS, Guinea exports nine times more primary products than the rest of the world. It first exports minerals, such as bauxite, aluminia, gold and diamonds, and then agricultural products such as coffee and fish. For SADC, Balassa's index for primary goods are really high, 3.21 on average for the whole 1995–2010 period. Conversely, few countries have a RCA index much higher than one for consumption goods, apart from the Seychelles, whose economic development goes through tourism and exports of a few agricultural product (tuna fish, cinnamon bark), though agriculture represents only 2 % of Seychelles' GDP (see World Factbook). Indeed, the Balassa's index for agriculture of the Seychelles is low, around 0.6.

Nevertheless, industry appears less developed for SADC: apart from the SACU, which has an index of around one, no country has a high index. Most of them export around half less than the rest of the world of intermediary goods. Flows for

Table 6 Top 10 average exported products (in value), SADC

1995–2000	1	Base metal nesoi cermets articles
	2	Nickel and articles thereof
	3	Pulp of wood, waste and scrap of paper
	4	Furskins and artificial fur, manufactures
	5	Cork and articles of cork
	6	Ores slag and ash
	7	Wool and fine or coarse animal hair, including yarns and woven fabrics thereof
	8	Organic chemicals
	9	Lead and articles thereof
	10	Inorganic chemicals, organic and inorganic compounds of precious metals, isotopes
2001–2004	1	Base metal nesoi cermets articles
	2	Nickel and articles thereof
	3	Furskins and artificial fur, manufactures
	4	Wool and fine or coarse animal hair, including yarns and woven fabrics thereof
	5	Cork and articles of cork
	6	Lead and articles thereof
	7	Ores slag and ash
	8	Pulp of wood, waste and scrap of paper
	9	Silk including yarns and woven fabrics thereof
	10	Musical instruments, parts and accessories
2005–2010	1	Base metal nesoi cermets articles
	2	Nickel and articles thereof
	3	Wool and fine or coarse animal hair, including yarns and woven fabrics thereof
	4	Cork and articles of cork
	5	Ores slag and ash
	6	Organic chemicals
	7	Silk including yarns and woven fabrics thereof
	8	Pulp of wood, waste and scrap of paper
	9	Furskins and artificial fur, manufactures
	10	Musical instruments, parts and accessories

Source: BACI database authors calculations
Level of disaggregation is HS2 (1992)

ECOWAS are sometimes scarce, we reported the number of trade flows when it was less than a hundred[11]. For consumption goods, ECOWAS's indexes are above one (on average for 1995–2010, 1.55), meaning that ECOWAS's countries are exporting relatively more consumption goods than the rest of the world. This highlights the need of diversification of ECOWAS economies, even if the difference between primary and consumption goods can be tenuous for edible products.

Table 7 Top 10 average exported products (in value), ECOWAS

1995–2000	1	Lead and articles thereof
	2	Products of animal origin (except fish)
	3	Nickel and articles thereof
	4	Tin and articles thereof
	5	Base metals nesoi, cermets, articles
	6	Lac gums, resins
	7	Ores slag and ash
	8	Ships, boats, floating structures
	9	Cork and articles of cork
	10	Organic chemicals
2001–2004	1	Base metals nesoi, cermets, articles
	2	Lead and articles thereof
	3	Products of animal origin (except fish)
	4	Lac, gums, resins
	5	Ships, boats, floating structures
	6	Nickel and articles thereof
	7	Organic chemicals
	8	Tin and articles thereof
	9	Silk, yarns and woven fabrics thereof
	10	Furskins and artificial fur, manufactures
2005–2010	1	Base metals nesoi, cermets, articles
	2	Products of animal origin except fish
	3	Lead and articles thereof
	4	Lac, gums, resins,
	5	Pulp of wood, waste and scrap of paper
	6	Ships, boats and floating structures
	7	Furskins and artificial fur, manufactures
	8	Ores slag and ash
	9	Nickel and articles thereof
	10	Raw hides and skins and leather

Source: Authors calculations. Level of disaggregation is HS2 (1992)

8 Conclusion

In this study, we used the gravitational model in order to browse the determinants of regional integration in three sub Saharan African REC, ECOWAS and SADC. These two CERs have experienced over the past 15 years economic growth, though less important than in the preceding decades. Trade expansion was marked by the rise of more peripheral countries than the leading SACU and Nigeria. We observe that regional integration does not appear to be sought per se, but as a second best relatively to global trade. Besides, over the period, the impact for leading countries is positive for all three RECs and for all sectors, even if differences in magnitude of these effects exist between sections and countries. The rippling effect of the leader's wealth always exists, only it is more or less strong depending on the sector and REC. In the case of SACU, the effect is ten times more important for consumption and intermediary goods, than for primary or capital goods.

Appendix 1: Evolution of Imports and Exports for SADC and ECOWAS

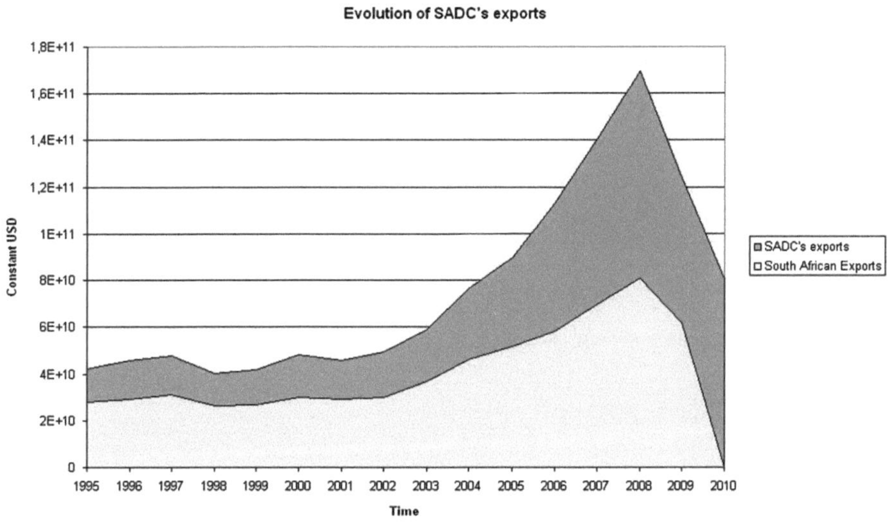

Fig. 2 SADC exports (WTO data)

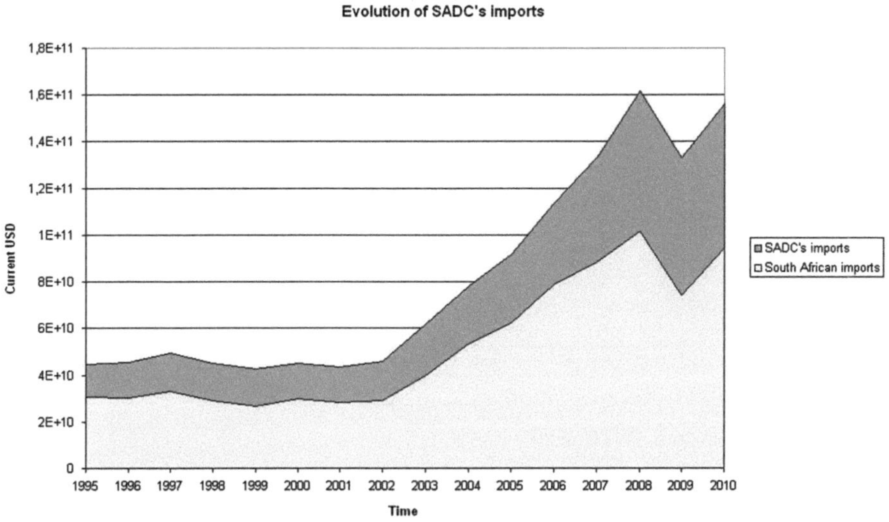

Fig. 3 SADC imports (WTO data)

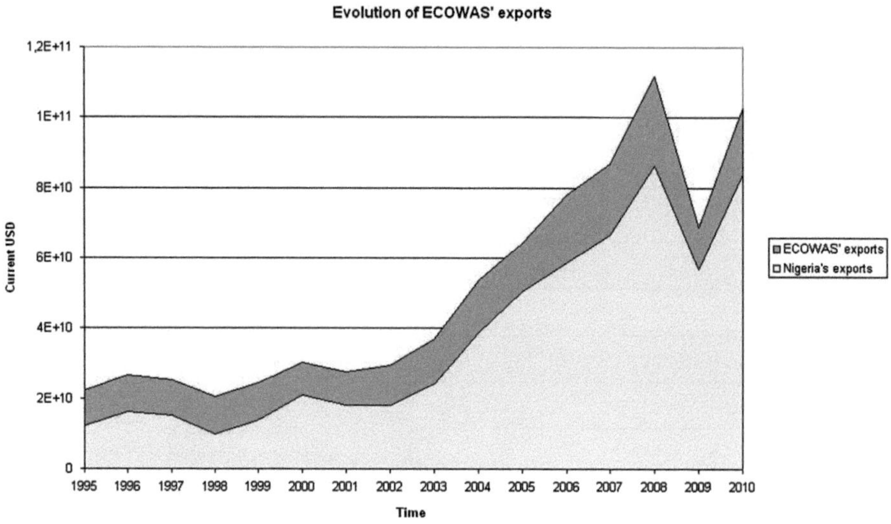

Fig. 4 ECOWAS exports (WTO data)

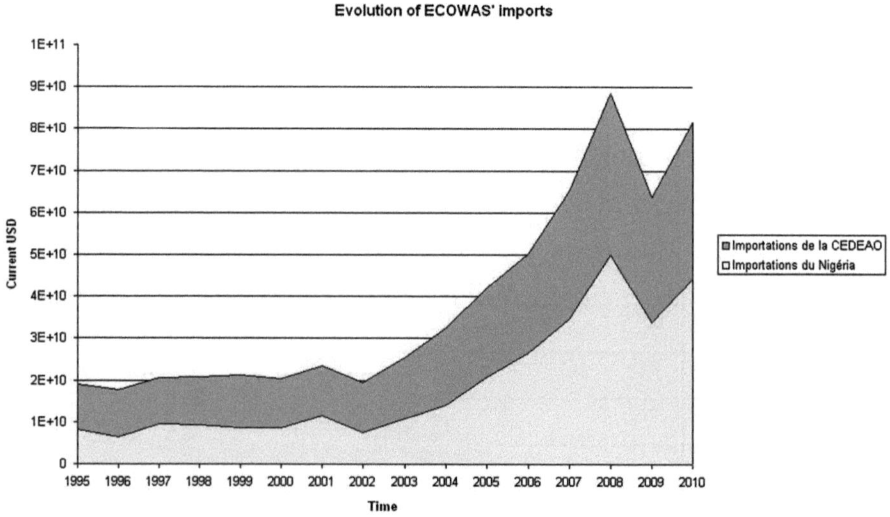

Fig. 5 ECOWAS imports (WTO data)

Appendix 2: Share of Global Flows in 2010

	Imports				Exports			
Country	Share of exchanges		Global rank		Share of exchanges		Global rank	
ECOWAS	Merchandises	Services	Merchandises	Services	Merchandises	Services	Merchandises	Services
Benin	0.01	0.02	148	148	0.01	0.01	140	151
Burkina Faso	0.01	0.02	151	142	0.01	0	142	163
Cote d'Ivoire	0.05	0.06	99	95	0.07	0.02	82	126
The Gambia	0	0	191	185	0	0	190	176
Ghana	0.07	0.07	86	90	0.05	0.04	94	105
Guinee	0.01	0.01	159	159	0.01	0	138	179
Guinee-Bissau	0	0	195	190	0	0	178	190
Liberia	na	na	na	na	na	na	na	
Mali	0.02	0.03	138	130	0.01	0.01	128	144
Niger	0.01	0.03	144	120	0.01	0	147	171
Nigeria	0.29	0.58	50	35	0.55	0.07	37	85
Senegal	0.03	0.03	119	122	0.02	0.01	125	118
Sierra Leone	na	na	171	174	na	na	165	180
Togo	0.01	0.01	157	154	0.01	0.01	155	148
ECOWAS	0.51	0.86	139.1	134.2	0.75	0.17	132.4	148.9
SADC	Merchandises	Services	Merchandises	Services	Merchandises	Services	Merchandises	Services
South Africa	0.61	0.51	32	39	0.53	0.36	38	44
Angola	0.12	0.46	73	na	0.33	0.02	53	na
Botswana	0.04	0.02	105	131	0.03	0.01	109	143
Lesotho	0.01	0.01	144	151	0	0.01	149	183
Malawi	0.01	0	147	180	0.01	0	145	167
Mauritius	0.03	0.06	124	101	0.01	0.07	124	83
Mozambique	0.03	0.03	121	118	0.02	0.02	119	131
Namibie	0.04	0.02	108	138	0.03	0.02	114	121
Democratic Republic of Congo	0.03	0.07	121	89	0.03	0.01	103	149
Seychelles	0	0.01	178	153	0	0.02	162	129
Swaziland	0.01	0.02	152	143	0.01	0.01	130	153
Tanzanie	0.05	0.05	100	103	0.03	0.05	113	93
Zambie	0.03	0.03	111	129	0.05	0.01	95	147
Zimbabwe	0.02	na	130	145	0.02	na	122	157
SADC	1.03	1.29	117.6	131.8	1.1	0.61	112.6	138

Fig. 6 WTO data for 2010. *na* not available

Country	Imports				Exports			
	Share of exchanges		Global rank		Share of exchanges		Global rank	
WAEMU	Merchandises	Services	Merchandises	Services	Merchandises	Services	Merchandises	Services
Benin	0.01	0.02	148	148	0.01	0.01	140	151
Burkina Faso	0.01	0.02	151	142	0.01	0	142	163
Cote d'Ivoire	0.05	0.06	99	95	0.07	0.02	82	126
Guinee-Bissau	0	0	195	190	0	0	178	190
Mali	0.02	0.03	138	130	0.01	0.01	128	144
Niger	0.01	0.03	144	120	0.01	0	147	171
Senegal	0.03	0.03	119	122	0.02	0.01	125	118
Togo	0.01	0.01	157	154	0.01	0.01	155	148
WAEMU	0.14	0.2	143.9	137.6	0.14	13.1	151.4	

Appendix 3: Exports Adressee Over Time

Percentage of exports by destination (in terms of revenue)

	SADC			ECOWAS			WAEMU		
	1995–2000	2001–2004	2005–2010	1995–2000	2001–2004	2005–2010	1995–2000	2001–2004	2005-2010
High income countries	72.65	71.75	59.65	63.32	56.2	47.32	51.15	39.78	37.7
Arab-world	2.07	1.65	2.9	1.57	1.1	1.86	2.51	1.81	2.57
Developing countries in SSA	12.04	13.56	18.45	12.1	19.43	20.4	21.35	34.91	33.71
Developing countries outside SSA	9.98	10.09	19.64	15.44	16.13	24.62	24.67	19.78	24.07

Source: World Bank Indicators

Appendix 4: Openness Rate

REC and leading country's openness rate over the period

REC	1995–2000	2001–2004	2005–2010
SADC	0.56	0.33	0.74
SACU	0.52	0.58	0.63
ECOWAS	0.35	0.36	0.36
Nigeria	0.80	0.75	0.70
WAEMU	0.63	0.66	0.70
Cote d'Ivoire	0.74	0.81	0.85

Source: Based on world development indicators

Appendix 5: Basic Gravitational Model and Augmented Equations

SADC OLS Estimates, 1995–2010

Fixed effects were controlled by time dummies and clustering of exporters

	Model 1 (gravitation equation)	Model 2 (1 + trade costs)	Model 3 (2 + economic dynamics)	Model 4 (3 + institutions)
GDP of exporter (current mn US$)	0.000000001	0.000000001	0.000000001	0.000000001*
	(0.000000000)	(0.000000000)	(0.000000000)	(0.000000000)
GDP of importer (current mn US$)	0.000000001**	0.000000000*	0.000000001*	0.000000000
	(0.000000000)	(0.000000000)	(0.000000000)	(0.000000000)
Weighted distance (population-weight, km)	−0.000003004***	−0.000002914***	−0.000002885***	−0.000001954***
	(0.000000838)	(0.000000811)	(0.000000800)	(0.000000512)
Exporter				
Cost to export (US$ per container)		−0.000012448	−0.000011709	−0.000011726
		(0.000006686)	(0.000006054)	(0.000006035)
Cost to import (US$ per container)		0.000008550	0.000007970	0.00000685
		(0.000005414)	(0.000005030)	(0.000005220)
Time to import (days)		0.000173185*	0.000198581*	0.000228833**
		(0.000078263)	(0.000085367)	(0.000083857)
Tariff rate, applied, weighted mean, all products (%)		0.000006846	0.000021378	0.000011251
		(0.000024706)	(0.000026089)	(0.000022954)

(continued)

	Model 1 (gravitation equation)	Model 2 (1 + trade costs)	Model 3 (2 + economic dynamics)	Model 4 (3 + institutions)
Cost to import (US$ per container)		0.000000132 (0.000000510)	0.000000401 (0.000000399)	−0.000000136 (0.000000294)
Tariff rate, applied, weighted mean, all products (%)		0.000032694 (0.000017001)	0.000026469* (0.000011181)	0.000013999 (0.000011366)
Roads, paved (% of total roads)			−0.000029349 (0.000020205)	−0.000010680 (0.000013149)
Imports of goods and services (annual % growth)			−0.000007605 (0.000053674)	−0.000018766 (0.000054253)
Exports of goods and services (annual % growth)			0.000070816 (0.000059433)	0.000056221 (0.000051594)
Industry, value added (annual % growth)			0.000009226 (0.000072071)	0.000004208 (0.000058474)
Agriculture, value added (annual % growth)			−0.000010594 (0.000070553)	−0.000013587 (0.000061138)
Services, etc., value added (annual % growth)			−0.000148587 (0.000140470)	−0.000166438 (0.000139898)
Manufacturing, value added (annual % growth)			−0.000114466* (0.000054550)	−0.000097469* (0.000047385)
Importer				
Roads, paved (% of total roads)			−0.000010782 (0.000006728)	0.000007247 (0.000007129)
Imports of goods and services (annual % growth)			0.000010774 (0.000011594)	0.000001520 (0.000014575)
Exports of goods and services (annual % growth)			−0.000016723 (0.000015576)	−0.000037042* (0.000016295)
Industry, value added (annual % growth)			0.000066738* (0.000029604)	0.000070025** (0.000025805)
Agriculture, value added (annual % growth)			0.000037383 (0.000021450)	0.000045505 (0.000023248)

(continued)

	Model 1 (gravitation equation)	Model 2 (1 + trade costs)	Model 3 (2 + economic dynamics)	Model 4 (3 + institutions)
Services, etc., value added (annual % growth)			0.000027666 (0.000050221)	0.000023322 (0.000046408)
Manufacturing, value added (annual % growth)			−0.000014076 (0.000012133)	0.000007503 (0.000014244)
Regional characteristics				
Gdp of leader (constant 2000 US $)			−0.000000000 (0.000000000)	−0.000000000 (0.000000000)
Gdp of region (constant 2000 US $)			0.000000000 (0.000000000)	0.000000000 (0.000000000)
Battle-related deaths (exporter) (number of people)				−0.000002088* (0.000000824)
Battle-related deaths (importer) (number of people)				−0.000001408*** (0.000000406)
One for contiguity				0.099817336*** (0.029764886)
One if a language is spoken by at least 9 % of the				0.004121298**
Population in both countries				(0.001508841)
Common legal origin				−0.000580729 (0.000898401)
One for common colonizer post 1945				0.001117352 (0.001974749)
Constant	0.028849828*** (0.007876255)	0.026713916*** (0.007193926)	0.029642768*** (0.008225510)	0.018059550*** (0.005087587)

ECOWAS OLS Estimates, 1995–2010

Fixed effects were controlled by time dummies and clustering of exporters

	Model 1 (gravitation equation)	Model 2 (1 + trade costs)	Model 3 (2 + economic dynamics)	Model 4 (3 + institutions)
GDP of exporter (current mn US$)	−0.000000960* (0.000000326)	−0.000001132* (0.000000465)	−0.000001173* (0.000000533)	−0.000015005* (0.000004826)
GDP of importer (current mn US$)	−0.000000087 (0.000000131)	−0.000000061 (0.000000101)	−0.000000151 (0.000000071)	0.000001939 (0.000004457)
Weighted distance (pop-wt, km)	0.000005193 (0.000009137)	0.000006148 (0.000010041)	0.000005238 (0.000009545)	0.000075857 (0.000190024)
Exporter				
Cost to export (US$ per container)		−0.000115243 (0.000091437)	−0.000108617 (0.000104151)	0.000459655* (0.000155192)
Cost to import (US$ per container)		0.000050395 (0.000083671)	0.000043277 (0.000079621)	−0.001066940 (0.000606337)
Time to import (days)		0.000924354 (0.002546651)	0.000736402 (0.002977881)	0.010367521 (0.007412750)
Tariff rate, applied, weighted (%) mean, all products		0.003520863 (0.003922823)	0.003746173 (0.003764270)	0.018791017* (0.006556396)
Cost to import (US$ per container)		0.000014441 (0.000015366)	0.000005392 (0.000006381)	0.000774740* (0.000296712)
Tariff rate, applied, weighted(%) mean, all products		0.000686430 (0.000551083)	0.000421525 (0.000431472)	−0.021068090 (0.013394095)
Roads, paved (% of total roads)			0.000036881 (0.001157985)	−0.002504209 (0.001797708)
Imports of goods and services (annual % growth)			0.000378399 (0.001039557)	−0.020548336 (0.022497233)
Exports of goods and services (annual % growth)			0.000276975 (0.001674619)	0.005332885 (0.007611829)
Industry, value added (annual % growth)			0.000453099 (0.002276938)	0.098618160* (0.033762821)
Agriculture, value added (annual % growth)			0.001121895 (0.001469741)	−0.006290263 (0.006273985)
Services, etc., value added (annual % growth)			0.002887031 (0.003784952)	0.014486231 (0.013672443)
Manufacturing, value added (annual % growth)			0.003395197 (0.002307559)	−0.077503931* (0.033539057)
Importer				
Roads, paved (% of total roads)			−0.000285483 (0.000275832)	0.000742602 (0.003777166)

(continued)

	Model 1 (gravitation equation)	Model 2 (1 + trade costs)	Model 3 (2 + economic dynamics)	Model 4 (3 + institutions)
Imports of goods and services (annual % growth)			−0.000302464	0.014471593
			(0.000453357)	(0.017789164)
Exports of goods and services (annual % growth)			−0.000308690	0.002742438
			(0.000398954)	(0.006664289)
Industry, value added (annual % growth)			0.000031377	−0.091392420
			(0.000318239)	(0.042510859)
Agriculture, value added (annual % growth)			0.000182207	0.006297388
			(0.000302425)	(0.006035650)
Services, etc., value added (annual % growth)			0.000198404	0.012793635
			(0.000445730)	(0.011674590)
Manufacturing, value added (annual % growth)			−0.000578954	0.057728605
			(0.000540759)	(0.034012653)
Regional characteristics				
GDP of leading country (current 2000 $)			0.000000000	0.000000000
			(0.000000000)	(0.000000000)
GDP of ECOWAS region (constant 2000 $)			−0.000000000	−0.000000000
			(0.000000000)	(0.000000000)
Battle-related deaths (number of people)				−0.000081264
				(0.000070125)
Battle-related deaths (number of people)				0.000068705
				(0.000060424)
One for contiguity				−0.059559681
				(0.271821973)
One if a language is spoken by at least 9 % of the				1.599560467
Population in both countries				(0.828583121)
Common legal origin				0.102372882
				(0.216002581)
One for common colonizer post 1945				−1.586363038
				(0.820105020)
Constant	0.187384902***	0.167476627***	0.137809526**	−0.079552334
	(0.041405699)	(0.039919778)	(0.042599790)	(0.495759783)

WAEMU OLS Estimates, 1995–2010

Fixed effects were controlled by time dummies and clustering of exporters

	Model 1 (gravitation equation)	Model 2 (1 + trade costs)	Model 3 (2 + economic dynamics)	Model 4 (3 + institutions)
GDP of exporter (current mn US$)	−0.000000000	−0.000000000	−0.000000000	−0.000000000
	(0.000000000)	(0.000000000)	(0.000000000)	(0.000000000)
GDP of importer (current mn US$)	−0.000000000*	−0.000000000*	−0.000000000	0.000000000
	(0.000000000)	(0.000000000)	(0.000000000)	(0.000000000)
Weighted distance (pop-wt, km)	−0.000001779***	−0.000001791***	−0.000001757***	−0.000000798***
	(0.000000401)	(0.000000399)	(0.000000389)	(0.000000214)
Exporter				
Cost to export (US$ per container)		−0.000009936*	−0.000009299*	−0.000008130*
		(0.000004289)	(0.000004572)	(0.000003976)
Cost to import (US$ per container)		0.000005274	0.000004745	0.000004186
		(0.000003494)	(0.000003494)	(0.000003209)
Time to import (days)		0.000064534	0.000058168	0.000032796
		(0.000096272)	(0.000097278)	(0.000096182)
Tariff rate, applied, weighted mean, all products (%)		0.000118866	0.000095386	0.000075451
		(0.000091782)	(0.000086703)	(0.000088764)
Cost to import (US$ per container)		0.000000942	0.000000770	0.000000942
		(0.000000840)	(0.000000775)	(0.000000758)
Tariff rate, applied, weighted mean, all products (%)		0.000111615	0.000087984	0.000076596
		(0.000074316)	(0.000072198)	(0.000079729)
Roads, paved (% of total roads)			−0.000055291***	−0.000037049**
			(0.000015385)	(0.000013674)
Imports of goods and services (annual % growth)			−0.000035008	−0.000012145
			(0.000029788)	(0.000031593)
Exports of goods and services (annual % growth)			−0.000048767	−0.000016545
			(0.000072200)	(0.000069934)
Industry, value added (annual % growth)			0.000148573*	0.000101431
			(0.000069662)	(0.000066706)
Agriculture, value added (annual % growth)			0.000086167	0.000057251
			(0.000050273)	(0.000044947)
Services, etc., value added (annual % growth)			0.000036206	0.000060004
			(0.000152650)	(0.000152550)

(continued)

	Model 1 (gravitation equation)	Model 2 (1 + trade costs)	Model 3 (2 + economic dynamics)	Model 4 (3 + institutions)
Manufacturing, value added (annual % growth)			−0.000041814 (0.000038035)	−0.000016755 (0.000039536)
Importer				
Roads, paved (% of total roads)			−0.000049864*** (0.000012704)	−0.000030800*** (0.000008273)
Imports of goods and services (annual % growth)			−0.000008420 (0.000022849)	0.000008147 (0.000025243)
Exports of goods and services (annual % growth)			−0.000053836** (0.000020593)	−0.000026318 (0.000018607)
Industry, value added (annual % growth)			0.000020976 (0.000026313)	0.000000716 (0.000019149)
Agriculture, value added (annual % growth)			0.000046383* (0.000020890)	0.000023266 (0.000015461)
Services, etc., value added (annual % growth)			−0.000010895 (0.000056939)	0.000026368 (0.000054923)
Manufacturing, value added (annual % growth)			−0.000006651 (0.000011822)	0.000013370 (0.000018074)
Regional Characteristics				
GDP of leading country constant 2000 $			0.000000000 (0.000000000)	0.000000000 (0.000000000)
GDP of UEMOA region constant 2000 $			−0.000000000 (0.000000000)	−0.000000000 (0.000000000)
Battle-related deaths, exporter (number of people)				−0.000000809 (0.000000492)
Battle-related deaths, importer (number of people)				−0.000000809*** (0.000000159)
One for contiguity				0.051125214*** (0.013101407)

(continued)

	Model 1 (gravitation equation)	Model 2 (1 + trade costs)	Model 3 (2 + economic dynamics)	Model 4 (3 + institutions)
One if a language is spoken by at least 9 % of the population in both countries				0.014887259*** (0.003690201)
Constant	0.016294816*** (0.003662205)	0.015272784*** (0.003283899)	0.017400122*** (0.003799242)	0.006183705** (0.001855934)

References

Adeaoti, Alii (2012) Foresight Africa top priorities for the continent on 2012. Annual report, Africa Growth Initiative at Brookings

Alemayehu G, Haile K (2002) Regional integration in Africa: a review of problems and prospects with a case study of COMESA. Final draft

Anderson JE, van Wincoop E (2001) Gravity with gravitas: a solution to the border puzzle, NBER working paper series 8079. NBER, Cambridge, MA

Bedossa B, Letilly G (2012) La crise _conomique mondiale de 2008–2009: quels impacts dans les pays d'Afrique subsaharienne? Macrodev 2

Behar A, Edward L (2011) Trends in intra-regional and extra-regional trade flows and policy, Policy research working paper 5625. World Bank Development Research Group, Washington

Behar A, Manners P (2008) Logistics and exports, Working paper series 2008–13. Centre for the Study of African Economies, University of Oxford, Oxford

Busson F, Villa P (1994) Croissance et sp_cialisation, Working paper 1994–12, CEPII, Paris

Chauvin S, Gaulier G (2002) Regional trade integration in South Africa. Discussion paper

Cottet N, Madariaga N, Gou NJ (2012) La diversification des exportations en zone franc: degr_, sophistication et dynamique, Macrodev 3. Discussion paper

Easterly W, Reshef A (2009) Big hits in manufacturing exports and development. Discussion paper

Ellison G, Glaeser EL (1997) Geographic concentration in U.S. manufacturing industries: a dartboard approach. J Polit Econ 105(5):889–927

Flatters F, Stern M (2006) SACU revenue sharing: issues and options. Policy brief, USAID RCSA and USAID South Africa (under Trade Policy Development Project and Support for Growth and Analysis II)

Freund C, Rocha N (2011) What constrains Africa's exports? World Bank Econ Rev 25 (3):361–386

Gaulier G, Zignago S (2010) BACI: international trade database at the product-level the 1994–2007 Version, Working paper 2010–23. CEPII, Paris

Hammouda B, Karingi N, Jallab S (2009) Why doesn't regional integration improve income convergence in Africa? Afr Dev Rev 21(2):291–330, Wiley

Head K, Mayer T, Ries J (2010) The erosion of colonial trade linkages after independence. J Int Econ 81(1):1–14

Kepaptsoglou K, Karlaftis MG, Tsamboulas D (2010) The gravity model specification for modeling international trade flows and free trade agreement effects: a 10-year review of empirical studies. Open Econ J 3:1–13

Krugman P (1980) Scales economies, product differentiation and the pattern of trades. Am Econ Rev 70(5):950–959

Krugman P (1991) Increasing returns and economic geography. J Polit Econ 99(1):483–499
Krugman P, Venables AJ (1990) Integration and the competitive of peripheral industry, Discussion paper 363. Centre for Economic Policy Research, London
Madariaga N (2010) Mesure et Evolution récentede l'intégration commerciale en zone Franc. Macrodev, n°1
Maringwa J (2009) SADC regional integration: what role has bilateral trade agreements played in promoting regional trade? Discussion paper, Trade & Industrial Policy Strategies, AusAID
Nunn N (2009) The importance of history for economic development. Annu Rev Econ 1(1):65–92

Terrorism and Regional Integration in Sub-Saharan Africa: The Case of the CFA Franc Zone

Juliet U. Elu and Gregory N. Price

Abstract To the extent that regional currency integration changes the cost of imported inputs used in the production of terror, it can change the supply of terror produced by rational terrorists. In this paper, we appeal to a theory of rational terrorism where a country's membership in a regional currency union conditions the cost of imported inputs that produce terror, and estimate the parameters of static and dynamic terrorism supply functions with Generalized Estimating Equation count data estimators for Sub-Saharan Africa between 1974 and 2006. Our parameter estimates reveal that regional currency integration has counter-terrorism benefits as countries with membership in the newly constituted CFA Franc Zone had fewer terrorism incidents relative to other Sub-Saharan African countries. Our parameter estimates also suggest that the CFA Franc Zone caused a decrease in terrorism. As terrorism constrains important drivers of economic growth, our results suggest that another potential channel by which regional currency integration improves living standards in Sub-Saharan Africa is through reducing terrorism.

Keywords Regional Integration • Terrorism • Sub-saharan Africa

1 Introduction

After the September 11, 2001 terrorist attacks on the World Trade Center and Pentagon in the USA, Sub-Saharan Africa has been increasingly recognized as a region warranting special counter-terrorism attention. (Abrahamsen 2004;

For critical but helpful comments, the authors thank participants of the Third Annual Conference on Regional Integration in Africa, Center for Research On Political Economy (CREPOL), Dakar, Senegal, July 4–5, 2012.

J.U. Elu (✉) • G.N. Price
Department of Economics, Morehouse College, 830 Westview Dr. SW, 30314 Atlanta, GA, USA
e-mail: jelu@morehouse.edu; gprice@morehouse.edu

D. Seck (ed.), *Regional Economic Integration in West Africa*, Advances in African Economic, Social and Political Development, DOI 10.1007/978-3-319-01282-7_10,

Cilliers 2003). This attention is underscored by the fact that since the late 1980s, sub-state terrorist activity in countries such as Burundi, Democratic Republic of the Congo, Liberia and Sudan have resulted in the loss of almost a million lives and significant destruction of physical property (Cilliers 2003). To the extent that terrorism is fueled by apocalyptic and radical religious beliefs, Abrahamsen (2004), notes that British counter-terrorism objectives in Sub-Saharan Africa recognize that there are more Muslims in Sub-Saharan Africa than there are in the Middle East – which may increase the likelihood of radical Islamist terrorism.[1]

To the extent that regional currency integration lowers transaction costs for all economic activities (Alesina and Barro 2002; Debron et al. 2003; Masson 2008; McKinnon 1963) and increases the gains to trade with member countries, regional currency integration, by changing the cost of importing terrorism inputs, could potentially have a negative or positive effect on terrorism in Sub-Saharan Africa. In this paper we examine the effects of membership in the CFA Franc Zone (CFAZ) on terrorism in Sub-Saharan Africa. We consider the time period 1974–2006 for which country-level terrorism incident data are available and which permits a consideration of the causal effects of country membership in CFAZ starting in 1999 when it was newly constituted by having all member country currencies pegged to the euro. Our inquiry contributes to a broad literature on the economic causes and consequences of terrorism (Abadie 2006; Abadie and Gardeazabal 2008; Chen and Siems 2004; Gould and Klor 2010). As we consider the extent to which terrorism in Sub-Saharan Africa is affected by regional currency integration, we add to the literature which views the decision to produce terror as a function of costs and benefits (Arce and Sandler 2003; Brandt and Sandler 2009; Elu 2012; Sautter 2010; Wintrobe 2006).

The remainder of this paper is organized as follows. In the second section we modify the rational terrorist framework of Elu and Price (2012) to generate a testable proposition about the effects of regional currency integration on terrorism in Sub-Saharan Africa. We postulate a causal nexus whereby regional currency integration conditions the cost of the informal inputs used to produce terror. The empirical methodology and data are discussed in the third section. In the fourth section, we report parameter estimates of a dynamic terrorism incident supply function with Generalized Estimating Equation count data estimators for the Sub-Saharan African countries in our sample. The last section concludes.

[1] Additional evidence on the empirical significance of terrorism in Sub-Saharan Africa is provided by Elu and Price (2012) who find that terrorism possibly constrains living standards by diverting financial inflows – remittances – that would otherwise be used to finance the drivers of economic growth toward the financing of growth-reducing terrorist acts.

2 Rational Self-Interest, Regional Currency Integration and the Supply of Terrorism

Following Elu and Price (2012), assume terrorists are the self-interested *homo economicus* of standard economic theory (Caplan 2006), where representative terrorist net utility is defined over the number of terrorism events N which he values at v, and is produced with two types of inputs: domestic inputs I_i' and foreign inputs I. Let domestic inputs cost k and following Ricci (2008), suppose inputs imported from other countries are marked-up by $\tau\ e\ k$ where τ is the transaction cost associated with converting domestic currency into foreign currency, and e is the foreign exchange rate – the amount of domestic currency per unit of foreign currency. The representative terrorist net utility maximum-value function is:

$$U\left(v, k_i', (\tau e)k\right) = argmax_{\left(\sum k_i' I_i', \tau ekI, N\right) \geq 0} \ vN - \sum k_i' I_i' - \tau ekI \quad s.t. \ f\left(I_i', I\right) \geq N$$

The production function $f(\cdot)$ is assumed to be continuous, and costs linear with $f'(\cdot) > 0$, strictly increasing, strictly quasiconcave, with $f\ (0,0) = 0$, and for all countries $\tau > 0$, and $e > 0$. Suppose further that the representative terrorist net utility maximum-value function is increasing in v, decreasing in (k_i', τek), and homogeneous of degree one, convex, and differentiable in (v, k_i', τek). Terrorists in each country have identical marginal cost, and for those who reside in countries that are regionally integrated, a fraction r of inputs are imported from member countries, and a fraction $(1 - r)$ is imported from non-member countries where $0 < r < 1$. This establishes:

Proposition (Supply of Terrorism, Transaction Cost, and Regional Currency Integration). *If the transaction cost of imported terrorism inputs under regional currency integration are less (greater) than the inverse of the exchange rate, the optimal supply of terrorism is lower (higher) in regionally integrated countries relative to other countries.*

A proof of this proposition follows from Hotelling's Lemma where $\partial\ U(v,k_i', \tau ek)/\partial\ v = N^*(\cdot)$, where $N^*(\cdot)$ is the optimal terrorism supply function. Evaluating N^* at $f\ (\sum k_i'{}^*, (\tau\ e)k^*)$, then $\partial^2 U\ (v^*, k_i', \tau ek)/\partial\ v\ \partial\ \tau ek^* = \partial\ N^*\ (\cdot)/\partial \tau ek^* = \partial\ f\ (\sum k_i'{}^*, \tau ek^*)/\partial\ (\tau e)k^* < 0$, and the optimal supply of terrorism varies inversely with the marginal cost of imported inputs. With regional currency integration $\tau = e = 1$ (Ricci 2008), and the marginal cost for imported terrorism inputs is $MC = r\,k_i + (1 - r)\,\tau e\,k_i$ so for an optimizing terrorist in a country where the currency is regionally integrated relative to one elsewhere, the optimal supply of terrorism will differ with respect to the difference in the marginal cost of imported terrorism inputs which is given by $\Delta\ MC = k_i r[1 - \tau e]$, where $\Delta\ MC > 0$ if $\tau < 1/e$, and $\Delta\ MC < 0$ if $\tau > 1/e$.

In general the implied causal nexus of the proposition implies that the effect regional currency integration on terrorism depends upon the extent to which it affects the costs of imported terrorist inputs. For example, if regionally integrated countries relative to non-integrated countries are better able to monitor illegal money laundering, which constitutes a transaction cost on imported inputs for terrorists, regional currency integration could have a negative effect on terrorism. Indeed, in the year 2000, the Inter-Governmental Action Group Against Money Laundering (GIABA) was established in Senegal – a CFAZ member country (Bolaji 2010). To the extent that GIABA enables CFAZ to monitor illicit inter-country cash flows that could finance terrorism among CFAZ members, it could also possibly enforce GIABA money-laundering prerogatives in a manner that manages transaction costs relative to the exchange rate in a way that deters terrorism. This motivates our econometric strategy below. Given data on terrorist incidents, membership in CFAZ, and other terror inputs, we estimate the parameters of a terrorism supply function for Sub-Saharan Africa that permits an assessment of the proposition above.

3 Empirical Methodology and Data

Our dependent variable is terrorism incidents in Sub-Saharan Africa from the 2010 Global Terrorism DataBase (2010) compiled by the National Consortium for the Study and Responses to Terrorism (START).[2] These data report the number of terrorist incidents for every country in the world between 1970 and 2008 that must satisfy three primary criteria, and at least two other secondary criteria. First, the incident must be the result of an intentional and conscious calculation on the part of a perpetrator. Second, the incident must entail some level of violence or threat of violence, including property violence, as well as violence against people. Third, the perpetrators of the incidents must be sub-national actors, which excludes acts of state terrorism. The secondary criteria are: (1) The incident must be aimed at attaining a political, economic, religious, or social goal, (2) There must be evidence of an intention to coerce, intimidate, or convey some other message to a larger audience (or audiences) other than the immediate victims, and (3) The incident must be outside the context of legitimate warfare activities.

Our measure of belonging to the CFAZ regional euro-currency zone is dichotomous, and based on a country's membership in the Central African Franc Zone as identified by Irving (1999).[3] Given the Sub-Saharan African countries START, we create dummy variables for a country's membership in: (1) CFAZ, and the sub-units: (2) West African Economic and Monetary Union (WAEMU), and

[2] START data are publicly available at http://www.start.umd.edu/gtd/.

[3] As of January 1, 1999 the currency arrangement among CFAZ member countries changed as the currency of these countries – the franc – was now pegged to the euro.

(3) Economic and Monetary Union of Central Africa (CEMAC). WAEMU includes the countries of Benin, Burkina Faso, Cote d' Ivoire, Mali, Niger, Senegal and Togo. CEMAC includes the countries of Cameron, Central African Republic, Chad, Congo Republic of, Equatorial Guinea, and Gabon.

As in Elu and Price (2012) we augment our empirical specifications with other inputs that may matter for the production of terrorism, with data from Penn World Table 6.3 (Heston et al. 2009).[4] In particular, we condition the supply of terrorism for each Sub-Saharan African country on real gross domestic product per capita, the ratio of export plus imports as a fraction of gross domestic product – a measure of trade openness, the exchange rate of national currency to U.S. dollars, and total population. Conditioning on these measures capture the effects of the formal inputs that can finance the supply of terror and are plausibly correlated with a country's formal income. For example, if the size of the informal economy is correlated with the size of the formal economy as suggested by the analysis of Schneider and Enste (2000), real gross domestic product per capita plausibly captures the effects of the size of the informal economy and the costs of informal inputs, on terrorism. In addition, total population plausibly captures any scale economies associated with the production of terrorism and any value of successful terrorist incidents that is correlated with increasing population.

Given that our measure of terrorism incidents in each Sub-Saharan African country is integer-valued, we posit that the number of terrorism incidents are realizations from a Negative Binomial distribution. The data also constitute repeated observations over time, rendering the possibility that for each country the number of terrorism incidents are correlated. This violates the independence assumption underlying Negative Binomial parameter estimation, and requires perhaps an erroneous specification of the source of individual country heterogeneity. As such, we estimate the parameters of Generalized Estimating Equations (GEE) specifications (Zeger et al. 1988).[5] Moreover, to the extent that assumptions about the source of individual heterogeneity under fixed effects Negative Binomial parameter estimation is limited to what's available in the data, GEE parameter

---

[4] Penn World Table 6.3 data are publicly available at http://pwt.econ.upenn.edu.

[5] See Zorn (2001) for an overview of estimating GEE specifications when repeated observations data are possibly correlated. A GEE specification is a semiparametric approach where for k explanatory variables and $j = 1,2 \cdots C$ possibly correlated clusters of observations on the number of terrorist incidents in country i (N_i), parameter estimates follow from solutions to a quasi-score function of the form:

$$U_k(\boldsymbol{\beta}) = \sum_{j=1}^{C} \mathbf{G}_i' \mathbf{V}_i^{-1} (\mathbf{N}_i - \boldsymbol{\lambda}_i) = 0$$

where $\mathbf{G}_i = \boldsymbol{\lambda}_i/\boldsymbol{\beta}$, and for scale parameter $\boldsymbol{\varphi} = 1$, $\mathbf{V}_i = [(A_i)^{1/2} R_i (\boldsymbol{\alpha}) (A_i)^{1/2}]/\boldsymbol{\varphi}$. The $\mathbf{A}_i$ are $T \times T$ diagonal matrices with $g(\boldsymbol{\mu}_{it})$ as the tth diagonal element, $\boldsymbol{\alpha}$ is a vector of unknown parameters, and $R_i(\boldsymbol{\alpha})$ is the working correlation matrix. A Negative Binomial (NB) GEE specification follows from specifying $\boldsymbol{\lambda}_i = h(\theta_i \boldsymbol{\beta}_i)$, and for dispersion parameter r, $N_i \sim NB(\lambda_i, \lambda_i [1 + r \lambda_i])$.

estimates provide population average responses to covariates are much closer to the data than parameter estimates based on specifying the source of individual heterogeneity (Zeger et al. 1988).

Parameter estimates from GEE provide measures of a population response to changing covariates. This is in contrast to simple Negative Binomial estimates that measure an observational unit response to changing covariates. Thus, GEE parameter estimates inform the extent to which the average propensity for terrorism incidents changes given variation in CFAZ membership change across all Sub-Saharan African countries. To the extent that this population average effect holds regardless of individual country changes in CFAZ membership over time, it is more relevant for assessing the effects of regional currency unions on terrorism in all of Sub-Saharan Africa, and not just for the countries that actually joined.

Our estimation of a Negative Binomial GEE specification will assume that for a given Sub-Saharan African country i, the correlation ρ between N_{it} and N_{it-1} is either autoregressive or stationary. We allow the order of autoregression and stationarity to range from 1 to 3, and specify the working correlation matrix accordingly. In particular let $\mathbf{R}_{jj'}$ be a working correlation matrix that includes for a given observation in a cluster the correlation between year j and j' for $j \neq j'$, then for an autoregessive process $\mathbf{R}_{jj^{t-1}} = \rho^{\left|j-\sum j^{t-1}\right|}$, and for order m stationarity $\mathbf{R}_{jj^{t-1}} = \rho_{\left|j-\sum j^{t-1}\right|} = \text{if } j - \sum j^{t-1} \leq m$, and zero otherwise. These correlation structures are in our view quite plausible given the data are repeated observations across time and particularly so in the case of our dynamic specification that includes the regressor N_{it-1}, as the error term is not likely to be independent and identically distributed.

4 Results

A terrorism incident summary of the countries in our sample is reported in Table 1. For the 41 Sub-Saharan African countries in our sample there were a total of 4,993 terrorism incidents for which 261 groups claimed responsibility for over the 1974–2006 time period. CFAZ member countries account for approximately 7 % of the observations. South Africa by far had the most terrorism incidents, and in all likelihood reflects the protracted conflict between black opposition groups and the government over white minority rule and apartheid. Judging by the name of the groups claiming responsibility, terrorist groups affiliated with Islam claimed responsibility for terrorism in approximately 26 % of Sub-Saharan countries – including Somalia. The non-Islamic sounding group names suggest that the majority of terrorist groups in Sub-Saharan Africa are belligerent tribal and opposition groups. Table 2 reports a summary of covariates utilized in our terrorism supply function specifications.

Table 1 Sub-Saharan African countries, terror incidents, CFAZ membership, and terror groups claiming responsibility in sample: 1974–2006

Country	Terror incidents	Terrorist groups claiming responsibility[a]
Angola	479	National Union for the Total Independence of Angola, Front for the Liberation of the Enclave of Cabinda, Popular Movement of the Liberation of Angola
Benin[c]	7	
Botswana	8	
Burkina Faso[c]	3	
Burundi	338	Anti-Government Guerrillas, Tutsi, Party for the Liberation of the Hutu People
Cameroon[b]	19	Foibe Tribe, Pirates, Muslim Youth, Muslim Militants, Kotoko Tribal Group
Central African Republic[b]	11	Central African National Liberation Movement
Chad[b]	32	Idriss Miskine Group, FACDM, Coup Plotters Against the Government, Zaghawa Ethnic Group, Movement for Democracy and Development, Armed Forces for a Federal Republic, Union of Democratic Forces, Movement for Democracy and Justice in Chad, United Front for Democratic Change
Democratic Republic of the Congo	78	Soviet and Cuban-backed rebels & mercenaries, Congolese National Movement-Lumumba, Congolese Liberation Party, Supporters of Opposition Leader Etienne Tshisekedi, Civil Guards, Former Hutu Soldiers,, Hutus, Tutsi, Banyamulenge Rebels, Mayi Mayi, Party for the Liberation of the Hutu People, Patriotic Front in Ituri, Rastas, Nationalist Integrationist Front
Djibouti	19	Afar Rebels, Armed Subversives, Extremist Nationalist Group, Front for the Restoration of Unity and Democracy
Equatorial Guinea[b]	1	
Eritrea	3	Nomadic Afars
Ethiopia	114	Tigray Peoples Liberation Front, Eritrean Liberation Front, Armed Guerrillas, Western Somalia Liberation Front, Ethiopian People's Revolutionary Party, Ethiopian-backed rebels,Issa and Gurgura Liberation Front, Amhara tribal group, Former members of Central Investigation Office,Oromo Liberation Front, Al-Gama'at al-Islamiyya, Al-Ittihaad al-Islami, Coalition for Unity and Democracy
Gabon[b]	4	Convention of Liberal Reformers
Gambia	3	
Ghana	17	Farighan, New Patriotic Party, Ningo tribe, Muslims, Al-Sunni muslim sect
Guinea	12	United Liberation Movement for Democracy in Liberia, National Patriotic Front of Liberia, Revolutionary United Front
Guinea-Bissau[c]	7	
Ivory Coast[c]	38	Federation of Students and Scholars of Cote d'Ivoire, Ivorian Popular

(continued)

Table 1 (continued)

Country	Terror incidents	Terrorist groups claiming responsibility[a]
(Cote d'Ivoire)		Front, Manatari Brotherhood, Liberian gunmen, Liberia Peace Council, Tribal group
Kenya	90	Popular Front for the Liberation of Palestine, Mwakenya Dissident Movement, Nandi Tribe, God's Oppressed Army, Forum for the Restoration of Democracy-Kenya, Sabaot Tribesmen, United Somali Congress, Tribesman, Muslim Youth, Islamic Party of Kenya, Kenyan African National Union, Toposa and Dongiro Tribes, Kenyan Rebels from Uganda, Ethiopian Dongiro Tribesmen, National Development Party, Al-Qa'ida, Borana Bandits, Oromo Liberation Front, Mugniki Sect
Lesotho	24	Lesotho Liberation Army, Opposition Militants
Liberia	26	National Patriotic Front of Liberia, Liberian Rebel Group, United Movement For Democracy in Liberia, Liberians United for Reconciliation and Democracy
Madagascar	20	Anti-Government Demonstrators, Militant Movement for Madagascan Socialism, Didier Ratsiraka's Militia
Malawi	4	Anti-Government Rioters, Young Pioneers
Mali[c]	34	Islamic Legion, Tuaregs, Tuareg Guerrillas, Black Malian Group, Association of Students and Pupils in Mali, Islamic Arab Front of Azawad, Gandi Koi, Black Africa Vigilantes, Salafist Group for Preaching and Fighting
Mozambique	221	Mozambique National Resistance Movement, South African Commandos, Mozambican Rebels, Anti-Communist Rebels, Right-Wing Group
Namibia	142	South-West People's Organization, Angolan Defense Force, African National Congress, White Wolves, National Union for the Total Independence of Angola
Niger[c]	40	Peoples's Liberation Front of Niger, Hizballah, Tuaregs, Tuareg Guerrillas, Air and Azawak Liberation Front, Islamic Terrorists, Popular Front for Liberation of the Sahara, Democratic Front for Renewal, Saharan Revolutionary Armed Front
Nigeria	156	Zimbabwe Patriotic Front, Gang, Katsina Muslim Society, Muslim Militants, Shiite Muslims, Effiat Ethnic Group, Jbibio Peoples, Muslims, Anti-Government Group, Katap Ethnic Group, Hausa Ethnic Group, Rioters, Igbo Tribal Group, Council for Popular Justice, United Front for Nigeria's Liberation, Modakeke Ethnics, Modakeke Ethnic Activists, Association of Mobil Spill Affected Communities, Ijaw Militants, Egbesu Youths of the Bayelsa, Odua People's Congress, Movement for Actualization of the Sovereign State of Biafra, People's Democratic Party, Egbema National Front, Bini-Oru, Al-Sunna wal Jamma, Movement for the Emancipation of the Niger Delta, Gugama Youth Federation, People's Democratic Party, The Joint Revolutionary Council

(continued)

Table 1 (continued)

Country	Terror incidents	Terrorist groups claiming responsibility[a]
Republic of The Congo[b]	25	Front for the Liberation of the Enclave of Cabinda, Congolese Armed Patriotic Group, Presidential Movement Militiamen, Pro-Government Militia, Congolese Rally for Democracy
Rwanda	131	Inkotanyi, Rwanda Patriotic Front, Hutus, National Republican Movement for Democracy and Development, Mayi Mayi
Senegal[c]	86	Mali Students, Liberation Front for the Senegalese People, Movement of Democratic Forces of Casamance, Separatists, Dioulas Tribal Group
Sierra Leone	88	National Patriotic Front of Liberia, Rebel Military Unit, Revolutionary United Front, Rebels, Kamajor Hunters, West Side Boys
Somalia	202	Front for the Liberation of the French Somali Coast, Somali Salvation Front, Somali National Movement, United Somali Congress, Islamic Terrorists, Somali National Alliance, Gunmen loyal to Mohammad Farah Aideed, Somali Guerrillas, Al-Ittihaad al-Islami, Mousa Ismail Sub-Clan, Habr Gedir Clan, Muslim Fundamentalists, Rahanwein Resistance Army, Majerten Clansmen, Rival Clan, Sa'ad Militia, Matan Abdulle, Musa Sudi Yalahow Militia, Islamic Courts Union, Islamic Tendency, Al-Qa'ida
South Africa	1918	African National Congress, South-West People's Organization, Urban Guerrillas, South African Liberation Support Cadre, Gang, Lesotho Liberation Army, Blacks, Students, Black Nationalists, Afrikaner Resistance Movement, Mandela Soccer Club, White Wolves, Right-Wing Extremists, Nazi Boerestat Party, Azania People's Organization, White Liberation Army, Civil Cooperation Bureau, Orde Boerevoik, Zulu Militants, Inkatha Freedom Party, Pan Africanist Congress, Xhosa Tribal Workers, Rival Zulu Group, Boere Aanvals Troepe, Muslims Against Global Oppression, People Against Gangsterism and Drugs, 28s
Sudan	124	Libyan, Liberation Front of Southern Sudan, Separatists, Sudanese Christian Rebels, Anti-Government Guerrillas, Black September II, Sudan People's Liberation Army, Islamist Sufi Group, Sudan Alliance Forces, Iraqis, National Democratic Alliance of Sudan, Ummah Liberation Army, Akfir wal-Hijra, Janjaweed, Justice and Equality Movement, National Redemption Front
Swaziland	12	African National Congress, Mozambique National Resistance Movement, Tigers, Swaziland Youth Congress, People's United Democratic Movement
Tanzania	9	Pan Africanist Congress, Left-Wing Terrorists, Bandits, Al-Qa'ida, Rebel Military Unit
Togo[c]	48	Togolese People's Rally, Togolese Dissidents

(continued)

Table 1 (continued)

Country	Terror incidents	Terrorist groups claiming responsibility[a]
Uganda	314	Save Uganda Movement, Uganda Freedom Movement, Anti-Government Rebels, Popular Resistance Army, Uganda National Liberation Front, Guerrillas, Uganda People's Army, New Ugandan Army, Uganda Federal Army, Holy Spirit Movement, Ugandan People's Democratic Army, Rwenzururu Rebels, Uganda Democratic Christian Army, Lord's Resistance Army, National Democratic Alliance, West Nile Bank Front, Uganda Federal Democratic Alliance, Rebels, Allied Democratic Forces, Hutus, National Army for the Liberation of Uganda
Zambia	58	Zimbabwe Guerrillas, Zimbabwe African People's Union, National Union for the Total Independence of Angola, Mozambique National Resistance Movement, African National Congress, Black Mambas
Zimbabwe	58	Zimbabwe African Nationalist Union, Zimbabwe African People's Union, Dissidents linked to Zanga, Guerrillas, Zimbabwe Patriotic Front, Anti-Government Rebels, Supporters of Joshua Nkomo, South African Guerrillas, Mozambique National Resistance Movement, Right-Wing Extremists, Movement for Democratic Change

Source: START global terrorism database

[a]These are the names reported in the START Global Terrorism Database of perpetrators of terrorist incidents for a particular country who claimed responsibility for terrorism incidents over the 1974–2006 time period. The terrorist incident counts are for years in which remittances data can be linked to the year of the terrorist incident

[b]Member of CEMAC

[c]Member of WAEMU

Tables 3 and 4 report respectively, static and dynamic GEE population-averaged parameter estimates for a the terrorism supply function. The six specifications account for autocorrelation and stationarity with orders that range from 1 to 4 respectively, as convergence was not realized with order 2 autoregression and stationarity. The explanatory adequacy of each regression is assessed with a Wald chi-square distributed test for the null hypothesis that the exogenous explanatory variables have parameters that are jointly insignificant. As our specifications have different error specifications, we also report for each the Quasi Information Criterion (*QIC*) statistic (Cui 2007; Pan 2001). A minimum *QIC* test statistic is also a measure of fit, as it enables selection of the best specification in terms of minimum description length (Rissanen 1978) – the specification that captures the most regularity of the data given uncertainty about the true specification.

Given the possibility of reverse causality and endogeneity of a country's membership in CFAZ, we also report for the static and dynamic GEE specifications a test for the exogeneity of CFAZ – the extent to which a country's membership in CFAZ causes terrorism – based on the test proposed by Robins et al. (1999). Developed for discrete random variables, the basic idea of the Robins-Greenland-Hu Causality test

Table 2 Terrorism and regional integration in Sub-Saharan Africa (1974–2006) covariate summary

Variable	Variable coding	Median	Mean	Standard deviation	Number of observations
Number of terrorism Incidents[a]	*Numeric*	3	10.84	27.55	495
Real gross domestic Product per capita 1996 Dollars[b]	*Numeric*	960.98	1607.93	1561.59	495
Trade openness 1996 Dollars[b]	*Numeric*	52.37	60.16	138.53	495
Total population[b]	*Numeric*	9885.66	19829.27	24945.66	495
Exchange rate 1996 Dollars[b] (*National Currency Units Per Dollar*)	*Numeric*	27.51	625.56	2125.40	495
CFAZ membership[c]	*Numeric* (Dichotomous)	0	0.073	0.259	495
Post-1999[c]	*Numeric* (Dichotomous)	0	0.285	0.452	495

Source:
[a]START global terrorism database
[b]Penn World Table 6.1: Trade Openness = (Exports + Imports)/gross domestic product
[c]Derived

is that if a treatment is unconfounded and exogenous, the expectation of the current value of the treatment does not depend on past or current outcomes of the presumed dependent variable, once past values of the treatment and other baseline covariates are known. Let **A** be a vector of treatments, **Y** the dependent variable vector which has a discrete probability distribution, and **X** a vector of other conditioning variables, Robins et al. (1999) show that if $E\,[\mathbf{A}_t \mid \mathbf{Y}_t, \mathbf{A}_{t-1}, \mathbf{X}_t] = E[\mathbf{A}_t \mid \mathbf{A}_{t-1}, \mathbf{X}_t]$, then **A** is exogenous and causes **Y**. To test the exogeneity of CFAZ(**A**) we report for both the static and dynamic specification, the parameter estimate of the coefficient on terrorism (**Y**) only, as the exogeneity of CFAZ membership implies that in an Ordinary Least Squares (OLS) regression of CFAZ membership against terrorism, one period lagged CFAZ membership, and the other conditioning covariates, the coefficient on terrorism should be insignificant.[6]

To account for the possibility that terrorism declined in Sub-Saharan Africa overall after 1999 – the year in which CFAZ membership was associated with currency being pegged to the euro – we add a dichotomous variable measuring years after 1999 to our specification of the terrorist supply function. This allows a

[6] Our implementation of the Robins-Greenland-Hu test estimates the auxiliary OLS linear probability regression with robust standard errors. The difference between the tests in the static and dynamic specification differs in what is included in $\mathbf{X}_t$ – the dynamic specification includes the one period lag of terrorism, whereas the static specification excludes it.

Table 3 Terrorism and regional integration in Sub-Saharan Africa (1974–2006) GEE population average negative binomial parameter estimates

Specification:	*AR1*	*AR2*	*AR3*	*Stationary (1)*	*Stationary (3)*	*Stationary (4)*
Regressand = number of terrorism incidents						
Regressors						
Constant	1.82	1.76	1.71	1.84	1.77	1.70
	(0.297)[a]	(0.251)[a]	(0.251)[a]	(0.304)[a]	(0.277)[a]	(0.252)[a]
Real gross domestic	0.00037	0.00032	0.00033	0.00038	0.00035	0.00038
Product per capita	(0.00007)[a]	(0.00006)[a]	(0.00007)[a]	(0.00007)[a]	(0.00008)[a]	(0.00006)[a]
Trade openness	−0.007	−0.007	−0.007	−0.008	−0.008	−0.007
	(0.004)[c]	(0.003)[b]	(0.003)[b]	(0.004)[b]	(0.004)[b]	(0.003)[b]
Total population	0.000005	0.000008	0.000008	0.000004	0.000007	0.000006
	(0.000005)	(0.000003)[b]	(0.000003)[a]	(0.000003)	(0.000005)[b]	(0.000003)[b]
Exchange rate	0.0001	0.0001	0.0001	0.0001	0.0001	0.0001
	(0.00002)[a]	(0.00002)[a]	(0.00002)[a]	(0.00002)[a]	(0.00002)[a]	(0.00001)[a]
Post-1999	−0.1349	−0.1948	−0.1717	−0.0983	−0.0021	−0.0763
	(0.1981)	(0.2277)	(0.2328)	(0.2116)	(0.2883)	(0.1688)
CFAZ membership	−0.8069	−0.5243	−0.5243	−0.9011	−0.6011	−0.6302
	(0.2805)[b]	(0.2794)[c]	(0.2828)[c]	(0.2982)[a]	(0.3940)	(0.2509)[b]
Diagnostics						
N	494	490	481	494	481	473
Robins-Greenland-Hu	0.0000001					
Causality Test:	(0.00009)					
E(CFAZ ∣ *Terrorism) =* $0\ \chi^2_{k-1}$: (H $_o$: $\beta_1 = \cdots \beta_k = 0$)	260.63[a]	116.43[a]	122.46[a]	293.90[a]	86.29[a]	156.99[a]
Quasi-likelihood information criterion statistic	680.96	685.395	693.044	681.339	707.437	680.017

Standard errors in parentheses
All standard errors are robust. Observations vary across the specifications as a result of estimation requiring per country observations to be equal to the number of lags in the error structure
[a]Significant at the 0.01 level
[b]Significant at the 0.05 level
[c]Significant at the 0.10 level

disentanglement of the CFAZ effects on terrorism versus the fact that terrorism may have declined for other reasons in Sub-Saharan Africa after 1999. Across the static and dynamic specifications in Tables 3 and 4, the years after 1999 have a negative effect on terrorism but never significant. Membership in CFAZ is negative and significant effect on terrorism in all but one instance. However, for the minimum

Table 4 Terrorism and regional integration in Sub-Saharan Africa (1974–2006) GEE population average negative binomial parameter estimates

Specification:	*AR1*	*AR2*	*AR3*	*Stationary (1)*	*Stationary (3)*	*Stationary (4)*
Regressand = number of terrorism Incidents						
Regressors						
Constant	1.88	1.86	1.83	1.88	1.85	1.84
	(0.233)[a]	(0.224)[a]	(0.231)[a]	(0.234)[a]	(0.236)[a]	(0.228)[a]
Number of terrorism	0.0155	0.0098	0.0089	0.0156	0.0086	0.0100
Incident(s) $_{t-1}$	(0.0029)[a]	(0.0026)[a]	(0.0027)[a]	(0.0030)[a]	(0.0027)[a]	(0.0026)[a]
Real gross domestic	0.0001	0.0002	0.0002	0.0001	0.0002	0.0002
Product per capita	(0.00005)[a]	(0.00005)[a]	(0.00006)[a]	(0.00005)[b]	(0.00006)[a]	(0.00006)[a]
Trade openness	−0.004	−0.005	−0.005	−0.004	−0.005	−0.005
	(0.003)	(0.002)[b]	(0.002)[b]	(0.003)	(0.002)[b]	(0.002)[b]
Total population	0.000003	0.000005	0.000005	0.000004	0.000007	0.000004
	(0.000003)	(0.000002)[b]	(0.000003)	(0.000003)	(0.000003)	(0.000003)
Exchange rate	0.00008	0.00009	0.00009	0.00008	0.00009	0.00009
	(0.00002)[a]	(0.00002)[a]	(0.00002)[a]	(0.00002)[a]	(0.00002)[a]	(0.00002)[a]
Post-1999	−0.1228	−0.1262	−0.1485	−0.1226	−0.1112	−0.1113
	(0.1369)	(0.1531)	(0.1462)	(0.1377)	(0.1531)	(0.1289)
CFAZ membership	−0.7471	−0.5999	−0.5950	−0.7522	−0.6533	−0.6357
	(0.2542)[b]	(0.2233)[b]	(0.2398)[b]	(0.2554)[a]	(0.2599)[b]	(0.2365)[b]
Diagnostics						
N	451	490	439	451	439	435
Robins-Greenland-Hu	−0.00002					
Causality Test:	(0.00008)					
E(CFAZ ∣ *Terrorism) = 0* χ^2_{k-1}: (H_o: $\beta_1 = \cdots \beta_k = 0$)	390.68[a]	180.89[a]	122.46[a]	389.21[a]	163.20[a]	254.39[a]
Quasi-likelihood information criterion statistic	524.981	547.975	551.116	525.147	555.017	544.109

Standard errors in parentheses
All standard errors are robust. Observations vary across the specifications as a result of estimation requiring per country observations to be equal to the number of lags in the error structure
[a]Significant at the 0.01 level
[b]Significant at the 0.05 level
[c]Significant at the 0.10 level

QIC specification which captures the most regularity in terrorism incidents in Table 4 – the autoregressive of order 1 error specification – CFAZ does have negative and significant effect on terrorism. As the Robins-Greenland-Hu test supports the exogeneity of CFAZ membership, this suggests that in Sub-Saharan Africa, CFAZ membership caused terrorism to decline in member countries over the 1974–2006 time period.

Overall, the parameter estimate for CFAZ membership is consistent with regional currency integration increasing the cost of formal inputs terrorist used to produce terror, and thus reducing the production of terror. As for the practical empirical significance of the CFAZ membership parameter estimate in the minimum *QIC* GEE specification, it suggests that if two countries in Sub-Saharan African differ in that one is a CFAZ member, and the other is not, the non-member country would have on average approximately 11 fewer terror incidents per year if it joined CFAZ.[7] Alternatively, and given the exogeneity of CFAZ membership based on the Robins-Greenland-Hu causality tests, over the 1974–2006 time period, CFAZ membership caused approximately 396 fewer terrorism incidents in Sub-Saharan Africa.[8]

5 Conclusion

This paper considered whether regional currency integration in Sub-Saharan Africa can have an effect on terrorism. Theoretically, if terrorists are rational, changes in the cost of terrorism inputs, ceteris paribus, input should condition the supply of terrorism. We postulated that regional currency integration can change the cost of imported terrorism inputs. With data on terrorism incidents, we estimated GEE count data specifications of terror supply functions for Sub-Saharan Africa between 1974 and 2006. Our parameter estimates reveal that CFAZ membership has a statistically significant, causal, and negative effect on terrorism in Sub-Saharan Africa. Empirically, our estimates suggest that CFAZ membership caused approximately 396 fewer terrorism incidents in Sub-Saharan Africa over the 1974–2006 time period.

Our results suggest that the pro-growth policy menu for Sub-Saharan Africa, as articulated for example in Ndulu et.al (2007) should indeed be expanded to include the formation of regional currency arrangements such as CFAZ. As terrorism crowds-out important drivers of growth in Sub-Saharan Africa, the formation of regional currency arrangements like CFAZ elsewhere in Sub-Saharan Africa can offset the effects that terrorism has on important determinants of economic growth such as investment in human and physical capital (Abadie and Gardeazabal 2008). In general, our findings suggest that another potential channel by which regional currency integration can improve living standards in Sub-Saharan Africa is through its effects on lowering terrorism.

---

[7] This computation follows from the fact that given $\lambda_{it} = (\beta^{'}\theta + \varepsilon_{it})$, for a given change in the population-average level of remittances from $I^{'}$ to $I^{'} + \delta$, the change in N_{it} is given by $[1 - (\beta_{I}^{'}\delta)] \times \overline{\lambda}$.

[8] This computation follows from scaling up the population average reduction in terrorism caused by CFAZ membership by the number – 36 – of CFAZ member countries in the sample.

References

Abadie A (2006) Poverty, political freedom, and the roots of terrorism. Am Econ Rev 96:50–56
Abadie A, Gardeazabal J (2008) Terrorism and the world economy. Eur Econ Rev 52:1–27
Abrahamsen R (2004) A breeding ground for terrorists? Africa and Britain's war on terrorism. Rev Afr Polit Econ 31:677–684
Alesina A, Barro RJ (2002) Currency unions. Q J Econ 117:409–436
Arce DG, Sandler T (2003) Terrorism and game theory. Simulat Gaming 34:319–337
Bolaji KA (2010) Preventing terrorism in West Africa: good governance or collective security? J Sustain Dev Afr 12:207–222
Brandt PT, Sandler T (2009) Hostage taking: understanding terrorism event dynamics. J Policy Model 31:758–778
Caplan B (2006) Terrorism: the relevance of the rational choice model. Public Choice 128:91–107
Chen AH, Siems TF (2004) The effects of terrorism on global capital markets. Eur J Polit Econ 20:349–366
Cilliers J (2003) Terrorism and Africa. Afr Secur Rev 12:91–103
Cui J (2007) QIC program and model selection in GEE analyses. Stata J 7:209–220
Debron X, Masson P, Pattillo C (2003) West African currency union rationale and sustainability. CESifo Econ Stud 49:381–413
Elu JU (2012) Terrorism in Africa and South Asia: economic or existential good? J Dev Areas 46:345–358
Elu JU, Price GN (2012) Remittances and the financing of terrorism in Sub-Saharan Africa: 1974–2006.Peace Econ Peace Sci Public Policy 18:1–42
Global Terrorism DataBase (2010) National consortium for the study of terrorism and response to terrorism. University of Maryland, College Park
Gould ED, Klor EF (2010) Does terrorism work? Q J Econ 125:1459–1510
Heston A, Summers R, Aten B (2009) Penn world table version 6.3. Center for International Comparisons of Production, Income and Prices/University of Pennsylvania, Philadelphia
Irving J (1999) For better or for worse: the Euro and the CFA Franc. Afr Recov 12:24–29, United Nations Department of Information
Masson PR (2008) Currency unions in West Africa: is the trade effect substantial enough to justify their formation? World Econ 31:533–547
McKinnon R (1963) Optimum currency areas. Am Econ Rev 52:717–725
Ndulu B, Chakraborti L, Lijane L, Ramachandran V, Wolgin J (2007) Challenges of African growth: opportunities, constraints, and strategic directions. World Bank, Washington, DC
Pan W (2001) Akaike's information criterion in generalized estimating equations. Biometrics 57:120–125
Ricci LA (2008) A model of an optimum currency area. Economics 2:1–31
Rissanen J (1978) Modeling by the shortest data description. Automatica 14:465–471
Robins JM, Greenland S, Hu F-C (1999) Estimation of the causal effect of a time-varying exposure on the marginal mean of a repeated binary outcome. J Am Stat Assoc 94:687–700
Sautter JA (2010) Variance, violence, and democracy: a basic microeconomic model of terrorism. J Strateg Secur 3:39–50
Schneider F, Enste DH (2000) Shadow economies: size, causes, and consequences. J Econ Lit 38:77–114
Wintrobe R (2006) Rational extremism: the political economy of radicalism. Oxford University Press, Oxford
Zeger SL, Liang K-Y, Albert PS (1988) Models for longitudinal data: a generalized estimating approach. Biometrics 44:1049–1060
Zorn CJW (2001) Generalized estimating equation models for correlated data: a review with applications. Am J Polit Sci 45:470–490

MIX
Papier aus verantwortungsvollen Quellen
Paper from responsible sources
FSC® C105338
FSC
www.fsc.org

If you have any concerns about our products,
you can contact us on
ProductSafety@springernature.com

In case Publisher is established outside the EU,
the EU authorized representative is:
Springer Nature Customer Service Center GmbH
Europaplatz 3, 69115 Heidelberg, Germany

Printed by Libri Plureos GmbH
in Hamburg, Germany